MW00778528

Russia's Foreign Policy

Change and Continuity in National Identity

Sixth Edition

Andrei P. Tsygankov

ROWMAN & LITTLEFIELD
Lanham · Boulder · New York · London

Published by Rowman & Littlefield
A wholly owned subsidiary of The Rowman & Littlefield Publishing Group, Inc. 4501 Forbes Boulevard, Suite 200, Lanham, Maryland 20706
www.rowman.com

Unit A, Whitacre Mews, 26–34 Stannary Street,

London SE11 4AB, United Kingdom

Copyright © 2022 by Rowman & Littlefield

First edition 2006. Second edition 2010. Third edition 2013. Fourth edition 2016. Fifth edition 2019.

All rights reserved. No part of this book may be reproduced in any form or by any electronic or mechanical means, including information storage and retrieval systems, without written permission from the publisher, except by a reviewer who may quote passages in a review.

British Library Cataloguing in Publication Information Available

Library of Congress Cataloging-in-Publication Data

Names: Tsygankov, Andrei P., 1964-author.
Title: Russia's foreign policy: change and continuity in national identity / Andrei P. Tsygankov.
Description: Fourth edition. | Rowman & Littlefield: Lanham, 2016. | Includes bibliographical references and index.
Identifiers: LCCN 2015043662 (print) | LCCN 2015044211 (ebook) | ISBN 9781442254015 (cloth: alk. paper) | ISBN 9781442254022 (pbk.: alk. paper) | ISBN 9781442254039 (electronic)
Subjects: LCSH: Russia (Federation)—Foreign relations. | Soviet Union—Foreign relations. | Great powers. | Russia (Federation)—Foreign relations—Western countries. | Western countries—Foreign relations—Russia (Federation) | Nationalism—Russia (Federation) | Social change—Russia (Federation)
Classification: LCC DK510.764 .T785 2016 (print) | LCC DK510.764 (ebook) | DDC 327.47—dc23
LC record available at http://lccn.loc.gov/2015043662

♾️™ The paper used in this publication meets the minimum requirements of American National Standard for Information Sciences—Permanence of Paper for Printed Library Materials, ANSI/NISO Z39.48-1992.
Printed in the United States of America

Contents

Tables

Note on the Transliteration

In transliterating names from the Russian, I have used "y" to denote "й," " ' " to denote "ь" and "ъ," "yu" to denote "ю," "ya" to denote "я," "i" to denote "й" and "ий," "iyi" to denote double "и," "e" to denote "э," "kh" to denote "х," "zh" to denote "ж," "ts" to denote "ц," "ch" to denote "ч," "sh" to denote "ш," and "sch" to denote "щ." I have also used "Ye" to distinguish the sound of "E" (such as "Yevropa") at the beginning of a word from that in the middle of a word (such as "vneshnei"). Everywhere, I did not distinguish between "e" and "ё." Original spelling is retained in quotations.

Chronology of Key Foreign Policy Events, 1979–2022

1979

December   Soviet Union sends troops to Afghanistan.

1983

March   US president Ronald Reagan announces the Strategic Defense Initiative.

1985

March   US–Soviet arms negotiations take place in Geneva.

April   Gorbachev announces a unilateral moratorium on deployment of intermediate-range nuclear missiles and proposes a moratorium on all nuclear weapons tests.

Eduard Shevardnadze succeeds Andrei Gromyko as Soviet foreign minister.

July   Soviet Union imposes five-month moratorium on nuclear weapons tests, making its extension contingent upon a similar US response.

September   Moscow proposes at Geneva negotiations that the United States and the USSR reduce long-and medium-range nuclear weapons by 50 percent.

1986

January   Gorbachev proposes a ban on all nuclear weapons by the year 2000.

June   Warsaw Pact meeting in Budapest proposes mutual Warsaw Pact–NATO troops reduction of 100,000 to 150,000 men and the reduction of military capabilities to those "necessary for defense."

July   Gorbachev announces in Vladivostok a five-point plan for cooperation in the Asia-Pacific region and advocates closer ties with China.

October	Reagan and Gorbachev meet in Reykjavik, Iceland.
1987	
May	General Dmitri Yazov is named the new Soviet defense minister.
December	Gorbachev and Reagan sign in Washington the INF treaty eliminating all 2,611 Soviet and US intermediate-range nuclear forces.
1988	
January	Gorbachev announces the need for "innovative policies" in Eastern Europe.
May	US–Soviet summit takes place in Moscow.
December	Gorbachev announces before the United Nations General Assembly a unilateral reduction of Soviet forces by some 500,000 men, 10,000 tanks, 8,500 artillery pieces, and 800 combat aircraft.
1989	
April	During Soviet crackdown on Georgian nationalists in Tbilisi, twenty demonstrators were killed and two hundred wounded. Unilateral withdrawal of Soviet forces from Hungary begins.
May	Gorbachev before Council of Europe promises not to interfere militarily in political events in Eastern Europe.
October	Shevardnadze proclaims before the Supreme Soviet that the Soviet invasion in Afghanistan in 1979 "violated the norms of proper behavior" and that the Krasnoyarsk radar installation is illegal under the 1972 Anti-Ballistic Missile Treaty.
December	The "Big Four" (United States, France, Great Britain, and USSR) meet to discuss the status of Berlin.
1990	
January	Soviet troops are deployed to Azerbaijan in the wake of massive anti-Armenian demonstrations.
February	"Two Plus Four" talks on German reunification announced.
March	In response to Lithuania's declaration of independence, Soviet paratroopers seize the headquarters of the Lithuanian Communist Party.
May	US–Soviet summit takes place in Washington.
July	Gorbachev and Chancellor Helmut Kohl announce agreement to allow reunified Germany to belong to NATO.
November	NATO and Warsaw Pact states sign the CFE treaty and the Charter of Paris at the CSCE Summit. Gorbachev proposes a new Union treaty.
December	Shevardnadze resigns as Soviet foreign minister.

1991

January	Soviet troops crack down on pro-independence forces in Lithuania and Latvia; nineteen protesters are killed.
March	In the Soviet referendum, voters choose to preserve the union; Baltics, Armenia, Georgia, and Moldova boycott the vote.
July	The Warsaw Pact is disbanded in Prague.
	US president George H. W. Bush and Gorbachev reach an agreement in Moscow on the Strategic Arms Reduction Treaty (START).
	Ten Soviet republics reach an agreement on a new Union treaty to be signed on August 20.
August	Coup against Gorbachev occurs.
December	Russia, Ukraine, and Belarus establish the CIS in Minsk; Gorbachev resigns as president of the USSR.

1992

February	Foreign Ministry conference "The Transformed Russia in the New World" takes place.
March	Foreign Minister Andrei Kozyrev briefly travels to China.
April	Bush, supported by Kohl, announces $24 billion assistance package for Russia.
	President Boris Yeltsin orders withdrawal of troops from Nagorno-Karabakh and asks for the deployment of NATO troops.
	Russia places the Fourteenth Army in Moldova under its control.
May	Russia supports the United Nations' sanctions against Yugoslavia.
	Russia signs the CIS Collective Security treaty.
	Russia joins the IMF and World Bank.
June	Russia and the United States agree on terms of START II.
July	Yeltsin attends G-7 summit.
	Yeltsin and Moldova's president, Mircea Snegur, sign peace agreement over Transdniestr conflict.
December	Yeltsin visits China.
	Kozyrev acknowledges the need to be more active on the eastern front.

1993

January	Yeltsin attends the Civic Union's congress; Bush and Yeltsin sign START II.
April	New Foreign Policy Concept signed into law.
May	Russia initiates the CIS Economic Union agreement at Moscow summit.

July	The Tokyo G-7 summit declares a $43.4 billion package of assistance for Russia.
October	Russia withdraws from the ruble zone.
	US secretary of state Warren Christopher promises Yeltsin not to push for NATO expansion immediately and to focus on Partnership for Peace instead.
November	Russia adopts new military doctrine.
December	Westernizers lose party elections to nationalist Vladimir Zhirinovski.

1994

January	US president Bill Clinton announces that the question of enlarging NATO is not whether it will happen, but when.
July	Kozyrev announces change in his foreign policy course.
September	At the Washington summit, Clinton pledges NATO enlargement will be guided by "three nos"—no surprises, no rush, and no exclusion of Russia.
December	Kozyrev refuses to sign up for Partnership for Peace; Yeltsin warns of "cold peace."
	Russian military launches offensive in Chechnya.
	Russia joins G-7.

1995

May	Russia begins dialogue with NATO and signs Partnership for Peace.
December	In Russian parliamentary elections, Westernizers lose to Communists.
	Kozyrev is removed from office.
	Yevgeni Primakov replaces Kozyrev as foreign minister.

1996

April	Treaty on the Formation of the Russia–Belarus Union State is signed.
May	IMF announces $10.2 billion to be disbursed to Russia monthly from March 1996 to March 1999.
June	Yeltsin approves the concept of the state nationalities policy of the Russian Federation and states the goal of a multiethnic Russia; he also initiates the search for a new "national idea."
July	Yeltsin is reelected as president.
November	Yeltsin and the Japanese prime minister meet and commit themselves to signing a peace treaty in 2000.
December	Primakov visits Tehran and declares that Russia–Iran relations are "developing along an ascending curve."
	Russia is admitted to the Asian and Pacific Economic Council (APEC).

1997

March   Yeltsin meets Clinton in Helsinki and insists that NATO not include former Soviet states.

               CIS adopts Concept of Economic Integrational Development.

April   Russia and China sign the "Joint Declaration on a Multipolar World and the Formation of a New International Order."

May   Yeltsin signs NATO-Russia Founding Act at summit with NATO leaders in Paris.

               Russia and Ukraine sign the "Big Treaty," which legalizes the borders.

June   Peace treaty to end the Tajik civil war is signed in Moscow.

October   Georgia, Ukraine, Azerbaijan, and Moldova establish a security group to balance Russia.

December   Russia adopts a new National Security Concept.

               Primakov responds to the US threat to attack Iraq by entering into an alliance with France and negotiating an agreement for the return of the UN inspections to Iraq.

1998

February   Russia and Ukraine sign the ambitious Program of Economic Cooperation.

May   Yeltsin and Clinton meet in Birmingham; Russia officially joins the G-8.

September   Primakov assumes the post of prime minister; Igor' Ivanov becomes foreign minister.

December   Russia withdraws ambassadors from London and Washington to protest US and British air strikes against Iraq.

               Primakov speaks of desirability of Russia-China-India alliance as a "new pole in world politics."

1999

February   Russian Duma narrowly ratifies the Russia–Ukraine "Big Treaty."

March   Russia begins negotiating the restructuring of its approaching $17.5 billion foreign debt payment.

               NATO's air strikes against Serbia begin; Primakov cancels the upcoming negotiations with the United States and the IMF in Washington.

April   Yeltsin appoints Viktor Chernomyrdin as Russia's special envoy on Yugoslavia.

               Russian Duma refuses to ratify START II.

May   Sergei Stepashin replaces Primakov as prime minister.

June   Chernomyrdin and Finnish president Martti Ahtisaari secure Milošević agreement to NATO terms for ending war.

Russian troops begin participation in the multilateral peace-keeping force in Kosovo.

The "Common Strategy of the EU on Russia" is adopted.

July   First meeting of Russia-NATO Permanent Council takes place since it was boycotted by Russia in March.

August   Russia sends troops to counter Chechen incursions into Dagestan.

Vladimir Putin replaces Stepashin as prime minister.

Chechen rebels occupy parts of Dagestan; Kremlin resumes military operation.

Bombs explode in Moscow, killing hundreds of residents.

October   Russia adopts new military doctrine.

December   Yeltsin resigns; Putin becomes acting president of Russia.

2000

March   Putin is officially elected president.

June   Putin holds summit with Clinton in Moscow.

September   Russia, India, and Iran sign an agreement, according to which all signatories will get relief from import tax and customs duties.

2001

February   The secretary of the Security Council, Sergei Ivanov, announces the new "pragmatic" course of bilateral relations in the former Soviet region.

June   Putin meets US president George W. Bush in Ljubljana, Slovenia.

September   Terrorist attacks on the United States occur.

Putin announces support for the United States and pledges intelligence assistance.

November   Putin and Bush meet in Crawford, Texas.

2002

February   Putin emphasizes Russia as a reliable energy alternative to the Middle East; he also proposes creating a "gas OPEC" group.

April   Putin proclaims Russia's European foreign policy a priority in a Duma address.

May   Russia and the United States sign a joint declaration on energy cooperation in Moscow.

October   Russia–United States "energy summit" takes place in Houston, Texas.

November   At the EU summit, Russia proposes to have a visa-free arrangement in Kaliningrad.

December   Russia shuts down the OSCE mission in Chechnya.

2003

January	Russia joins the antiwar coalition and argues for the United Nations as the only legitimate body to sanction the use of force in Iraq.
April	Russia and Turkmenistan sign a strategic gas agreement.
May	Russia and five other ex-Soviet states form the Collective Security Treaty Organization (CSTO) for fighting terrorism.
June	Putin proposes that visas between EU countries and Russia be abandoned altogether by the year 2006.
August	Putin seals a joint venture with British Petroleum worth over $6 billion.
	Moscow withdraws its peacekeeping mission from Bosnia and Kosovo.
September	Russia signs an $800 million deal with Iran and pledges to build two more nuclear reactors in Iran.
	Russia signs a partnership agreement with Azerbaijan.
	Russia signs an agreement with Saudi Arabia pledging co-operation in the energy sector and in setting the international price of oil.
October	The head of Russia's state electric company, Anatoli Chubais, announces that Russia's main goal is to build a "liberal empire" in the former USSR.

2004

March	Putin is reelected president.
May	EU incorporates ten new members.
	Russia and the EU agree on conditions to extend the Partnership and Cooperation Agreement with the EU to the ten new members.
September	Terrorist attack occurs in Beslan, North Ossetia.
	Putin announces reform in the political system.
November	Orange Revolution in Ukraine; Russia supports Viktor Yanukovich in Ukraine's presidential election.

2005

January	Putin–Bush summit takes place in Bratislava.
March	Change of power occurs in Kyrgyzstan through a mass protest; Russia takes no side.
April	Putin visits Middle East.
	Russia and Germany agree to build a gas pipeline under the Baltic Sea.
May	Celebration of victory in World War II takes place in Moscow.
	After riots and their brutal suppression in Uzbekistan, Russia supports the government.

June	Russia-China-India meeting takes place in Vladivostok to discuss prospects of strategic partnership.
	Russia and Georgia reach agreement on withdrawal of Russia's military bases.
December	Russia–Ukraine dispute over natural gas takes place.

2006

June	Russia declares opposition to Ukraine and Georgia joining NATO.
September	Russian imposes economic and political sanctions against Georgia.
December	Russia–Belarus dispute over natural gas takes place.

2007

February	Putin delivers speech at the Munich Conference on Security Policy.
March	The Foreign Ministry report "A Review of the Russian Federation's Foreign Policy" is released.
April	The United States announces plans to deploy elements of a missile defense system in Eastern Europe.
May	Kazakhstan, Turkmenistan, and Uzbekistan agree to increase exports of energy via Russia's pipelines.
	Putin announces a moratorium on implementing the Conventional Forces in Europe treaty.
	Russia–EU summit takes place in Samara.
December	Russia announces plans to re-equip its new SS-27 missiles with multiple warheads.

2008

March	Dmitri Medvedev is elected president.
April	Russia blocks Georgia and Ukraine from receiving the Membership Action Plan for NATO.
June	President Medvedev proposes a new pan-European treaty beyond NATO.
	Russia–EU summit takes place in Khanty-Mansiysk.
July	Russia and China complete border demarcation.
August	Russo–Georgian war begins.
	Russia recognizes the independence of Abkhazia and South Ossetia.
December	Russia's new National Security Strategy through 2020 is released.

2009

April	Russia expresses concern over the EU's Eastern Partnership project.
May	NATO conducts a military exercise in Georgia.
	Russia–EU summit takes place in Khabarovsk.
June	SCO summit takes place in Ekaterinburg.
July	US–Russia summit takes place in Moscow.
	Russia agrees to US military overflights to and from Afghanistan.
	Russia conducts a large military exercise in the Caucasus.
September	Medvedev critically assesses Russia's prospects in the article "Go, Russia!"
October	Russia proposes that Iran send spent nuclear fuel outside for reprocessing.
	Russia agrees to supply natural gas to China beginning in 2014–2015.
November	Medvedev proposes to judge the effectiveness of foreign policy "by a simple criterion: Does it improve living standards in our country?"

2010

February	The Foreign Ministry report focuses on strengthening Russia's economic position.
April	The United States and Russia sign the new START treaty.
	Ukraine agrees to extend the lease on Russia's Black Sea Fleet for twenty-five more years in exchange for the reduction of gas prices by 30 percent.
May	Russia and Turkey sign agreement to carry oil from the Black Sea to the Mediterranean.
June	Violent change of power occurs in Kyrgyzstan; Russia does not interfere.
	Russia supports UNSC sanctions against Iran and refuses to supply Iran with an S-300 air defense system.
July	In a meeting with Russia's ambassadors, Medvedev highlights the need to establish "modernization alliances" with foreign powers.
	Customs Union of Russia, Belarus, and Kazakhstan comes into force.
September	Russia completes an oil pipeline to China, and two gas pipelines are planned.
November	Russia and China agree to use national currencies in bilateral trade.

December	Medvedev expresses disappointment with the lack of progress on the proposed pan-European treaty.

2011

January	Hamid Karzai visits Moscow to meet Medvedev.
March	Russia abstains in the UNSC resolution that authorized air strikes against Libya.
April	Russia invites Ukraine to join Customs Union.
	Russia creates a new antiterrorism center in Kyrgyzstan.
	The Russia-controlled CSTO amends its mission by pledging to defend its members from internal "unconstitutional disturbances."
August	Russia hosts a trip by North Korea's leader Kim Jong-il; the idea of a trans-Korean pipeline is explored.
September	Russia's state oil company, Rosneft, concludes an agreement with ExxonMobil to develop Russia's Arctic Basin.
	Putin announces his decision to run for the presidency.
October	Putin proposes to build a new Eurasian Union among the CIS states.
December	Russia completes negotiations over WTO membership.

2012

February	Russia and China veto UNSC Syria resolution.
March	Putin is elected president in the first round.
	The Kremlin approves NATO use of an airport in Ulyanovsk as a transit point for moving soldiers and cargo to and from Afghanistan.
May	Russia warns the US Congress against adopting a bill imposing visa bans and asset freezes on human rights violators in Russia.
June	Putin's first foreign trips include Belarus, Germany, France, Uzbekistan, China, and Kazakhstan.
	Putin meets US president Barack Obama in Mexico.
July	Putin addresses Russian ambassadors and permanent representatives in international organizations.
August	Russian court sentences members of the punk band Pussy Riot to two years in jail for hooliganism; Western governments express their strong disagreement with the decision.
October	Russia refuses renewal of the Nunn-Lugar Cooperative Threat Reduction Program and additional cuts in strategic nuclear warheads; Putin stresses the need to address the US MDS plans in Europe.
December	Putin addresses the Federation Council and speaks of new demographic and moral threats.

The US Congress, while normalizing trade relations with Russia, passes the Magnitsky bill that imposed sanctions against human rights violators in Russia.

The Russian Duma passes the "Anti-Magnitsky Act" that bans the adoption of Russian children by US citizens.

2013

February   Russia releases a new Foreign Policy Concept that discusses competition of different "values and development models."

June   Former CIA employee Edward Snowden defects to Russia; the Kremlin refuses to turn him over to the United States.

The Russian Duma passes a law against "propaganda of non-traditional sexual relations among minors"; Western governments express their disappointment.

August   Russia grants Snowden asylum; Obama expresses his disappointment and cancels a bilateral summit with Putin.

The United States accuses Syria of using chemical weapons against opposition and threatens force; Russia disagrees and proposes a process of eliminating Syrian chemical weapons.

September   The United States and Russia reach an agreement on phased elimination of Syria's chemical weapons.

The G-20 summit takes place in St. Petersburg.

Putin visits Japan and signs investment and trade agreements.

October   Putin's speech on "the desire for independence and sovereignty in spiritual, ideological and foreign policy spheres" takes place at the Valdai Club.

November   Ukraine refuses to sign an Association Agreement with the EU; mass protests take place in Kyiv, pressuring the government to reverse the decision.

December   In his address to the Federation Council, Putin positions Russia as a "conservative" power and the worldwide defender of traditional values.

2014

February   Russia and the West disagree on Syria in Geneva negotiations.

Russia holds successful Olympics in Sochi.

A revolutionary change of power takes place in Ukraine; Russia sends additional troops to Crimea.

The West condemns Russia's actions and threatens to apply sanctions.

March   Russia annexes Crimea after its referendum and desire to join Russia.

	The United States introduces sanctions against the Russian economy.
April	A Malaysian airplane with 286 passengers on board is downed.
	The EU joins the US sanctions against Russia.
May	Putin travels to China to sign massive natural gas deals.
	Moscow writes off North Korean debt and agrees to build a gas and rail link into South Korea.
July	The sixth BRICS summit is held in Fortaleza, Brazil.
September	The Minsk-I agreement on cease-fire in Ukraine is signed.
	At the Valdai forum Putin is critical of the United States' "destabilizing" role in world affairs.
October	The ruble loses about 40 percent of its value.
November	Russia participates in the APEC summit.
	Another massive natural gas deal is struck between Russia and China.
December	In his address to the Federation Council Putin justifies the incorporation of Crimea in terms of consolidating Russia's centuries-old "civilizational and sacred significance."

2015

January	Putin travels to Istanbul and proposes a gas pipeline through Turkish territory to Europe's borders.
February	The Minsk-II agreement on cease-fire in Ukraine is signed.
May	The seventieth anniversary Victory Day parade in Moscow is not attended by Western leaders.
	China's president attends the Victory Day parade and signs important economic agreements in Moscow.
	Leaders of Russia and China sign an agreement on cooperation between the Eurasian Union and the Silk Road.
	Russia and the Eurasian Union sign a free trade treaty with Vietnam.
	US secretary of state John Kerry arrives in Moscow to discuss the Middle East.
	Putin signs law on "Undesirable" Organizations, giving prosecutors the power to shut down international organizations deemed "nontraditional."
July	Russia hosts summits of SCO and BRICS in Ufa, Russia.
	The United States, the UK, France, Russia, China, and Iran sign an agreement limiting the Iranian nuclear program in exchange for the lifting of international sanctions.
September	Putin travels to the United States and the UN to make a case for intervening in Syria.

October	Russia begins its intervention in Syria.

2016

June	The United Kingdom votes to leave the European Union. Putin supports the idea of Greater Eurasia, or cooperation between the Eurasian Economic Union, the European Union, and China.
August	Unknown hackers attack the site of the Democratic National Convention in the United States and release confidential materials on Hillary Clinton to WikiLeaks.
November	Donald Trump is elected president of the United States. Putin signs the New Concept of Foreign Policy.

2017

January	The United States expels thirty-five Russian diplomats accused of spying and cyber interference in American elections.
April	The United States bombs Syria's military base, partly exploited by Russia.
May	US secretary of state Rex Tillerson visits Moscow. Putin meets French presidential candidate Marine Le Pen.
June	Putin travels to France to discuss bilateral relations with President Emmanuel Macron.
July	Putin and Trump meet in Hamburg on the sidelines of G-20. US Congress approves new sanctions against Russia, alongside Iran and North Korea. Russia orders hundreds of US diplomats to leave the country.
September	The United States closes Russia's Consulate General in San Francisco. Russia attends the BRICS summit in China. Putin proposes to deploy UN peacekeepers in eastern Ukraine. The Syrian government regains control of over 90 percent of the country.
October	King Salman of Saudi Arabia visits Russia.
December	The United States agrees to assist Ukraine and provide lethal weapons for its army.

2018

March	Former Russian spy Sergei Skripal and his daughter are poisoned in Great Britain. The British government introduces sanctions against Russia, supported by many in the European Union. Germany approves the building of the Nord Stream 2 pipeline with Russia.
July	Putin–Trump summit takes place in Helsinki, Finland.

August	The US Congress approves new sanctions against Russia.
	President Trump promises new sanctions against Russia.
October	Putin visits Azerbaijan and central Asia.

2019

January	The United States announces withdrawal from the INF Treaty.
	Russia refuses to attend and pay its dues to the Parliamentary Assembly of the Council of Europe (PACE).
	Russia supports Nicolás Maduro in Venezuela's elections.
February	Putin addresses Russian Duma and proposes to amend the constitution.
	Putin and Aleksandr Lukashenko meet to "deepen integration" of Russia–Belarus union.
April	Volodymyr Zelensky is elected president of Ukraine.
	Robert Mueller's report on Russia is published in the United States.
	Putin meets with North Korean leader Kim Jong-un in Vladivostok.
May	US secretary of state Michael Pompeo visits Russia.
June	The European Union extends sanctions against Russia.
	Russia returns to PACE.
July	Putin and Zelensky agree on prisoners' exchange.
	The United States and Russia fail to agree on START renewal.
	Russia and India agree to pay for military supplies in national currencies.
	Putin extends support for new leadership in Kyrgyzstan.
August	The United States announces future INF deployment in Asia.
	The United States announces withdrawal from START.
October	Russia and Turkey sign agreement on Syria and joint patrol of area in northern Syria.
December	Gazprom signs a new contact with Ukraine until 2024.
	Russia and OPEC sign agreement to reduce oil production in 2020.

2020

January	Putin visits Syria.
	Putin's annual address to Federation Council stresses domestic issues.
March	New Russia–Turkey agreement on Syria is signed.
May	Gazprom demands that Belarus pay its gas debt in full.
June	Fraudulent elections take place in Belarus, followed by mass protests against Lukashenko.

August	Putin supports Lukashenko and expresses readiness to help in stabilizing Belarus.
	Alexei Navalny is poisoned and transported to Germany.
	Russia registers Sputnik V vaccine against COVID-19 after two rounds of tests.
September	Russian foreign minister cancels trip to Germany.
October	Russia proposes a mutual moratorium on INF deployment in Europe.
November	Russia brokers peace between Armenia and Azerbaijan.
December	Putin calls Joe Biden to congratulate him on his election as US president.
	The United States accuses Russia of new cyberattacks.

2021

January	Alexei Navalny is arrested upon his return to Russia.
	Normandy meeting on Ukraine fails to reach any results.
February	Russia warns the West against interfering in Russian elections.
	EU foreign chief Josep Borrell visits Moscow but fails to resolve differences.
	Russia and the United States renew START for five years.
March	Russia recalls its ambassador following Biden's reference to Putin as "a killer."
	The United States introduces sanctions against Russia's sovereign debt.
	Ukraine approves the strategy for "de-occupation and integration" of Crimea.
April	The cease-fire in eastern Ukraine is violated.
	Russia amasses 100,000 troops on the border with Ukraine.
	Russia sanctions the United States and recommends that the US ambassador leaves Moscow.
	Biden calls Putin and proposes a summit.
	Czech government sends eighteen Russian diplomats home.
May	Putin meets with Lukashenko in Sochi.
	Russia and the EU issue mutual sanctions.
	Russia takes part in US-organized international conference on climate change.
June	Putin–Biden summit takes place in Geneva.
	Biden calls on Putin to think about Russia's dependence on China.
	COVID infections reach a new record high in Russia.
July	The United States accepts Russian–German gas pipeline Nord Stream 2 as "nearly completed."

August	The Taliban takes power in Afghanistan.
	Russia and China agree to rely on SCO in helping to stabilize Afghanistan.
	Russia and Ukraine issue mutual sanctions.
September	A sharp rise of natural gas prices in Europe occurs.
	Separate visits by leaders of Syria and Turkey to Moscow take place.
	United Russia wins elections to State Duma.
October	Putin is ready to increase gas supplies to Europe but not through Ukraine.
	US under secretary of state Victoria Nuland visits Moscow.
	Leaders of Armenia and Azerbaijan visit Moscow in two separate visits.
	Russia closes NATO's mission in Moscow.
November	Putin delivers online presentation at Glasgow climate summit.
	Sergei Lavrov accuses Kyiv of dragging Russia into the Donbas conflict.
December	Putin's official visit to India takes place.
	Putin and Biden hold an online meeting.
	Russia publishes proposals of security guarantees from the West.

2022

January	Russia assisted Kazakhstan by leading the CSTO mission to defend the country from internal destabilization.
February	Following shelling in the Donbas region and Russia's recognition of the independence of two breakaway territories in eastern Ukraine, the Kremlin began its "special military operation" against Kyiv.
March	The Russian ruble lost 40 percent of its value.

Sources:

Partly adapted from: Coit D. Blacker, *Hostage to Revolution: Gorbachev and Soviet Security Policy, 1985–1991* (New York: Council on Foreign Relations, 1993), ix–xviii; Strobe Talbott, *The Russia Hand* (New York: Random House, 2002), 423–29; Karen Dawisha and Bruce Parrott, *Russia and the New States of Eurasia* (Cambridge, UK: Cambridge University Press, 1994), 298–310; Ted Hopf, *Social Construction of International Politics: Identities and Foreign Policies, Moscow, 1955 and 1999* (Ithaca, NY: Cornell University Press, 2002), 212–13.

Preface

Winston Churchill once famously observed that the key to understanding Russia's "enigma" is its national interest. However, he failed to explain what that interest was. It is therefore our scholarly task to uncover what Russians themselves understand to be their foreign policy interests and objectives. In contrast to the direction of Churchill's thought, there has been a great deal of change in Russia's perceptions of its national interest. Thus, President Boris Yeltsin and his first foreign minister, Andrei Kozyrev, defined national interest as that of integration with Western economic and security institutions. The second foreign minister, Yevgeni Primakov, saw the need to restore Russia's great power status and balance hegemonic aspirations of the United States. Finally, Vladimir Putin and Dmitri Medvedev adopted their own distinct vision of national interest, which balanced Russia's great power status with the need to have special relationships with the West in general and the United States in particular. Confronted with global instability, Western sanctions, and rise of non-Western powers, Russia is yet again reassessing its interests and relations with the West.

This book seeks to contribute to our understanding of the national interest formation in Russia's foreign policy. Instead of assuming that national interest is about power or modernization, as mainstream international relations theories tend to do, I maintain that we ought to study the complex forces behind its formation. Upon closer inspection, we discover that much of Russia's foreign policy and national interest can be understood in the context of the country's relations with the West. Russia's attempts to embrace Western liberalism, as well as its insistence on great power status, make sense when we consider the significance of Western recognition in affirming Russia's actions. Western actions serve to reinforce or undermine dominant political forces inside Russia. Extending recognition emboldens Russian liberals insisting on their country's belongingness with the West. Withholding such recognition strengthens Russia's traditionally strong supporters of greater independence from the West. It is therefore domestic identity coalitions

xxv

competing for influence in the context of Western actions that help to make sense of Russia's foreign policy formation. Chapter 1 explains my approach in greater detail.

This book does not claim to break new ground in empirical research. My objectives are more modest: to assist fellow academics in their teaching needs, and to suggest a plausible interpretation of Russia's foreign policy. In my own teaching, I continue to feel a deficit of broadly targeted textbooks appropriate for senior undergraduate and graduate courses in the field of post-Soviet studies. With the fourth decade of post-Soviet changes under way, there is still surprisingly little written that would meet this criterion. Fortunately, there are exceptions. There is also a good deal written by specialists on various specific aspects, issues, and periods in the development of Russia's foreign policy after communism. In my book, I relied heavily on this literature in attempting to synthesize it into a relatively broad overview of the subject. In addition to highlighting in endnotes the impact of some specific sources on my thinking, I list in a "further reading" section some of the readings that influenced this book.

While writing with teaching needs in mind, I have advanced an argument and taken an explicit analytical perspective. My choice of explaining Russia's foreign policy turns by changes in the nation's identity, rather than by material capabilities or leadership's perspectives alone, was a conscientious one. I fully realize that for the purpose of advancing scholarship, many of the book's assertions would require much greater documentation. I hope, however, that my framework is helpful for presenting material, asking interesting questions, and organizing in-class discussion. After all, no textbook is neutral, and instructors usually try to balance the dominant text(s) by assigning additional materials with conflicting viewpoints and perspectives. In my own teaching, I also commonly employ articles and materials by authors holding diverse views. Provoking thinking and sparking debates in class is essential for learning, as it is through arguing—and sometimes only through arguing—that we deepen our understanding. Although this may seem like a challenging way of teaching, our students deserve nothing less. I therefore intentionally present material in a somewhat polemical way, as a debate among different social and political groups in Russia.

I also make an effort to differentiate myself from more common treatment of Russian foreign policy in the West. My own perspective on the development of Russia's foreign policy is neither pro-Western liberalism nor anti-Western nationalism. Both of these perspectives have influenced Russian foreign policy formation, but, in my judgment, each has defended views of relatively narrow elite circles and ultimately failed to respond to broader needs of Russian society. I hope that scholars across the world pay close attention to future developments in Russia's foreign policy. Russia retains its political significance, and engaging it as a legitimate member of world society remains a key to peace and security in the new era. Such engagement requires that we improve our knowledge of Russia's perceived national interests.

The book is divided into six chapters. Chapter 1 provides a brief historical overview of Russia's foreign policy and spells out the book's approach to understanding Russia's post-Soviet international behavior. I situate my approach relative to more mainstream international relations theories, realism and liberalism, and I argue the insufficiency of these traditional theoretical perspectives for understanding Russia. The rest of the book is a detailed analysis of several distinct concepts of national interest that guided Russia's international policies in the late Soviet and post-Soviet years. The latter parts are broken down further in order to cover such stories as the International Monetary Fund (IMF), the North Atlantic Treaty Organization (NATO), China, Yugoslavia, Iran, Commonwealth of Independent States (CIS) ties, the United States, the Iraq war, bilateral relations with newly independent states, and others. These are cases that instructors can choose from in order to stimulate a more focused discussion in class. Instructors may elect to assign longer articles or those materials that interpret Russia's actions differently than I do.

Chapter 2 analyzes Gorbachev's New Thinking philosophy and what it meant for the country's foreign policy. Chapter 3 explores Russia's attempts at cooperation with Western nations. In particular, it analyzes the formation and consequences of three distinct visions of national interest—integration with the West (early Yeltsin and Kozyrev), great power balancing (late Yeltsin and Primakov), and pragmatic cooperation (early Putin). Chapter 4 then reviews Russia's assertiveness in relations with the West by analyzing great power assertiveness (Putin since 2007), renewed pragmatic cooperation under Medvedev, and return to Putin's assertiveness since the spring of 2012. Chapter 5 looks into changes in Russian foreign policy since 2019. In each of the substantive chapters, I specify the international and domestic context of foreign policy formation. I provide a brief overview of domestic debates on national interest, and then review Russian policies toward the West, the East, and the former Soviet region. Furthermore, in each chapter, I offer an assessment of each period's foreign policy record. Criteria for my assessment are spelled out in the first chapter. Chapter 6 summarizes my explanation of change and continuity in Russia's foreign policy and its implications for Russian and Western policymakers.

Writing this book would have been impossible without the support of my friends, colleagues, students, and family. Naturally, full responsibility for the book's content is my own. For financial assistance, I wish to thank the Office of the President at San Francisco State University, which granted me an Award for Professional Development of Probationary Faculty and therefore made it possible for me to complete this book.

I owe special thanks to Susan McEachern and Andrzej Korbonski. In the spring of 2002, they each, independently, suggested to me the idea of a textbook on Russian foreign policy. Comments and criticism by Ronald Linden and anonymous reviewers have been instrumental in improving the book. During the years since the book was first published, I also have received many helpful comments from reviewers, teachers, scholars, journalists, and members of the policy community in reaction to the published book and my other writings on Russia's international policy. While revising the book for various editions, I have greatly benefited from their comments and suggestions.

Many thanks to Rowman & Littlefield Publishers for smoothing out my prose and for all of their assistance. I also wish to thank many of my students in classes on Russia and foreign policy. The writing process would have been much less rewarding without their reactions to various portions of the book. Finally, I have a special debt to my family for their love and support. I dedicate this book to my children and grandchildren.

1

Understanding Change and Continuity in Russia's Foreign Policy

When political formulas, such as "national interest" or "national security," gain popularity they need to be scrutinized with particular care. They may not mean the same thing to different people. They may not have any precise meaning at all.

—Arnold Wolfers[1]

This chapter provides analytical tools for understanding the subject of this book. It reviews Russia's international behavior across history and identifies several patterns of change and continuity in the country's foreign policy. Russia's traditional foreign policy debates survived the fall of the Soviet system, and Russia's postcommunist behavior should therefore be understood in the historical context. The chapter offers a framework for understanding Russian foreign policy, comparing and contrasting it with some prominent analytical perspectives. My approach focuses on Russia's relations with the outside world, and it views Russia's behavior as particularly influenced by the development and behavior of Western nations. What often determines Moscow's foreign policy choices is whether or not the West's international actions are perceived by Russian officials as accepting Russia as an equal and legitimate member of the world. The chapter also develops standards for evaluating Russia's foreign policy record. Finally, it orients the reader regarding the book's methodology and organizational structure.

RUSSIA'S FOREIGN POLICY:
CHANGE AND CONTINUITY

Russia's foreign policy was formed in different external contexts, while responding to some similar sets of security challenges. This combination provides Russia's historical foreign policy with elements of change and continuity.

Changing Contexts

At least since Peter the Great, Europe and Western nations, in general, played an especially prominent role in creating for Russia the system of meanings in which to act. To many Russians, the West represented a superior civilization whose influences were to be emulated or contained but never ignored. Yet Western contexts were changing over time, presenting Russia with different policy dilemmas. More specifically, different Wests have been associated respectively with sovereign monarchy, the rise of a liberal political system, and finally, the consolidation of a liberal political system.

Sovereign monarchy emerged as a dominant political form in seventeenth-century Europe after the era of religious wars. It was the era of increasingly secular sovereign statehood, and it was in this context that Peter the Great assumed power in 1694. In the context of European secularism, Peter introduced a new ideology of state patriotism or loyalty to the state—a sharp break with the religious autocratic Russia that had emerged after the two-centuries-long rule by the Mongols. Despite opposition from the Eastern Orthodox Church, the czar decisively turned Russia in the secular national-ist direction. Although religion was still playing an important role, it was increasingly subjected to considerations of the state. European international politics, and with it Russia's international politics, was becoming the politics of accumulating national power rather than affirming religious values.

The liberal and egalitarian ideals of the French Revolution of 1789 further changed Europe by splitting it into progressive and antirevolutionary camps. The era of the rising Europe of Enlightenment, constitutionalism, and capital-ism presented Russia with new international dilemmas. Russian rulers had to decide between the old monarch-centered vision of sovereignty and the new popular sovereignty, and this choice was then to shape the nation's interna-tional behavior. Some rulers—most prominently, Alexander II—attempted to yet again redefine the country's identity in line with the new European ideas of freedom and equality. Their moderate foreign policies reflected the need for Russia to undergo considerable domestic changes. Other rulers were fearful of the new Europe and sought to defend the basic features of the old monarchic regime. Thus, Alexander I insisted on the need to defend the status quo in post-Napoleonic Europe and embraced antirevolutionary Germany and Austria, rather than progressive France, as his role models. Alexander III also continued policies of siding with European autocracies and repression at home.

As Europe was fighting its way through the crisis of rising liberal ideas, some Russians began to advocate a break with both old and new Europe. Alexander Herzen, for instance, grew disappointed with European conservative restorations of the 1840s and argued for Russia's own, non-European way of "catching up" economically and socially. The Bolsheviks pushed this line of thinking to its extreme and adopted a fundamentally different political system and foreign policy. The Bolshevik revolution of October 1917 reflected the crisis of European identity and the Russian leadership's inability to choose between the two Europes. The czar failed to prevent the country from nearing destruction, revolution, and civil war. The rule of Nicholas II was symbolic in this respect. In 1904, he dismissed his finance minister, Count Sergei Witte, a proponent of the new Europe and an economic reformer, and chose to sacrifice domestic reforms to the goals of foreign policy expansionism by going to war against Japan. By then entering World War I, Nicholas further brought the European crisis closer to home and made it impossible to prevent the spread of extremist Marxist ideas in Russia, a move that brought his downfall in the Bolshevik revolution of 1917. In recognition of the West's world role, however, even the Bolsheviks sought to engage Western nations and related to their technological and material power. The Bolsheviks' concept of Soviet power and proletarian democracy was also a response to egalitarian ideas of the French Revolution. Furthermore, Bolsheviks' foreign policy, after the early efforts to overthrow the "bourgeois" governments in Europe, was that of rapprochement and pragmatic cooperation with the West.

As Europe reemerged as a consolidated liberal-democratic continent after World War II, the Soviet rulers sought to preserve a connection with the new West. The intercourse with the West grew stronger under Nikita Khrushchev and then Mikhail Gorbachev. Soviet leader Nikita Khrushchev's famous de-Stalinization speech at the XXth Communist Party congress broke many taboos of the old thinking and was meant, among other things, to bring Soviet Russia closer to Europe.[2] Despite Khrushchev's removal, the impact of de-Stalinization proved to be irreversible—a considerable part of a new intellectual generation now referred to themselves as the "children of the XXth party congress" and worked within and outside the establishment to bring Soviet Russia closer to the West. The post-Stalin period saw, in particular, growth of specialized institutions in which researchers carefully analyzed Western viewpoints, such as those generated by American international relations (IR) scholars.

Ultimately, the new Western influences contributed greatly to the discourse of human rights and democracy in the Soviet Union, creating the environment for reformers and helping Gorbachev come to power. Although he never meant for the socialist system to be replaced by that of Western liberalism, Gorbachev proclaimed a new era in relationships with the West and therefore greatly contributed to the new fundamental change. In addition to Khrushchev's policies of de-Stalinization and peaceful coexistence, Gorbachev drew from ideas of Russian liberal-minded scientists, such as Vladimir Vernadski, Pyotr Kapitsa, and Andrei Sakharov—all long-term advocates of developing relationships with the West. The leader of perestroika was also building on European social-democratic ideas, as well as American theories of transnationalism and interdependence. The Soviet collapse of 1991 completed the process of the country's difficult adjustment to the new international context and laid the groundwork for the establishment of Russia's liberal foreign policy orientation. The new liberal context continues to be highly contested in Russia and will be shaped further by the country's interaction with Western nations. If the West remains a relatively consolidated liberal entity with a clear and unambiguous message to the world, the new liberal identity has a good chance of taking stronger root in post-Soviet Russia.

Three Schools of Foreign Policy Thinking

Although Russia's foreign policy was a response to various international contexts, it also displayed a remarkable degree of historical continuity. Across the eras of monarchy and liberalism, Russia's engagement with the world followed several persistent patterns of thinking and behavior. As a borderland nation in an uncertain, often volatile external environment, Russia had to continuously respond to similar challenges to its security. These challenges included unrest in neighboring territories, threats of external invasion, and difficulties in preserving internal state integrity. Over time, the country has developed three distinct traditions, or schools, of foreign policy thinking— Westernist, Statist, and Civilizationist. Throughout centuries, Westernizers, Statists, and Civilizationists sought to present Russia's international choices in ways consistent with the schools' historically established images of the country and the outside world.

Westernizers placed the emphasis on Russia's similarity with the West and viewed the West as the most viable and progressive civilization in the world. The early Westernizers sought to present Russia as a loyal member in the family of European monarchies. Historically the emergence of this school of thinking can be traced back to Peter the Great's military Westernization. Peter was the first to admire the West for its technological superiority and to raise the possibility of borrowing Western technology to overcome Russia's backwardness. Alexander I was more consistent in defending the values of the old Europe and vigorously opposing the spread of French egalitarian ideas. After the defeat of Napoleon, Alexander championed the so-called legitimist policies and established the Holy Alliance with Germany and Austria in order to suppress revolutionary activities on the Continent.

Liberal Westernizers identified with the Western values of constitutional freedoms and political equality. After the era of great reforms and Russia shifting its relations from Germany to France and Britain under Alexander II, the czarist government seemed more willing to embrace the new European values of constitutionalism. Pavel Milyukov, once a foreign minister and a leader of Russian liberals, took the most active pro-European position by insisting that Russia must stay in World War I as an active member of the anti-German coalition. To Milyukov, support for the European allies—despite all the devastation that the war had brought to Russia—was a matter of principle and the country's identity orientation. Westernizers within the Soviet system saw Russia as standing not too far apart from European social democratic ideas. For instance, one of Gorbachev's favorite lines of thinking was that the Soviet Union had to "purify" itself of Stalinist "distortions" and become a democratic, or "human," version of socialism (*gumannyi sotsializm*). In his foreign policy, Gorbachev pursued the notion of mutual security with the West and presided over a series of revolutionary arms-control agreements with the United States, as well as over the Soviet military withdrawals from Europe and the third world. By introducing the idea of a "common European home," Gorbachev meant to achieve Russian–European integration based on the principles of European social democracy.

Finally, the liberal Westernizers in post-Soviet Russia argued for the "natural" affinity of their country with the West based on such shared values as democracy, human rights, and a free market. Liberal Westernizers warned against relations with former Soviet allies and insisted that only by building Western liberal institutions and joining the coalition of what was frequently referred to as the community of "Western civilized nations" would Russia be able to respond to its threats and overcome its economic and political backwardness. Andrei Kozyrev and Boris Yeltsin's vision of "integration" and "strategic partnership with the West" assumed that Russia would develop liberal democratic institutions and build a market economy after the manner of the West. Throughout 2009–2012, President Dmitri Medvedev advocated a new era of improving relations with the Western nations based on a common assessment of security threats and greater openness in economic and political systems. He initiated a new pan-European security treaty and argued for liberalizing the economic and political system in order to overcome Russia's backwardness, corruption, and rigidity.

Statists have emphasized the state's ability to govern and preserve the social and political order. This is, arguably, the most influential school of Russia's foreign policy thinking. It is explicit in choosing values of power, stability, and sovereignty over those of freedom and democracy. Critical to Statism is the notion of external threats to Russia's security. Ever since the two-centuries-long conquest by the Mongols, Russians have developed a psychological complex of insecurity and a readiness to sacrifice everything for independence and sovereignty. Multiple wars in Europe and Asia further reinforced this mentality and provided Statism's supporters with extra justifications for their reasoning. For instance, when justifying the need for rapid industrialization, the leader of the Soviet state, Josef Stalin, famously framed his argument in terms of responding to powerful external threats.

> The history of the old Russia was the continual beating she suffered because of her backwardness. She was beaten by the Mongol khans. She was beaten by the Turkish beys. She was beaten by the Swedish feudal lords. She was beaten by the Polish and Lithuanian gentry. She was beaten by the English and French capitalists. She was beaten by the Japanese barons. All beat her—for her backwardness. . . . We are fifty or a hundred years behind the advanced countries. We must make good this distance in ten years. Either we do it, or we shall be crushed.[3]

The Statists, however, are not inherently anti-Western; they merely seek the West's recognition by putting emphasis on economic and military capabilities. The Statists of the monarchical era valued Russia's autocratic structure of power, partly because such were the structures of European monarchies as well. In foreign policy, Statists often trace their intellectual and policy origins to Prince Alexander Gorchakov. Gorchakov labored as Alexander II's foreign minister to recover Russia's lost international positions after the defeat in the Crimean War. He pursued the policy of "concentration" by developing a system of flexible alliances and limiting Russia's involvement in European affairs.[4] Other Statists trace their roots to Peter the Great. Unlike Westernizers emphasizing Peter's Europeanness, Statists relate to Peter's military competitiveness. It was state security and military competitiveness, they argue, that brought about the czar's notion of getting closer to Europe.

The socialist Statists insisted on the importance of the Communist Party's firm control over the society for the purpose of maintaining political order and averting external "capitalist" threats. Within the Soviet leadership, this school was always suspicious of efforts to activate political institutions outside the party and opposed Gorbachev's democratization reform. In foreign policy, some Statists advocated relative accommodation with the West, while others favored balancing strategies. Maksim Litvinov, for instance, supported a "collective security" system in Europe in order to prevent the rise of fascism. Nikita Khrushchev, too, wanted to break taboos of isolationism and bring Soviet Russia closer to Europe. He also called for a return to Lenin's principles of "coexistence" with the capitalist world, although he later slipped into several incidents of confrontation with the West. Both Litvinov and Khrushchev saw themselves as supporters of the late Lenin's course toward giving up the idea of the world revolution and learning to live and trade with the potentially dangerous capitalist world.

On the other hand, Stalin's pact with Hitler, as well as Leonid Brezhnev's "correlation of forces" strategy, reflected the will to balance perceived dangerous influences from the outside world. By signing the treaty of friendship with Nazi Germany, Stalin hoped to isolate Russia from World War II, or at least to buy enough time to prepare for it. His successors operated on a world scale and, with the "correlation of forces" doctrine, they meant to respond to the perceived growing global influence of the West. Both strategies meant to preserve Russia's independence in world affairs and had some elements of Gorchakov's described strategy of concentration.

The liberal Statists of the post-Soviet era no longer supported a single-party state, and they agreed with the importance of building a market economy and political democracy. However, they were not ready to sacrifice to these new values the historically tested notion of a strong state, and they argued that liberal values should be established to strengthen, not weaken, the state. The liberal Statists believed that Russia continued to be exposed to external threats and must remain a great power capable of responding to those threats anywhere in the world. Yet they proposed different strategies to achieve the great power status.

The distinction between Primakov's and early Putin's policies is a case in point. Both camps have at one point or another referred to Gorchakov as their inspiration, and both viewed Russia's greatness and strength as key goals of their foreign policies. In their domestic policies, both wanted to bring more order and control to social and political life. Primakov sought to control big business. Putin continued in the same vein, but also tightened his grip over the legislature, party building, regions, and electronic media, while at the same time declaring his commitment to the newly established political institutions and economic liberalization. The critical foreign policy difference between the two, however, is that Primakov was trying to rebuild the former Soviet Union and contain the United States through a strategic alliance with China and India, whereas Putin emphasized bilateral relations in Russia's periphery and was ambitious to develop a partnership with the United States to deter terrorism.

Finally, Civilizationists have always seen Russian values as different from those of the West, and they have always attempted to spread Russian values abroad, outside the West. Their response to Russia's security dilemmas has been more aggressive than that of the more status quo–oriented Statists. As a foreign policy philosophy, Civilizationism dates back to Ivan IV's ("Ivan the Terrible's") "gathering of Russian lands" after the Mongol Yoke and to the dictum "Moscow is the Third Rome," which was adopted under Ivan. Unlike Westernizers and Statists, Civilizationists have sought to challenge the Western system of values, insisting on the cultural distinctiveness of Russia and Russia-centered civilization. Some representatives of this school advocated a firm commitment to the values of Orthodox Christianity, while others viewed Russia as a synthesis of various religions.

The early Civilizationists advocated the identity of the "Russian empire." They recognized the constraints set by the West-centered external context and recommended that Russia expand beyond its eastern and southern borders. Yet they were eager to defend what they saw as a cultural unity in their outer area. For instance, in the nineteenth century, Civilizationists defended the notion of Slavic unity, and their ideology of Pan-Slavism affected some of the czar's foreign policy decisions.

The socialist Civilizationists went further and challenged the West in a most direct fashion. The Lenin-Trotski doctrine of the world revolution was the Soviet version of Civilizationist thinking. Although it had died as an official philosophy in 1921 with Lenin's commitment to coexistence with capitalism, many in the official and social circles remained convinced of the virtues of the thinking. For example, in the late Soviet and the post-Soviet context, some hard-line political and intellectual movements often defend a widespread external expansion as the best means of ensuring Russia's security. The so-called Eurasianists view Russia as a constantly expanding land-based empire in a struggle for power against sea-based Atlanticism, associated especially with the United States.[5] Born out of the agony of two Europes, Soviet Russia saw itself as superior to the "decadent" and "rotten" Western capitalist civilization. Yet even the Soviet Civilizationists sought to justify their foreign policy expansionism by the need to respond to the "global imperial expansion" of the West. The expansionism, therefore, was seen by Russian rulers as legitimate and permissible in the international context. It remains to be seen which forms Russia's post-Soviet liberal Civilizationism might take.[6]

The continuity of Russian schools of foreign policy thinking in different external contexts is summarized in table 1.1.

EXPLAINING CHANGE AND CONTINUITY
IN RUSSIAN FOREIGN POLICY

This section introduces various explanations of Russian foreign policy and argues for the insufficiency of traditional approaches. In attempting to address

Table 1.1. Russia's Foreign Policy: Change and Continuity

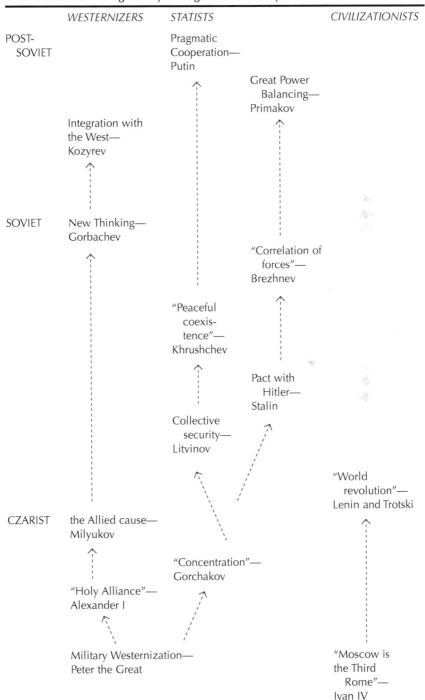

	WESTERNIZERS	*STATISTS*	*CIVILIZATIONISTS*
POST-SOVIET		Pragmatic Cooperation—Putin	
			Great Power Balancing—Primakov
	Integration with the West—Kozyrev		
SOVIET	New Thinking—Gorbachev		
			"Correlation of forces"—Brezhnev
		"Peaceful coexistence"—Khrushchev	
			Pact with Hitler—Stalin
		Collective security—Litvinov	
			"World revolution"—Lenin and Trotski
CZARIST	the Allied cause—Milyukov		
		"Concentration"—Gorchakov	
	"Holy Alliance"—Alexander I		
	Military Westernization—Peter the Great		"Moscow is the Third Rome"—Ivan IV

the shortcomings of these approaches, I offer a framework for understanding Russian behavior as shaped by the nation's interaction with the West.

The Insufficiency of Traditional Explanations

The most influential tradition of international thinking, commonly referred to as realism, has focused on historical patterns and continuity in Russia's foreign policy. In particular, scholars have sought to explain Russia's consistent commitment to the status quo, as well as foreign policy expansionism. Scholars in this tradition have often emphasized Russia's national interest as the driving force behind its international behavior. Defining it as preservation and enhancement of power within the existing international system, many scholars and statesmen alike saw national interest as a geopolitically enduring reality, rather than something open to interpretations. Other factors, such as ideology, the nature of government, and political culture, mattered, too. Yet their role was to specify—and sometimes to cover for, but never to contradict—"genuine" national interest. Realists have typically argued that the Soviet leaders, while employing a revolutionary ideology and acting under a totalitarian system of government, defended Russia's traditional interests.

> Soviet leaders did not act as though the demands of ideology and those of the Russian national interest were in conflict. Lenin, in negotiating the Treaty in Brest-Litovsk, and Stalin, in negotiating the Nazi-Soviet Pact and in the wartime summit conferences, were constantly aware that their first priority was to ensure the survival of the Russian state and to seek ways to enhance its security. . . . When they had opportunities to expand, the territories that interested them were identical to those that the tsars had sought, for identical strategic reasons.[7]

Others have pointed to underlying consistencies in Soviet policy. For instance, Nathan Leites, in his seminal study of Bolshevik ideology, identified three rules guiding the Soviet behavior: "never risk already conquered major positions for the sake of uncertain gains," "anything less than the exertion of maximum pressure is ineffective," and "mastery in the skill of retreating is as necessary as mastery in the skill of advancing."[8] For Western policymakers, realist studies implied the need to stay firm in resisting Russia's power aspirations, rather than to keep searching for common solutions, and to apply what during the Cold War would be called "containment." As Winston Churchill put it in his famous "iron curtain" speech, "There is nothing they [Russians] admire so much as strength, and there is nothing for which they have less respect than for . . . military weakness."[9]

More recent developments in realist thinking point to the structure of the international system—namely, the absence of legitimate authority (anarchy)—as the central force that affects Russia's international behavior. For example, some realists have explained Russia's liberal momentum of the late 1980s–early 1990s and the searches for active accommodation with the West by the Soviet defeat in the Cold War and the need to respond to the emergence of an America-centered global unipolar system. In this perspective, Russia's hegemonic policy in the former Soviet area and a nonconfrontational engagement with the West is the only rational strategy, given the fundamental weakness of Russia's post–Cold War capabilities.[10] The new or structural realists continue to view power and national interest as the underlying force of Russia's international behavior. Even when they employ factors other than power, such as perceptions and domestic politics,[11] they assign to these factors secondary roles relative to the role attributed to the structure of the international system. Introducing perceptions and domestic politics, therefore, does not change the overall thrust of the realist analysis, according to which the international environment is anarchic in nature and states have a constant drive for security and power (national interest).

By focusing on foreign policy continuity, realists employ a very narrow perspective on "change," limiting it to fluctuations of available power capabilities. In the realist tradition, there is little room for foreign policy patterns shaped by considerations other than power, such as indigenous ideas or cultural beliefs. As a result, realists typically overlook and wrongfully interpret some far-reaching changes in Russia's foreign policy that are potent for cooperation with Western nations. Realism seems to work when the actual policies at play are of a zero-sum nature, but it errs when the zero-sum reality is not in place.

For example, in his engagement with two leading realists, Robert English pointed to the inaccuracy of presenting Gorbachev as the overseer of the Soviet strategic retreat. He argued that the origins of Gorbachev's New Thinking dated back to the late 1950s and 1960s and had to do with domestic changes and the revival of cultural links to the West, not defense calculations and economic needs.[12] If this criticism is correct, realism is unable to account fully for Russia's liberal changes. It has a built-in tendency to misrepresent the scope and the origins of Russia's foreign policy changes. It follows that it is simply unfit for fully understanding Russian liberal-minded statesmen, such as Pavel Milyukov, Mikhail Gorbachev, or Andrei Kozyrev. Even when realists are able to correctly identify the direction of Russia's "realist" policy-makers, such as Primakov and Putin, their excessive emphasis on the international structure of power makes them neglectful of important domestic/local sources that often shape Russia's foreign policy.[13]

A less prominent, but still influential, tradition in international relations concentrates on understanding foreign policy changes. Western scholars working in this tradition have challenged the realist notion of foreign policy continuity by pointing to such episodes as Khrushchev's early arms control efforts, the Soviet policies of détente, and Gorbachev's sweeping international initiatives. Frequently referred to as liberals, these scholars have also sought to undermine the concept of national interest as something objective and geographically defined. In particular, they have pointed to considerable disagreements among state elites regarding Russia's international priorities and interests. They have also identified multiple coalitions and interest groups with different foreign policy agendas and ways to influence the policymaking process. Furthermore, they identified some learning curves in Russian/Soviet foreign policymaking.[14]

The end of the Cold War produced new expectations of increasing policy convergence across nations and pushed liberals toward developing theories of foreign policy that would be more sensitive to the structure of the international system. The liberal view of the international system is principally different from that of the realists. Unlike realists, who emphasize international anarchy and cyclical development, liberals have argued the global and progressive ascendancy of Western political and economic values. Francis Fukuyama pioneered the claim and insisted on the arrival of "the universalization of Western Liberal democracy as the final form of human government."[15] In this spirit, many scholars and policymakers took the end of the Cold War as an opportunity to assert that economic and political modernization, rather than geopolitically defined national interest, should serve as the primary foreign policy goal. Theories on the transition to a free-market economy and pluralistic democracy became dominant in academic and political discourse. Behind those theories lay a deep conviction in the progressive nature of international relations and the ability of market democratic institutions to turn the world into a more peaceful and prosperous place.

Despite the increased sophistication of its foreign policy analysis, liberalism is a limited guide in understanding Russia's foreign policy. It cannot offer a comprehensive theory of foreign policy because of its unrealistic assumptions and selective focus. While rejecting the anarchy-based perspective as inaccurate, liberals produced a vision of an international system that is restrictive in its own way. Unlike that of realists, the liberal vision of foreign policy change is progressive and cumulative. However, this vision does not account fully for conservative turns in Russia's foreign policy. Such turns are normally viewed as "setbacks" that imply Russia's future "return" to the track of progressive liberal changes. For instance, in acknowledgment of scholars of Clinton's Russia policies, "for the Clinton team, Yeltsin the man *was* reform, while his enemies represented regression and the possible return of communism."[16] It is not surprising that the Clinton White House miscalculated many of Russia's developments and often did not want to admit some obvious facts. For instance, as late as the second half of 1993, American officials believed that Russia's transition was on track and, as a result, they were completely unprepared for the nationalist victory in Russia's December 1993 parliamentary election.

Liberals have also failed to fully understand the changes that Yevgeni Primakov and Vladimir Putin brought to Russia's foreign policy. Unlike realists, liberals tend to view Primakov and Putin as unsuccessful statesmen because of their attempts to advance foreign policy that principally differed from Western priorities. Such differences are often attributed to Russia's "non-democratic" political system or Russian leaders' "wrong" assessment of their country's interests. With such thinking, liberals can be caught off guard by Russia's sustained assertiveness. For example, they are puzzled by the Kremlin's revisionism. They have long argued that Russia remains economically and politically vulnerable and is in no position to challenge America's global leadership. The conventional wisdom in liberal circles is that Russia is a declining autocratic power with unsustainable international behavior.[17]

Social Constructivism and Its Promise

Overall, there are two problems with realist and liberal accounts of foreign policy. First, both theories tend to emphasize one aspect of the international system at the expense of others. Rather than acknowledging the validity of both power and modernization/democratization imperatives in foreign policy formation, they choose to highlight one or the other. In so doing, the two approaches refrain from developing a comprehensive and complex explanatory framework. In such a framework, realism would need to be modified to account for liberal changes in Russia's foreign policy, whereas liberalism should be revised to explain Russia's periodic retreats to great power thinking.

The second problem is that both realism and liberalism are ethnocentric in the sense that they view Russia's foreign policy through similar Western cultural lenses and do not pay sufficient attention to Russia's indigenous history and system of perceptions. While realists are committed to the notion of Western power and dominance in the world, liberals advocate economic and political modernization by making little effort to apply any but the Western definition of the notion. Developed in the West, by the West, and for the West, these two approaches are increasingly problematic in a world that is multicultural and multi-meaningful. In order to address their limitations, they both need to be sensitized to social conditions in which the various changes in Russia's foreign policy take place. If we are to understand the diversity of national foreign policies, we ought to first understand what "national" is.

In the field of international relations, the perspective that begins the analysis by asking what "national" is and that exposes the "nation" to various meanings and interpretations is called social constructivism. Constructivists are different from realists and liberals in viewing the international system as a social or cultural phenomenon. In addition to military and institutional constraints or facilitators of state actions, as emphasized by the other two theories, constructivists concentrate on the cultural contexts and meanings in which these actions take place. From this perspective, the international system is not merely a terrain for applying available military, economic, and diplomatic instruments; rather, the role of the international system is in assisting states in their socialization and understanding of interests in world politics. The international environment constructs state actions and interests. Such actions and interests are not rationally uniform, and they differ depending on individual states' experiences with the international system and its parts. Constructivists argue that because particular social contexts define national interests, the formation of such interests should be carefully studied, rather than merely assumed to be rational or irrational. In the words of a leading constructivist, "It is striking how little empirical research has been done investigating what kind of interests state actors actually have."[18]

The central category of the constructivist theory of international politics is identity. Before nations figure out how to best defend their interests with available material and diplomatic means, they first seek to understand what these interests in the international society are. By interacting with other members of international society, nations develop affiliations, attachments, and—ultimately—their own identities. Historically, some nations or cultural communities emerge as more important than others, and it is through these significant Others that national Selves define their appropriate character and types of actions. The very existence of the Self becomes difficult without recognition from the Other. National identity therefore is a system of meanings that expresses the Self's emotional, cognitive, and evaluative orientations toward its significant Other. The significant Other establishes the meaningful context for the Self's existence and development and therefore exerts decisive influence on the Self. Through its actions, the Other may reinforce or erode the earlier established sense of national identity. Depending on whether these influences are read by the Self as extending or denying it recognition, they may either encourage or discourage the Self to act cooperatively. (Table 1.2 summarizes the constructivist perspective on foreign policy, relative to those of realism and liberalism.)

At the same time, one must not privilege international social practices at the expense of those of local origins. Local conditions, such as the state of the economy, relations among different social groups, or the type of political regime, are just as important in shaping national perceptions. These and other conditions have long been part of foreign policy analysis, and the initially international system–oriented constructivism is now moving toward

Table 1.2. International Relations Theories and Their Perspectives on Foreign Policy

	International Influences	*Foreign Policy Actor*	*Foreign Policy Objective*
Realism	Anarchy	State	State power
Liberalism	Western economic and political progress	Individuals, groups	Modernization and democratization
Constructivism	Significant Other	National Self	Self's acceptance by the Other

incorporating domestic-level variables.[19] Foreign policy begins when a state manages to transcend the dichotomy of internal/external pressures and develops multiple strategies for responding to world challenges.[20] With distinct social conditions in place, nations have distinct concerns and therefore view the world in their own ways. For instance, perceptions of reality by rich nations will differ from perceptions of reality by those that are considered poor. Some local concerns are more historically stable and are formed across a relatively long time, while others are more immediate and emerge in response to short-term developments. But in both cases, they serve as cultural lenses through which a nation views the outside world.

A nation, however, is not a homogenous entity. Different traditions or schools of thinking about the world develop in response to international and local conditions, and these schools compete for political influence. They hold different images regarding a nation's identity, the nature of the external world, and appropriate policy response. In a relatively open society, they compete openly for the dominant position and are supported by various social groups or coalitions. Constructivists do not view foreign policy as a product of a unitary state's advancing power, as in realism, or as a particular group pursuing modernization interests, as in liberalism. Rather, the role of a coalition is to put forward a particular image of national identity that will speak to the existing local conditions and be recognized by the significant Other. Identity coalitions are broader and more fundamental than interest coalitions, and they seek to achieve social recognition, rather than to maximize wealth or power.

To summarize, both international influences and local conditions are critical in understanding the processes of foreign policy formation and change. International influences by the Other create the meaningful context in which the national Self evolves and then shapes foreign policy. Past interactions with the external environment, as well as local conditions, establish identity as a relatively stable system of meanings with a well-consolidated context in which to act. Therefore, a nation has relative autonomy in influencing foreign policy, and that autonomy is historically established.

On a more contemporary level, however, identity is a product of discursive competition among different groups and coalitions, drawing on different actions of the Other and interpreting contemporary international and local influences in a way that suits the groups' interests. The process that links international and local conditions, national identity and foreign policy, is a complex one, and it includes vigorous debates over the nature of national identity and national interests. Because international society contains multiple norms and influences, some of them may conflict in influencing the Self. For instance, realists emphasize the need to be strong, while liberals insist that the world revolves around values of free economy and society. Both strength and liberty can serve as powerful normative messages the modern West sends to the outside world. However, just as realists and liberals disagree, the norms of strength and liberty can conflict in shaping the identity of the Self.

At this point, identity becomes highly contested. Different identity coalitions form to promote their visions. Promoted by various identity groups in both public and private spaces, identity contestation is especially intense until one of the available visions becomes predominant. Activities of political entrepreneurs, appropriate material and ideational resources, conducive institutional arrangements, and historical practices can considerably facilitate this process of persuading the general public and elites. When this persuasion part of the process is complete, the state appropriates the dominant national identity vision as a guide in policymaking (national interest). Foreign policy, then, is a highly political phenomenon. It evolves with the rise and fall of various identity visions, as advocated by different social and political groups. Individual leaders' views and ideologies, as creative and autonomous as they may be, too frequently reflect group visions of national identity. Other factors and influences may interfere with a decision-making process, yet if all the other factors are equal, one can expect a reasonable degree of foreign policy consistency based on an adopted image of national identity. (Table 1.3 spells out the causal influences on foreign policy as viewed from the constructivist perspective.)

The Social Construction of Russia's Foreign Policy

In Russia's case, Europe and the West, in general, played the role of the significant Other and prominently figured in debates about national identity. It was Europe and the West that created the meaningful environment in which Russia's rulers defended their visions of national identity and national interest. Russia has historically sought to be recognized by the Western Other and to modernize after the manner of the West. In 1917—partly because of the West's own agonizing split between autocracy and liberalism, and partly because of the special local conditions and the leadership's errors—Russia went through the experience of a social revolution and ceased experimenting with liberal reforms. The liberal West, therefore, rejected Russia as one

Table 1.3. Constructivist Explanation of Foreign Policy: A Causal Process

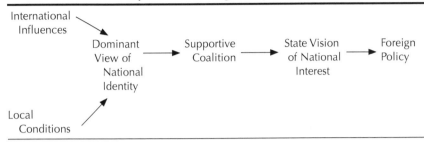

of its own, and Bolshevik leaders sought to be recognized for their strength, rather than for the nature of their domestic institutions. Statist thinking prevailed in the Soviet discourse, reflecting the desire to maintain the balance of power with the West. As the West consolidated its liberal institutions after World War II, liberal thinking returned to the Soviet Union, paving the way for possible future changes. Gorbachev's arrival signaled that Soviet liberalism had grown strong enough to challenge the tenets of the old Statist and Civilizationist thinking.

However, Gorbachev was unable to stay his course. Under the conditions of extreme polarization between the old Statists and Civilizationists and the new liberal Westernizers, Gorbachev lost his initial support among elites and the general populace and subsequently had to resign. Although he never meant for Russia's socialist identity to be replaced by that of pro-Western liberalism, Gorbachev undoubtedly greatly contributed to the rise of domestic Westernizers. The 1991 collapse of the Soviet Union presented Russia's new liberals with an opportunity to fashion a pro-Western course of foreign policy. President Boris Yeltsin and his foreign minister Andrei Kozyrev pursued policies of strategic partnership and integration with the West and its institutions. Externally, they were inspired by the Western promises of support, and they expected to "join" the West within a few years. They saw the West's victory in the Cold War as the promise and the opportunity of the new liberal era. Domestically, the Westernizing coalition included—in addition to liberal-minded leadership—intellectuals, human rights activists, and new pro-capitalist elites, particularly those with export interests in the West. The new identity coalition pursued a revolutionary agenda of transforming the old Soviet institutions into those of a pro-Western nation-state. It seemed as if the new liberal identity was finally to be established in Russia.

But Soviet disintegration did not end the old identity debates. In fact, partly because of the Soviet breakup, the new post-Soviet identity became deeply contested, and the liberal momentum did not last. Soon the pro-Western policies were met with a formidable opposition, in which the new Statists played the key role. The new Statists were different from their Soviet counterparts in acknowledging the necessity of building a market economy and democratic institutions. At the same time, they shared the old line of Statist reasoning, according to which all reforms had to be subjected to the main objective of strengthening the state. The new Statist coalition included military industrialists, the army, and the security services—those who saw only marginal benefits in adopting the Western model. Led by presidential adviser Sergei Stankevich and then the chief of foreign intelligence Yevgeni Primakov, the new Statists insisted that the national interest had not changed significantly and still had to do with defending Russia's great power status. Over time, this reasoning won the support of the elites and the masses, and the state had to adopt the Statist concept of national interest. Primakov—now Russia's newly appointed foreign minister—argued for more restrained relations with the West and for a more "balanced" and "diverse" foreign policy. Primakov believed that Russia's new liberal values did not erase the need to maintain the status of a distinct Eurasianist great power and to balance Western influences. One of his prominent proposals was that Russia develops a strategic alliance with China and India.

Statists were able to defeat Westernizers because of the power of the old Statist identity, the establishment of which could be traced as far back as the 1920s. The Statists were also successful in using the weakness of the new liberal state and mobilizing various informal channels for influencing policymaking. In particular, they benefited politically from the failure of Westernist radical economic reform. Externally, the identity struggle between Statists and Westernizers took place in the changed context. Looking to protect Russia's security, Statists were soon able to identify several threatening developments. Newly emerged instabilities and conflicts in the former Soviet republics and inside the country (Chechnya) in the early to mid-1990s made it extremely difficult for Westernizers to sustain their policies of disengagement from the periphery. Importantly, the West—Russia's significant Other— greatly strengthened the Statist discourse by making a decision to expand the North Atlantic Treaty Organization (NATO) eastward and exclude Russia from the process. This strengthened the sense that the West was not accepting Russia as one of its own. All of these developments provided the context for constructing the sought-after image of external threat and solidified the influence of the new identity coalition. On the other hand, Westernism did not have sufficient public support to be able to reduce the power of the Statists.

The arrival of Vladimir Putin as the new president signaled yet another change in policies and a renewed interest in engaging the West. In a stunning strategic reversal, the state adopted another distinct view of national interest—different from those of Westernizers and Primakovites. Although Putin insisted on Russia's priority of preserving great power status, his strategy for achieving this objective differed considerably from Primakov's. Instead of continuing the policy of balancing against the West, Putin explicitly sided with Europe and the United States and insisted that Russia was a country of European and Western, rather than Asian, identity.

Why such a modification in the previous Statist thinking? The unresolved identity question, the shifting balance in the Statists–Westernizers debate, and the new international context help to explain Putin's strategic innovation. Domestically, Putin's course of "Pragmatic Cooperation" with the West was the project of a mixed-identity coalition that included both Westernist and Statist interests. Sometimes referred to as the alliance of oligarchs and chekists,[21] the new domestic coalition brought Putin to power and gained strength in the new world context, which held both threats and opportunities for Russia. Opportunities came from domestic economic stabilization and cooperation with the United States after the September 11, 2001, terrorist attacks, and threats were defined by the new leadership as being of a terrorist nature and emanating from both inside and outside of Russia.

The public strongly supported Putin's approach. His vision of the national interests, which included the preservation of Russia's security and identity, socioeconomic development, and the strengthening of political institutions,[22] resonated with the domestic public better than the security-underplayed Westernism of Kozyrev or the security-overplayed Eurasianism of Primakov. In response to the colored revolutions and perceived Western pressures, Russia's policy obtained a more assertive dimension. The Kremlin sought to consolidate Russia's position by challenging the Western nations to open their markets to Russian business and not expand their military infrastructure closer to Russia's borders.

Once the international context began to change, Russia's identity competition resumed. With the global financial crisis severely undermining the country's economy, the liberal Westernizers reemerged to promote Russia's modernization according to Western standards of free-market competition, political pluralism, and transparency. They embraced Medvedev's vision of a cautious modernization and sought to push it toward a radical revision of Putin's Statist model and assertive relations with the West. Medvedev's foreign policy was based on the notion of international alliances for modernization and served to bring Russia closer to Europe and the United States. Although a number of serious issues remained unresolved, Russia and the West signed a new START (Strategic Arms Reduction Treaty) treaty, cooperated on securing Afghanistan, and occasionally coordinated their policies toward the Middle Eastern region. In 2012, Russia also joined the WTO (World Trade Organization).

However, the international context continued to encourage Statist thinking inside Russia. The Western expansion of military infrastructure, such as the Missile Defense System in Europe, attempts to limit Moscow's influence in the former Soviet region, and promotion of Western values contributed to Putin's perception of the West as seeking to internally weaken Russia. The Ukraine crisis in 2014 and Russia's military intervention in 2022 further exacerbated Russia's sense of strategic vulnerability by pushing it further away from the West toward non-Western nations, especially China.

Neither realism nor liberalism is fully satisfactory in explaining the identified changes and continuity in Russia's foreign policy. For example, realist arguments that post-Soviet Russia was merely looking to consolidate its great power capabilities fail to acknowledge the socialist Westernist nature of Gorbachev's policies and the liberal Westernist vision of Russia's first post-Soviet foreign minister. Both Gorbachev and Kozyrev were thinking in terms of the priority of cooperation and engagement with the world, rather than preserving or reviving Russia's material power. They had roots in domestic international thinking, but were also motivated and encouraged by the West's liberal developments. Because of the failure to acknowledge the true origins of the identified liberal foreign policy developments, realists also misrepresented the scope of changes resulting from these developments. Both changes implied fundamental breaks with the Statist past and went far beyond strategic adaptation to the growing military power of the West. Liberals, on the other hand, have difficulty making sense of Russia's retreat to great power thinking. To them, this retreat does not seem rational, since in the world of globalization, preoccupation with great power status may be an impediment to development and, ultimately, the survival of the country. Indeed, it is all too common to see Western politicians' references to Putin as a paranoid and irrational thinker.[23]

Ultimately, both realism and liberalism are inadequate in identifying the genuine nature and origins of various concepts of national interest guiding Russia's international behavior. In particular, they miss the fact that national interest is not about power or modernization. Instead, it is about social adaptation to the constantly changing international and local conditions, and it is about recognition by the identified significant Other. For both Westernizers and Statists, the West is a key point of reference, although each school understands its nature differently. Even Civilizationists, who rarely held a prominent position in domestic discourse, aspired to be respected by the West. What matters in national-interest formation is how the debate about national identity is shaped by (1) a population's most pressing local concerns and (2) contemporary behavior of Western nations toward Russia that vindicates or erodes the earlier established images of the West.

In addition, as I try to show in the following chapters, each school must work hard to make use of available material and institutional resources in society. Ultimately, it is the described local conditions combined with considerations of international recognition and respect, rather than a position in the international economy or the balance of power, that determine the concept of national interest adopted by the state as a foreign policy guide. Russia's post-Soviet concepts of national interest and their formation are summarized in table 1.4 (see facing page). The remaining chapters of the book further develop the above-suggested explanation of Russia's foreign policy.

EVALUATING RUSSIA'S FOREIGN POLICY

In addition to describing and explaining Russia's foreign policy, one should also attempt to evaluate the record of its efficiency. This section introduces the evaluative standards adopted in this book and briefly illustrates their application with examples from the post-Soviet era. The remaining chapters offer a more detailed assessment of the accomplishments and losses of each of the described foreign policy courses.

Evaluative Standards

Four criteria deserve to be carefully considered in evaluating a foreign policy record—security, welfare, autonomy, and identity. Security typically refers to the absence of military threats to the nation, particularly (but not limited to) from outside. The welfare criterion implies that foreign policy assists the nation in creating external conditions for the improvement of standards of living that may have to do with economic growth, new jobs, and social services. Autonomy has to do with the state's ability to make decisions by withstanding possible pressures of special interests from inside and outside the country. Finally, a successful foreign policy is not fundamentally disruptive to the existing system of cultural values. Rather, such a policy relies on these values by reshaping and mobilizing them in a manner that would further the nation's interests and assist the nation in accomplishing its principal goals.

In general, a foreign policy is about protection of a nation's external security, economy, and social lifestyle. Each of these criteria or objectives can be measured by a variety of indicators. A more secure nation, for example, is one that has relatively few military threats from outside and therefore can afford to reduce its military expenditures. A more prosperous nation has stable growth and improving living standards for the general population. A more autonomous nation has a state that is capable of defending the interests of the people as a whole and is not hostage to some powerful influences at home, such as big business or military, or from abroad. Determining the state's foreign policy autonomy requires comparing how the proclaimed goals of defending the interests of the national majority stand against specific international actions of the state, as well as to what extent these actions represent

Table 1.4. Explaining Russia's Foreign Policy after Communism

Local Conditions

Behavior of the West	*National-Democratic Revolution*	*Economic Depression; Political Instability*	*Economic Recovery; New Security Threats*	*Economic Decline; Remaining Security Threats*	*Economic Decline; Political Mobilization*
Support	INTEGRATION WITH THE WEST				
NATO expansion		BALANCING			
Renewed support			PRAGMATIC COOPERATION		
Regime change			ASSERTIVENESS		
Engagement				ALLIANCES FOR MODERNIZATION	
Political and economic pressures					CIVILIZATION AND ASYMMETRIC ASSERTIVENESS

interest groups at the expense of the rest of the society. Finally, a culturally sensitive foreign policy reflects the already-established historical patterns and usually has the population's support with regard to the asserted relationships with the nation's significant Other. Approval of the society in each of these categories expressed through public opinion polls (should such polls be available) may serve as additional evidence for evaluating a foreign policy record.

The foreign policy of each time period can be evaluated using these criteria as they apply during a specified period. Foreign policy is successful if at a given time it has provided a balanced defense of all the listed objectives using the available resources.

From New Thinking to State-Civilization

Russia's foreign policy record is complex. Overall, the country's leadership has tried to defend its security by relying on the limited resources available and without resorting to an imperialist course. After the collapse of the economy in the early 1990s, Russia began a difficult process of recovery, and society on the whole began to feel the difference of the post-Yeltsin era. Under Putin, during the 2000s the state restored a good measure of policy autonomy, and key international decisions became more reflective of the social consensus than those of the early to mid-1990s. Polls of the general public on some pressing international issues during the past two years or so consistently demonstrate that people on the whole are satisfied with the country's foreign policy. Finally, as a result of a more moderate foreign policy course, Russia has been able to strike a better cultural balance between the necessity to rethink the old Soviet legacy and the need to respect some traditional values, such as the defense of Russian-language speakers abroad. Geopolitically, Russia's foreign policy reflects the nation's desire to have strong ties with European, or Western civilization, while preserving special relations with Muslim and Asian neighbors.

In none of the specified areas, however, has Russia's foreign policy been perfectly efficient. For instance, terrorism continues to pose a serious challenge to the nation's internal and external security. The economic improvement is still more of a product of the 1998 currency devaluation and favorable world oil prices than of competitive domestic restructuring. In a number of areas, interest groups have preserved their influence on state policy. And the crisis of Russia's post-Soviet identity has not yet been fully resolved. The transition to a relatively balanced foreign policy course has also not been easy or straightforward. Rather, it has emerged as a result of zigs and zags of different strategies that different leaders have pursued in concert with their views of Russia's national interest. Nevertheless, the overall improvement in foreign policy efficiency has been evident if one examines the record over the past thirty years. Polls of the general public on some pressing international issues during the past two years or so consistently demonstrate that people, on the whole, are satisfied with the country's foreign policy. What follows is a brief assessment of four distinct periods in Russia's international activities.

Gorbachev's foreign policy course was based on an innovative understanding of national interest that called for rethinking the Soviet system and its international environment (New Thinking). Its most important accomplishment was a radical improvement of Russia's national security, which resulted mainly from fundamentally changed relationships with the West. Thanks largely to Gorbachev's personal leadership and commitment, several key arms-control agreements were concluded, and the whole era of highly adventurous arms races was gone forever. The disappearance of the threat from the West liberated a lot of resources that had been previously spent to feed one of the most powerful military machines in the world.

The New Thinking record is not as impressive in areas outside security. Gorbachev's preoccupation with matters of arms control did not assist him in reforming the Soviet economy or improving people's standards of living. From 1988 to 1989, polls began to register growing disappointment with reforms and a lack of trust in the central leadership. While Moscow was busy negotiating with Western nations over security matters, such as thresholds of nuclear sufficiency and withdrawals of troops from the third world and Eastern Europe, the economy was increasingly losing control, eventually collapsing in 1990. This development severely handicapped Gorbachev in his ability to pursue the originally designed international course. Already in 1990, this course was on its way to changing from the Soviet one in terms of initiative and design into a largely West-controlled one. The leader of New Thinking was weakened and had to make many more concessions to Western leaders than he had envisioned. He no longer had the initiative or policy autonomy required for sustaining his course, and US president George H. W. Bush was, therefore, correct to proclaim the West's "victory" in the Cold War in his 1992 State of the Union address. In addition, Gorbachev's foreign policy failed to mobilize Russian cultural identity. Introduced to reinvigorate the country's social energy and initiative, New Thinking left the nation's citizens deeply divided and unsure about their future. Already in 1989, 34 percent of the public felt that the Soviet Union could not serve as an example to the outside world, compared with only 5 percent in 1988.[24]

The course of Integration with the West, pursued by President Yeltsin and his foreign minister Kozyrev, was meant to capitalize on the already-achieved security and improved relations with Western nations. The post-Soviet leaders went much further than Gorbachev in their proclaimed convergence of the interests of new Russia with those of the West. Whereas Gorbachev saw the Soviet Union and the West as culturally distinct entities, the new leadership proposed that Russia become a full-fledged member of Western civilization by borrowing key Western values, such as individualism, the market economy, and political democracy. Partly, the new concept of national interest, which emphasized rapid economic and political modernization, was designed to attract Western economic assistance and therefore address the welfare criterion of foreign policy. Yeltsin and Kozyrev hoped that after proclaiming their commitment to Western values and adopting principles of rapid marketization, or the so-called shock therapy, private investments and financial assistance would quickly revive the half-alive and continuously deteriorating economy.

The reality was different. Western investments remained scarce. Through the use of IMF and World Bank loans, the economy was stabilized, but at the heavy price of stagnation, collapsed social services, and skyrocketing poverty. The failure of shock therapy to bring Russia into the family of rich Western nations alienated a considerable portion of the elites and general public, making it difficult to defend the foreign policy record of the pro-Western leadership. Increasingly, the populace felt that strategic partnership with the West was not working, and many developed resentments toward Western nations, particularly the United States. For instance, during 1993–1995, the number of those viewing the United States as a threat increased from 26 to 44 percent among the general public and from 27 to 53 percent among the elites.[25] In addition, many judged that Russia was effectively ceding its policy autonomy to the West in economic and other affairs. In 1995, 75 percent of the population believed that the economy was essentially in foreign hands.[26] The number of those perceiving the West as seeking to weaken Russia also increased. The increased dependency on the West in economic affairs went hand in hand with loss of autonomy in security affairs, as Washington was often dictating Moscow's foreign policy in such critical areas as the Balkans and Iraq.

Perhaps worst of all, security issues returned to the agenda. Partly the result of Kozyrev's overconcentration on the Western direction, the security threats reemerged in the form of ethnic and military conflicts in the former Soviet Union and even inside Russia (Chechnya). All of these developments further exacerbated the sense of Russian hurt pride and identity. The pro-Western foreign policy course did little to address those feelings. Accompanied by failures to protect the nation's security, economy, and policy autonomy, this course in fact deepened the sense of cultural loneliness among Russians. Shrunken in size after the Soviet Union's disintegration and confronted with NATO's decision to expand eastward, Russia was bound to seriously rethink the assumptions of its pro-Western foreign policy.

When the leading critic of the West-oriented course, Yevgeni Primakov, replaced Kozyrev as foreign minister, Russia's foreign policy changed greatly. As much as was possible under Yeltsin's leadership, the new foreign

minister pursued policies of restoring great power status. He addressed the
new security threats through intense diplomatic involvement in the former
Soviet region, particularly in the areas of military confrontations (Moldova)
and civil wars (Tajikistan), and through the initiation of economic and security projects aimed at tightening the ties among the former Soviet republics
under the leadership of Russia. Primakov was also successful in restoring
some measure of foreign policy autonomy. While Russia's dependence on
Western lending agencies continued, the new course was pursued with greater
respect for public perception of the national interest, and it was considerably
less tolerant of Washington's attempts to shape Russia's policies toward the
Balkans, Iraq, and the former Soviet region. Both elites and the general public
expressed their strong support for the new course, welcoming its greater independence and concentration on solving security issues in the former Soviet
Union. In line with the new course, the public was supportive of strengthening the army and relations with the former republics.[27]

The strategy of Great Power Balancing was not as successful in improving the welfare of Russians. The project of integrating the former Soviet
region proved to be excessively geopolitically driven and not as founded on
economic grounds. The economy continued to stagnate, not bringing any
foreign investments and increasing the burden of foreign debt. The new foreign policy strategy was also dubious with respect to the criterion of identity.
Primakov addressed the new cultural fear of the West by attempting to pragmatically defuse the crisis in relations with NATO and by proposing to build a
strategic triangle of Russia, China, and India to balance American hegemonic
growth in world politics. NATO's military intervention in Yugoslavia in 1999
further pushed Russia away from the West. Yet the Westernist component
of Russia's cultural identity is a well-established reality, and the strategy of
Eurasia-oriented Great Power Balancing failed to address this part of the
Russian national psyche.

Vladimir Putin's course of Pragmatic Cooperation has been more successful in terms of meeting the criteria of security, welfare, autonomy, and
identity. Creatively borrowing from both Westernist and Statist thinking of
the post-Soviet era, the president forcefully responded to the new security
challenge of terrorism in Chechnya, the Caucasus, and central Asia, simultaneously improving somewhat damaged relations with the West. Dmitri
Medvedev's policy of modernization continued the effort to pragmatically
engage the West in order to strengthen ties with most advanced economies
while preserving a good measure of state autonomy. As a result, the economy
and social welfare have improved. Russia finally gained membership in the
World Trade Organization (WTO) in 2011—in part to continue with the
country's efforts of economic modernization. Finally, Pragmatic Cooperation
helped to preserve both Westernist and Statist components of Russia's

identity by orienting Russians to adjust to the West while preserving their own cultural legacy and long-standing relations with non-Western nations in Asia and the Muslim world.

However, since the early 2010s, the course of Pragmatic Cooperation has demonstrated limitations, as Western nations declined to recognize Russia's distinct security interests and values. Following the Orange Revolution in Ukraine, Russia sought to consolidate its political system in order to prevent the Ukraine-like destabilization and the West's potential interference in Russia's internal affairs. Putin's new vision of Russia as a State-Civilization with distinct interests and values since 2012 sought to compensate for the weaknesses of Medvedev's cooperative and West-centric approach. Russia's new course has aimed to stand its ground on security issues by not allowing Ukraine to be absorbed by the West's political and military institutions. Russia also wanted to take advantage of new opportunities presented by the rise of non-Western powers. This course resulted in Russia's military intervention in Ukraine in 2022, new political and military tensions with the West, and increased isolation of Russia from the global markets.

METHODOLOGY AND ORGANIZATION OF THE BOOK

This study combines two methods. In order to explore the indigenous system of Russian perceptions, I explore the content and intensity of Russian foreign policy debates by comparing arguments made by the identified schools of thinking. For understanding the process of contestation of national interests, I employ the method of "schools of thought" analysis. Following Martin Wight's conceptualization,[28] I identify three distinct schools of thinking about the national interest that existed in Russia before and after Gorbachev's perestroika (Westernism, Statism, and Civilizationism). Careful exploration of the arguments made by various schools and participants in Russian discourse allows me to identify existing foreign policy alternatives and to present a comprehensive picture of the country's international thinking.

For understanding changes in Russia's post-Soviet foreign policy, I employ a method of "overtime comparison." Beginning with the next chapter, I offer a detailed analysis of the rise and fall of several distinct concepts of national interests—New Thinking, Integration with the West, Great Power Balancing, Pragmatic Cooperation, Assertiveness, Alliances for Modernization, and Civilization—as well as policies that stemmed from each of these concepts. I present these concepts by dividing them into two broad periods of Russia's relations with the West, following Gorbachev's New Thinking (chapter 2); attempts at cooperation from Integration to Pragmatic Cooperation (chapter 3); and attempts to assert Russia's interests from Assertiveness to Civilization (chapter 4). The final substantive section (chapter 5) then analyzes Russia's search for a new direction following 2019. I trace how each of these visions first emerged outside the state and the process through which it then came to define leadership's perceptions and adopted international policies. The book's central argument is that it is these visions of national interest, rather than Russia's position in the international economy or balance of power, that have determined the country's foreign policy after communism. During the 1990s through the early 2000s, neither structural power conditions nor the international economic position of Russia has changed sufficiently to fully account for its foreign policy choices.

The book's organization is straightforward. The chapters that follow study national interests and foreign policy formation through several distinct periods from the late 1980s until 2022. In each period, I describe the international and local contexts in which Russian debates about national interest took place. I analyze the process through which one of the foreign policy visions prevailed and obtained the status of state vision. I then review specific international policies pursued by leaders toward the former Soviet Union and the outside world in attempting to satisfy their visions of national interest. Finally, I attempt to evaluate the accomplishments and losses of each of the pursued foreign policy courses. The concluding chapters reflect on the future choices of Russia's foreign policy and summarize the analysis by comparing the diverse concepts of national interest and evaluating their relative performance. The final section (chapter 6) also draws lessons for Russian and Western policymakers.

NOTES

1. Arnold Wolfers, " 'National Security' as an Ambiguous Symbol," in *Classics of International Relations*, 2nd ed., ed. John A. Vasques (Englewood Cliffs, NJ: Prentice Hall, 1990), 135.

2. Khrushchev's Europeanism was limited, and it pursued the objective of greater European independence in the context of a power struggle with the Americans. Yet his position that the European Economic Community become a reality emboldened those in domestic politics who wanted to improve relationships with Bonn and other European nations. See Iver B. Neumann, *Russia and the Idea of Europe: A Study in Identity and International Relations* (London: Routledge, 1996), 140–41.

3. As cited in Richard Sakwa, *The Rise and Fall of the Soviet Union, 1917–1991* (London: Routledge, 1999), 187–88.

4. See Yevgeni Primakov, "Rossiya v mirovoi politike," *Mezhdunarodnaya zhizn' 5* (1998); I. Ivanov, *Vneshnyaya politika Rossiyi* (Moscow: Mezhdunarodnyye otnosheniya, 2001), 313–30; *Strategiya dlya Rossiyi: Povestka dlya prezidenta—2000.* Russian Westernists, on the other hand, are often critical of Gorchakov's diplomacy

(see, for example, Yuri Fedorov, "Krizis vneshnei politiki Rossiyi," *Pro et Contra* 6, nos. 1–2 [2001]).

5. Aleksandr Dugin, *Osnovy geopolitiki* (Moscow: Arktogeya, 1997); Aleksandr Mitrofanov, *Shagi novoi geopolitiki* (Moscow, 1998).

6. Interestingly enough, Yeltsin's former privatization czar and former head of Russia's state electric company, Anatoli Chubais, wrote that Russia's main goal in the twenty-first century should be to build up a "liberal empire" through the strengthening of its position in the former Soviet Union. "EES Head Calls for Russia to Become a 'Liberal Empire,' " RFE/RL Newsline, September 26, 2003; Anatoli Chubais, "Missiya Rossiyi v XXI veke," *Nezavisimaya gazeta*, October 1, 2003.

7. Robert H. Donaldson and Joseph L. Nogee, *The Foreign Policy of Russia* (Armonk, NY: M. E. Sharpe, 1998), 59.

8. Nathan Leites, *The Operational Code of the Politburo* (New York: McGraw Hill, 1951), as cited in Celeste A. Wallander, "The Sources of Russian Conduct," in *The Sources of Russian Foreign Policy after the Cold War*, ed. C. A. Wallander (Boulder, CO: Westview Press, 1996), 5.

9. Sakwa, *The Rise and Fall of the Soviet Union*, 295.

10. Neil MacFarlane, "Realism and Russian Strategy after the Collapse of the USSR," in *Unipolar Politics*, ed. Ethan B. Kapstein and Michael Mastanduno (New York: Columbia University Press, 1999); Allen Lynch, "Realism of Russian Foreign Policy," *Europe-Asia Studies* 53, no. 1 (2001).

11. Gideon Rose, "Neoclassical Realism and Theories of Foreign Policy," *World Politics* 51, no. 1 (1998).

12. Robert English, "Power, Ideas, and New Evidence on the Cold War's End," *International Security* 26, no. 4 (Spring 2002): 78–82.

13. In fact, both Primakov's and Putin's foreign policies can be understood in terms of Russia's responses to new domestic challenges, such as economic poverty and insecure borders. As some scholars have argued, outside the Western Hemisphere, states' international responses often explain the need to stabilize political regimes internally. See, for example, Mohammed Ayoob, *Third World Security Predicament: State Making, Regional Conflict, and the International System* (Boulder, CO: Lynne Rienner, 1995).

14. For a more detailed overview of Russia's foreign policy studies, see Wallander, "The Sources of Russian Conduct."

15. Francis Fukuyama, "The End of History?" *National Interest* (1989): 4.

16. James Goldgeier and Michael McFaul, *Power and Purpose* (Washington, DC: The Brookings Institute, 2003), 11.

17. For analysis of liberal errors in assessing both Primakov and Putin, see Seva Gunitsky and Andrei P. Tsygankov, "The Wilsonian Bias in the Study of Russian Foreign Policy," *Problems of Post-Communism*, 2018.

18. Alexander Wendt, *Social Theory of International Politics* (Cambridge: Cambridge University Press, 1999), 133.

19. As one scholar suggests, "Identity explanations are likely to become 'foreign policy-ized' by connecting identity to other factors and theories that have long been part of the FPA agenda." Juliet Kaarbo, "Foreign Policy Analysis in the Twenty-First

Century: Back to Comparison, Forward to Identity and Ideas," *International Studies Review* 5 (2003): 160. International relations scholars have recognized the internal/external bind by referring to it as a "two-level game." Robert D. Putnam, "Diplomacy and Domestic Politics: The Logic of Two-Level Games," *International Organization* 42, no. 2 (1988).

20. For additional hypotheses about international influences and their interaction with local conditions, see Jack Snyder, "International Leverage on Soviet Domestic Change," *World Politics* 42, no. 1 (1989); James Richter, *Khrushchev's Double Bind: International Pressures and Domestic Coalition Politics* (Baltimore, MD: Johns Hopkins University Press, 1994).

21. *Chekist* originates from the Russian *CheKa*, the original name of the Bolsheviks' security service. It was led by People's Commissar Feliks Dzerzhinski. Oligarchs are, of course, superrich captains of Russia's privatized economy.

22. See Vladimir Putin, "Rossiya na rubezhe tysyacheleti," *Nezavisimaya gazeta*, December 2, 1999.

23. Suffice it to recall German chancellor Angela Merkel's remarks to President Barack Obama following Russia's intervention in Crimea, that Putin is living "in another world" (Peter Baker, "Pressure Rising as Obama Works to Rein in Russia," *New York Times,* March 2, 2015, http://www.nytimes.com/2014/03/03/world/europe/pressure-rising-as-obama-works-to-rein-in-russia.html?hp).

24. Yuri Levada, ed., *Est' mneniye! Itogi sotsiologicheskogo oprosa* (Moscow: Progress, 1990), 284.

25. William Zimmerman, *The Russian People and Foreign Policy* (Princeton, NJ: Princeton University Press, 2002), 91.

26. Zimmerman, *The Russian People*, 92.

27. Zimmerman, *The Russian People*, 91; Fond Obschestvennoye Mneniye, at www.fom.ru.

28. Martin Wight, *International Theory: The Three Traditions* (Leicester, UK: Leicester University Press, 1991).

2

The Cold War Crisis and Soviet New Thinking, 1985–1991

Taking into account the new situation in the world, the problem of interests must be addressed in a new way.

—Mikhail Gorbachev[1]

With Gorbachev, Russia's story of engagement with the West took a sharp turn. While being a convinced socialist, Gorbachev pursued a radically different interpretation of Russia's socialist identity, which he viewed as distinct yet compatible with Western ideas of democracy, and which eventually collapsed under the heavy weight of Western modernity. Before we analyze the leader of perestroika's worldview and perceptions, we must, however, review the context in which Gorbachev formulated his foreign policy vision. For it was this context that shaped Soviet Russia's new understanding of national interest.

THE COLD WAR AND SOVIET FOREIGN POLICY

During the Cold War, the Western Other changed in some fundamental ways. These changes, as well as their influences on the Soviet Union, can be viewed in at least two different lights. On the one hand, the West emerged as a more unified civilization committed to values of democracy, liberal capitalist reconstruction, and human rights. The success of the Marshall Plan in post–World War II Europe, as well as a considerable improvement in living standards, made a positive impression on some officials in Soviet Russia and encouraged reformers inside the country.

On the other hand, the Cold War warriors in the West pushed for increased military expenditures and a tougher stance toward Russia, which made it more difficult for the Soviet reformers to advocate change and rapprochement with Western nations. As the logic of confrontation was gaining the upper hand in Russia–West relations, the two sides were increasingly losing sight of many other important international issues, such as poverty and environmental degradation. In this context, everything was progressively viewed through the lens of who gains more power and who manages to more successfully weaken the opponent.

In this contradictory context, the Soviet schools of foreign policy thinking drew their inspiration from different developments in the West. The Soviet Westernizers emphasized the West's democratic consolidation and policies of détente. They sought to acquire Western recognition by conducting domestic reforms and advocating a more robust international cooperation. In Europe, it was social democratic ideas that most closely resembled this group's views. Through support of détente, European social democrats made it easier for the Soviet reformists to press on with their international and domestic agenda.[2] Gorbachev, as well as his reformist predecessors, such as Nikita Khrushchev, did not see the West as inherently evil. They identified with the West of reform and moderation, rather than with that of containment or defeat of the Soviet "evil empire" in an arms race competition. Outside the political class, this nonconfrontational vision appealed to the Soviet middle class—the highly educated social strata that were eager to break the taboos of Soviet isolationism and develop mutually beneficial relationships with the West.

A more nationalist group within the Soviet establishment, the Statists, took note of détente, but also saw the West's militarism and policies aimed at preventing the Soviet Union from influencing world affairs. Many in the Soviet bureaucratic and military establishment, therefore, did not believe in any far-reaching changes and instead advocated limited reforms and coexistence with the "world of capitalism." This group was not closed to changes in world politics, but was prepared to cooperate with the West in a reciprocal manner only. Continuation of détente was viewed to be possible, but only to the extent that the West itself was committed to it. Similar to Western realists who insisted on reaching a balance of power between the Soviet and Western poles, this group advocated the notion of "correlation of forces" between socialism and capitalism. Members of the group saw the goal of achieving international status and acceptance in terms of preservation of strength, both military and economic.

Finally, there were also some die-hard Bolsheviks committed to the ideology of winning the competition between socialism and capitalism. Unlike Westernizers and pragmatically oriented nationalists, this group stood for the authentic "socialist values" that were deemed to be superior to those of capitalism. The supporters of such views, or Civilizationists, had zero trust in détente and rapprochement with the West and associated all Western activities with aggressive "imperialist" intentions. There could be no middle ground in the struggle with imperialism, and the Cold War was ultimately a competition between the two systems' cultural values rather than merely economic or military systems. It was through the spreading of values that the group planned to achieve the appropriate recognition of the Soviet Union by the outside world. This group included some leading Communist Party ideologists and eventually emerged as the main opposition to the future New Thinking.

It was Statists who were primarily in control of the actual foreign policy-making during the Cold War era. Immediately after the 1917 revolution, the Bolsheviks were conducting two foreign policies—one was aimed at stabilizing relations with the Western leaders and conducted by the Commissariat on Foreign Affairs, whereas the other sought to undermine the West through the activities of the Comintern. That duality receded into the past as Stalin took charge and shifted the effort away from the highly ideological communist rhetoric and toward winning recognition of Soviet Russia as a "Great Power" and, later, a "Superpower."[3] Stalin's Statism therefore won over the Comintern-like Civilizationism in foreign affairs. Only during the so-called second Cold War of the late 1970s through the early 1980s did the Soviet Civilizationists regain some of their former prominence, partly in response to the rise of hard-line thinking toward Soviet Russia in the West.

The arguments about the need to expand into Afghanistan and other third world countries were partly provoked by the West's own military buildup, opposition to the ratification of the Strategic Arms Limitations Talks (SALT II), and the decision by NATO to deploy American missiles in Europe. In addition to aiding Afghanistan, the Soviets supplied communists in Vietnam and Angola. When in 1983 US president Ronald Reagan announced the Strategic Defense Initiative, also known as the Star Wars program, the Soviet leaders were divided between the more status quo–oriented Statists and the more expansionist Civilizationists. Westernizers were hardly in the picture; they occupied much less prominent positions and could not be taken very seriously given the extent of tensions with the West. After the death of Konstantin Chernenko, Gorbachev was elected general secretary of the Communist Party for his vigor and youth rather than his policy beliefs. At the time, his worldview and policy beliefs were hardly known to his comrades in the Politburo.

GORBACHEV AND THE CONCEPT OF NEW THINKING

In the mid-1980s, Gorbachev was not known for his radical international ideas. After being elected general secretary, he moved cautiously and first proposed the strategy of accelerating scientific and technological progress as a way to improve the state of the Soviet economy. The idea, although well received by the ruling establishment, brought little practical results, and the new leader used the momentum to advance his more radical vision of economic, political, and international changes known as perestroika. Gorbachev also insisted that perestroika could take place only if accompanied by New Thinking, or radical transformation of the traditional outlook on world affairs.

The New Vision of World Politics

By introducing New Thinking, Gorbachev did not mean to replace the Soviet system with one similar to that of the West. He was a product of the system and a firm believer in the Soviet Union's principal viability. At the same time, Gorbachev was highly critical of how the system had performed in the past and wanted to renew it in some fundamental way. In particular, he dreamed of releasing human potential and social creativity that, in his opinion, were suppressed under the Stalinist regime. Eventually Gorbachev meant to bring the system closer to the model of Scandinavian societies, in which democracy was combined with strong egalitarian principles in the economy.

Yet Gorbachev proved to be especially innovative in the area of world politics. Seeking to break the Cold War hostilities and be accepted by the Western nations as an equal member of the world, Gorbachev proposed a vision that required the Cold War enemies to cooperate.[4] The new vision sought to present the old enemies with a notion of a common threat, leaving them little choice but to abandon their old hostilities. At the heart of the vision lay the notion of a global and principally non-divisive world, which was argued to be in danger of annihilation. The Cold War, with its arms races and power struggle, put humankind on the verge of nuclear, ecological, and moral catastrophe. New Thinking diagnosed the catastrophe as one that was global in nature and could be resolved only through global efforts. To quote from the author of New Thinking, "For all the contradictions of the present-day world, for all the diversity of social and political systems in it, and for all the different choices made by the nations in different times, this world is nevertheless one whole. We are all passengers aboard one ship, the Earth, and we must not allow it to be wrecked. There will be no second Noah's Ark."[5]

It was therefore critical to acknowledge the primacy of values "common to all humankind" and to understand that security could only be mutual. The reasons for this were the threat of mutual destruction in a nuclear war, as well as an increased level of economic and ecological interdependence in the world.

The origins of New Thinking therefore had little to do with the necessity of a strategic retreat in the face of the growing economic and military strength of the West—the argument often advanced by realists.[6] To argue this is to neglect Gorbachev's domestic intellectual roots. It is true that the Soviet

Table 2.1. Gross National Product Growth for the USSR and the United States, 1960–1985 (%)

	1965	1970	1975	1980	1985
USSR	4.8	4.9	3.0	1.9	1.8
United States	4.6	3.0	2.2	3.4	2.5

Source: David Kotz and Fred Weir, *Revolution from Above: The Demise of the Soviet System* (London: Routledge, 1997), 42.

economy was in decline by the time of Gorbachev's arrival (see table 2.1). Yet the new leader did not make sense of the world in terms of economic or military capabilities. He was not a member of the Statist school, and his entire thinking about international politics was shaped by a desire to reach out to a liberal and social democratic West. This thinking also had a distinct domestic tradition stretching back at least to Nikolai Bukharin's and Nikita Khrushchev's foreign policy liberalizations.

Achieving recognition by Western nations was extremely difficult given the legacy of the Cold War. For at least a decade, conservatives were in power, and they originally received the arrival of Gorbachev and his ideas of perestroika and New Thinking with suspicion. Such recognition was all the more difficult because Gorbachev was not a believer in the primacy of the Western values of political democracy and the market economy. Instead, he envisioned some global unity from contributions of both capitalist and socialist systems. He was prepared to learn from other systems and other nations[7] while remaining a socialist and a believer that the whole world would continue to be influenced by the socialist experience and "socialist values."[8]

The Domestic Appeal

The new vision of world politics was designed to appeal to all the main groups of the Soviet political class. Westernizers were to be attracted to ideas of democratization, reform, and rapprochement with the West. Gorbachev himself was influenced by the ideas of European social democrats, as well as liberal-minded scientists such as Vladimir Vernadski, Pyotr Kapitsa, and Andrei Sakharov. His concept of a "common European home" also had its roots in Nikita Khrushchev's efforts to bring Soviet Russia closer to Europe. Khrushchev saw Russia as culturally close to Europe, and at one point he even proposed the concurrent disbandment of NATO and the Warsaw Pact. New Thinking also sought to appeal to at least some of the Statists, who understood the necessity of responding to Western military pressures by reducing diplomatic tensions and moving in the direction of a new détente. Finally, Gorbachev's vision meant to engage some of the most forward-thinking members of the Civilizationist school because it offered a new, admittedly very unorthodox way of capitalizing on "socialist values." The leader of perestroika traced his origins to the late Lenin's notion of coexistence with capitalism, and he kept emphasizing that his project was a development, not an abandonment, of socialism. As utopian as it was, the vision had global ambitions and even elements of a moral messianism. It was therefore a creative synthesis that attempted to engage representatives of the entire political class.

But Gorbachev's vision was never a purely elite product. Socially, it reflected the worldview of the Soviet middle class that grew stronger during the 1960–1986 period. The proportion of highly educated and qualified urban specialists had quadrupled during the indicated period. The overall number of urban dwellers in the total population had grown by over two-thirds, by some calculations.[9] The Soviet middle class was dissatisfied with Brezhnev's unwillingness to initiate change, and increasingly expected reforms in the rigid economic and political system. Many representatives of this class were also in touch with the outside world's technological developments, and their perceptions of the world began to conflict with those of Brezhnev's nomenklatura and hard-line military. Increasingly, Soviet society supported accommodation, not confrontation, with the outside world. Although the Soviet system's resources were far from exhausted, the anticipation of and the eagerness for change were already in the air.

Redefining National Interest

The above-described vision left little room for national interest as pursued independently of the interests of other members of the global society. Gorbachev did not expect the Soviet Union or any other nations to give up what they perceived to be in their interests. Yet he called for acknowledging the futility of class and narrowly viewed national gains and for developing a globally integrated approach based on the notion of mutual responsibility and "balance of interests." Practically speaking, he proposed compromises and multilateral negotiations as a way to implement the new vision.

For the Soviet Union, New Thinking implied the necessity of formulating its national interest and foreign policy objectives in a way that would be respectful of world opinion and nonthreatening toward others. In particular, Gorbachev proposed rethinking the nature of capitalism. The old ideological vision assumed that the Soviet Union had to contain the influence of world capitalism, because at its highest stage of development—imperialism— capitalism was intrinsically related to expansion and war. Without containing imperialism, the Soviet Union would be destroyed. As Josef Stalin said in a slightly different context, "Either we do it, or we shall be crushed."[10]

The Gorbachev vision posited something very different. In February 1988, he criticized the very notion of imperialism as being no longer accurate. He argued that capitalism had developed domestic democratic mechanisms for resisting expansion and war and was therefore self-containing. Such criticism had its roots in the Soviet postwar debates. Already in the late 1940s, Yevgeni Varga, director of the Moscow Institute of World Economy and World Politics, began arguing that postwar capitalism could regulate its contradictions and had relatively stabilized. After Stalin's death, those emphasizing the depth of imperialist contradictions and the inevitability of the capitalist decline gathered around Richard Kosolapov, the editor in chief of *Kommunist* and a member of the Central Committee of the Communist Party, while those opposing this hard-line view assembled at the Institute of World Economy and World Politics.[11]

Siding with supporters of the anti-imperialism view of capitalism allowed Gorbachev to present the notion of military sufficiency in an entirely different light, and to call for a reevaluation of Soviet defense expenditures. It provided the basis for terminating the arms race in which the Soviet Union had been previously heavily involved. Clarifying the new approach, the foreign minister Eduard Shevardnadze argued that an attempt to reach military parity with all potential enemies was in fact against Soviet national interests.[12] (Table 2.2 summarizes the New Thinking view of national interest.)

The introduction of the notion of "national interest" was partly strategic, and was designed to preempt possible criticism that New Thinking was nothing but a series of concessions to capitalism. Multiple withdrawals from Eastern Europe and the third world, as well as proposals to eliminate entire classes of nuclear missiles, could now be presented as something that was part of a long-term strategy. For example, the "loss" of Eastern Europe after the 1989 fall of the Berlin Wall could now be presented as a net "gain" in a general calculus of creating a favorable international environment. In February 1990, Shevardnadze insisted along these lines, "Our national, as well as historic and everyday, interest is that our neighbors are stable and prosperous. We will only benefit from this."[13]

Table 2.2. New Thinking (NT): View of National Interest

What?	Global responsibility and "balance of interests"
How?	Military sufficiency Multilateral negotiations Diplomatic compromises

DOMESTIC CRITICS OF NEW THINKING

Despite Gorbachev's efforts to be a consensus builder, his New Thinking was soon attacked from two different directions. Conservative forces charged that Gorbachev was "selling out" the Soviet interests to the West, whereas liberals saw him as indecisive in abandoning the "outdated" Soviet outlook. Revolutionary changes in the country further polarized the process of foreign policy formation, making it impossible to sustain the originally devised plan with appeal to all main social groups. The original coalition of New Thinkers was fairly broad, representing the industrial, military, party, and academic establishment. Over time, however, that coalition began to fall apart, and the struggle of ideas around New Thinking suggested in which directions some future social and politico-economic groups were to emerge.

Conservative Opposition

Conservative opposition to Gorbachev consisted of some representatives of Statist and Civilizationist schools. Intellectually heterogeneous, conservatives were united in their hatred of New Thinking, perceiving it as leading to the Soviet Union's social and political disintegration. Conservative Statists remained highly skeptical of the ideas of détente and domestic reform and were prepared to discuss only military modernization. Conservative Civilizationists put their emphasis on what they saw as key socialist values, such as economic and political centralization of the system. Both groups had much to agree on and enjoyed sufficient support in the military and party establishments, as well as in the wider society.

Conservatives rejected the idea that the West had made a considerable contribution to world development and insisted that Soviet Russia had little to learn from Western modernity. To them, the moral authority in the world lay unquestionably outside the West, whereas the West was viewed as an inferior community united by the aspiration to become rich at the expense of the world. The global crisis diagnosed by Gorbachev could therefore not be solved by appeals to the West itself. Nor could there be dialogue with those who exploited the world economically and corrupted it morally. To Statists, New Thinking would result in destroying the Soviet military capabilities, and to Civilizationists, it would erode the very spirit of Soviet society. Religious nationalists—who followed the philosophy of the nineteenth-century Slavophiles, and viewed Russia as a holder of Orthodox religious beliefs, not to be corrupted by Western Christianity—reinforced the position of the latter.[14]

Not tempted by New Thinking's emphasis on common human values, conservatives recommended that the Soviet Union stay firm and preserve its own historical and cultural tradition. They insisted on the need to continue to resist the influences from the West. Some proposed to accumulate power through economic and technological development, and to abstain from global military conflicts, while others suggested an offensive strategy of expansion to fill the geopolitical vacuum between the Soviet Union and the West.[15]

Liberal Opposition

Conservative perspectives initially remained marginalized in Soviet society. As Gorbachev's reforms were failing to live up to rising expectations, there was still little in Western behavior that could have justified the conservative fears of the West attempting to destroy Russia. On the contrary, a number of successful negotiations with Western leaders made Russians trust the West more and attracted them even more to its values. This situation improved the position of liberal-minded Westernizers in the national discourse and provided conditions for the consolidation of a Westernist coalition. Originally sympathetic to Gorbachev's agenda, members of the new coalition now felt that he was too slow and inconsistent in his policies. The coalition included representatives of the Soviet middle class, liberal intellectuals, and some party nomenklatura, all of whom were growing impatient with the pace of Gorbachev's domestic and external changes. Eventually Boris Yeltsin, a former provincial party secretary, emerged as the leader of the Westernist coalition. Supported by some ethnic republics, liberals were attracted to the "Western" model of development and were disappointed in Gorbachev's "socialist" character of reform.

Liberal critique of New Thinking was just the opposite of that of conservatives. It insisted that Gorbachev's philosophy failed to attribute most common human values to Western civilization. In the view of one scholar, common human values are those "that are based on the criteria of the Western civilization, with its liberal-democratic values and the level of scientific-technological development."[16] Whereas Gorbachev was proposing a globally integrated approach based on the notion of mutual responsibility, liberals viewed the West as the ultimate moral authority and the model to follow. With the nineteenth-century thinker Petr Chaadayev, who believed that "we [Russians] are placed somewhat outside of the times,"[17] the Soviet liberals had little faith in the national tradition of development. In their view, the dilemma before Soviet Russia was either modernization-Westernization or autarchy and backwardness. Any alternative ways of development were no longer available, and Gorbachev's renewed socialist project was nothing but a harmful utopia.

Table 2.3 summarizes contending views on New Thinking.

Table 2.3. New Thinking (NT): Contending Views

Conservatives:		Liberals:
NT weakens the Soviet state	vs.	NT fails to change the Soviet system

NEW THINKING ABROAD: BANKING ON THE WEST'S RECOGNITION

It follows that both conservative and liberal critics of New Thinking had a tendency to view national interest in zero-sum terms. While conservatives saw the Soviet national interests as anti-Western, liberals tended to equate them with those of the West. Gorbachev's complex and dialectical perspective on the Soviet Union in world politics was hardly acceptable to either one of his opponents. To stay his course at home, he needed major support from the West. Obtaining such support in response to New Thinking initiatives could have improved Gorbachev's domestic credibility and assisted him in keeping together his fragile coalition of support. Banking on recognition from the West became a crucial part of the new Soviet strategy. The inadequacy of Western reciprocity, along with Gorbachev's own errors in reforming the economic and political system, ultimately contributed to his failure.

Promises and Disappointments

Gorbachev's ambitious foreign policy agenda included far-reaching disarmament measures, particularly in the area of Soviet-American relations; withdrawal of military assistance and troops from the external imperial territories in Eastern Europe and the third world; and strengthening global institutions (see the chronology earlier in this book for a summary of key events during Gorbachev's tenure). The latter was crucial for fighting militarization, poverty, and environmental degradation across the world, and Gorbachev placed a high premium on the United Nations in accomplishing these goals. The New Thinking vision assumed the emergence of a new global community, in which diverse socioeconomic systems would cooperate in the spirit of mutual trust and reciprocity.

Initially, Gorbachev planned to engage the West through multiple disarmament and demilitarization initiatives. Already in 1985 he argued that military doctrine should become more defensive, announced a unilateral moratorium on nuclear tests, insisted on the need to dissolve military blocs, and made known the Soviet readiness to make disproportionately large cuts in conventional forces.[18] He followed up by proposing more far-reaching changes during several summits with Western leaders. In January 1986, Gorbachev proposed to eliminate all nuclear weapons by 2000, and he offered some major cuts in strategic weapons. He then made several significant concessions on the issue of intermediate nuclear forces, and at the end of 1987, he traveled to Washington to sign the agreement that dismantled the whole class of medium-range and short-range missiles (see table 2.4 for a summary of Gorbachev's security record).

No less crucial were decisions to withdraw military assistance and troops from Eastern Europe and the third world. In 1987, the Eastern European leaders were informed that the Soviets were considering troop withdrawal, which was fully consistent with New Thinkers' beliefs in freedom of choice and noninterference in Eastern European domestic affairs. In early 1988, Gorbachev announced the decision to withdraw from Afghanistan, as well as from other third world countries. Gorbachev himself had made these decisions much earlier; indeed, he came to office convinced of their necessity.[19]

Finally, in the spirit of strengthening global institutions, the leader of New Thinking took to heart the idea of reforming the United Nations. He supported more extensive resources for peacekeeping forces, proposed to renounce the use of force by the permanent members of the Security Council,

Table 2.4. Gorbachev's Legacy in Security Policy

The INF Treaty (December 1987). The United States and the USSR agreed to eliminate 1,600 intermediate-range missiles. Also eliminated were approximately 1,100 shorter-range missile systems (500–1,000 km) deployed in Europe.

The CFE Treaty (November 1990). Signed by sixteen NATO states and six members of the Warsaw Pact, the Treaty on Conventional Armed Forces in Europe placed restrictions on the number of conventional weapons within the agreed-upon zone. The treaty deprived the USSR of the ability to mount a credible attack against NATO in Europe.

START (July 1991). The Strategic Arms Reduction Treaty limited each side to a total of 1,600 long-range ballistic missiles and heavy bombers.

Withdrawals of troops from Eastern Europe. Gorbachev decided not to interfere in Eastern Europe before or after anticommunist revolutions there and began to withdraw the Soviet troops in April 1989.

The unification of Germany. Gorbachev endorsed the "Two Plus Four" formula to produce the final settlement on Germany, to acquiesce to West Germany's virtual absorption of its eastern neighbor (largely on Western terms), and to accept a united Germany becoming a full member of NATO.

The radical upturn in US–Soviet relations. By the time of the Bush–Gorbachev summit in December 1989, the two sides had converged on many international issues, such as the desirability of a negotiated peace in Nicaragua and El Salvador and a reduction of Soviet assistance to Cuba. Bush was at first reluctant to accept the reality of the December 1991 Soviet breakup, when the leaders of Ukraine, Russia, and Belarus announced the creation of the Commonwealth of Independent States.

Adapted from: Coit D. Blacker, *Hostage to Revolution: Gorbachev and Soviet Security Policy, 1985–1991* (New York: Council on Foreign Relations, 1993), 184–89.

and argued for a number of new agencies and agreements. Consistent with these proposals, the new Soviet leadership paid the United Nations $200 million for peacekeeping operations that the old leaders had refused to support since 1973. It also contributed to mediating political resolutions of conflicts in Africa and Latin America.[20]

Despite all of these efforts, Western leaders were not as cooperative as Gorbachev had hoped. Although Ronald Reagan and British prime minister Margaret Thatcher liked Gorbachev personally, they did not feel convinced by his arguments against nuclear deterrence and nuclear weapons as an "absolute evil." During 1985–1987, they were also not persuaded that the Soviet Union was sincere about renouncing the "Brezhnev doctrine" in Eastern Europe or withdrawing its troops from the third world. The core of the mistrust had to do with the uncertain nature of Soviet reform and a fear of a conservative comeback to power. As a result, many of Gorbachev's initiatives were met with skepticism. For instance, the Geneva Summit in November 1985 produced nothing but a declaration of the inadmissibility of nuclear war. Reykjavik, too, failed, as the Soviet proposals were left unreciprocated. Gorbachev also found no support on the issue of nonuse of force and nonintervention in the internal affairs of other states,[21] which was crucial for him to reciprocate his "freedom of choice" principle with regard to the former outer empire of the Soviet Union. Increasingly, he was left in a difficult position to respond to conservative critics at home.

Conservatives in the party and military establishment opposed New Thinking with a growing vigor. Initially, Gorbachev's coalition was a fairly broad one and even included the chief of the general staff Sergei Akhromeyev and the Politburo member Yegor Ligachev, who agreed with a number of military cuts and withdrawals. In particular, both supported Gorbachev's decision to withdraw from Afghanistan. Yet the more radical the New Thinkers were in their proposals, the more vigorous was the opposition. The military was critical of Reykjavik and of the notion of defense "sufficiency," which was meant to make military doctrine more defense-oriented and to prepare the ground for future military cuts. Party officials objected to the principle of "freedom of choice" with regard to Eastern Europe. For instance, Oleg Rakhmanin, head of the Central Committee department for relations with socialist countries, publicly defended the Brezhnev doctrine of limited sovereignty and denounced any changes in bloc relations.[22] Gorbachev fought back by pushing for more military cuts and concessions to the West. He took advantage of the system's failures, such as Chernobyl's nuclear accident and a foreign private aircraft's landing in Red Square, using them as a pretext for replacing hard-liners with those more loyal to his course. In addition, although there was initially no direct connection between his foreign policy initiatives and the state of the Soviet economy, the leader of perestroika was constantly making this connection to maintain conservative support for his course.

Decline and Capitulation

After 1988, the domestic situation took a sharp turn. An economic slowdown, a dramatic worsening of people's living standards, and political separatism of some of the Soviet republics severely affected Gorbachev's ability to stay the course that had already been undermined by the West's reluctant cooperation. The economy was especially important. Although it was growing at the rate of 2.2 percent after the cyclical decline of the early 1980s, it began to decline again during the 1987–1989 period, and then collapsed after 1989[23] (see table 2.5). The collapse of the economy was likely a reaction to the vacuum of power resulting from the abolition of state orders. The "law of state enterprise" that came into effect in 1988 replaced state orders with nonbinding control figures. The economy that for decades had been state-regulated had not yet developed market-based incentives and was now in a free fall.

As a result, the state of domestic politics was growing increasingly polarized, with conservatives and liberals pulling in opposite directions. Conservatives feverishly tried to restore control over the system and argued for preservation of the class perspective in international relations. But with the Eastern European revolutions under way, the reality was hitting. The spring 1989 elections in Poland and Hungary brought to power anticommunist forces, and November 1989 saw a key symbol of the Cold War, the Berlin Wall, falling. As the old system was largely discredited, political attention was turning to liberals, who attacked Gorbachev for his indecisiveness and unwillingness to follow the West's model of development. As the leader of New Thinking was losing control, liberal forces were consolidating around Boris Yeltsin, who was soon elected president of the Russian Federation.

Table 2.5. Growth Rates for the Soviet Economy, 1985–1991

	Western Estimates (gross national product)	Official Soviet Data (net material product)
1985	1.8	3.2
1986	4.1	2.3
1987	1.3	1.6
1988	2.1	4.4
1989	1.5	2.5
1990	−2.4	−3.9
1991	−12.8*	−15*

* Estimate excludes Georgia and the Baltic republics.

Source: David Kotz and Fred Weir, *Revolution from Above: The Demise of the Soviet System* (London: Routledge, 1997), 75.

Even Gorbachev's closest supporters, such as Aleksandr Yakovlev and Eduard Shevardnadze, were now leaving him disappointed. Finally, the general public, too, grew dissatisfied with the results of reform. For instance, in 1989, 39 percent of the public associated the difficulties of reforms with the government's indecisiveness, while only 22 percent attributed such difficulties to the activities of conservative forces.[24]

These domestic changes affected the course of New Thinking negatively. Initially designed as a middle ground between Western capitalism and Stalinist socialism, New Thinking was now seriously endangered and increasingly looked like a failure. After 1988, as Gorbachev was losing ground at home, his foreign policies toward the West were losing their momentum and originality. Symptomatically, in November 1989, foreign minister Eduard Shevardnadze publicly admitted a lack of "conceptual ideas" and a "deficit of counterarguments" in responding to conclusions about the coming triumph of Western liberal ideology.[25]

In the meantime, the general public was losing its faith in the country. While in 1988 only 5.3 percent of respondents had felt that the Soviet Union could not serve as an example to the outside world, in 1989 the share of those expressing that feeling reached the level of 34 percent.[26] Western leaders understood Gorbachev's inability to sustain his originally globalist course and pressed for more concessions, without offering much in return. Yegor Ligachev, Gorbachev's powerful conservative opponent, had reason to charge that certain forces in the United States were "linking perestroika with the dismantling of socialism."[27] Gorbachev still tried to save what was left of his course by resisting unified Germany's membership in NATO and insisting on diplomatic solutions to the Persian Gulf crisis. But the Cold War was over, and after having initiated the change, the Soviet Union had little say in negotiating its outcomes. Banking on the West's recognition proved to be a flawed strategy.

On balance, Gorbachev contributed greatly to improving his country's security by relieving an extremely heavy burden of military expenditures that by the time of his arrival had reached the share of some 16.5 percent of the gross national product (GNP).[28] Yet, even if judged by Gorbachev's own standards and expectations, New Thinking was a failure and a capitulation before the West. As an identity project, it did not serve the formulated purposes. Few of Gorbachev's hopes matched the reality.

One of them was that far-reaching disarmament initiatives would break down the old Western mistrust and produce some global commitments to demilitarization. Convinced of the viability of socialism, Gorbachev also declared the "freedom of choice" principle with regard to Eastern Europe and the third world. He hoped that these areas would remain neutral and might eventually turn social democratic. He expected the old bipolar security system to be gradually replaced by that of nonconfrontation and cooperation. The old military blocs, such as the Warsaw Pact and NATO, were to recede into the past, and European security would have been organized around the inclusive Organization for Security and Cooperation in Europe (OSCE), the origins of which were in the 1975 Helsinki Accord signed by the Soviet Union. Finally, the United Nations was expected to develop enough muscle to successfully deal with the possible vacuum of power and rising instabilities in the third world after the Soviet withdrawals.

Such were the hopes. The reality, however, was quite different. Western leaders expressed a willingness to negotiate arms-control agreements but showed no desire to go as far as Gorbachev expected them to. Neither Margaret Thatcher nor Ronald Reagan shared Gorbachev's vision of complete demilitarization and denuclearization. Eastern European states had their own memory of being a part of the Soviet outer empire and, once the opportunity presented itself, rushed to join Western economic and security institutions, first and foremost NATO. Germany reunited. The Warsaw Pact disappeared, but NATO persisted, and even decided to expand all the way to the Russian borders. The United Nations remained relatively weak and unable to adequately deal with growing violence in the third world. Afghanistan in particular is a case in point; the Soviet withdrawal from that state ultimately resulted in its collapse. Afghanistan's leader Mohammad Najibullah was executed, while the new regime of the Taliban became a safe haven for terrorists and their training camps.

THE CRISIS FOR NATIONALITIES AND THE REVENGE OF NEW THINKING AT HOME

The Soviet Union was an empire, in which the center effectively controlled the sovereignty of the peripheral republics. The Kremlin, rather than Russia and the Russians, played the role of the center; in many ways, Russia was just as heavily exploited by the authorities for the sake of maintaining the empire's economic and political cohesion. Although the Soviet authorities maintained the principle of representation of indigenous nationalities in the power structures, they also relied on political coercion, economic redistribution, and forceful migration—all the traditional tools of empire building. Yet the principle of nationalities' representation developed and reinforced the sense of peripheral distinctiveness from the empire. Historically, it paved the way for nationalist mobilization during imperial decline,[29] particularly among those republics that had developed a sense of national Self before incorporation into the Soviet empire.

Given this nature of relationships between Moscow and the Soviet republics, changing the Soviet territorial power structure should have been high on Gorbachev's list of priorities. If, externally, the Soviet national interests were to be pursued in balance with the interests of other nations, that principle should have applied internally as well. Yet until the early 1990s, Gorbachev failed to address the problem, and his way of dealing with the imperial decline and nationalities crisis presents us with another illustration of how naive and divorced from power considerations New Thinking ideas were. Gorbachev failed to recognize the Soviet Union as an empire and simply did not see the need for major power changes. By not reacting to national uprisings in a timely and systematic manner, he lost some valuable time (table 2.6 summarizes the rise of ethnonationalism in the Soviet Union). Only in March 1990 did he raise the question of a new union treaty as a way to avoid political disintegration. By that time, nationalists in the Baltic republics and elsewhere had been active for more than three years. Six republics—the Baltic ones, Georgia, Moldova, and Armenia—announced their intent to not participate in the new union treaty, and Russian liberal critics of Gorbachev were already debating the idea of confederation. Later, the leader of perestroika himself admitted that he had "underestimated the strength of national feelings and aspirations."[30]

By the time Gorbachev had formulated his concept of a revived union, he had to defend it against the well-elaborated positions of conservatives and

Table 2.6. The Rise of Ethnonationalism in the Union Republics, 1989–1991

Union Republic	Main Ethnonationalist Movement (date of foundation)	Sovereignty Declaration (rank)
Armenia	Karabakh Committee (Feb. 1988)	July 1990 (8)
Azerbaijan	Azeri Popular Front (July 1988)	Sept. 1989 (4)
Belarus	Renewal (Andradzhen'ne) (June 1989)	June 1990 (7)
Estonia	Estonian Popular Front (July 1988)	Nov. 1988 (1)
Georgia	Committee for National Salvation (Oct. 1989)	Nov. 1989 (5)
Kazakhstan	Nevada Semipalatinsk Movement (Feb. 1989)	Sept. 1990 (9)
Kyrgyzstan	Openness (Ashar) (July 1989)	Nov. 1990 (10)
Latvia	Latvian Popular Front (July 1988)	May 1989 (2)
Lithuania	Sajudis (June 1988)	July 1989 (3)
Moldova	Moldovan Popular Front (Jan. 1989)	May 1990 (6)
Russia	Democratic Russia (1990)	May 1990 (6)
Tajikistan	Openness (Ashkara) (June 1989)	July 1990 (8)
Turkmenistan	Unity (Agzybirlik) (Jan. 1990)	July 1990 (8)
Ukraine	Popular Front (Rukh) (Nov. 1988)	June 1990 (7)
Uzbekistan	Unity (Birlik) (Nov. 1988)	May 1990 (6)

Adapted from: Graham Smith, *The Post-Soviet States: Mapping the Politics of Transition* (London: Arnold, 1999), 39; Ann Sheehy, "Factsheet on Declarations of Sovereignty," *Report on the USSR*, November 9, 1990.

Westernizers. Conservatives advocated the idea of empire. Some popularized the essentialist notion of Soviet Eurasia as a new continental empire and a distinct civilization, and recommended the use of force in preserving territorial integrity. Liberal Westernizers around Yeltsin and his supporters criticized the Soviet Union as a hyper-centralized state, attacking it from a colonial nationalist perspective. Increasingly, they saw the solution in separating Russia from the center and building Russia's own state institutions. Gorbachev's perspective was not an essentialist one. Rather than advocating an empire or a nation-state, he argued for the Soviet Union as a reformed federation and a community of various peoples. Culturally, he saw this community in transnational terms. A European in his social and political outlook, Gorbachev saw the need to maintain a cultural balance. After 1987, he upgraded his "common European home" formula by adding the Asian dimension and more frequently referring to the Soviet Union as an Asian, as well as a European, country. His foreign minister Eduard Shevardnadze also touted this vision. For example, in October 1988 in his welcoming message to foreign guests attending the Asia-Pacific region conference in Vladivostok, he stressed that the Soviet Union was a "great Eurasian space" and a "world of worlds" (mir mirov), and argued that Russia had to live in a complex world of both European and Asian nations.

That vision had broad popular support. For example, even as late as during the March 1991 referendum on the future of the new union—a referendum that was conducted in all of the Soviet republics except the Baltics, Armenia, Georgia, and Moldova—147 million people voted and 76.4 percent approved the preservation of the union. The wording of the question was: "Do you support the preservation of the union as a renewed federation of sovereign republics in which the rights of a person of any nationality are fully guaranteed?"[31]

Yet it was a struggle of elites, rather than involvement of the general public, that was about to determine the future of the Soviet Union. The referendum for a renewed union took place in the context of Gorbachev's struggle against liberal elites on the one hand and conservatives on the other. Yeltsin's umbrella organization, Democratic Russia, openly called for the dissolution of the Soviet Union and even tried (unsuccessfully) to convince Yeltsin to campaign for a "no" vote in the referendum. Liberals turned nationalists presented the Soviet Union as an "empire" that was to be dismantled for the sake of Russian prosperity. Throughout the political campaigns of 1990 and 1991, Yeltsin had advanced the "Russia-victim" argument, and it was his advisers who eventually wrote a scenario for dissolving the union. Conservatives, too, did what was in their power to sabotage Gorbachev's efforts.

In early 1991, Soviet troops cracked down on the rebellious Lithuania and Latvia. Gorbachev denied responsibility by putting the blame on his defense minister, Dmitri Yazov. Yet liberals in Russia widely associated the crackdown with Gorbachev, and this association worsened the problem. The conservative coup in August was meant to prevent the scheduled signing of the new union treaty between the center and nine republics, but it only made the Soviet disintegration inevitable. The nationalism of the republics' political leadership then reached its highest degree, with Russia and Ukraine playing a particularly important role. On December 25, 1991, after Russia, Ukraine, and Belarus had concluded a separate treaty creating the Commonwealth of Independent States (CIS) without consulting the center, Gorbachev resigned.

Paradoxically, New Thinking contributed to the breakup of the Soviet Union. By aiming for the West's support and recognition, it inserted itself into the arena of Western, modern nation-states, making it increasingly difficult to discourage the Soviet ethnic republics from embarking on nationalist projects. Soon after the beginning of perestroika, nationalists were openly referring to the Soviet Union as the last empire in the "age of decolonization." By announcing glasnost and democratization, New Thinking also provided nationalists in Russia and other republics with the required channels for political mobilization. The organization of mass demonstrations in the Baltic republics and then election to national parliaments of those who saw the future only in terms of complete independence greatly facilitated the undermining of the Soviet Union. Finally, Gorbachev's own vision made little room for timely changes in nationalities policy. Despite mounting evidence of strong secessionist sentiments displayed by several republics, he kept insisting that the republics formed a natural historical unity and that they should be "grateful" to the Soviet Union for their social and economic development. Such "New Thinking" undoubtedly stimulated peripheral nationalism. Although public support for the preservation of the union was sound, the extreme polarization of the political space by elites deprived Russia of a chance to reformulate its transnational identity.

UTOPIA AND REALITY: ASSESSMENT OF GORBACHEV'S FOREIGN POLICY

Gorbachev's New Thinking project was introduced to renew the Soviet national identity and to save it as the idea of a reformed socialism open to an outside world yet loyal to some of the already developed social values. Over time, however, the project of saving the national idea regressed into a national defeat. Most of New Thinking's expectations regarding the outside world failed to materialize. The Cold War ended on terms that Gorbachev himself found difficult to accept. The Soviet Union unilaterally withdrew from most areas of the world where it had been present, and it did so without receiving the satisfaction of strengthening global institutions, such as the United

Nations, or being given credit for changing the world's thinking. Instead, it was widely accepted that the Soviets lost the Cold War to the West, and it was the West that emerged as the triumphant civilization and the guarantor of peace and security in the world. As if this were not enough, the forces of nationalism in Russia and several other republics added to Gorbachev's domestic defeat. He acknowledged the defeat and resigned as president of a country that was no more. His overall project of external openness and domestic liberalization had been initially widely supported in Soviet society and among elites, who felt ready to move away from the stiffening bureaucratic and militaristic system. But in the process of being implemented, New Thinking lost appeal both externally and domestically, and it contributed to the loss of governance in the country.

The following section offers a more detailed assessment of Gorbachev's foreign policy record, reflecting on the causes of what happened and highlighting lessons learned from the failure of New Thinking.

The Record: Accomplishments and Losses

Gorbachev and his team should be given great credit for initiating a new progressive thinking about the future of the country and the world. Liberals worldwide have been appreciative of the intellectual effort expended to reactivate social initiative and put a human being in the center of state policy. It is highly misleading to view New Thinking as driven by some power necessities or as an ideology meant to cover the Soviet system's prime desire to rebuild its economic and military capabilities. Gorbachev may have been naive in his expectations and strategic design, but he certainly was not a cynical power calculator whose main concern was to save the Soviet economic and military machine from defeat in the Cold War. In fact, he did not need to be a New Thinker for power purposes, as the old system could have survived for another generation or so.[32] Nor did he believe, when he came to power, that the Soviet economy was in serious trouble. Gorbachev could have continued to enjoy power without introducing any changes, or he could have introduced limited measures to reform the economy and fight corruption, as favored by his predecessor Yuri Andropov and the majority of the leadership. Instead he initiated what he himself liked to refer to as a "social revolution."

One undisputed accomplishment of New Thinking has been a break with the old Soviet-style isolationism and a radical improvement in military security (see tables 2.4 and 2.7 for summaries). It is only thanks to major theoretical innovations and subsequent arms-control agreements that the Soviet leadership was able to avert the threat of war and move to a realistic military budget. After the 1987 agreement with Washington about the elimination of an entire class of nuclear forces, the very idea of a war with Western countries

Table 2.7. Limits on Arms Accepted or Proposed by Gorbachev, 1983–1991

Delivery Systems (warheads)	START, 1983	START, 1991*
Strategic nuclear delivery vehicles	12,580	6,000
Ballistic missiles	10,180	4,900
Heavy ICBMs	3,080	1,540
Sea-launched ballistic missiles	3,080	Limits
Bombers	2,400	1,100

* As proposed in 1987.

Adapted from: Michael McGwire, *Perestroika and Soviet National Security* (Washington, DC: Brookings, 1991), 79.

seemed anachronistic. The state could now concentrate on what it declared as its major tasks—improving people's lives and making the system more accountable to society.

Yet it was in the areas outside military security that the state failed to deliver. Gorbachev's foreign policy failed when judged by the three key criteria of social welfare, policy autonomy, and cultural identity. First, New Thinking did little to improve living standards at home, and it did not result in the expected active participation of the West in reforming the domestic economy. In some ways, Gorbachev's active foreign policy even harmed the domestic reforms, as it precluded the leader of New Thinking from concentrating on what required his full attention at home. Although Gorbachev visualized partial privatization of the economy, he never seriously tried it. Partly, he was too busy with his revolutionary foreign policy. But he was also fearful that private property would lead to a capitalist system at home, subverting what he saw as the accomplishments of socialism.

For instance, in September 1990, several Soviet and Western economists developed the "500 Days" plan, which included economic restructuring, privatization, and active involvement of foreign capital. Gorbachev backed away from the plan, viewing it as leading to a restoration of capitalism. But even before then he missed many opportunities to introduce a more decentralized system and economic incentives. Unlike his more pragmatic teacher Vladimir Lenin, who was not afraid of large foreign concessions and a "dual economy" with a relatively large private sector during the post–civil war reconstruction, Gorbachev proved to be a much less flexible reformer. As a result of his hesitancy, even a mixed economy, in which only small and medium-sized businesses are in private hands, never appeared. The economy remained heavily centralized, and it was unrealistic to expect considerable Western participation in the process of economic reform. It was even less realistic to expect such participation after the Soviet economy had collapsed.

As a result of the collapsing economy, Gorbachev was increasingly perceived abroad as weak and unable to sustain his foreign policy course.

Western leaders pressed for more concessions, as in negotiations over Germany's reunification and its role in European security, and the leader of New Thinking was surrendering one position after another. Increasingly, the West, in its own policy calculations, successfully used him. Although this did not yet amount to a loss of Soviet foreign policy autonomy or the ability to make independent decisions, it may have created preconditions for future diminished sovereignty.

Finally, Gorbachev's foreign policy failed to deliver what New Thinking saw as perhaps the most important of its promises—reformulation of the Soviet cultural identity. Isolation from the world and the West was to be replaced by an image of a more open, democratic, and yet socialist nation confidently looking forward and even providing the world with an example to follow. Instead, Russia found itself a deeply divided nation, with an identity crisis extending well into the post-Soviet era.

Table 2.8 summarizes the record of New Thinking.

Lessons Learned from the Failure of New Thinking

New Thinking failed to achieve its objectives abroad and at home not because it had developed a wrong vision for the world's future, but because it had chosen a wrong course to implement that vision by largely divorcing itself from domestic and international power considerations. No grand idea can materialize if it is promoted without due consideration for the existing political context. Although Gorbachev had started his reforms supported by a relatively broad coalition, which included intellectuals and members of the middle class, the military, and party bureaucracy, he was ultimately left alone with his vision. The larger society also began to withdraw its support as early as 1988–1989, and this registered in polls as well as in growing support for Gorbachev's liberal opposition. Sadly, this did not lead to a major rethinking of the initial strategy, or to attempts to rebuild the coalition of support.

Externally, giving due attention to the political and power context would have meant an effort to achieve genuine reciprocity from the West in response to the breathtaking Soviet initiatives. One after another, countries in the

Table 2.8. The Record of New Thinking

Security	New arms-control agreements
	End of Soviet isolationism
Welfare	State disintegration
	Collapsed economy
Sovereignty	Voluntary concessions
	Growing dependence on the West
Identity	A culturally divided nation

West politely declined or ignored Gorbachev's initiatives—on nuclear disarmament, abandonment of the principle of deterrence, nonuse of force and
nonintervention in the internal affairs of other states, and strengthening the
United Nations. Yet the leader of New Thinking kept going with his own
agenda of unilateral withdrawals and military concessions. Believing that his
efforts would somehow be rewarded and appreciated externally and at home
was naive, all the more so because he was rapidly losing important bargaining chips in promoting his own revolutionary agenda, just as he was losing
domestic support for his course. Gorbachev and his team simply did not think
in the categories of preserving power and the capabilities of the state. This
was enormously costly to them, because the West was not as naive in negotiating with New Thinkers in the Kremlin, and the Western leaders did give
power factors their due consideration.

It was also very costly to the New Thinkers because over time they lost the
ability to sell the course at home. And if the first lesson to learn from their
failure is that a successful foreign policy requires reciprocity, then the second
lesson should be that a foreign policy must match domestic needs and have
strong roots at home. Trying to revolutionize foreign policy simultaneously
with fundamental reforms in the economy, the political system, and the area
of center-periphery relations is an admirable but ultimately impossible task.
Priorities should have been chosen, and such priorities should have been
domestic rather than external.

Ironically, the harder Gorbachev seemed to push for foreign policy
changes, the less control he had left at home. First, in 1988, he lost control over the economy after replacing state orders with nonbinding control
figures. Then, he lost control over the political situation after his leading
opponent, Boris Yeltsin, was elected president of Russia—first by the parliament and then by popular vote—while Gorbachev remained an essentially
nonelected politician. Before 1989, Gorbachev still had a chance to acquire
more domestic legitimacy and to strengthen the status of the Soviet president
through nationwide elections; after that, such an opportunity was no longer
available. By not dealing with the nationalities crisis in a timely manner, he
further worsened his domestic standing, and the public had difficulties trusting his course. Symptomatically, during 1988–1989, the percentage of those
viewing nationalities relations as worsening increased from 38 percent to 72
percent, and in 1989, 30 percent of the respondents thought that a future civil
war was likely.[33]

In sum, liberal ideas cannot succeed when they are not backed by power,
and they can succeed only to the degree they successfully shape power and
use it to achieve their own agenda. Such power can include the support of
influential elites, the general public, or developed states abroad, but it must
remain a part of the course's support. Liberal ideas should guide a course

strategically, but their promoters should also take care to retain sufficient domestic and foreign support of their efforts.

NOTES

1. Mikhail Gorbachev, *On My Country and the World* (New York: Columbia University Press, 2000), 190.

2. For instance, the human rights provisions of the Helsinki Accords, signed by the Soviet Union during détente, emboldened domestic reform–oriented forces and, albeit indirectly, gave rise to a network of committed activists in the Soviet Union and Eastern Europe. For details, see Robert G. Herman, "Identity, Norms, and National Security: The Soviet Foreign Policy Revolution and the End of the Cold War," in *The Culture of National Security*, ed. Peter J. Katzenstein (New York: Columbia University Press, 1996), 292; Robert D. English, *Russia and the Idea of the West: Gorbachev, Intellectuals and the End of the Cold War* (New York: Columbia University Press, 2000), 154–55.

3. Eric Ringman, "The Recognition Game: Soviet Russia against the West," *Cooperation and Conflict* 37, no. 2 (2002).

4. On Gorbachev as a thinker who sought to improve the Soviet Union's world status through an innovative strategy of engaging the West, see Deborah Welch Larson and Alexei Shevchenko, "Shortcut to Greatness: The New Thinking and the Revolution in Soviet Foreign Policy," *International Organization* 57 (Winter 2003).

5. Mikhail Gorbachev, *Perestroika: New Thinking for Our Country and the World* (New York: Harper & Row, 1987), 12.

6. See, for example, Stephen M. Walt, "The Gorbachev Interlude and International Relations Theory," *Diplomatic History* 21, no. 3 (1997); Stephen G. Brooks and William C. Wohlforth, "Power, Globalization, and the End of the Cold War: Reevaluating a Landmark Case for Ideas," *International Security* 25, no. 3 (Winter 2000/2001).

7. Gorbachev, *Perestroika*, 152.

8. For example, in his book *On My Country and the World*, Gorbachev discusses at length the October Revolution's global significance.

9. Graham Smith, *The Post-Soviet States: Mapping the Politics of Transition* (London: Arnold, 1999), 23. See also Moshe Lewin, *The Gorbachev Phenomenon: A Historical Interpretation* (Berkeley: University of California Press, 1991).

10. As cited in Richard Sakwa, *The Rise and Fall of the Soviet Union, 1917–1991* (London: Routledge, 1999), 188.

11. For a detailed analysis of debates between Old and New Thinkers, see English, *Russia and the Idea of the West*.

12. Stephen Sestanovich, "Invention of Soviet National Interest," *National Interest* 20 (1990).

13. Sestanovich, "Invention of Soviet National Interest," 10.

14. See, for example, Igor Shafarevich, "Russofobiya," *Nash sovremennik* 6, no. 11 (1989); Yuri Borodai, "Treti put," *Nash sovremennik* 9 (1991).

15. Sergei Kurginyan et al., *Postperestroika* (Moscow: Politizdat, 1990); Aleksandr Prokhanov and Shamil Sultanov, "Izmenit'sya, chtoby vyzhit," *Den'* 6 (1991); Aleksandr Dugin, "Anatomiya mondializma," *Den'* 16 (1991).

16. El'giz A. Pozdnyakov, "Formatsionnyi i tsivilizatsionnyi podkhody i mezhdunarodniye otnosheniya," in *SSSR v mirovom soobschestve*, ed. Nodar A. Simoniya (Moscow: Progress, 1990), 143. For a broader context, review the articles published in Russia's academic and literary journals during 1987–1991.

17. Petr Chaadayev, "Apology of a Madman," in *Readings in Russian Civilization, 2nd ed.*, ed. Thomas Riha (Chicago: University of Chicago Press, 1969), 304.

18. English, *Russia and the Idea of the West*, 201–02.

19. English, *Russia and the Idea of the West*, 203–04.

20. Larson and Shevchenko, "Shortcut to Greatness," 98.

21. Larson and Shevchenko, "Shortcut to Greatness," 99.

22. English, *Russia and the Idea of the West*, 204.

23. David Kotz and Fred Weir, *Revolution from Above: The Demise of the Soviet System* (London: Routledge, 1997), 76.

24. Yuri Levada, ed., *Est' mneniye! Itogi sotsiologicheskogo oprosa* (Moscow: Progress, 1990), 290.

25. Eduard Shevardnadze, "Vneshnyaya politika i nauka," *Mezhdunarodnaya zhizn'* 2 (February 1990): 17, 18.

26. Levada, *Est' mneniye*, 284.

27. Sovetskaya Rossiya, February 6, 1991.

28. Some estimated the defense budget at 20 percent of the GNP and even higher (English, *Russia and the Idea of the West*, 200, 323n31). The official Soviet figures were 8.1 percent for 1975 and 4.6 percent for 1984. See Finansy i statistika (Moscow, 1985) as quoted in Janos Kornai, *The Socialist System: The Political Economy of Communism* (Princeton, NJ: Princeton University Press, 1992), 137.

29. Yuri Slezkine, "The USSR as a Communal Apartment, or How a Socialist State Promoted Ethnic Particularism," *Slavic Review* 53, no. 2 (1994).

30. Mikhail Gorbachev, *Dekabr' 1991: Moya pozitsiya* (Moscow: Novosti, 1992), 175–76.

31. Kotz and Weir, *Revolution from Above*, 147.

32. Michael Ellman and Vladimir Kontorovich, eds, *The Disintegration of the Soviet Economic System* (London: Routledge, 1992); see also Michael Ellman and Vladimir Kontorovich, "The Collapse of the Soviet System and the Memoir Literature," *Europe-Asia Studies* 49, no. 2 (1997); and Vladimir Kontorovich, "Economists, Soviet Growth Slowdown and the Collapse," *Europe-Asia Studies* 53, no. 5 (2001).

33. Levada, *Est' mneniye*, 280, 288.

The Post-Soviet Decline and Attempts at Cooperation, 1991–2004

The United States and other Western democracies are as natural friends and eventual allies of the democratic Russia as they are foes of the totalitarian USSR.

—Andrei Kozyrev, August 1992[1]

Such a country as Russia can survive and develop within the existing borders only if it stays as a great power.

—Vladimir Putin, March 2003[2]

Soviet disintegration ended the previously established sense of national identity in Russia and opened up a space for identity reformulation by the new state. The leaders of post-Soviet Russia proceeded from different visions of national identity and foreign policy, which was consistent with their vision of the world. This chapter describes their visions and respective policies, identifying their differences and the general effort to come to terms with the globally dominant West. All of these efforts took place under conditions of economic and state weakness, although the domestic decline began to be reversed in the first half of the 2000s.

INTERNATIONAL AND DOMESTIC CONDITIONS

The assessed foreign policy perspectives had their roots in distinct international and domestic contexts. While changing, these contexts were not

fundamentally incompatible, and contained elements of similarity and continuity that resulted in a continuous foreign policy for the country.

From Liberal World Order to New Security Threats

The most powerful force that shaped the worldview of new Russia's leadership in the late 1980s to the early 1990s was the economic and political rise
of the West. The economic power and political cohesiveness of Western
civilization contrasted with the disarray in the former Soviet Union. Many
Western commentators were in a self-congratulatory mood, which also contributed to the perception of the worldwide ascendancy of Western values and
institutions. By the time conservatives had been in power for a good decade,
and with the decline of Soviet power, they became convinced of the West's
victory in the Cold War struggle.

For example, Francis Fukuyama's argument about the "end of history"
defended the worldwide ascendancy of Western-style liberal capitalism and
captured the vision dominant in American policy circles.[3] In Europe, such
admirers of civil society and "participatory democracy" as Andrew Arato,
Ralf Dahrendorf, and Timothy Garton Ash expressed similar Western democratic triumphalism, and saw the Soviet decline as a catalyst for a revival of
civic norms of plurality and publicity in Eastern Europe. British journalist
Timothy Garton Ash forcefully stated the mood by maintaining that European
revolutions "can offer no fundamentally new ideas on the big questions of
politics, economics, law or international relations. The ideas whose time has
come are old, familiar, well-tested ones"—liberal ideas about the rule of law,
parliamentary government, and an independent judiciary.[4]

Although politically Western leaders were supportive of Gorbachev's
gradual efforts to dismantle the Soviet system, most of them were critical
of his socialist intentions and hoped for the emergence of a Western-like
system in place of the Soviet Union. Many increasingly perceived the Soviet
system as "the grand failure,"[5] and as early as 1989 such a perception had
won the support of the mainstream intellectual and political discourse in the
West. The leading policy establishment journal *Foreign Affairs* soon issued
the verdict that "the Soviet system collapsed because of what it was, or
more exactly, because of what it was not. The West 'won' because of what
the democracies were—because they were free, prosperous and successful,
because they did justice, or convincingly tried to do so."[6] The vision was
finally legitimized on the highest policy level when US president George H.
W. Bush announced the Cold War "victory" of the United States in his 1992
State of the Union message.

However, several years after the Soviet dissolution, Russia was confronted
with gathering security threats both inside and outside the country. At home,

Russia faced the growing challenge of secessionism and instability in one of its key southern regions, Chechnya. Outside Russia, threats emerged from instabilities and ethnic conflicts in Moldova, central Asia, and the Caucasus. No less importantly, the West extended little recognition to Russia as one of its own, instead treating it increasingly as a potential threat. The rise of ethnic conflicts and the Western decision to expand NATO despite Russia's opposition greatly contributed to the return of Statist thinking to the country, undermining the power of Westernizers in the second half of the 1990s. Statism assumes that respect and recognition can come only from strength, and weakness is not worthy of respect. Instability in Eurasia and the decision to expand NATO by excluding Russia from the process strengthened the Russian perception of the West as playing power games and attempting to take advantage of Russia's temporary weakness. Nationalists felt vindicated, whereas liberals were confused and at a loss for arguments in their defense. Many politicians and intellectuals, including those with a liberal orientation, saw NATO's expansion as a dangerous and threatening development.

As important as the decision to expand NATO was, it reflected the broader change in the West's perception of the world. From the rhetoric of victory in the Cold War and the "end of history," the Western political community moved to a feeling of anxiety over its growing inability to preserve peace and stability across the globe. The new ethnic conflicts in Europe and the former Soviet Union, the perceived threat from the undefeated regime of Iraqi leader Saddam Hussein, and environmental and demographic pressures from Asia and Africa seemed to pose great risks. Various intellectual projects emerged to reflect the rising pessimism among US policymakers about the future of the world order, rejecting earlier rosy perceptions. With the growing awareness of new dangers came fear and suspicion of the non-Western world, which was best summarized by Samuel Huntington's thesis of the "clash of civilizations." Just as Fukuyama once expressed the West's optimism, even euphoria, about the future world order, Huntington expressed growing feelings of anxiety and frustration. He insisted that instead of expanding globally, the West should go on the defensive and prepare to fight for its cultural values in coming clashes with non-Western "civilizations."[7] In this new intellectual context, Russia, with its authoritarian past and politically unstable present, was often viewed as a source of threat rather than as a "strategic partner." The once newly born liberal ally was now increasingly perceived to be driven by traditional imperial aspirations, or as a failing state unable to govern itself.

In the early 2000s, the international context changed yet again, reinforcing Russia's growing sense of insecurity while also undermining the security and confidence of Western nations. The horrific terrorist attacks on the United States on September 11, 2001, created a principally different social and political atmosphere inside Russia while also changing the US perception of the world. President George W. Bush proclaimed terrorism to be "pure evil" directed at freedom-loving people throughout the world, and argued the necessity of launching a strategy of preemption. Several leading intellectuals called for the capture or killing of Osama bin Laden and linked the violent attacks to Islam and the Middle Eastern region. In Russia, these develop-ments provided Putin with a formidable opportunity to bolster his domestic and international posture and to vindicate his conception of security threats. Russia's new president wasted no time in taking advantage of September 11 to reshape Russia's relations with the United States and to redefine the threats to Russia as being characterized by global terrorism.

Three distinct international conditions that affected Russia's foreign policy during the period of 1991 through 2004 are summarized in table 3.1.

Domestic Weakness and Recovery

Russia's domestic conditions during 1991–2004 changed from economic and political instability to a time of relative recovery and stabilization.

The Soviet decline and dissolution were accompanied by drastic economic changes. In contrast to steadily growing Western economies, Russia's gross domestic product (GDP) showed about a 60 percent cumulative decline from 1985 to 1992.[8] Economic weakness remain a major issue in Russia through-out the 1990s. Russia was receiving financial assistance from the West's lead-ing lending agencies, while foreign debt and the domestic budget deficit of the Russian government figured prominently. The heaviest debt approached in 1999 when Russia had to pay $17.5 billion, at a time when its domestic budget was around $20 billion.[9] The budget deficit—which resulted mainly from the government's inability to collect taxes—had been consistently siz-able since the beginning of Yeltsin's economic reform (see table 3.2).

The government was desperate to find noninflationary ways to reduce the deficit and to restructure and reschedule the growing debt. The room for political maneuvering was severely limited, and the government continued the practice of borrowing from the International Monetary Fund (IMF). In turn, the IMF required a tight conditionality and secured a more politically compliant Russia. For all of its talk about depoliticized relations with recipi-ent countries, the political side of the IMF–Russia relationship was always visible. The 1995–1996 lending, for example, was conducted in the context

Table 3.1. Russia and International Conditions, 1991–2004

	1991–1993	1994–1999	2000–2004
International Conditions	Economic and political rise of the West	Ethnic conflicts and NATO expansion	Rise of terrorism

Table 3.2. Russia's Government Revenue and Expenditures, 1992–1998 (% of GDP)

	1992	*1993*	*1994*	*1995*	*1996*	*1997*	*1998*
Revenue	15.6	13.7	11.8	12.2	13.0	11.9	10.2
Expenditures	26	20.2	23.2	17.6	22.0	18.9	16.1

Source: Nigel Gould-Davies and Ngaire Woods, "Russia and the IMF," *International Affairs* 75, no. 1 (1999): 15.

of the approaching presidential elections, in which Yeltsin's victory was the number-one priority for the West. The Western intervention in Yugoslavia—against which Russia objected vehemently—took place as the Russian government was in the process of negotiating the restructuring of the approaching $17.5 billion payment.[10]

As the proposed vision of radical reform and strategic partnership with the West was failing to bring any visible improvements in people's living standards, the population was becoming disillusioned and skeptical. At home, Russians experienced a drastic decline in living standards. Externally, the prospects of NATO expansion toward Russia's borders and military conflicts in the Russian periphery created a sense of insecurity. The disintegration of the Soviet Union added to the change in attitude; many Russians felt that economic failures were now exacerbated by the significant loss of territory and world status. Public support for pro-Western development fell. According to one poll, support for the US model of society declined from 32 percent in 1990 to 13 percent in 1992, or by more than two-thirds. A similar trend was observed with regard to Russian popular opinion about Japanese and German models of society.[11] The biggest demonstration of declining support for Yeltsin and Kozyrev's policies came during the December 1993 parliamentary elections, when liberal parties lost to those of nationalist orientation.

The Russian economy began to recover after the August 1998 financial crisis. By that time, the government had largely completed market reforms, and the country was in a relatively favorable structural position. The growth had been steady, and other indicators were encouraging (see table 3.3). Commercially, too, Russia was in a relatively advantageous position. Its foreign trade had been enjoying a structural surplus, and the economy was wide open for commercial operations. The share of foreign trade had been around 50 percent of the GDP, making Russia's economy, on that measure, about as open as Germany's. The stock of foreign direct investment accumulated since 1989 remained low: about ten times less than in China, and five times less than in Brazil.[12] Yet, rising world oil prices provided Russia with additional new opportunities to explore.

The second internally significant development had to do with ethno-political developments in the Caucasus. Yeltsin's failure to respond to Chechnya's announcement of independence in 1991, as well as the largely political nature

Table 3.3. Russia's Economic Recovery, 1998–2001 (% of 1998)

	GDP	Consumption	Government Investment	Capital Spending	Flight
1998	100	100	100	100	100
1999	105.4	87.2	104.6	105.4	94
2000	114.1	96.2	122.7	131.4	123.6
2001	120	101.3	131.1	133.7	73.6

Source: Philip Hanson, "The Russian Economic Recovery: Do Four Years of Growth Tell Us that the Fundamentals Have Changed?," *Europe-Asia Studies* 55, no. 3 (2003): 386.

of his decision to intervene in late 1994, contributed to a long and bloody confrontation. For Yeltsin, the decision was an attempt to shift public attention away from his own promises to improve or, at least, sustain the living standards of ordinary Russians. In the meantime, the actual income of ordinary Russians, most of whom were wage earners and pensioners, fell drastically, and the economy shrank considerably. Partly as a reaction to Yeltsin's opportunism, the public remained largely skeptical of his military intervention. With little support at home, the army was unable to solve the conflict by force, as disorder and terrorism were increasingly spreading throughout Chechnya and beyond.

By the mid-1990s, terrorist activities intensified in the Caucasus and worldwide. In Russia, the Kremlin's inaction in the aftermath of the 1996 peace agreement with Chechen rebels led to the further spread of anarchy inside the republic, not to political stabilization. The newly elected leader of Chechnya, Aslan Maskhadov, failed to maintain order, and mass kidnapping and extortion by local warlords continued. In August 1999, Chechen rebels led by Shamil Basayev and the Arab fighter Khattab had occupied parts of the neighboring republic of Dagestan, in response to which the Kremlin resumed military operations in the region. Also in August, two bombs exploded in apartment buildings in Moscow, killing hundreds of civilians. The sheer magnitude of violence was unprecedented. Russians united behind Putin, who was running for president on the platform of "eradicating extremism" in Chechnya and reestablishing a "strong state" throughout the entire Russian territory. Initially, the popularity of then prime minister Putin was at the level of only 2 percent, but in two months, it jumped to 26 percent, and as the war in Chechnya progressed, it reached an unprecedented 58 percent in January 2000.[13]

THREE PERSPECTIVES ON NATIONAL IDENTITY AND INTEREST

Distinct combinations of international and domestic conditions resulted in diverse identity coalitions and three dominant perspectives on Russia's national interest. Table 3.4 summarizes these perspectives. Each of these perspectives was domestically contested and opposed by different politico-economic and identity groups.

Westernizers, 1991–1993

The Perspective on National Identity and Interest

Loyal to the intellectual tradition of Westernism, the new Russia's leaders saw their country as an organic part of Western civilization whose "genuine" Western identity had been hijacked by Bolsheviks and the Soviet system. In the Westernist perspective, during the Cold War Russia had acted against its own national identity and interest, and now it finally had an opportunity to become a "normal" Western country. Thus, Kozyrev argued that the Soviet Union was not merely a "normal" or "underdeveloped" country, but a "wrongfully developed" one.[14] This vision was a clear product of a long tradition of Russia's Westernist thinking. While such eminent nineteenth-century historians as Vasili Klyuchevski and Pavel Milyukov recognized Russia's national characteristics, they insisted that their country would nevertheless develop in the same direction as the West and go through the same stages of development.

The new Westernist coalition consisted of idealistic reformers and pragmatic representatives of the former Communist *nomenklatura*. The reformers, such as Gennadi Burbulis, Yegor Gaidar, and Andrei Kozyrev, advocated radical policies that they hoped would bring Russia in line with

Table 3.4. Russia's Perspectives on National Interest, 1991–2004

	Westernizers (Yeltsin–Kozyrev)	Statists-Balancers (Primakov)	Statists-Pragmatists (Putin)
What?	"Natural partnership" with the West	A great power in a multipolar world	A great power in the West-centered world
How?	Rapid membership in Western organizations Isolationism in the former Soviet region Radical economic reform	Flexible alliances Reintegration of the post-Soviet region Economic reform	Counterterrorist cooperation with Europe and the US Limited integration into the world economy Market-based principles in the former Soviet region

the politico-economic standards of Western countries within a limited period of time. Typically, these reformers talked about one or two years of necessary reforms, after which Russians were to considerably improve their living standards. Members of the former party *nomenklatura* realized that the return to the Soviet past was no longer possible. Some of them, especially those originating from the Komsomol (the youth branch of the Communist Party) apparatus and directors of large state enterprises, had entered private business during 1989–1991 and now wanted to obtain control over the state property that had previously been managed under the leadership of the Central Committee. The goals of reformers and the former *nomenklatura* were compatible: Reformers wanted pro-Western capitalist reforms, while the party *nomenklatura* was eager to become a class of new capitalists.

United by the popular president Boris Yeltsin, the Westernist coalition found itself in a position to act on its foreign policy beliefs. Gorbachev's reforms had been effectively discredited, and the failed coup of August 1991 eliminated the appeal of the old communist ideas.

The defeat of Gorbachev by liberal Westernizers led to the assertion of a different concept of national interest. While accepting the general premises of New Thinking, the new Russia's leaders developed these premises in a more sweeping philosophy of Integration with the West and its economic, political, and security institutions. In Kozyrev's words, the country's very system of values was to be changed, as Russia was to accept the priority of the individual and the free market over society and state. As a result, a "natural partnership" with Western countries was to develop, and Russia was to be brought to the front-rank status of such countries as France, Germany, and the United States within ten to twelve years. In the spirit of liberalism, Kozyrev formulated the national interest, which was basically "transforming Russia into a free, independent state, formalizing democratic institutions, setting up an effective economy, guaranteeing the rights and freedoms of all Russians, [and] making our people's life rich both materially and spiritually."[15]

It is worth emphasizing three key components of the asserted vision of national interest—radical economic reform, rapid membership in the Western international institutions, and isolationism from the former Soviet states.

First, Yeltsin and Kozyrev advocated a strategy of radical economic reform, the so-called shock therapy, so that Russia's transition to a Western-style system would be both fast and irreversible. The argument was made that in the contemporary post–Cold War world, Russia should stop worrying about military power and geopolitics and, instead, invest its resources in the creation of a modern economy and political system. The new leadership linked the idea of radical reform to that of strategic partnership with the West, and the calculation was that the latter would be instrumental in implementing the former. Russian Westernizers hoped that the West had finally recognized Russia as one of its own, and would therefore invest the required resources in Russia's transition. For instance, in addressing a joint session of the US Congress in June 1992, Yeltsin saw no reason to hide his expectations for massive external assistance in reforming the country's economy. He even chose to be dramatic in linking the success of Russia's reform to US aid, telling the joint session that his country had only one chance to survive: "There will be no second try . . . the reforms must succeed. . . . If we [that is, you Americans] do not take measures now to support Russia, this will not be a collapse of Russia only, it will be a collapse of the United States, because it will mean new trillions of dollars for the arms race."[16]

Joining international organizations was the second critical element in the strategy of Integration with the West. Since the United States and other Western countries were now "natural allies," Russia should gain a full-scale status in such transatlantic economic and security institutions as the European Union, the North Atlantic Treaty Organization (NATO), the International Monetary Fund (IMF), G-7, and so on. In this brave new world of economic interdependence and Western institutional predominance, Russia would no longer need to pursue its "greatness"; it should instead prepare for a relative decrease of status in a post-confrontational world and try to solve its problems by way of joining the Western "community of civilized nations."[17]

Finally, the new concept of national interest assumed that Russia's Integration with the West would take priority over its relationships with the ex-Soviet republics. The new leadership believed that, just as Russia had suffered from isolation from the West, it had also taken on the excessively heavy Soviet imperial burden. The argument was made that the Soviet Union had been a constant drain on Russian resources, as Russia had had to subsidize other republics. Russia was therefore turned into an "internal colony" of the Soviet Union. The solution was found in the eventual separation of the country from the former republics economically, politically, and culturally.

The concept of "little Russia" was introduced to assist the leadership in justifying little, if any, responsibility for the former Soviet region. In the economic realm, Russia's leaders planned to stop subsidies for the ex-republics. In the security area, they wanted to gradually withdraw Russia's military and to rely on the assistance of international organizations, such as the Organization for Security and Co-operation in Europe (OSCE), in solving possible conflicts in the region. Politically, they viewed the organization newly established in place of the Soviet Union—the Commonwealth of Independent States—as a mechanism for completing the republics' separation from Russia, rather than for promoting or preserving their integration.

The liberal Westernist concept of national interest shaped the new foreign policy concept prepared in late 1992 and signed into law in April 1993. The concept heavily influenced by the documents and charter of the OSCE

favored the promotion of Russia's interests in the first place through participation in different international organizations. The foreign minister's
emphasis on Western international institutions in part reflected his own professional experience; for sixteen years (1974–1990), Kozyrev had worked in
the Directorate of International Organizations at the Soviet Foreign Ministry.
He saw international institutions as the main avenue for resolving conflicts
outside the essentially peaceful and prosperous Western Hemisphere, including between the former Soviet republics.

This concept of national interest was in many ways unprecedented—never
before had Russia's officials been as supportive of dismantling their imperial
institutions, as critical of their own history, and as trusting of Western intentions. In Yeltsin and Kozyrev's design, Russia was not only supposed to cooperate with the West on a broad range of international issues, as Gorbachev had
planned, but it was also to become more like the West at the expense of its
own historically developed identity. Gorbachev wanted the Soviet Union to
be more respectful of other nations, but he did not propose abandoning what
he saw as his country's socialist values and interests. He argued that security
must be mutual, especially in the context of US–Soviet relations, and that it
should be broadened to incorporate various aspects of economic and environmental interdependence.

Contrary to what realists might assert, the new Russia's leaders did not pursue the strategy of Integration with the West because of a weakness of Soviet
material capabilities. The reformers' idealistic worldview could hardly be
likened to pragmatic calculations of a weakened superpower. On the contrary,
many reformers saw the Soviet collapse as an opportunity to establish a new
identity for Russia. Liberal theorists of international relations are closer to
the truth when they point to the impact of Western ideas of modernization on
Russia's liberals. Yet these theorists could hardly have predicted the intensity
of growing opposition to Russia's new Westernist course.

Opposing Perspectives

The Westernist vision of Russia's identity and foreign policy turned out to be
deeply contested and soon was challenged by various elites, as well as the
larger society.

Social Democrats were the former supporters of Gorbachev. They supported the elements of international openness and cooperation present in
Kozyrev's thinking, but criticized his excessively pro-Western orientation
and isolationism in relation to the ex-Soviet republics.[18] Social Democrats
recommended that Russia actively participate in building a new international
order, but they condemned any attempts to shape the world in accordance
with a particular culture's standards. In addition, they argued that it was

relations with the whole world, not just the West alone, that were of key significance.[19] Despite the significance of the Social Democrats' critique, their public visibility in debates on Russia's foreign policy was low. Closely associated with Gorbachev, this group was yet to recover from the devastating blow of the Soviet breakup.

Civilizationists argued that the West was interested only in global hegemony and weakening Russia. One group—the National Communists—was merging some old communist ideas with those of nationalism and was particularly influenced by Josef Stalin's doctrine of "socialism in one country," which acknowledged the need for Russia to focus on developing military and economic capabilities within Soviet boundaries. The most active promoter of this group's ideas was Gennadi Zyuganov, the leader of the Communist Party of the Russian Federation.[20] Another hard-line group referred to itself as Eurasianists, and viewed the world in terms of the geopolitical struggle between land-based and sea-based powers. Unlike National Communists, who portrayed themselves as adherents to conservative beliefs, such as religion and social stability, Eurasianists argued that conservatism was not enough, and advocated the notion of a "conservative revolution" and geopolitical expansion.[21] While National Communists had no ambitions beyond restoring the Soviet Union, Eurasianists wanted to build a larger geopolitical axis of allies—such as Germany, Iran, and Japan—in order to resist American influences. They attracted some support from hard-line military and nationalist political movements, such as Vladimir Zhirinovski's Liberal Democratic Party.

Civilizationists attacked Kozyrev's course as serving the interests of the West at the expense of Russia. To them, Russia's national interest was, almost by definition, anti-Western. They had no regard for the market economy and political democracy, and viewed Russia's institutions as diametrically opposed to those of the West. The West's liberalism, they argued, was nothing more than United States–based unipolarity in the making. Russia's adequate response should include rebuilding military capabilities, reforming the economy on the model of China's gradual state-oriented style, and preserving control over Eurasia, or the post-Soviet world. In the words of the conservative periodical *Molodaya gvardiya*, "The historical task before Russia and other nations of the world is not to allow for the twenty-first century to become the American century."[22]

Statists and Their Institutional Advantages

Under the new geopolitical and economic situation, a number of members of the political class began to advocate a principally different vision of national interest that included a stronger role for the state and revival of Russia's great power status. Influenced by both Westernizers and Civilizationists, Statists positioned themselves to unite supporters of the old and the new Russia. Under the leadership of Yevgeni Primakov, at the time heading the Foreign Intelligence Service, the new coalition united many former Soviet industrialists, state bureaucrats, and members of the military and security services. The members of the new coalition had no faith in the West's willingness or ability to integrate Russia. Instead, they believed in the state's role in preserving security and conducting a less painful economic reform. Statists also had in mind a different model of Russia's relationships with the outside world, and the Westernist vision of the country's identity was soon to be defeated. In late 1995, Kozyrev was removed from office and replaced by Primakov, his prominent critic and the father of Russia's new Statism.

Table 3.5 summarizes contending views on the Westernist perspective of national interest.

In addition to the West's disengagement and Russia's domestic instabilities, the rise of Statism became possible because of various institutional channels available to the school's advocates. The combination of a historically dominant nationalist political culture and low centralized democratic system provided the new Statists with some institutional advantages. Effective use of institutions, such as parliament, media, and influential nongovernmental organizations, helped Statists to promote their vision and undermine that of Kozyrev.

One of the earliest critics of Kozyrev's foreign policy inside the establishment was the chairman of the Foreign Affairs Committee of the Supreme Soviet, Yevgeni Ambartsumov, who had defined the former Soviet region as the sphere of Russia's vital interests by drawing parallels with the early-nineteenth-century policy of American special rights in the Western Hemisphere (the Monroe Doctrine).[23] Another critical agency with direct access to Yeltsin was the Primakov-led Foreign Intelligence Service, which responded to NATO expansion by stressing the dangers of security disintegration in the post-Soviet area. Other important government channels included the Presidential Administration and Security Council. Presidential adviser Sergei Stankevich and the head of the Security Council, Yuri Skokov, each

Table 3.5. Westernism: Contending Views

Social Democrats: Westernism undermines Russia's social democratic potential	**Statists:** Westernism undermines Russia's statehood
vs.	
National Communists: Westernism destroys Russia's socialist system	**Eurasianists:** Westernism eliminates Russia's geopolitical independence

challenged the pro-Western foreign policy by promoting the vision of Russia as a cultural bridge between Europe and Asia and insisting on the defense of the rights of ethnic Russians in the former Soviet republics.[24]

Outside the state, several prominent organizations advanced the Statist vision. Among them, the think tank Council for Foreign and Defense Policy and the political movement Civic Union served to express views of industrialists, businessmen, intellectuals, and mass opinion leaders while advocating Russia's more "Near Abroad"–oriented policies and pragmatism in relationships with the West.[25] In January 1993, the Civic Union adopted its own Concept of Russian Foreign Policy, which advocated Russia's national interest defined in terms of achieving a great power status in Eurasia.

The End of Russia's Westernist Momentum

The Westernist course began to lose its momentum toward the end of 1992. The absence of practical outcomes was all too visible. The calculations of Yeltsin and Kozyrev—that the West would recognize Russia as its own, and provide all the necessary assistance to integrate it into its midst—proved to be flawed. Although Western governments provided some substantial financial aid to Russia and were willing to cooperate on matters of security and arms control (the next section returns to this point), these measures could not meet the existing highly inflated expectations for Western assistance. Credit and investment were too negligible to buttress the credibility of the liberal Westernist vision, let alone transform Russia's institutions. In the realm of security, the importance of the Russia-favored OSCE declined visibly, and Russia made no progress in getting closer to NATO. Although Russia gained a nominal standing within an expanded G-8, its formal inclusion did not come about until July 1994. In addition, some influential foreign policy experts in the West spoke of "the premature partnership" with Russia,[26] a statement that came as a cold shower to the Yeltsin-Kozyrev team.

Under these conditions, the opposition's criticisms were beginning to bite. Geopolitics was quickly becoming the name of the national discourse, and Westernizers could no longer be taken seriously without framing what they had to say in geopolitical terms. Kozyrev had to acknowledge the end of the "honeymoon period" in relations with the West.[27] Yeltsin expressed similar feelings by criticizing the United States for its tendency to "dictate its own terms." Echoing Statist sentiments, he declared that Russia's relations with the West "had to be balanced. After all, we are a Eurasian state."[28] The radical Westernist coalition was falling apart, with some of its members joining the ranks of moderate or even radical opposition. The rhetoric and the agenda of the Statists were gaining currency.

Statist-Balancers, 1994–1999

The Perspective of Statist-Balancers

In this context of growing security threats, the Statist insistence on viewing Russia as first and foremost a great power resonated with the elites and
the broader public. Primakov and his supporters thought about the international system in terms of power poles and favored the United Nations as the
key institution for maintaining a multipolar balance of power, particularly
among great powers.[29] They appealed to the historical notion of Russia as a
Derzhava, which can be loosely translated as a holder of international equi-
librium of power. A *Derzhava* is capable of defending itself by relying on its
own individual strength, and its main goal should be the preservation of that
status. Many Statists also used the notion of Eurasia as symbolic in describing Russia's special geopolitical location and multiethnic nature. Taking issue
with Westernizers, Statists pointed to the need to maintain a multicultural
balance inside Russia.

Unlike Civilizationists, however, Statists were more pragmatic and were
prepared to cooperate with anyone defending the existing balance of international power and Russia's role in it. While viewing the world primarily in
terms of disparities and competition among great powers, Statists were not
anti-Western and did not see Russia as inherently hostile to the West. The
school maintained that, although Russia's interests and values differed from
those of the West, it had historically interacted with the West, and this limited interaction had not threatened Russian sovereignty. Although the school
understood security as resulting more from the state's individual strength than
from collective efforts, it saw the value of tactical coalitions and alliances.

The Statist coalition combined the military industries, army, and security
services that saw the largely ignored potential for generating revenue through
the development of new technologies and exportation of conventional weapons. In one of its documents, the Council for Foreign and Defense Policy,
an influential nongovernmental organization, expressed the attitude typical
of Statist circles when it described the military-industrial complex as "a
key, possibly, the key factor of Russia's struggle for a dignified place in the
twenty-first century."[30] Over time, the large Russian "security class" gained
strength and was able to challenge the emerging and still nascent "commercial
class" that promoted the Westernist image of Russia's identity. By appointing Primakov, President Boris Yeltsin has "signaled that he cares more about
assuaging Statism at home than soothing U.S. fears."[31] Primakov served as
foreign minister from January 1996 through September 1998, and as prime
minister he remained a guiding influence on foreign policy until May 1999. It
was now up to the Statists to define and defend the country's national interest.

Primakov and his team proposed two central elements for recovering Russia's status as a great power in a multipolar world: balancing the United States' unipolar ambitions in a coalition with other states, and integrating the former Soviet region under tighter control from Moscow. Primakov understood that Russia was weak and had limited resources for foreign policy grandeur. Yet his thinking was, counterintuitively, that the country had to pursue "active" foreign policy (*aktivnaya vneshnyaya politika*)[32] in order to compensate for currently limited resources in reforming the economy and preserving territorial integrity. He believed that Russia was in a geopolitically dangerous environment and simply could not afford to concentrate on purely domestic issues (see table 3.4 for a comparative summary of the Statist view of national interest).

In relationships with the West, Primakov insisted that Russia be motivated primarily by its own interests, and he proclaimed the vision of a multipolar world. The Statist logic was simple: The power dictates its rules, and under the conditions of a unipolar world, Russia would have no independent voice in international politics. The unipolar world was not going to be liberal or democratic, despite American promises, and Russia should not succumb to the rhetoric of the strongest. Instead, it must use a combination of both cooperation and balancing policies for the purpose of undermining the unipolarity. Primakov believed that a limited and pragmatic cooperation with either the "strongest" or the West was both feasible and important. Unlike the Westernizers, however, Primakov and his supporters insisted that the principle of absolute power equality must be honored in each instance of cooperation.

In addition to cooperating with the West, Statists believed that Russia also had to engage in balancing tactics against the strongest power, the United States. In a multipolar world, which Russia wanted to see built, Russia had to be able to prevent the formation of an opposing coalition by using balancing tactics in relating to all of its foreign partners—Western, Eastern, and Southern. Russia's policy orientation in the world, then, should have been multilateral, or "multivector," aiming to develop balanced relations with Western and non-Western countries. In Yevgeni Primakov's words, "Russia is both Europe and Asia, and this geopolitical location continues to play a tremendous role in [the] formulation of its foreign policy. Its [geopolitical interests] include China, India, and Japan, and not just the United States or Europe. They also include the Middle East and the 'Third World.' Without such geopolitical scope, Russia cannot continue to be a great power and to play the positive role it has been destined to play."[33]

Primakov made it explicit that his strategy was reminiscent of State Chancellor Alexander Gorchakov's "concentration" course after Russia's defeat in the Crimean War. After the March 1856 Paris peace treaty, which legitimized Russia's defeat, Gorchakov recommended to Czar Alexander II that, in facing the new conditions, Russia temporarily "will have to focus persistently on the realization of [its] internal development and the entire foreign policy will have to be subordinated to this main task."[34] In combination with flexible alliance making, Russia at least partially achieved the goal: In 1870 it felt strong enough to act unilaterally and partially renounce the conditions of the Paris peace treaty. Primakov, too, was hoping that, after rebuilding the economy, Russia would "return" to world politics.

In the former Soviet Union, Statists defended the notion of a tightly integrated region with Russia's informal control over policies of the former republics. Unlike neocommunists or Eurasianists, the new foreign minister wanted no formal responsibility for the "postimperial space" and preferred to refer to Russia's relations with its post-Soviet neighbors as "multilateral integration."

Such thinking about Russia's national interest was adequately reflected in official documents. The country's National Security Concept of 1997 described "the new geopolitical and international situation" followed by "negative processes in the national economy" as key threats to Russia. It identified Russia as an "influential European and Asian power," and it invariably termed the country's relationships with "other great powers" as an "equal partnership." Furthermore, it recommended that Russia maintain equal distancing in relation to the "global European and Asian economic and political actors," and presented a positive program for the integration of the efforts of the Commonwealth of Independent States (CIS) in the security area. The government's official Foreign Policy Concept of 2000 referred to the Russian Federation as "a great power . . . [with a] responsibility for maintaining security in the world both on a global and on a regional level," and warned of a new threat of "a unipolar structure of the world under the economic and military domination of the United States."[35]

Although Primakov's perspective was definitely the closest to realist thinking, it is difficult to apply realism as an international relations theory for explaining Russia's turn to Great Power Balancing. Realists expect that policy change follows evolution in state material capabilities. Yet Russia's capabilities did not improve. As table 3.5 indicates, the country's economic decline continued, and there was hardly a material basis for developing a more assertive foreign policy. What changed, however, was the behavior of the West toward Russia and its local conditions; this contributed to an altered domestic perception and brought to power the identity coalition of Statists.

Other Perspectives

The new foreign policy vision found broad support in Russian society and, especially, among the political elites. After Kozyrev's departure, Yeltsin embraced the rhetoric of great power and multipolarity and pronounced the discussion of Russia's foreign policy priorities to be "completed" and the new foreign policy concept to be supported by a "consensus of various social and political forces."[36] Statists and many Social Democrats welcomed the new foreign policy course. Some Social Democrats praised the new foreign policy for its proclaimed pragmatism, restraint, and sense of priorities.[37] Civilizationists, too, accepted some of Primakov's arguments while at the same time pushing him to adopt a more confrontational line in relations with the West. To them, the notion of a great power implied the restoration of the Soviet Union, and multipolarity meant isolation from and competition with the West.[38]

Westernizers stood out from the rest of the political class in their most irreconcilable critique of the course of Great Power Balancing. Westernizers drew attention to the fact that ordinary Russians were concerned primarily with the state of the Russian economy and internal security, and not the issues of military capabilities and great power status. Insisting, as before, on Russia's politico-economic integration with European institutions, they saw as fundamentally misplaced Primakov's priorities of reviving the CIS as a vehicle of post-Soviet integration, resisting the eastern expansion of NATO, developing military cooperation with Iran, and trying to build the Russia-China-India security axis. Furthermore, they challenged the relevance of Gorchakov's "concentration" on contemporary foreign policy. In their view, Gorchakov's flexible alliances had deprived Russia of a chance to side firmly with democratic France, and, ultimately, contributed to the rise of Germany and Russia's own revolution. They charged that, by not siding firmly with the West and trying to play Europe or China against the United States, Primakov's policy, too, was likely to result in failure.[39]

While echoing many of the old Westernist arguments, the new Westernizers became more pragmatic and less ideological in their reasoning. Increasingly, they were concentrating on various material benefits of Russia's pro-Western orientation. Some spoke of the need in "pragmatic liberalism" for successfully opposing Primakov's "pragmatic nationalism," whereas others acknowledged that the road to Europe would not be an easy or straightforward one.[40]

Table 3.6 summarizes contending views on the Statist perspective of national interest.

Table 3.6. Great Power Balancing (GPB): Contending Views

Civilizationists:		Westernizers:
GPB must more decisively confront the West	vs.	GPB leads to confrontation with the West

Statist-Pragmatists, 2000–2004

The Perspective of Statist-Pragmatists

In response to these global developments, Putin put forward the ideology of pragmatism and self-concentration. This ideology articulated the vision of a new identity coalition, which combined both Westernist and Statist influences. With Westernizers, Putin came out as critical of past practices of overextending foreign policy resources—a possible reference to both the Soviet and Primakov periods. However, he also committed himself to traditional values typically emphasized by Statists and Civilizationists. For instance, in his programmatic article "Russia at the Turn of the Millennium," which he addressed to his electorate, the future president emphasized patriotism, a strong state, and social solidarity as his country's key values. Unlike Gorbachev or Kozyrev, Putin was not eager to replicate Western social democratic or liberal values on Russian soil, and he made it clear that Russia would never become the "second edition of . . . the U.S. or Britain."[41] Rather, he saw his country as a modern great power capable of adapting to a changing world under state leadership. In the tradition of Statism, priority is given to governability and the state's ability to exercise its power, whereas democracy comes second.[42]

The Statist thinking therefore proved to be resilient in post-Primakov Russia. Putin spoke of the Eurasianist dimension of Russia's identity, and was determined to continue the war in Chechnya as he saw fit, despite criticism from his Westernist opponents inside and outside the country.

Yet, unlike Primakov, who tended to view the world primarily in terms of new threats to Russia's security, Putin pointed to both threats and opportunities. In particular, he saw security threats to the modern system of international relations coming from terrorist activities, rather than state-organized military capabilities. In this, his Statism was also distinct from that of Primakov. Putin's "no one is going to war with us" was a reference to states, yet he was convinced that terrorists had an interest in attacking Russia. His support for Western countries and the United States' efforts in fighting international terrorism after September 11 was therefore not tactical, but came from his principal belief system.

This new vision represented the interests of the new mixed social coalition. Because commercial elites often defended Russia's Westernist identity, whereas military and security elites promoted Statism, the new coalition was sometimes referred to as the alliance of oligarchs and *siloviks*, or chekists (from the Russian CheKa, the original name of the Bolshevik security service). Liberal and commercially oriented Westernizers strongly supported

Putin's election. Especially important were Russia's oligarchs, the group of superwealthy businessmen that had emerged as a powerful force in 1996. At that time, they had managed to overcome their differences and pull together enough financial resources to reelect Boris Yeltsin, who was unpopular then. At the same time, many Statists and Civilizationists felt compelled to embrace Putin. Statists and various members of Russia's military elite supported him because of his background in the security service and his stated beliefs in strengthening the state and social order. The new identity coalition rose to prominence in the post-1998 new domestic and external context. The relative recovery of the Russian economy improved the oligarchs' position, and the intensification of terrorist activities in the Caucasus and worldwide strengthened the *siloviks'* position. In the new world context of both threats and opportunities, the oligarchs and *siloviks* each hoped to increase their influence on the president.

In his turn, Putin was planning to take advantage of the unstable coalition's resources, while exercising his authority as he saw fit. He did not hide his preference for the state-dominant model of economic development, and made known his lack of respect for how oligarchs had emerged and enriched themselves. But he also expressed his readiness to honor privatization and market reforms, already under way.[43] The president was being ruthless to those oligarchs, such as Boris Berezovski, Vladimir Gusinski, and Mikhail Khodorkovski, who he perceived as violating his new deal. The first two had to emigrate, and the third, the heir of the oil giant Yukos, was arrested on charges of multiple fraud and tax evasion. The president had more respect for security elites, especially the army, which had been much humiliated under Yeltsin. The first war in Chechnya taught the military, among other things, that it could not count on the civilian leadership for adequate financial assistance. Putin moved to change that by proposing a considerable reduction in the army's personnel—from 1.2 million in 2001 to between 800,000 and 850,000 by 2005[44]—along with modernization and a considerable increase in the military budget (see table 3.7 for details of the budget increase).

Consistent with the new vision of Russia's identity, a new conceptualization of national interest was adopted. Putin soon revealed his differences from Primakov's Great Power Balancing. For Putin, the most important national

Table 3.7. Russia's Increased Military Budget, 1999–2002

Year	1999	2000	2001	2002
Billions of Rubles	109.0	111.0	218.9	284.1

Source: Dale R. Herspring, "Putin and the Armed Forces," in *Putin's Russia: Past Imperfect, Future Uncertain,* ed. Dale R. Herspring (Lanham, MD: Rowman & Littlefield, 2003), 170.

interest lay in Russia's modernization and economic growth, not in balancing American influences in the world. Such a perspective assumed that in today's world, geoeconomics had gained the upper hand over geopolitics, and thus Russia had to learn to defend its national interest by economic means. It also implied that Russia had to economize its resources and not overstretch itself in world political affairs. Balancing, therefore, needed to yield to Pragmatic Cooperation. Finally, it meant that any integration in the former Soviet area had to be open to and compatible with domestic private interests and the task of Russia's gradual integration with the world economy.

To substantiate his vision, Putin warned of the danger of turning into a third-world country. Ridiculing overly noisy great power rhetoric—"let us not recollect our national interests on those occasions when we have to make some loud statements"—Russia's new leader compared Russia to Portugal, the EU's poorest member. He then drew the uncomforting conclusion, "It would take us fifteen years and an eight percent annual growth of our GDP to reach the per capita GDP level of present-day Portugal."[45] The reality was that, despite Russia's economic recovery after the 1998 financial crisis, the size of its economy and purchasing power was less than one-fourth the size of the economies of China and Japan, and less than one-tenth the size of the economies of the United States and the European Union.[46] Putin's support for the concept of multipolarity was also more muted, and the key emphasis of the new National Security Concept was on economic decline, organized crime, corruption, terrorism, and separatism. After September 11, his support for multipolarity continued to decline, and the focus was on pragmatism and self-concentration in foreign policy. Despite some common anti-Western sentiments among the members of Russia's political class, the president became far more active in promoting Russia's relationships with the United States and Europe, and more passive on the Eastern and Asian fronts.

Putin's vision of Russia as a defensive and pragmatically pro-Western power was therefore different from the earlier described visions of Integration with the West or balancing the West's global influences (see table 3.4 for a summary). He saw the first task as improving the state of the Russian economy by capitalizing on domestic oil reserves and increasing the ability to export to the West in order to confirm Russia's great power status and to preserve the required space to maneuver to defend Russia's political interests in world politics. Without antagonizing the West, and given the West's need to have Russia as an ally, Putin planned to promote its interests in relations with Chechnya, Iran, and Iraq as he saw fit.

Opposing Perspectives

Putin's decision to support the United States in the post–September 11 struggle against terrorism and his redefinition of national interest led to an important change in the Russian discourse. Liberal Westernizers threw their support behind his post–September 11 vision. Yet they urged him to go beyond a tactical alliance with the West and toward forging a development of common identity and cultural values. A leader of the liberal Yabloko party, Grigori Yavlinski, in an article titled "A Temporary Friendship or an Eternal Alliance?," insisted that Putin's vision of national interest had to be viewed as a "choice in favor of a long-term unity with Western or European civilization, of which Russia is an organic part."[47] Ideologists of another liberal party, the Union of Right-Wing Forces, went even further by viewing the events of September 11 as a clash between "civilization" and "barbarians," who had yet to learn the "universal" rules of "civilization."[48]

While Westernizers were critical of the new vision's pragmatism, Statists and Civilizationists were worried about its pro-Western component. Statists who were former supporters of Primakov's foreign policy course aimed to preserve Russia's independence and great power status in world politics. Primakov himself felt uneasy about Putin's post-9/11 strategy, referring to it as "justified, yet a big risk," and worrying about the American military presence in the Caucasus and central Asia.[49] Other Statists emphasized the "harmful" aspects of American unilateralism as one of the reasons for the attacks of September 11, and insisted on a tactical rather than a strategic focus when it came to cooperation with the United States.[50]

Table 3.8 summarizes Putin's view of national interest.

The National Communists and Eurasianists went much further in criticizing Putin's vision as not sensitive to American hegemony. The problem, in their minds, was not merely the American strategy and hegemonic ambitions; such strategy and ambitions themselves should be viewed as inevitable products of Western culture and its creature: modern civilization. For this group, the politics of the West were inseparable from its culture and economics.[51] Much like President Bush and some Westernizers, the hard-line Civilizationists

Table 3.8. Putin's View of National Interest

What?	**A great power in the West-centered world**
How?	Counterterrorist cooperation with Europe and the United States
	Limited integration into the world economy
	Market-based principles in the former Soviet region

viewed the post–September 11 world in terms of a struggle between "good" and "evil," except they found themselves on the other side of the barricade. For their side to win in this struggle, they recommended building a broad coalition of anti-American cultures and civilizations.

The political class's cautious reaction, described above, was broadly representative of the feelings within Russia's general public, which remained wary of Western intentions. The country's most traumatic postcommunist experience and the failure of Gorbachev's and Yeltsin's early attempts to develop a strategic partnership with the West made the Russian political class, military, media, and general public skeptical of the new efforts at rapprochement. Few factions in the Russian Duma initially supported Putin's decision to side with the United States after 9/11. Russia's Muslim leaders reacted critically to the American military campaigns in Afghanistan and Iraq. Of special importance was a series of published "open letters" signed by retired generals, including one of Yeltsin's former defense ministers, accusing Putin of "selling out" the country and "betraying" the nation's vital interests. Even the mainstream media described what they perceived as a sense of Russian "encirclement" by US and NATO troops.[52] The Russian general public, although supportive of Putin's leadership, also showed signs of increased concern over American actions in the world. According to data from the Russian Center for the Study of Public Opinion, 63 percent of all Russians felt that the terrorist attack on the United States was a form of "retribution for American foreign policy."[53]

THE WESTERNIST MOMENT, 1991–1993

As brief as Russia's Westernist momentum was, Yeltsin and Kozyrev did try to act on their beliefs. This section reviews their policies toward the outside world, which demonstrate the depth of their convictions about Western civilization's primacy in the world. Russia's leaders turned their full attention to the West, while remaining neglectful of relationships with the rest of the world.

Toward Integration with the West

The new Russia's leaders hoped that the West would provide all the required material and moral support for reform when it saw how committed Russia was to a liberal transformation. At times the Russians sounded dramatic and even desperate for massive Western material and moral support because they believed that, short of such support, their reforms were doomed to failure. There is no reason to doubt the sincerity of Russia's leaders. Their utopian ideological considerations were the primer in shaping Russia's perception of the world. Rational interests came in a distant second and reemerged as a key foreign policy motivation only at a later stage. It is consistent with Westernist ideological beliefs that Russia's leaders were ready to do everything in their power to gain membership in Western international organizations and support the West's agenda in international security affairs.

Striving to Join Western International Organizations

The leaders of the new Russia had very high expectations about joining Western international organizations. In economic affairs, they did not merely expect loans or assistance in debt restructuring and currency stabilization; they also wanted a flow of massive Western investments, and they were correct to measure the success of Russia's integration into the world economy by such investments, rather than high-interest loans. For instance, in July 1992 Yeltsin declared at a G-7 summit that a $24 billion package would not save Russia and that foreign direct investment in the amount of several hundred billion dollars was necessary to do the job. Most Russian politicians expected a grand bargain with Russia, something comparable to the Marshall Plan or the "500 Days" plan that had been articulated but never implemented during the Gorbachev era. The latter included $100 billion of support over four years for reforming the Soviet Union, alongside an orthodox IMF program.[54]

Such expectations, of course, assumed an unprecedented level of trust in the new Russia by Western leaders and the world business community—a condition that was hardly in place. The West was neither willing nor able to launch something similar to the massive Marshall Plan for postcommunist Russia. All Western nations could offer was to work through the IMF in trying to reform Russia. Germany embarked on the reunification project, which soon proved to be extremely costly. The United States—at the time, the key supporter of the new Russia—also was going through an economic downturn and was hardly in a position to put all its eggs in the highly uncertain basket of what was once the largest economy of the communist world.

Gaining the required assistance, not surprisingly, proved to be very difficult, and Russia's overall record was mixed at best. In June 1992, Russia was able to join the International Monetary Fund and the World Bank, which it saw as crucial for creating a market economy. IMF credits were essential for achieving macroeconomic stabilization and balancing the budget, but they did not (and could not) do much to assist Russia with integration into the world economy. Russia also managed to join the G-7 in July 1992, despite the opposition of both British prime minister John Major and German chancellor Helmut Kohl. Yet the membership did not change much in Russia's economic status. Even psychologically, progress was disappointing—Western leaders saw Russia as an aid recipient, not a donor, and did not treat the newcomer as an equal partner.

The biggest gains resulted from Russia's emphasis on relationships with the United States. First, in the politically charged atmosphere of Russia's high expectations, Bush, supported by Kohl, announced a $24 billion package in April 1992. At the time, Yeltsin faced particularly strong opposition to his reform at home, as the Congress of People's Deputies revealed the commitments of many to fight privatization and land reform. US president Bill Clinton was even more supportive of Yeltsin, arguing for a global alliance to support democracy and preventing a world "more dangerous in some respects than the dark years of the Cold War." As a result of the new American president's efforts to mobilize the West to support Russia, the Tokyo G-7 summit declared a $43.4 billion program of assistance for Russia. Aside from that, the progress in either joining Western organizations or mobilizing them to assist Russia in its integration strategy was hardly satisfactory to the Kremlin leadership.

In security affairs, Russia invited the peacekeeping forces of the United Nations and the OSCE into Europe to provide security in the former Soviet Union. Kozyrev wanted to rapidly integrate with European security institutions and even stated Russia's desire to gain membership in NATO. However, in dealing with new security challenges, Russia soon discovered the need to rely on its own army.

Supporting the West's International Security Agenda

Until approximately mid-1993, the new Russia's leaders also loyally supported the West's international security agenda. In Europe, Russia was working toward gaining full membership in all European security institutions, including NATO. Even when NATO announced its plans to expand east, Russia's new rulers initially raised no objections to the process.

Despite traditionally strong ties with Serbia, Russia's leaders also supported the West's agenda in the Balkans. Initially, they avoided even meeting with the leaders of Yugoslavia and sided with the West in condemning the Serbs for atrocities against the Muslims over the independent Bosnian state. In the spring and the summer of 1992, Russia also supported the United Nations' economic sanctions against Yugoslavia and suspension of the country's membership in the OSCE, although Russia's leaders had initially favored negotiations regarding the punishment of Yugoslavia. Furthermore, Moscow did not object to the United Nations security resolutions authorizing the possible use of force against Yugoslavia, and it did not use its veto power when the UN General Assembly voted to expel the country from the United Nations. Later, Yeltsin also supported the Western plan, devised by US secretary of state Cyrus Vance and British foreign secretary David Owen, for a weak confederation in Bosnia and Herzegovina.

The new Russian leaders also shared—even at the cost of the country's traditional ties—the West's arms-control agenda. Yeltsin slashed strategic nuclear arsenals by half and also agreed to eliminate all land-based intercontinental ballistic missiles (ICBMs) armed with multiple warheads, while the United States retained such warheads in submarines. The terms of the new agreement, START II, were agreed upon at the June 1992 summit and signed in January 1993. This was an unprecedented move: For the first time in the history of the nuclear arms race, Russia abandoned the heart of its strategic arsenals, while the United States preserved its own. Even Russia's liberal commentators, such as Aleksei Arbatov, criticized the agreement as unbalanced.[55] Yeltsin acknowledged that Russia was sacrificing strategic parity with the United States, but stated that the parity was "ominous," and did not make any sense now that "the fundamental change in the political and economic relations between the United States of America and Russia"[56] had taken place. Until September 1993, Yeltsin also did not see the need to revise the Conventional Forces in Europe (CFE) treaty, which restricted the internal distribution of forces in Russia and gained strong opposition from the military establishment.

In its efforts to rapidly integrate with the West, Russia forfeited billions of dollars in arms sales by abandoning lucrative markets in the third world and supporting Western sanctions against Libya, Iraq, and Yugoslavia. On Iraq, Kozyrev even supported US bombing, as well as UN sanctions. This policy stance began to change only in 1993 under the pressure of those arguing that Russia could not afford to lose Iraq's $7 billion debt to it. Kozyrev also went along with the United States' attempts to restrict Russia's military ties with China, Iran, and India. In the meantime, while Russia was going out of its way to persuade the West that it had been sincere in its integration drive, the West continued to play power politics and did not seem to care to reciprocate. In the arms markets, as the liberal *Izvestiya* noted, whereas Russia's share from 1991 to 1993 dropped from 38 to 17 percent, the US share increased from 30 to 58 percent.[57]

The Neglect of Asia and the Muslim World

Russia's new Westernism had a clear zero-sum component, which was particularly visible in the attitude toward Asia and the Middle East. More partnership with the West meant less of a relationship with the non-Western regions. In the highly ideological mind-set of Kozyrev's team, the East was associated with "backwardness" and "authoritarianism" rather than the "prosperity" and "democracy" of the Western "civilized nations." Again, the identity argument was made: Russia had been too Asiatic already, and it was now time to move away "from its Asian roots of oriental despotism and toward the Western democratic camp."⁵⁸ Many in the Westernist camp believed that the non-Western systems, such as China and the Middle Eastern countries, would soon follow the Soviet and Eastern European example and collapse precisely because these systems were "nondemocratic." China was especially despised because of the Tiananmen massacre of Chinese democrats in 1989 and Beijing's support of the anti-Gorbachev coup in Moscow in August 1991.

Russia's relations with China are a clear example of the new leadership's passivity in the eastern direction. Although Gorbachev laid out preconditions for improving relations with China by signing two important joint communiqués and the border treaty, the progress in the relationship between the two sides was stalled by their growing ideological differences. In February 1992, the border treaty was ratified by Russia's Supreme Soviet, but Yeltsin and Kozyrev remained wary of China as anti-Western and critical of Russia's democratic development. The relationships were on hold until late 1992. Russia's leaders and politicians were avoiding even meeting Chinese officials. In March 1992, Kozyrev traveled to China in an attempt to stimulate economic cooperation between the two. However, the trip lasted only thirty hours, and the two sides disagreed on human rights issues by officially concluding that in Russia–China ties, "elements of considerable agreement coexist with different approaches to some quite significant questions."⁵⁹

A similar pattern could be observed in Russia's relations with the Muslim world. Russia's leaders were initially dismissive of the region's significance. Yeltsin ordered the withdrawal of the CIS troops from Nagorno-Karabakh in the Caucasus and simultaneously asked for the deployment of NATO troops as a peacekeeping force there. Despite the growing instability in Afghanistan and central Asia, he also refrained from any serious involvement in the region, leaving the stage to Iran and Turkey. In April 1992 after the mujahideen takeover of Kabul, Kozyrev visited Afghanistan, but that visit, too, was a goodwill gesture more than an effort to develop the mutual relationship. Despite various complaints from the domestic opposition, Russia's officials had no problems with the increased activism of the United States in the region, evident, for instance, in the February 1992 visit of Secretary of State James Baker to central Asia. Finally, Russia was slow to recognize the role of India and Korea in its foreign policy. Russia's Westernism meant a reduction of Russia–India trade, particularly in the military area. In the Korean Peninsula, Yeltsin and Kozyrev pursued the one-sided policy of favoring the South over the North. In 1992, both Russian leaders proposed signing a treaty of friendship with South Korea to cement their relationship, despite the assessments of Korea specialists that Russia's interests required balanced relations with the two. The ideological dichotomy between the "civilized" pro-Western South and the "barbaric" Stalinist North severely weakened the link to the North, while the anticipated economic benefits of a Moscow–Seoul relationship were not forthcoming. In June 1993, the North announced its first withdrawal from the Nuclear Non-Proliferation Treaty, and Moscow responded by supporting the United States–sponsored sanctions against North Korea.

The Westernizers insisted that relationships with the "barbaric" East were to be limited to those of issues of national security. When in March 1992 leading Statist Sergei Stankevich proposed that Russia reactivate its relations with the Muslim world, Kozyrev replied negatively. The foreign minister denied that Russia had any specific interests in Asia aside from those of maintaining security, and even those had to be addressed within the Western institutional framework. He singled out the need to put joint pressure on North Korea to relinquish its ambitious nuclear program. Later, when the Statist pressures on Kozyrev to view Russia as a "great power" in Eurasia had increased, he reframed his pro-American argument by linking Eurasia to the United States. Writing in *International Affairs* in early 1993, he asserted that Russia's Eurasian location is part of its status: "Anyone who looks at the map will see that the United States is our next-door neighbor in the East." To stress his point, Kozyrev added: "In the East, not the West."[60]

Isolationism in the Former Soviet Region

Yeltsin and Kozyrev's isolationism toward the former Soviet republics was an extension of their radical Westernist beliefs. Eager to integrate with the West, the new leaders had no time to wait for the republics to pursue similar policies. Nor did they feel responsible for assisting their neighbors in their transformation. Russia had to go West alone, and, in order to overcome potential resistance from the ex-leaders of the republics, it had to erect nationalist economic, political, and security barriers against the former Soviet nations.

Isolationist Thinking

Westernizers justified the isolationist course on economic, political, and cultural grounds. Economically, they argued, Russia had been turned into an "internal colony" of the Soviet Union and, as a result, suffered from being a core of the Soviet empire even more than all other republics. As the largest and the wealthiest nation in the region, Russia had to subsidize the republics instead of selling its raw materials, such as oil and natural gas, at the world market's prices. Were Russia to continue to serve as an economic locomotive, the argument went, it would become the first victim of such generosity. The roots of this argument can be traced to Gorbachev's era when Yeltsin's umbrella organization, Democratic Russia, presented itself as an anti-imperial movement by emphasizing the autonomy of Russia and other republics and even openly calling for the dissolution of the Soviet Union. The Soviet

Union was presented as an "empire" that was to be dismantled for the sake of Russian prosperity. Throughout the political campaigns of 1990 and 1991, Yeltsin had advanced the "Russia-victim" argument, and it was his advisers who eventually wrote a scenario for dissolving the union. Ironically, the argument was borrowed from Russian anti-Western nationalists, who often complained about the Russian burden of providing for the rest of the union (although they never wanted to break up the union).

Furthermore, the post-Soviet Westernizers believed that during the Soviet era Russia also suffered politically and culturally, and it should now rebuild its identity in nonimperial or "civic" terms. Valeri Tishkov, the director of the Institute of Ethnology and Anthropology and the minister for nationalities in 1992, had provided the intellectual justification and first put forward the concept of a civic nation publicly in 1989. The central thrust of viewing Russia as a civic nation was its deethnification, or the removal of the categories of ethnicity and religion from the identity-building project. Tishkov argued that Russia should form a civic Russian (*rossiyskaya*) nation, or a community of all citizens of the Russian Federation regardless of their cultural and religious differences, rather than any form of ethnic Russian (*russkaya*) nation. Domestically, the new vision categorized Russia within its current post-Soviet borders as a political nation, and one of "co-citizenship."[61] Externally, it meant to relieve the new Russia of responsibility for the Soviet policies and their historical legacies in the region. In particular, Russia was not to be responsible for the well-being of twenty-five to thirty million ethnic Russians—about 30 percent of the homeland Russians—who resided in the former Soviet republics outside Russia.

The liberal foreign policy community supported the isolationist component in the country's national interest. For instance, one prominent report of the Foreign Ministry's Institute of International Relations warned against Russia's assuming the role of a new core in the Commonwealth of Independent States. It insisted that Russia's key interest was in entering the G-7 as a full-fledged participant and therefore being prepared to "give up the CIS in favor of orientation toward Europe."[62]

Isolationism in Practice

Politically, Russia's isolationism aimed at separating from the ex-Soviet republics institutionally. Yeltsin and Kozyrev concentrated on strengthening sovereignty and independence from the former Soviet region and its transnational institutional umbrella, the CIS. The organization emerged to do away with the Soviet Union, and initially—before it included all ex-republics except the Baltic ones—had had only Russia, Ukraine, and Belarus as members. Yeltsin, who had proposed the CIS mainly in order to defeat his political opponent, Gorbachev, never meant for the organization to facilitate cooperation and interdependence in the region. Rather, he wanted it to complete the ex-Soviet republics' political and economic separation, and that vision permeated the organization's founding agreements and subsequent seminal documents, such as the CIS charter.

In its practical policy, Russia preferred to deal with its neighbors on a bilateral, rather than multilateral, basis. It was also far from active in relations with the states of the region. Despite Kozyrev's rhetoric about the priority of the CIS in Russia's foreign policy, his first trips were to Western Europe, North America, and other regions of the world. Apart from a quick visit to Estonia, he first traveled to the former Soviet region only in April 1992. By July of the same year, Russia had opened only one embassy in the region, in Kyiv. Moscow assumed that, even if some of the former states were to eventually gravitate toward Russia, this would happen much later, and on a market basis. That attitude began to change in 1993 when Russia initiated the CIS Economic Union agreement, which was supposed to develop multilateral economic cooperation.

In security matters, Russia's isolationist policies reflected the desire to reduce to a minimum responsibility for maintaining order in the former Soviet region. The Russian analyst Alexander Pikayev captured four specific goals that the Kremlin sought to accomplish: the fastest possible withdrawal of Russian troops from outside Russia; tacit support of the control introduced by governments in the former Soviet republics on former Soviet troops; ignoring separatist tendencies within individual CIS states and maintaining relations with the central governments; and inviting foreign participation in settling conflicts in the post-Soviet region.[63]

Russia's officials tried to accomplish those goals until approximately mid-1992. Yeltsin ordered the withdrawal of troops from Nagorno-Karabakh, while simultaneously asking for the deployment of NATO troops as a peacekeeping force there. When Chechnya proclaimed independence in November 1991, Yeltsin ruled out military intervention as a policy option. He also did not initially oppose Ukraine, the largest CIS state outside Russia, taking control over the former Soviet troops located on the republic's territory. Furthermore, by establishing Russia's Ministry of Defense in April 1992, Yeltsin indicated his unwillingness to maintain the collective status of the former Soviet Armed Forces, which had been favored by the central Asian leaders. A signatory of the CIS collective security treaty (May 1992), Russia did little to activate the treaty, and over the year, it continued to seriously discuss the possibility of deploying UN or NATO peacekeeping troops in the areas of ethnic conflict. Nor did it show serious concern over the status of ethnic Russians in the former Soviet states.

The leadership's position showed signs of change only when military conflicts in various parts of the former Soviet Union threatened to spill over to
Russia. The first challenge came from Moldova in the spring of 1992. The
intention of Moldova's leadership to reunite with Romania had provoked
violent secessionism in the Transdniestr area, which gravitated toward Russia
economically and culturally. Moldova's efforts to involve the OSCE had
failed to produce any results in a timely manner, and Russia intervened to
stop widespread fighting. It put the fourteenth former Soviet division under
its control, negotiated a cease-fire, and took on the task of maintaining peace
in the region. Kozyrev at first condemned the army involvement and rejected
the opportunity to establish ties with the separatist Transdniestr leaders.
By late June, however, even he favored an intervention and deployment of
Russia's military forces. This proved critical for preventing a further spread
of violence and civil war in Moldova. It also established the precedent for
further interventions in Tajikistan, Georgia, and elsewhere.

In economic matters, Russia planned no coordination with the former
republics. In the aftermath of the failed coup of August 1991, Yeltsin first
formulated the idea of Russia going it alone as a matter of economic strategy.
In his speech to the Russian Congress of People's Deputies, he committed
himself to the strategy of shock therapy—or freeing up all prices by the end
of the year, rapid privatization of both industry and land, large reductions in
state spending, and a tough monetary policy. He argued that Russia must go
first and that, by so doing, it would provide an example for other republics.[64]
Yeltsin shared the widely held liberal convictions that the republics were
nothing but a "burden [*girya*] on the Russian legs," and that Russia had little
choice but to "break away" (*uiti v otryv*) from the former Soviet Union.

Acting on those convictions, Russia reformed its currency by unilaterally
withdrawing from the ruble zone. In July 1993, it stopped money supplies to
the ex-republics and withdrew old Soviet/Russian ruble notes from circula-
tion in its territory. Russia had earlier pledged to consult with the republics
in matters of economic policy, which had been written into the CIS founding principles in the Minsk agreement of December 1991. Yet, despite those
obligations, it chose to proceed with the currency reform, as well as price
deregulation, which immediately created a crisis for the republics relying on
the ruble in their transactions. In addition, Russia began erecting trade barriers as soon as the Soviet Union fell apart, and maintained them at a relatively
high level even after most-favored nation and free-trade agreements with the
republics were concluded. In part, those policies responded to relative trade
disadvantages for Russia, since it had continued to export goods to the republics at prices considerably below those of the world market. Such policies also
reflected Russian dissatisfaction with the state of payments by a number of
republics in the aftermath of the Soviet disintegration. Both considerations

further reinforced the leadership's belief that economic isolationism from the cash-stripped republics and extensive ties with the West would serve Russia's national interest best.

Finally, Russia acted on some of its cultural isolationist beliefs. Until 1993, the government subscribed to the civic identity policies as outlined by Minister of Nationalities Tishkov. Tishkov argued for understanding nationality as citizenship; for abolishing the principle of ethnic autonomies; and for giving priority to individual, rather than collective, rights. In November 1991, the government confirmed its commitment to the civic identity project by adopting the citizenship law. The law recognized all those living in the territory of the Russian Federation as citizens, regardless of their ethnic characteristics, and called a citizen of the Russian Federation *rossiyanin* (Russian defined in civic terms), not *russki* (ethnic Russian). In foreign relations the government denied any responsibility for ethnic Russians outside territorial Russia. Although Yeltsin had made some statements about the need to defend "our compatriots abroad," Kozyrev argued until the autumn of 1992 that ethnic Russians outside Russia did not constitute a special problem for the Russian government.

Setbacks and Reassessment

The Yeltsin-Kozyrev course could not be sustained and had already begun to backfire by late 1992. The IMF-recommended "shock therapy" was introduced in January 1992 and led to severe economic hardship for ordinary people. Political opposition to reform had emerged and had become vocal. The general population was disillusioned with Western aid and disappointed in Yeltsin's overall reform design. Instead of gaining support at home, the reformers' strategy of integrating with the West resulted in public resentment toward the Western Other. A late 1993 poll showed, for example, that two-thirds of Russians were convinced that the West's economic advice represented a deliberate effort to weaken Russia[65]—precisely the message the hard-line opposition to reformers meant to convey to the larger society. In such a context, opposition—particularly that of the Statists and conservative Civilizationists—was increasingly successful in challenging the Westernist foreign policies.

The first wake-up call came when Yeltsin had to cancel his trip to Japan to settle the old territorial dispute over the Kuril Islands. To Russia's leaders, Japan was a part of the West and therefore deserved the appropriate attention. The initial strategy was to embrace the 1956 Soviet–Japanese agreement as the basis for regulating the issue and to return two of the four northern islands, seized by Stalin at the close of World War II, to Japan. Yeltsin's visit was planned for September, yet—in a stunning reversal—he canceled the trip, scheduled to begin four days later. The argument about returning the islands provoked immediate negative reaction from Russia's parliament and the military-security lobby. The Supreme Soviet held a special hearing, and the Ministry of Defense openly insisted that geostrategic interests dictated against any military withdrawals from the Kurils. This was a serious blow to Russia's course, and revealed that it had major limitations.

Yeltsin-Kozyrev's Balkan policy also came under heavy attack. The former Supreme Soviet emerged as especially active in criticizing the official policy toward the Balkans and even engaged in its own shuttle diplomacy with Belgrade. In December 1992, the Supreme Soviet passed a resolution calling for sanctions on all the warring sides and demanding that Russia use its veto in case of UN consideration of military intervention in the region. As a result of those pressures, Russia first abstained from a UN vote on additional sanctions against Yugoslavia and then refused to send its blue-helmet troops from Croatia into Sarajevo to help police a UN-brokered military agreement. The opposition's pressures on Russia's foreign policy in the Balkans further intensified in 1994 when NATO launched air strikes against the Bosnian Serbs.

The opposition also challenged the isolationist course in the former Soviet region. The Civic Union and its Russian heir, the Union of Industrialists and Entrepreneurs, consolidated ties with trade unions and established branches throughout the entire post-Soviet space. It was impossible to ignore these groups' arguments because of collapsing economies in all the successor states. In the two years after 1991, all of these states experienced negative economic growth rates and a breakdown of their trade, production, labor, and energy ties. Many newly independent states were asymmetrically dependent on Russia's market, fuel, and supplies, and this dependence further complicated the task of creating independent economies. A number of the republics— such as Armenia, Belarus, Kazakhstan, Kyrgyzstan, and Tajikistan—were especially critical of Russia's isolationism. Russia, too, was hit hard, and its economy contracted severely.

The army grew especially prominent in opposing the Kremlin's security policies. Responding to growing pressures of instability in the post-Soviet area, some military branches openly challenged civilian authorities. Moldova is a case in point. When in May 1992 Yeltsin publicly announced the upcoming withdrawal of the Fourteenth Army, the defense minister, General Pavel Grachev, immediately corrected him, saying that the division could leave only after the conflict in the area had been defused. Military and security services were also especially active in opposing NATO's decision to expand eastward by incorporating members of the former Soviet bloc in Eastern Europe. In November 1993, the military adopted a new doctrine, which now proclaimed Russia's immediate periphery the area of its geopolitical interests and most vital concerns. Russia's military, military industrialists, and security services also opposed concessions to the West in arms reductions and sales.

The larger population, too, opposed the isolationist policies. Ethnic autonomies resisted the civic nation project out of fear of losing their own identities. Many Russians also could not accept Russia's new national identity and continued to favor the preservation of strong cultural ties across the former Soviet region. Polls indicated that most Russians supported voluntary reunification of the ex-Soviet republics with Russia.[66] A powerful identification of many Russians outside Russia with their homeland, and vice versa, emboldened conservative Civilizationist thinking and organizations, such as the Congress of Russian Communities, to speak on the Civilizationists' behalf. Kozyrev attempted to protest against the growing influence of the military and nationalists on foreign policy, but without much effect. Yeltsin and Kozyrev therefore saw their agenda being taken away by the military, the Ministry of Defense, and conservative members of the political class.

Table 3.9 summarizes various dependencies and interdependencies between Russia and other former republics.

Table 3.9. Russia and the Ex-Republics: Economic, Military, and Cultural Dependencies

	Share of Russia in a Republic's Trade in 1987	Russian Interrepublican Trade (% of Foreign Trade in 1990)	Ethnic Military Bases and Troops, 1993	Russians (% of Population in 1989)	Fluency in Russian by Titular Nationality (% of Population in 1989)
Armenia	49.7	90	5,000	1.6	44.3
Azerbaijan	52.7	88		5.6	31.7
Belarus	62.6	87	30,000	13.2	60.4
Estonia	58.3	92	5,000	30.3	33.6
Georgia	55.5	86	20,000	6.3	31.8
Kazakhstan	64.4	89		37.8	62.9
Kyrgyzstan	48.2	86		21.5	36.9
Latvia	53.5	89	18,000	33.9	65.7
Lithuania	64.9	90		9.4	37.4
Moldova	50.0	88	8,000	12.9	53.3
RUSSIA	—	61			
Tajikistan	45.0	87	23,000	7.6	30.0
Turkmenistan	45.2	93		9.5	27.6
Ukraine	72.9	82		22.1	59.5
Uzbekistan	51.4	89		8.4	22.2

Sources: Michael Bradshaw, *The Economic Effects of Soviet Dissolution* (London: Royal Institute of International Affairs, 1993), 27; Constantine Michalopoulos and David Tarr, *Trade and Payments Arrangements for States of the Former USSR* (Washington, DC: World Bank, 1992); *New York Times*, November 30, 1993, A12; Graham Smith, *Post-Soviet States* (London: Arnold, 1999), 36.

In mid-1993, largely in response to growing domestic criticism, the attitude of Russia's leaders began to change. The devastating December elections made it painfully clear that the sought-after Integration with the West was not meant to happen and that Westernizers needed to adjust to new realities. The elections brought many anti-Western forces into the parliament, partly the result of the state's uncompromisingly pro-Western policies. The victory of Vladimir Zhirinovski's extreme nationalist party reflected, in part, state neglect of the army and its needs. In response, Kozyrev spoke of a serious correction of his course. Immediately after the December elections, he announced changes in Russia's foreign policy according to the voters' preferences. Kozyrev proclaimed that these changes would include declaring the former Soviet region the sphere of Russia's vital interests, and the continuation of a military presence in regions where Russia had traditionally been dominant. Russia's leaders also refused to cooperate with NATO. Furthermore, faced with hard-line opposition at home, they had to reject the offer to join the Partnership for Peace program, which was designed to preserve cooperative military ties with the alliance.

The official Foreign Policy Concept of the Russian Federation adopted in 1993 further signaled change. In response to pressures from the Statists, the officials spoke about Russia's "special responsibility" in the former Soviet Union. In June 1993, Yeltsin told a group of military officers that Russia must maintain and formalize its military presence in Moldova, Georgia, Armenia, and central Asia. Kozyrev echoed these sentiments by emphasizing the former Soviet region as a "zone of special responsibility and special interest."[67] The concept of involving international institutions, such as the OSCE or NATO, in solving conflicts in the region was also receding into the past. Convinced that Russia's troops would be most effective in maintaining security, Moscow also asked the UN to grant Russia special peacekeeping power in the region. In addition, Moscow no longer seemed to be as eager to predicate its policies upon the West's recognition. This was the case even once the champion of Westernist thinking, Kozyrev, complained about Western claims of Russian neoimperialism in the former Soviet region and insisted that Russia would not listen to the West's "lectures."[68]

The reevaluation of rhetorical policy had been completed in early 1994, when the foreign minister announced the need to follow the preferences of the voters after the nationalist victory in the December elections. The emphasis on the civic nation identity stance had changed, with Tishkov resigning and the government proclaiming its commitment to promoting dual citizenship in the former Soviet region. It looked as if the leadership had indeed learned its lessons from the Statist coalition. Some of the former opponents, such as the parliamentarian Ambartsumov, even conceded that Kozyrev's approach had changed sufficiently to make him retract his call for the minister's resignation.[69]

The new foreign policy project of Integration with the West proved to be a flawed one and was soon defeated by the opposing Statist coalition. Several developments assisted the Statists in defeating the Westernizers. First, the West itself did not satisfy Yeltsin's and Kozyrev's expectations when it treated Russia more as a dependent client than as a full participant in a coalition of Western nations. By not extending to Russia's leadership the sought-after recognition, the West contributed to the already growing feelings of public alienation from the new Westernist course. Second, the Russian domestic context greatly favored the revival of Statist thinking. The political culture was supportive of independent state and great power status, and new threats both inside (Chechnya, growing crime, and sharp decline in living standards) and outside the country (military conflicts in the periphery) created an environment that was permissive to the rise of Statist opposition. In challenging the Westernizers, the Statists also successfully exploited some cultural affinities of ethnic Russians, as well as institutional channels available in the new political system.

The overall record of the Westernist course was not impressive. New security threats reemerged in the former Soviet region in the form of military conflicts in Moldova, central Asia (Tajikistan), and the Caucasus (Georgia and Chechnya), and Russia's leaders did little to preempt those threats or to react to them in a timely fashion.

Nor could Westernizers convincingly defend their foreign policy record in social and economic welfare. Their hopes that a proclaimed commitment to Western values and shock therapy, as the strategy of marketization, would bring sufficient private investments and assistance to quickly revive the economy did not materialize. The heavy reliance on IMF and World Bank loans only allowed Russia to stabilize the economy in macroeconomic terms. Meanwhile, the old economic structure remained in place, and the state did little to conduct an institutional reform or to assist former Soviet managers and workers in their difficult transition to a capitalist type of economy. The radical policies alienated a considerable portion of the elites and the general public, and many Russians developed resentment toward Western nations, particularly the United States. For instance, during 1993–1995, the number of those viewing the United States as a threat increased from 26 to 44 percent among the general public and from 27 to 53 percent among elites.[70]

In addition, Russia developed a considerable dependency on Western lending agencies, with negative implications for its policy autonomy. The number of those viewing the West as seeking to weaken Russia increased. The increased dependency on the West in economic affairs went hand in hand with a loss of autonomy in security affairs, as Washington was often dictating

Table 3.10. The Record of the Westernist Course

Security	New threats in Moldova, central Asia, and the Caucasus
Welfare	Macroeconomic stabilization
	New poverty and collapsed social services
	Industrial stagnation
Autonomy	Dependence on Western lending agencies
	Dependence on Western security policies
Identity	Hurt Russian pride

Moscow's foreign policy in such critical areas as the Balkans and Iraq. In the meantime, Russia was losing its traditional allies in Asia and the Middle East.

These developments indicated the pro-Western course's inability to alleviate Russian hurt pride and identity. Not only had the foreign policy course failed to provide the nation with security and welfare, but it had also failed to engage the Statist component of Russia's identity. Collapse of the Soviet state, the Western encouragement of shock therapy in Russia's economic reform, and the decision to expand NATO toward Russia's borders prompted the Kremlin to reevaluate the course of Integration with the West.

Table 3.10 summarizes the record of Westernism.

Hard-line opposition did not come to power, as Yeltsin and Kozyrev had feared. But the economic and political systems that emerged were hardly reminiscent of those of the West, and were far from the ones the Westernizers had hoped for. In the economic realm, Russia built not a free-market model of capitalism, but rather what scholars call oligarchical capitalism. Under oligarchical capitalism, the economy is largely controlled by and divided among those with business interests in the West. In this environment, the Western assistance enriched the elites and provided support for the new regime that was evolving away from democracy. Oligarchs began to play the role of the new post-Soviet *nomenklatura* and influenced many key decisions of the state. In both Russia and the West, observers raised questions of the aid donors' responsibility for such developments.[71] In the realm of political and legal institutions, Russia developed a super-presidential system with few effective checks and balances. Under the 1993 constitution, the president gained enormous power and could exercise it to prevent a strongly integrated opposition from emerging.

Such was the irony of the radically pro-Western course that it could produce only non-Western—at times, even anti-Western—economic and political outcomes.

Table 3.11. Russia's Power Resources Relative to Other Powerful States (%)*

	United States	Japan	Germany	France	RUSSIA	China
Population (1995)	4.7	2.2	1.4	1.0	2.6	21.2
Territory (1994)	7.1	0.3	0.3	0.4	13.2	7.3
GNP (1995)	25.2	18.7	8.7	5.5	1.2	3.0
Manufacturing (1995)	22.6	25.4	11.7	5.9	3.1	5.3
Merchandise Exports (1995)	12.1	9.2	10.8	5.9	1.7	3.1
Nuclear Weapons (1996)	46.8	—	—	2.9	46.1	2.5
Military Expenditures (1993)	41.0	5.9	5.4	5.3	4.3	4.1
Military Personnel (1996)	6.7	1.4	1.6	1.8	5.7	13.2

* Share as a percentage of the world's total.

Source: Robert A. Pastor, ed., *A Century's Journey: How the Great Powers Shape the World* (New York: Basic Books, 2001), 19.

THE STATIST CHALLENGE, 1994–1999

Containing Western Influences

Primakov's strategy for dealing with the West included two central elements—upholding the power of the United Nations as the key agency for defining and enforcing rules of international conduct; and developing close ties with influential states outside the Western Hemisphere, such as China and India. As a permanent member of the Security Council, Russia planned to exercise its voting power as it saw fit, while at the same time contributing to world peace and stability as a member of the world "concert of great powers." It sought to mobilize Russia's power resources to pursue that goal. (For a summary of these resources relative to other nations, see table 3.11.)

The East had a special role in this dual-track strategy. Unlike Westernizers, Primakov was a firm believer in special relations with Asian and Middle Eastern countries. This belief was firmed up during his long career as a Middle East specialist and policymaker. For many years, the future minister worked in several Middle Eastern countries as a correspondent for the leading communist newspaper *Pravda*. Primakov subsequently moved to academia to serve as director of the Institute of Oriental Studies and, later, of the prestigious Institute of World Economy and International Relations. He then began to work for Gorbachev. However, while advocating for strong ties with Asia and the Muslim world, he differentiated sharply between the Islamic states and the Taliban's form of Islam, which he described as "Islamic extremism." Primakov wanted to engage the former for the sake of balancing against growing Western influences, and to isolate the latter.

Opposing NATO Expansion

The key focus of Primakov's policy was undoubtedly NATO's eastward expansion and Russia's adaptation to this new reality. The decision to expand the alliance was made in January 1994 in response to several security crises in the Balkans and pressures from the former Eastern European states. By the time Primakov had assumed his responsibilities, it became clear that NATO, rather than the Russia-desired Organization for Security and Co-operation in Europe (OSCE), was turning into the cornerstone of European security. It was also clear that, despite Russia's original hopes, it was not about to be considered for membership in the organization.

Many in Russia saw the expansion as the most serious foreign policy challenge and made their opposition to the process explicit.[72] The expansion was incomprehensible in light of Russia's historical commitments, its new relationships with the Western countries, and the West's own promises not to expand the alliance. Many Russians felt deceived, as the expansion followed Gorbachev's military withdrawals from Eastern Europe, Kozyrev's restriction of some profitable arms sales in order to comply with Western rules, and Russia's general commitment to developing a strategic partnership with the West. Overwhelmingly, the Russian foreign policy community perceived the expansion as a violation of the norm of reciprocity and the very spirit of the post–Cold War transformation. Eventually, even radical Westernizers, such as Kozyrev, announced their disappointment with the decision. The general public, too, expressed concerns, and those concerns only increased over time. As former US defense secretary William Perry put it, Russian reaction to NATO expansion "ranged from being unhappy to being very unhappy. . . . This is a very widely and very deeply held view in Russia."[73]

Under these conditions, Primakov saw his task as limiting the potential damage of the expansion. His very appointment, in fact, served the purpose of further ameliorating the anti-NATO backlash because of his already-established reputation as a tough defender of Russia's national interest. Primakov soon recognized that the expansion of the alliance had become inevitable, and that Russia had to shift from the mode of resistance to that of adaptation. Although he was highly critical of the Western decision, he recognized the reality for what it was—"the expansion of NATO is not a military problem; it is a psychological one."[74] To narrow the gap of perception, Russia had little choice but to work on establishing closer diplomatic and political ties with the alliance. The result was the negotiated document signed by the two sides in May 1997 and titled "Founding Act on Mutual Relations, Cooperation and Security between Russia and NATO." Russia saw this as a quasi institutionalization of its relationship with NATO, and it also received the opportunity to join NATO in establishing a special body, the

Permanent Joint Council, to consult about and—when appropriate—even join in decision-making and joint action. In December 1997, in his speech to the State Duma, Primakov referred to the Founding Act as a major accomplishment and evidence of Russia's diplomacy in obtaining its own objectives.

Admittedly, the Founding Act did not give Russia the veto power it sought, and the subsequent intervention in the Balkans demonstrated this situation all too painfully. Domestic critics, such as the leader of the communists, Zyuganov, went so far as to compare the charter to a new Yalta, in which Russia was a defeated party signing its own act of capitulation. Even some of Primakov's supporters felt he went too far in acquiescing to the West. Yet his strategy worked in terms of shifting Russia's focus to adaptation to the new reality and attempting to influence outcomes through diplomacy and bargaining from within. Despite the Kosovo crisis (described below), Russia was brought closer to NATO, and the question of the alliance's expansion was largely defused in domestic politics, depriving hard-line critics of the ability to pressure the government. Russia now had a mechanism for permanent consultations with the alliance. In addition, NATO reaffirmed in writing its commitment to not deploy nuclear weapons or substantial new forces on the territory of new member states. Russian diplomats extracted what they could given Russia's weak bargaining position.

Working to Improve Economic and Military Independence

A Statist, Primakov made an effort to improve Russia's economic and military capabilities, without which his strategy of containing Western influences could hardly have been sufficient. In economic affairs, rather than continuing with Kozyrev's policy of joining Western international organizations, he worked to restore a measure of Russia's independence. He argued against a West-dependent economic recovery and entering the world economy as a supplier of raw materials, and he insisted on separating the economic issues from those related to politics and security. At the time, many of the government's critics charged that the assistance served to further corrupt the circles of the ruling elite and to entice them to "sell" Russia to the West.

Despite Primakov's efforts, there was little he could do to restore the country's economic independence. By the time of his arrival in office, Russia's foreign debt and domestic budget deficit figured prominently. After assuming the responsibilities of prime minister, Primakov realized ever more painfully the difficulties of maintaining the independence posture; even with what was considered to be a "leftist government," he had to submit to the State Duma a tight budget and fully comply with the IMF conditions.

In military affairs and arms control, the foreign minister turned prime minister sought to reduce the heavy economic burden of maintaining the largest nuclear arsenal in the world. Primakov believed in the political power of nuclear weapons, but advocated a relatively small arsenal. Against the hard-line opposition and even some of his own supporters, he argued for ratification of START II, which had been signed in January 1993. Yet his efforts, accompanied by support from the Ministry of Defense, failed because of the United States' bombing of Iraq and, subsequently, NATO's military intervention in Yugoslavia. These events strengthened conservative Civilizationists and other hard-liners in the Duma, who feared US intentions to develop a missile defense system and consequently blocked the ratification. START II, which promised to reduce the number of nuclear missiles to the new 3,000–3,500 threshold, remained formally dead until the arrival of Putin.

Resisting Military Solutions in Iraq

However dependent Russia was on Western creditors, Primakov could not support the United States–sanctioned military interventions, as did his predecessor. Intervention in Iraq emerged as one of the two key issues—the other being Yugoslavia—on which he felt compelled to forcefully disagree with the American position. In his view, there were at least three major reasons why Russia could no longer limit its policy to supporting the US bombings and opposing lifting the United Nations' sanctions in Iraq. First, because of his opposition to "unipolarity," he wanted to contribute to opposition to the United States–promoted military methods of dealing with Saddam Hussein. The second reason was Iraq's sizable debt—around $7 billion—to Russia, which could not be repaid without lifting sanctions. Third, Russia's growing energy companies, such as Lukoil, were eager to acquire contracts in Iraq and the Arab markets in general.

It was this perception of Russia's interests that shaped Primakov's handling of two main crises in late 1997 and early 1998. In the first crisis, Primakov responded to the US threat to attack Iraq following the latter's unwillingness to comply with the UN inspections and the inspectors' subsequent departure. In alliance with France, Primakov negotiated a deal whereby all the inspectors were allowed to return in exchange for a vague promise to work for the lifting of sanctions. The deal did not last long, however, as the sanctions were never lifted, and Saddam Hussein made it difficult for inspectors to access "presidential sites," some of which were suspected of activities related to weapons of mass destruction. This time, Russia seemed to have failed to produce a mutually acceptable agreement, and the UN secretary-general assumed the diplomatic initiative. Primakov, at least, felt satisfied that the issue was left to the United Nations, and not solved unilaterally by the United States.

In the meantime, Saddam Hussein was playing his own game, trying to pressure Moscow to be more aggressive on the issue of lifting sanctions.[75]

During 1999, Russia—in part dissatisfied with Baghdad's uncooperative behavior, in part as a trade-off for the United States' not raising at the UN Security Council the issue of Russia's ruinous war in Chechnya, and in part having an insufficient number of options in the face of US military pressures—was less willing to work with Iraq. Much to Iraq's dismay, Russia eventually chose not to exercise its veto on Security Council Resolution 1284 (it abstained), which demanded Baghdad's compliance with the inspectors' ruling and promised lifting the sanctions on the importation of civilian goods to Iraq.

Primakov's approach appeared to have accomplished little. Sanctions remained in place, negotiations did not produce any visible results, and therefore Russia's economic interests were left unsatisfied. Yet, in one important respect Russia held its ground—the key political decisions with regard to Iraq remained the United Nations' prerogative, and those decisions were different from those favored by the United States. This remained so until the March 2003 decision of President George W. Bush to attack Iraq.

Confronting NATO's Intervention in Yugoslavia

Until the Western military intervention in the Balkans, Primakov followed the policy of pragmatic cooperation with NATO members. When he took over, the Dayton Accords of November 1995 had been signed with minimal input from Russia, and the hard-line opposition insisted on realignment with Serbia. The new foreign minister indeed moved to reevaluate the role of Belgrade in European security, but he did not go nearly as far as hard-liners wanted him to. While advocating pragmatism over Kozyrev's ideological commitment to the West, Primakov actively worked through the Contact Group, the framework for diplomatic coordination among Russia, the United States, France, Britain, and Germany, created in response to Yeltsin's call in February 1994. Although Russia opposed NATO's command of peacekeeping and in some cases objected to specific acts of force against the Bosnian Serbs, in general it did not interfere with UN-sanctioned Western actions in Bosnia.[76]

NATO's decision to begin air strikes against Belgrade in March 1999 changed this framework of relationships. Despite a number of important disagreements between Russia and the West, the military intervention came as a shock to Russia's foreign policy community. This was illustrated by Prime Minister Yevgeni Primakov's decision to cancel the upcoming negotiations with the United States and the IMF in Washington on March 24, 1999. Although his airplane had already been approaching the United States, he ordered it to return home. Russia's official reaction was harsh and included issuing a statement on NATO's aggression in violation of the United Nations' jurisdiction and the Helsinki Act on the preservation of sovereignty, suspension of participation in the Founding Act agreement, withdrawal of the military mission from Brussels, and ordering NATO representatives to leave Russia.

Such reactions reflected the largely negative attitudes toward NATO within Russian society and its foreign policy community. The overwhelming majority believed that the Western actions were driven by power and hegemonic ambitions, rather than by concerns over Yugoslavian leader Slobodan Milošević's actions against Kosovo Albanians. Among the general public, about 90 percent opposed NATO's bombing of Belgrade and felt threatened by the alliance's actions.[77] It was the expansion of NATO, rather than the ethnic war in the Balkans, that shaped Russia's perception of the intervention in Yugoslavia. By that time, the Western alliance had already invited the Czech Republic, Poland, and Hungary to apply for membership. At the Madrid summit in the summer of 1997, the US secretary of state Madeleine Albright specifically promised to extend the invitation to the Baltic states, which had been a part of the Soviet Union before 1991. Primakov's foreign ministry insisted again on the unacceptability of the alliance expansion. Despite the Founding Act agreement of May 1997, the post-Madrid atmosphere of Russia–West relationships was tense. The clash over Kosovo manifested the depth of the Russian fears. It brought in some elements of political escalation and, at times, came close to military confrontation. Russia's Duma, for instance, fell short by two or three votes of passing a resolution on accepting Yugoslavia into the Russia-Belarus Union, which would have made Russia a participant in the war.

Primakov had no plans to throw his support behind Serbia, as some conservative Civilizationists called on him to do. Instead, he got involved in mediating the conflict. Using the West's interest in Russia's involvement, he formulated tough conditions for ending the war, which included guarantees for Yugoslavia's preserved sovereignty, a broad autonomy for Kosovo, and the UN's assuming leadership in the postwar settlement. Yet the peace was reached more on the West's than on Russia's terms. Out of fear of further Russia–West political escalation, Yeltsin dismissed Primakov as the key negotiator and replaced him with former prime minister Viktor Chernomyrdin, who was much too pro-Western and inexperienced in foreign affairs to negotiate the peace that Primakov had in mind. In early June, under pressure from Chernomyrdin, Serbia finally accepted the conditions for peace, but Russia's initial conditions had not been honored. As one Russian observer described the outcomes of the war, "Russia took part in Yugoslavia's acceptance of the same NATO conditions that it had previously called unacceptable."[78]

Primakov and the larger Statist community drew some tough lessons from Russia's engagement with the West. This engagement widened the gap between the two sides in perception and reinforced the sense of Russia's identity as distinct from that of the West. To reduce what Statists saw as the country's external insecurity, they recommended a series of steps. First, the main external threat was perceived to be from NATO, even though previously many analysts had seen China as equally threatening. After the war in Yugoslavia, many now viewed Kosovo as a template of NATO's future strategy. This found its reflection in proposals to increase the defense budget, as well as in official documents. The new draft military doctrine emphasized that the threat of direct aggression against Russia and its allies could only be "deterred by conducting active foreign policy and maintaining high readiness of conventional and nuclear forces." The Security Council further proposed extending and updating strategic and tactical nuclear weapons, among other measures.[79] In this context, many argued against the ratification of START II. Second, Russian elites insisted on strengthening the UN Security Council in its decision-making and peacekeeping capacity at the expense of NATO. Third, many called for tightening the defense space in the former Soviet Union.

Capitalizing on Relations outside the West

The active foreign policy defended by Primakov meant the development of geostrategic and economic ties outside the West. Both objectives were designed to improve Russia's relative power position in the world at the expense of Western nations, particularly the United States. An Arabist by training, Primakov was notably more active in the Middle East than his predecessor. In addition to expressing interest in playing a more active role in the peace process, Primakov considerably increased Russian arms sales in the region. Outside the Middle East, Russia was especially interested in the Asia-Pacific region, often describing the Association of Southeast Asian Nations (ASEAN) as an influential center of the developing multipolar world. Everywhere he traveled the new minister spread his message about the necessity of building a multipolar world order. However, three states played an especially important role in his vision—China, Iran, and India.

China's significance for Russia is difficult to overestimate. China shared a 4,300-kilometer-long border with Russia and demonstrated a very high rate of economic development. China was also the main buyer of Russian weapons; it purchased almost all of its arms and military equipment from its northwestern neighbor. Politically, the two shared concerns about the United States' global dominance and perceived as threatening developments NATO's expansion, the United States' plans to build a national missile defense system, and interventions in Iraq and Kosovo. Finally, both countries faced similar threats to internal security, with the separatist activities of the Chechens in Russia and the Muslim Uighur minority in China's province of Xinjiang.

All of these factors brought the two countries closer together. In April 1996, the sides affirmed that they were entering into a new stage of partnership, and a year later the countries' leaders signed the "Joint Declaration on a Multipolar World and the Formation of a New International Order," which reflected Primakov's vision of multipolarity as a work in progress. The late 1998–1999 developments, such as US military strikes against Iraq, plans for the creation of a US-Japanese theater of missile defense, NATO expansion, and the bombing of Yugoslavia again brought the two together to actively coordinate their responses to what they saw as threatening developments in world affairs. Economic relations between Russia and China did not progress as fast as the countries had desired, but they did improve in areas of border trade and arms sales.

Yet despite pronounced progress, the Russia–China relationship did not go as far as Primakov would have wanted. His efforts met with opposition across the political spectrum. China was leading Russia in GDP terms by a factor of five, and that worried both Westernizers and conservative Civilizationists, who sensed the danger of a Chinese encroachment in the Far East. Westernizers were particularly critical of Chinese authoritarianism, arguing that, sooner or later, it would translate into foreign policy expansionism. The strong Chinese gravitation toward the global economic markets also complicated Primakov's geostrategic calculations. The full-fledged strategic partnership of Russia and China, therefore, remained only a possibility.

Another potentially strategic partner in Primakov's calculus was Iran. Politically, he saw the country as a regional ally in containing the influence of the Taliban regime in Afghanistan and Turkey, particularly on the states of central Asia and Azerbaijan. Globally, Iran was yet another potential ally in resisting the US-controlled unipolarity. Economically, Russia was building nuclear reactors, supplying industrial equipment, and planning on forming a common policy in developing energy pipelines in the Caspian region. As with China, Primakov's record on Russia's cooperation with Iran was mixed. The two sides cooperated on economic matters and in arranging a cease-fire in Tajikistan and resisting the Taliban in Afghanistan. Despite objections from Washington that Iran was building a nuclear weapon in violation of the existing nonproliferation regime, Russia continued to cooperate with Iran while denying all the allegations.

Over time, however, Russian–Iranian relations demonstrated their limits. Politically, Russia did not want to see Iran emerging as a possible military threat in the region, and some officials publicly spoke against such a development. The issue subsequently became even more pronounced as Iran became the head of the Islamic Conference and emerged as more supportive of the Chechen rebels and Kosovo Muslims. Furthermore, while acting in concert with Russia in trying to block the Baku-Ceyhan and Trans-Caspian pipelines,

Iran developed an interest in serving as an alternative export route for central Asian oil and gas. Finally, neither Yeltsin nor Primakov was willing to go too far with testing the United States' patience. The end result was what one scholar labeled a "minimax" policy, in which Russia tried to minimize the damage to US–Russian relations while at the same time maintaining the maximum amount of influence in Iran.[80]

Finally, Primakov's diplomacy sought to engage India as a partner of strategic importance. The foreign minister was capitalizing on the old Soviet ties in trying to revive Russia as India's key rearmament agent. In 1997, the Indian prime minister announced that his country had purchased $3 billion in arms from Russia in the previous two years, and that the two sides had discussed potential contracts worth another $7 billion—a level that would move India ahead of China in the ranks of Moscow's arms customers.[81] Politically, Primakov was interested in building closer relations with Russia, India, and China to balance the power of the United States, which was a marked shift from the previous policy of balancing China through an alliance with India. In December 1998, Primakov spoke of the desirability of the three's alliance as a "new pole in world politics." This, however, remained wishful thinking, as neither India nor China had a similar interest.

Integrating the Former Soviet Area

The Concept of Integration

Integration of the former Soviet area was another key pillar of Primakov's strategy of balancing Western power and resisting NATO expansion. The new foreign policymakers defined Russia's interests in terms of accumulating national power and sought to accomplish three objectives. First, being pressured by the new conflicts in the former Soviet Union, they wanted to maintain Russia's military presence in the area. Second, they wanted to protect the status of ethnic Russians living outside of Russia. Furthermore, Moscow was interested in obtaining valuable economic assets and facilities in the post-Soviet world.

Using strong bargaining power in relations with the former republics, Russia was planning to obtain more informal control over their economic and security policies, without being overly responsible for the costs of such control. The country did possess considerable power to take a more assertive approach in the former Soviet Union. It had the most sophisticated weaponry, as well as the largest and the most experienced army in the region. Russia was also economically powerful due to the large size of its domestic market, rich endowment with natural resources, and more diversified commercial ties with countries beyond the former Soviet region. Politically, it was the only

Table 3.12. Russia's Power Capabilities Relative to Former Soviet States

Country	Population, 1989 (millions)	GNP, 1993 (billions)	Military Personnel
Armenia	3.4	1.9	60,000
Azerbaijan	7.5	4.4	86,700
Belarus	10.5	16	98,400
Estonia	1.6	1.7	3,500
Georgia	5.7	2.3	?
Kazakhstan	17.4	18.2	40,000
Kyrgyzstan	4.7	2.9	7,000
Latvia	2.6	1.6	6,950
Lithuania	3.8	2.9	8,900
Moldova	4.5	4.1	11,850
RUSSIA	148.9	1,160	1,520,000
Tajikistan	5.9	2.5	2–3,000
Turkmenistan	3.9	3.8	11,000
Ukraine	51.9	54.2	542,000
Uzbekistan	22.3	14	25,000

Source: Neil MacFarlane, "Realism and Russian Strategy after the Collapse of the USSR," in *Unipolar Politics*, ed. Ethan B. Kapstein and Michael Mastanduno (New York: Columbia University Press, 1999), 225–26.

state in the region with the recognized reputation of a United Nations Security Council member, and it had also obtained membership in the prestigious G-8. Furthermore, it had a diversified linguistic diaspora of twenty-five million people, many of whom identified with their "homeland" and, therefore, could assist Russia in projecting its influence abroad. Some indicators of Russia's relative power in the post-Soviet region are summarized in tables 3.8 and 3.12.

The concept of integration was first clearly articulated on September 14, 1995, when Yeltsin issued a wide-ranging decree titled "The Establishment of the Strategic Course of the Russian Federation with Member States of the CIS." The eight-page document had been developed out of one of the Primakov-led Foreign Intelligence Service reports, and it was transformed into the CIS Concept of Economic Integrational Development adopted in March 1997. For the first time since the Soviet breakup, the Kremlin acknowledged the priority significance of the CIS for Russia's national interest and defined Russia as the leading power in the formation of a new system of interstate political and economic relations in the region. The Kremlin sought to revive the social, economic, and political coherence of the former Soviet region, without reviving the empire.

The strategy of integration had a good portion of pragmatism in responding to the new challenges Russia was facing both inside and outside of the region. While a major departure from Kozyrev's early isolationism, integration could not be likened to a restoration of the empire or a revival of aggressive imperial nationalism. Certainly, Primakov's supporters did not see it that way. For instance, the influential Council for Foreign and Defense Policy, which was also close to Primakov, issued a report titled "Will the Union Be Revived?" in which it referred to the idea of the Soviet restoration as a "reactionary utopia."[82] At the same time, the report argued that a reasonable alternative to post-Soviet integration was not available and that Russia should assume the role of leader of such an integration.

For Primakov, the security context, particularly NATO's expansion, prompted the strategy's necessity. For the politically driven Yeltsin, however, the strategy was a way to neutralize his opposition and to restore the state-diminished capacity to conduct foreign policy. Yeltsin's opposition included members of the military, industrialists, and some hard-line nationalists who had ties with Russians outside of Russia. In security affairs, the Primakov-recommended strategy helped to seize the initiative that the military had increasingly been taking away from civilian authorities. Under Primakov, the Ministry of Foreign Affairs took considerable power away from the Ministry of Defense. For instance, it led the resolution of the Tajik civil war and the Moldovan conflict, and in both cases it produced peace treaties. In economic and cultural affairs, integrationism meant promoting Russian state interests by taking the initiative away from nongovernmental organizations that sought to restore the Soviet Union.

The new course also had considerable social support at home. The general public was strongly supportive of Russia's closer economic, political, and cultural relations with the ex-Soviet states, although it did not favor the empire's restoration. For instance, in December 1997, 61 percent of Russian citizens were sorry that the Soviet Union had collapsed—up from 33 percent in December 1992. At the same time, most respondents did not approve of military interventionism to integrate the former Soviet region. Even more telling, in 1996 about 65 percent were convinced that the only way to regain the former great power status was through the successful development of the Russian economy.[83]

Integration Attempts

The new conflicts in the region pushed the leadership to revise its originally isolationist stance with regard to the former Soviet Union. Primakov's appointment led to the reestablishment of a balance between political and military tools of policy and helped to facilitate the end of the Tajik civil war and a peace treaty that was signed in June 1997 in Moscow. When it came to the Caucasus, however, Russia's stabilizing efforts were far less successful. Despite Primakov's more firmly established control of peacekeeping forces, he failed to stabilize the situation in Georgia. The earlier support by Russia's military of the Abkhaz separatist movement backfired and contributed to Moscow's inability to mediate the conflict. It also resulted in Georgia's declining to support the CIS's collective security efforts. Finally, Russia intervened in Chechnya in order to respond to the republic's secessionism and to maintain a presence in the Caucasus. In addition to territorial integrity, Russia sought to defend the important Baku-Novorossiysk pipeline that runs through Chechnya. However, after the first Chechen war (1994–1996) and the May 1997 Chechen presidential elections, Moscow developed no specific policy in the republic, and Chechnya continued its slide into anarchy.

Russia and Belarus developed a common perception of security threats and a close coordination of foreign policies, and they pledged the establishment of a defense alliance. Russia also activated political ties with Ukraine, which the new foreign minister saw as his first priority. As a result of Primakov's efforts, the two sides signed in May 1997 the so-called "Big Treaty," which settled the fleet issue and legalized the borders. The treaty provoked some criticism on both sides, but Primakov's support was instrumental in its ratification in February 1999. Both Primakov and his successor Igor' Ivanov saw the political normalization with Ukraine as a step toward improving the two's relations, rather than as a concession to Ukrainian aspirations to join NATO. This attitude found broad social support at home, as 70 percent of Russians supported the "Big Treaty."[84] As for the policy toward the most pro-Western Baltic states, Russia sought to minimize the negative consequences of NATO's expansion by offering those states security guarantees, and by making explicit its position that Baltic membership in NATO would endanger Russia's good relations with NATO.

Economic integration was another important aspect of Primakov's strategy. During the Soviet era, Russia and the former republics were tightly integrated economies (see table 3.9) and could not successfully break the multiple bonds of their mutual dependency. Primakov's approach was state-oriented. He wanted to actively practice "economic diplomacy"—the Kremlin's label for both negative and positive sanctions—to strengthen Russia's political interests in the region. He had in mind to capitalize on Russia's relative economic power (see table 3.12) in facilitating Russian-favored bilateral and multilateral political ties with the post-Soviet states. In the Statist spirit, Primakov reasoned that the state interests were superior to those of the private sector, and therefore one had to be prepared to invest in projects with the potential to facilitate the reintegration of the former republics.

Yet the outlined strategy of multilateral integration remained largely unrealized, partly because of Russia's own economic difficulties and partly because some republics were eager to diversify their ties away from the former imperial core. These republics perceived the CIS economic integration projects as Russia's thinly veiled imperialism and therefore resisted even some commonsensical measures to coordinate economic policies. For instance, the Payment Union, as well as interstate investment cooperation, never materialized. Other economic agreements were not working effectively. The only major exception was the Customs Union, which was signed by Russia, Belarus, Kazakhstan, Kyrgyzstan, and Tajikistan in March 1995 and continued to function during Primakov's tenure. Russia made more progress in developing bilateral relations than it did multilateral relations in the region. In some cases, it successfully applied its economic power to achieve important political goals. In central Asia, for example, Russia used Turkmenistan's and Kazakhstan's dependence on Russia's energy pipelines to negotiate a more favorable treatment of ethnic Russians residing in these states. It also further consolidated its economic and political relations with Belarus.

The vision of post-Soviet integration also had a cultural component to it. Primakov felt that Russia had an obligation to respond to the political and cultural feelings of twenty-five million Russians who had found themselves outside their "homeland" and continued to identify with it. The issue was closely related to preserving cultural balance inside Russia, which included by far the largest number of ethnic groups (some 140), with only five of its twenty-one ethnic republics having a clear majority of the titular nation (Chechnya, Chuvashia, Ingushetia, Tuva, and North Ossetia).

The challenge, as Primakov and Yeltsin saw it, was to find a way to revive the identity of the transnational community in the former Soviet area without giving ground to the hard-line Civilizationist opposition. Primakov's supporters cautioned against pushing the Russians-first vision too far and argued that such a vision could jeopardize Russia's own fragile multicultural balance. The solution, Primakov's supporters argued, was to embrace and to cautiously promote the idea of Eurasia as a multicultural, multiethnic, and multireligious community in place of the former Soviet Union.[85] To promote it, the government first developed and began to promote the idea of dual citizenship in the former Soviet states. The government also hoped to curb the uncontrolled flow of migrants to Russia. Russia aggressively promoted dual citizenship, but by 1995 all the post-Soviet states, with the exception of Turkmenistan and Tajikistan, rejected the idea. In response, the Russian government began to advocate CIS citizenship, but was not successful.

Assessing Primakov's Statism

Primakov's foreign policy had a number of successes, particularly in the realm of security. His attention to the former Soviet area and intense diplomatic involvement made a difference in negotiating peace in Moldova and Tajikistan (although not in Georgia). He also negotiated and pushed through ratification of the "Big Treaty" with Ukraine, which put the two countries' relations on a new security footing. The minister could also be credited for making progress in Russia's negotiations with NATO. Despite a number of setbacks in their relationship, Russia had developed a mechanism of permanent consultations with the alliance and obtained its written commitment not to deploy nuclear weapons or substantial new forces in the territory of new member states. In addition, the new minister worked hard to improve ties with the countries of Asia and the Asia-Pacific region.

Through his course, Primakov also restored some attributes of foreign policy autonomy. Although Russia continued to be highly dependent on the West in economic affairs, it made Washington more attentive to its national interest in the area of security issues. On such issues as arms sales and security in Yugoslavia, Primakov took a much tougher line than his predecessor, who, in the words of one journalist, "had corrupted Americans" by his willingness to follow in Washington's footsteps.[86] Both the elites and the general public expressed their strong support for the new course, welcoming its greater independence and concentration on solving security issues in the former Soviet Union. For example, on the issue of sending troops to the former Soviet republics, provided that Russia was asked to do so, the general public support grew from 35 to 56 percent during the 1993–1999 period. The elite's support on the same issue over the same period increased from 56 to 72 percent.[87]

Table 3.13 summarizes the foreign policy record of Great Power Balancing.

As analysts have acknowledged, Primakov accomplished these positive changes despite Russia's continuous decline in 1992–1997 and lack of balancing options. This policy activism from the position of weakness suggests yet again the limitations of realism as an international relations theory for understanding Primakov's foreign policy. Rather than being driven by material power alone, that policy was a response to a particular combination of international and domestic factors of a political and cultural nature.

However, Great Power Balancing had some major flaws as well. Primakov's failures to assert his vision in Iraq and Kosovo—as well as his uninspiring attempts to establish a strategic triangle of Russia, China, and India to contain the United States' global hegemony—are cases in point. In the world of US

Table 3.13. The Foreign Policy Record of Great Power Balancing

Security	Peace agreements in the former Soviet region
	Mechanism of permanent consultations with NATO Improved ties with Asian world
Welfare	Failed economic union in the CIS
	Continued industrial stagnation at home
Autonomy	Less dependent decision-making
Identity	Continued identity crisis

unipolarity and global economic interdependence, none of these countries was eager to enter into the Russia-sought balancing coalition.

Even more obvious were his failures to improve Russia's welfare. Integration was partly meant to respond to the imperative of improving life throughout the region, but it proved to be excessively geopolitically driven and not as founded on economic grounds. Most multilateral CIS-based economic agreements were not working properly, and the former Soviet states continued to drift separately. Most of them also rejected Russia's citizenship initiatives. Faced with Primakov's state grandeur in the former Soviet region, the Russian private sector was not willing to invest in the relationships in the former Soviet Union. The energy companies, for example, grew strong by the time of the integration strategy, but often did not feel compelled to back up the state with their resources and subsidize the former republics or supply them at lower energy prices in exchange for their political loyalty to the Russian state.

The new foreign policy also did not make serious progress in resolving Russia's identity crisis. Symptomatic of the identity search was, for example, the discussion about Russia's new "national idea" that Yeltsin had initiated immediately following his 1996 reelection as president. Primakov addressed the crisis by proposing a Eurasianist foreign policy orientation in building strategic relations with China, Iraq, and India. His cooperation with the West was merely pragmatic, as opposed to strategic, and NATO's intervention in Yugoslavia pushed Russia further away from the West. Yet the Westernist component of Russia's cultural identity had been confirmed by Russia's post-Soviet developments, and many Russians continued to identify with the West. The strategy of Eurasia-oriented Great Power Balancing was not successful in addressing this part of the Russian national psyche.

PUTIN'S PRAGMATIC COOPERATION, 2000–2004

With the introduction of the philosophy of pragmatic Statism and pragmatic cooperation, the West remained at the center of Russia's foreign policy. The new policy was, however, to reengage the West in order to acquire its recognition of Russia as a great power. Therefore, while insisting on Russia's own interests in many areas of world politics, Putin sought to frame those interests as consistent with strategic commitments to Western values, such as international law, personal freedoms, and a market economy. His strategy of engaging the West was to propose a new agenda, the implications of which might be more far-reaching than those stemming from addressing the old issues of NATO expansion or the missile defense system. While not giving up on the old issues easily, Russia's leader did not want to be cornered on those issues.

He therefore proposed some new areas in which Russia could develop some long-term advantages. Two of these areas were counterterrorism and energy cooperation.

Reengaging the World after 9/11

Strengthening Relations with the United States

Putin's efforts to engage the United States predate the September 11 attacks. The new leader wanted to start fresh after the Kosovo experience, which had considerably soured Russia–West relations, and he began to cultivate ties with the American administration soon after he came to office. Washington's initial reaction was cold. The new administration in the United States made it clear that it did not foresee any breakthroughs in relations with Russia. As late as February 2001, Bush's national security adviser Condoleezza Rice insisted that Russia was a threat to the United States and its European allies. Putin persisted and finally got his break when he met with the American president in Ljubljana, Slovenia, in the summer of 2001. The relationship began to change, largely thanks to personal chemistry between the two leaders. It was after the summit that Bush made his famous remarks on Putin: "I was able to get a sense of his soul."[88]

September 11 presented Putin with a unique opportunity to implement his new vision of national interest. Soon after the terrorist attacks on the United States, he offered that country's leaders broad support for antiterrorist operations in Afghanistan. The measures included intelligence sharing, opening Russian airspace to relief missions, taking part in search-and-rescue operations, rallying central Asian countries to the American cause, and arming anti-Taliban forces inside Afghanistan. As our earlier analysis indicates, the domestic public was wary of rapprochement with the United States, and that constrained Putin's freedom of action. Determined, he pressed forward by stressing the positive potential of the new Russia–US relations. In particular, beginning with his interview in the *Wall Street Journal* in February 2002, Putin emphasized Russia as a reliable alternative to traditional Middle Eastern sources of oil and natural gas. Russia was the world's single largest non-OPEC (Organization of Petroleum Exporting Countries) oil exporter, with 10 percent of the known oil reserves and 9 percent of the world output. Yet this oil accounted for only 1 percent of American imports in 2001.[89] In May of the same year at their summit in Moscow, the US and Russian presidents signed a joint declaration on energy cooperation. Then followed the Houston "energy summit" in October, where Russian officials said that they could export as many as a million barrels a day to the United States within five years.

Eager to engage the United States, Putin was careful not to overplay his opposition on traditional issues, such as NATO, the Balkans, and the ABM (Anti-Ballistic Missile) Treaty. Rather than insisting on Russia's membership in NATO or the alliance's not admitting new members—both demands being entirely unrealistic although not uncommon for previous diplomacies—Putin moved to organize security relations with Western countries on the common basis of counterterrorism. After initial support for Slobodan Milošević, he opted to minimize involvement in the affairs of the post-Kosovo Balkans. In August 2003, Moscow withdrew its peacekeeping mission from Bosnia and Kosovo. And, despite formidable domestic resistance, Putin made little of his opposition to the US desire to abandon the ABM Treaty, which had prohibited the unilateral building of a nuclear missile defense system. In his opinion, the United States' decision was a "mistake," but it presented no threat to the national security of the Russian Federation.

Capitalizing on Ties with Europe

In addition to developing new relations with the United States, Putin put a new emphasis on ties with European partners, especially Germany, France, and Italy. Russia's energy markets were primarily in Europe—they accounted for 40 percent of Russia's foreign trade, relative to the United States accounting for a mere 5 percent of trade. In fact, if Europe is understood in the wider sense—as the one that includes the EU, Central and Eastern Europe, Norway, and Switzerland—then Europe's share of Russia's trade was up to 55 percent.[90] In June 2003, Putin also sealed a joint venture with British Petroleum worth over $6 billion. His vision of global security, too, proved to be quite compatible with those of large European nations. During the crisis over the American decision to go to war against Iraq, Russia joined the antiwar coalition and argued that the United Nations was the only legitimate body for sanctioning the use of force. In siding with the Europeans, Putin was firmly supported at home, but he was also careful not to present his views as anti-American, positioning himself instead as a voice of moderation and even reconciliation between the American and the European side in the West. Putin continued making efforts to bring Russia and Europe closer culturally. During the celebration of St. Petersburg's three-hundred-year anniversary, he went as far as to suggest that visas between EU countries and Russia be abandoned altogether by the year 2006.

As was the case with Russia's new relations with the United States, Putin's efforts to demonstrate his commitment to European values were unmistakably pragmatic. In those issues where the new leadership perceived European powers to be infringing upon Russia's interests, the Kremlin preferred to maintain a distance from Brussels. Most symptomatically, for all the rhetoric

on developing closer relations with the EU, there was relatively little cooperation in the area of security. For instance, Moscow continued to be mistrustful
and rejected European ideas for joint peacekeeping missions in the former
Soviet states, such as Moldova. It also shut down the OSCE mission in
Chechnya. In addition, Putin's government decided to put an end to the activities of US Peace Corps volunteers in Russia; this action became a source of
irritation in relations with the United States. All of this indicated that Russia
continued to differ from its Western counterparts in its evaluation of national
interest and security threats. Consistent with the earlier specified strategy
of modernization, Russia continued to be interested primarily in economic
cooperation with Europe, defined in terms of growing investments and sales
of energy and weapons abroad.

In their turn, Europeans continued to advance their economic and political standards of behavior, of which Russia had been suspicious, arguing that
Europe treated it, in the perception of Putin's adviser, as a "mischievous
student in the school of democracy."[91] Some of these suspicions were visible in discussions about the issue of visas for Russian transit travelers to
and from Kaliningrad. Kaliningrad was the Russian enclave that became
surrounded by EU members after Lithuania's admission into the EU in May
2004. The Europeans were especially worried about corruption of the local
administration in the Kaliningrad region, as well as the miserable economic
situation there. On that basis, they declined Russia's proposal to have a
visa-free arrangement, but the two sides reached a compromise agreement in
Luxembourg on April 2, 2004. The agreement spelled out measures aimed at
ensuring the free transit of goods from Russia to Kaliningrad, and it ensured
that Russian train travelers to the Kaliningrad enclave were to obtain a
Lithuanian permit only. More broadly, the historical enlargement of the EU
and the incorporation of ten new members on May 1, 2004, underscored the
policy of constructing Europe without any meaningful role for Russia.[92]

Supporting the United States in Afghanistan, But Not in Iraq

The pragmatism in defining national interest helps to interpret Russia's
divergent foreign policy responses toward two major military crises after
September 11—Afghanistan and Iraq. Putin's support of the United States
after 9/11, on the one hand, and his decision to oppose the war in Iraq, on
the other, were both shaped by a sober calculation of payoffs in state power
and autonomy.

The pragmatism of Putin's support for the United States' war against the
Taliban regime in Afghanistan was quite obvious; for a long time, Russia
supported the Northern Alliance and was eager to have its long-term rival
removed from power without a single shot fired. While offering his support,

Putin made it clear that he would not commit Russian troops to operations inside Afghanistan because the Russian constitution proscribed such operations and the United Nations had yet to authorize them. Another expected payoff from the extended intelligence cooperation was American support for Putin's policies in Chechnya, the absence of which had been complicating Russia's efforts to develop a positive image in the eyes of the West. Other expectations were of an economic nature and related to Moscow's plans to increase energy sales abroad. Finally, Putin had in mind to eventually gain membership in the World Trade Organization (WTO), but on relatively favorable terms. On all of these accounts, the president was counting on the support of the United States.

The war in Iraq was a different matter, however. Here, Putin decided to join the coalition of those opposing the war on American terms. Along with Russia's foreign policy officials, he warned against going over the head of the United Nations, which would authorize the use of force. The same vision of national interest underlined Putin's decision. As in Afghanistan, he wanted to reduce terrorist threats to Russia, and he wanted to provide his country with better conditions for economic modernization. Not convinced by arguments about the existence of a nuclear program in Iraq and links between Saddam Hussein's regime and the Al Qaeda terrorist network—both being the key arguments of the Bush administration—he saw the war as a deviation from the global war on terrorism. Along with many others in Russia's political circles, Putin believed that terrorism, as a stateless phenomenon, was a challenge to the very system of states. In his view, terrorism could be defeated only through the coordination of state efforts, and not through taking on relatively established states, such as Iraq.

The economic modernization consideration was also prominent in Putin's calculations. This consideration included Russia's ties with Europe and Iraq. The strategy of pragmatism assumed cooperation with the United States, but not at the expense of ties with Europe, the latter being far more extensive. In addition, Russia had important oil interests in Iraq, and Saddam Hussein skillfully exploited those by promising to Russian private companies more lucrative contracts. In the wake of the military intervention, many Russian experts forecasted a drastic fall in world oil prices in the near future—another nightmare for Russia, where a considerable part of revenue came from exporting natural resources. There was also the issue of Iraq's sizable debt to Russia—$7 to $8 billion, by different calculations; Russia was worried it would never see the money as a result of the war.

The two divergent decisions found support at home. If Putin had lost any of his credibility for throwing his support behind American intervention in Afghanistan, he certainly regained it all during his opposition to the war in Iraq. Russian elites grew highly skeptical of the idea of siding with the United

States. Even some of the Westernizers viewed the war in Iraq as a dangerous precedent of jeopardizing the role of the United Nations. Very few supported the war, insisting on the primacy of Russia's "strategic partnership" with the United States and Russia's future role in Iraq. Statists and Civilizationists, predictably, saw the war as George W. Bush's drive for global hegemony and warned of his appetite for Russia's resources and territory.[93]

Outside the West: Economic Modernization at Any Cost?

Putin's view of the world outside the West was shaped by the same belief that Russia must do everything in its power to conduct successful economic modernization. Like Primakov, he believed in the necessity of Russia having a strong presence on the world's political stage, but he chose a different method of achieving that goal. The issues that for Primakov had the political significance of balancing American power were reduced to considerations of economic recovery under Putin. Unlike his predecessor, Putin was not a committed Eurasianist and did not seem to have much trust in the East. In some ways, his thinking about Russia's Asian neighbors was similar to that of Westernizers, and was marked by fear and defensiveness. For example, he shared the Westernizers' concern that if Moscow failed to improve the economic situation, neighboring nations could exploit Russia. In one of his speeches, the president issued an explicit warning: "I do not want to dramatize the situation, but if we do not make every real effort, even the indigenous Russian population will soon speak mostly Japanese, Chinese, and Korean."[94]

Therefore, Putin's policies outside the West, as active as they were, are best understood as serving the purpose of modernizing Russia, rather than developing strategic diplomatic alliances or deep cultural affinities. In building ties with Asian neighbors, Russia was especially determined to win markets in arms and energy. It was interested in selling its arms in the West as well, but many Western forces dismissed Russian products as inferior. China and India, on the other hand, had emerged as Russia's largest buyers. Given that the two countries had been the world's largest and second-largest arms importers, the economic prospects of cooperating with them were quite promising. Characteristically, while promoting weapons sales in Asia, at no point did Putin raise the issue of balancing the United States or creating some new strategic "axis" to serve this purpose. Even in the midst of signing a friendship treaty with China and knowing Russia's opposition to US plans for a national missile defense, Putin stressed that "Russia plans no joint actions with other states in this sphere, including China."[95]

While selling arms, Putin was typically dismissive of Western concerns about weapons proliferation. Russia's president was convinced that his country's actions were perfectly legitimate. Russia pledged to build two more nuclear reactors in Iran and signed an \$800 million deal with the Iranian government. The deal had been signed before Putin visited the United States in September 2003, and President Bush's efforts to change Putin's mind produced no results. To substantiate the Kremlin's claims about the commercial nature of Washington's pressures, some Russian analysts argued that, in the absence of official contracts, the US–Iranian trade turnover was around \$1 billion, which was higher than that of Russia, despite the Russian–Iranian strategic partnership agreement.[96]

Another key area of concentration of Russia in Eurasia was energy and transportation projects. Here again, Russia was closely cooperating with China, Japan, Iran, and India. In the south, one key idea had been to build the so-called north–south transport corridor that would pave the way for the delivery of goods from India and the Arabian Peninsula through Iran and the Caspian region to Russia and Europe, and vice versa. In September 2000, Russia, India, and Iran signed the agreement, according to which all signatories would get relief from import tax and customs duties. The transportation route was expected to reduce transport costs by 20 percent and reduce delivery times by fifteen to twenty days, compared with the old route via the Suez Canal. In the east, Russia was planning to capitalize on rich Siberian oil reserves by building pipelines to the neighboring countries. During 2003–2004, Russia's government was deciding between a shorter Chinese route and a longer route that would connect Siberian oil sources with Japanese markets. The Chinese Angarsk-Daqing project was agreed on by Russia's Yukos and China National Petroleum, and in May 2003, the twenty-five-year oil-supply deal was signed by the new Chinese president, Hu Jintao, on his first trip to Russia. The alternative project would connect East Siberia to Nakhodka and, from there, to Japan. It was extensively lobbied for by the Japanese side, which promised to finance the whole project if Russia agreed to it.

Pragmatism in Eurasia

Putin's approach to the former Soviet region was in line with his overall foreign policy philosophy of pragmatic modernization. Along with Primakov, he valued the region's political and geostrategic significance, but he placed the key emphasis on post-Soviet Eurasia's "advantage on the scale of global economic competition."[97] The new vision of the region assumed a more open, multilevel, politico-economic space planned by the Russian state, but built with the close participation of the Russian private sector. In addition, Putin stepped up cooperation on issues of counterterrorism and attempted to assemble his own coalition of the willing in the region.

The New Westernist-Statist Consensus

The new vision rested on firm social support at home. Westernizers were critical of the "integration" strategy for its underestimation of domestic business interests and for continuing what they saw as harmful practices of paying the former republics in exchange for their political loyalty to Russia. Boris Berezovski, a prominent oligarch and a one-time CIS executive secretary, attacked the Primakov-inspired vision for its "antimarket spirit."[98] As early as 1994, pro-Western reformers such as Economics Minister Yegor Gaidar and Finance Minister Boris Fedorov resigned, due partly to their opposition to the negotiations over an economic union with Belarus. To Westernizers, the former republics were unreliable partners—too corrupt and conservative to develop economic relationships with Russia.

Some of Primakov's Statist-oriented supporters, too, began to withdraw their support for the strategy of post-Soviet integration. Driven by nationalist, rather than free-market, considerations, they spoke against what they saw as Russia's one-sided concessions and unwarranted exploitation of its resources. The new liberal-nationalist consensus was summarized in the document of the influential Council for Foreign and Defense Policy titled "Strategy for Russia: Agenda for President—2000." The authors found Primakov's vision of a multipolar world to be outdated, expensive, and potentially confrontational. Instead, they proposed the concept of "selective engagement," which they compared with Russia's nineteenth-century policy of "self-concentration" after its defeat in the war in the Crimea and with China's policy since Deng Xiaoping. Regarding the former Soviet area, the authors recommended a "considerable revision" of policy, which would involve abandoning the "pseudointegration at Russia's expense" and "tough defense of our national economic interests."[99]

The Vision of Three-Level Ties in the Region

Consistent with the newly formed consensus, the new leadership adopted the rhetoric of pragmatism and self-concentration regarding the former Soviet area. In February 2001, the secretary of the Security Council, Sergei Ivanov, publicly announced the new course, acknowledging that it would mean a serious rethinking of Russia's previous policies in the region. By the time of this announcement, the debt of the CIS states to Russia had reached $5.5 billion.[100] Vice Premier Viktor Khristenko clarified the new approach by emphasizing its reciprocal nature: "The essence of the current policy of Russia toward the CIS states is an energetic bilateral cooperation based on pragmatism and a reciprocal account of interests. We develop multilateral contacts only in those spheres that received support from the parties."[101]

In the words of the parliament's CIS committee member Igor Glukhovski, Russia's relations with the former Soviet states would now exist on three separate levels—bilateral, subregional, and regional. In addition to bilateral relations, Russia would participate in subregional arrangements, such as the Collective Security Treaty signed by Russia, Belarus, Armenia, Kazakhstan, Kyrgyzstan, and Tajikistan. Another subregional arrangement was the Eurasian Economic Union, which was formed by Russia, Belarus, Kazakhstan, and Kyrgyzstan, with Ukraine joining in October 2003. Finally, Russia would develop regional forms of participation, particularly when it came to defending the region from international terrorist threats.[102]

New Bilateral Relations

Putin's objective of strengthening Russia's economic presence in the region materialized in aggressively asserting control over the ex-republics' strategic property and transportation. For example, in Georgia, Russia's state electric company obtained the right to be the main electricity provider, which provided it with a formidable opportunity to influence Georgian economic development. In Armenia, Russia obtained several strategic assets, such as an atomic electric station, to offset a debt of $40 million. Outside the Caucasus, Russia was covering 30 percent of the energy needs in Belarus, and the head of Russia's state electric company, Anatoli Chubais, also expressed an interest in participating in energy privatization in Ukraine and other states of the former Soviet region.[103] Russia continued to press for control of oil pipelines in the Caucasus, central Asia, Ukraine, and the Baltics. Its most important achievement was a strategic energy accord with Turkmenistan, under which virtually all of Turkmenistan's gas fell into Russia's sphere of influence for the following twenty-five years. The accord effectively eliminated the plans to utilize Turkmenistan's gas fields for laying pipelines through Afghanistan with the assistance of the United States.

This strategy of economic domination also implied Russia's cultivation of relationships with the already-existing political regimes in the former Soviet Union, however democratic or authoritarian they were. In the fall of 2003, Russia quickly endorsed elections in Azerbaijan and Armenia, despite their questionably democratic nature. Putin's emphasis on economic ties assisted here as well. In late September 2003, he visited Azerbaijan to sign an agreement dividing the two countries' rights to Caspian oil and gas, which mattered greatly to Azerbaijan. Russia also secured continued use of the Gabala radar station, which was located in Azerbaijan and which Russian media speculated Moscow was using to monitor the United States–led war on Iraq. In Georgia, Russia chose not to comment on another fraudulent parliamentary election that eventually caused President Eduard Shevardnadze to resign, and it quickly moved to start afresh with the newly elected president, Mikhail Saakashvili. Here, in addition to its economic interests, Russia wanted to secure the border with Chechnya and, especially, the Pankisi Gorge, which was long recognized as a transit point for terrorists.

In central Asia, Putin actively coordinated counterterrorist efforts with the local regimes, and he provided them with substantial military assistance in exchange for Russia's expanded military presence. He secured a strategic partnership with Kazakhstan, in part through the division of Caspian resources. As a part of the gas deal with Turkmenistan, he also promised President Saparmurat Niyazov some unspecified extra security services "to combat international terrorism." In Ukraine, Putin decisively supported the incumbent president Leonid Kuchma in his conflicts with the opposition. Here, too, the expectation was that the next president would continue Kuchma's policies of cooperation with Russia, and Russia would therefore continue to expand its economic presence in the country. In his turn, Kuchma agreed to sell Russia parts of Ukraine's natural gas transit system to offset the debt of roughly $2 billion to Moscow for energy deliveries. Finally, in Belarus, Russia continued to support President Aleksandr Lukashenko and supply energy at a discounted rate, but raised new demands regarding further steps in developing the Russia–Belarus union.

In addition to developing its economic presence in the region, Moscow sought to offset the growing geoeconomic influences of the West. Joint US–British companies controlled 27 percent of the Caspian's oil reserves and 40 percent of its gas reserves. The United States also supported the Baku-Ceyhan oil pipeline, which passed through Georgia and Turkey to Europe and bypassed Russia. It provided resources for GUUAM, an economic and security group of five former Soviet states—Georgia, Ukraine, Uzbekistan, Azerbaijan, and Moldova—established in 1998 as a counterweight to Russian influence. And after September 11, it opened military bases in several central Asian states.

Russia responded to these developments by preserving and strengthening its military presence in the Caucasus, central Asia, and Belarus through bilateral and multilateral efforts. Bilaterally, it negotiated the establishment of a new air force base in Kyrgyzstan and a base in Tajikistan, in addition to the already-existing other arrangements, such as the Baikonur Cosmodrome, the ballistic missile testing range in Kazakhstan, and a major early-warning radar in Tajikistan. Russia also moved to consolidate its naval supremacy on the Caspian Sea with the planned induction of dozens of new warships in its Caspian flotilla over the next few years.

Pragmatic Multilateralism

Although Putin abandoned the Primakov-like effort to revive the CIS, he did not give up multilateralism as a way to strengthen Russia's position in the region. Through both economic and security multilateralism, Putin was patiently assembling his own coalition of the willing. In the economic area, a notable development was the creation of an economic agreement with Belarus, Kazakhstan, and Ukraine, which aimed at eliminating trade barriers and devising shared energy-transport policies.

In the security realm, Russia concentrated on counterterrorist activities by developing the Shanghai Five, with China as a prominent member, and rebuilding the old Tashkent Collective Security Treaty. The Shanghai Five, or the Shanghai Cooperation Organization (SCO), emerged out of a Russia–China treaty on significant reduction of the number of border troops. The treaty was signed in 1997 along with Kazakhstan, Tajikistan, and Kyrgyzstan. After September 11, both Russia and China reactivated the SCO to address terrorism and a security vacuum in central Asia. A perceived threat of Islamic separatism was a matter of concern for Beijing, due to outbreaks of unrest among the Muslim Uighur minority—a Turkic-speaking group in China's Xinjiang region, which borders central Asia, Afghanistan, and Pakistan. Even Uzbekistan, once the central Asian state most interested in reducing Moscow's power in the region, was now more inclined to cooperate with Russia. Uzbekistan joined the Moscow-created center to fight terrorism, and called Russia "not only the guarantor of our security, but also a reliable strategic partner." Uzbekistan joined the SCO in late 2001, and in June 2004, it signed a strategic cooperation agreement with Russia that included some important economic and military dimensions.

In addition, Russia's long-advocated collective security action to deal with perceived threats in central Asia found its expression in transforming the old Tashkent treaty into a full-fledged regional defense pact. In April 2003, six states—Russia, Belarus, Kazakhstan, Kyrgyzstan, Tajikistan, and Armenia—formed the Collective Security Treaty Organization (CSTO), pledging to pool their resources to fight terrorism in the area. The organization sought to mimic the Cold War–era Warsaw Pact in Eastern Europe, complete with a joint headquarters and armed forces and a written commitment to respond to aggression against any member state.

Transportation Initiatives

Accelerating the development of a transportation system through transnational and transregional projects was an especially prominent focus of Putin's activities in the post-Soviet region. Most of these projects involved transporting oil and gas, of which Russia is one of the world's largest producers. The Caspian Sea was a particularly prominent area of attention from the Russian state. Here, the idea was to quickly establish a gas supply network to Turkey and Europe in order to undermine some Russia-competitive pipelines in the region. One such pipeline—from Baku to Ceyhan—was completed in May 2005, and by connecting northern Caspian structures to the Russian oil pipeline system, Russia would emerge as more competitive. Russia also discussed the idea of a trans-Caspian pipeline to bring oil underwater from Aktau in Kazakhstan to Baku and then to outside markets via the Baku-Ceyhan line. In February 2002, the Russian president also proposed an ambitious "gas OPEC" project that would involve Russia's pooling its natural gas resources with those of the central Asian states for the purpose of dominating the world markets.

Russian policymakers have been actively promoting transregional projects besides those related to the Caspian Sea. One of these projects is the Trans-Siberian Railroad, both an east-west route and a north-south one. The Russian Transportation Ministry has strongly lobbied for the Trans-Siberian project, which involves a completion of the 8,500 miles of railroad for transporting up to 100 million tons of cargo a year. While developing the project, the Russian government sought to be globally competitive, with potential competition coming from TRASEKA, the Brussels-planned international transportation corridor for connecting Europe, the Caucasus, and Asia. In addition to the Trans-Siberian route, Moscow's plans included developing a China–Kazakhstan–Russia–Europe route (east-west) and one that would connect Russia with India, Iran, Kazakhstan, Turkmenistan, and other Persian Gulf states (the north-south route). Other initiatives included the April 2005 agreement between Russia and Germany on a project to deliver Russian gas directly to Germany by a pipeline under the Baltic Sea, bypassing the Baltic states and Poland.[104]

The new vision assumed that post-Soviet Eurasia is a relatively economically open region, but one in which Russia occupies a central role and derives considerable economic, as well as political, benefits. The Russian foreign policy community had been debating the benefits of such geoeconomic thinking for quite some time. For instance, in his Eurasian Strategy for Russia, Sergei Rogov proposed that Russia focus on building the "communicational bridge" linking its southern, western, and eastern peripheries through the development of ground, air, and electronic transportation routes.[105] Although market-oriented, this vision meant to preserve Russia's leadership in the region and was broadly supported by various political movements, as well as a regionally oriented private sector. It bore little resemblance to Kozyrev's philosophy of integration with the West at the expense of Asian and former Soviet partners.

Assessment of Putin's Policy

Putin's policy continued and changed the previous Statist course of Great Power Balancing. Putin picked up where Primakov left off and remained focused on the objective of preserving great power status. Yet, the new leader abandoned the old strategy for achieving the objective. A multipolar world and post-Soviet integration—key tenets of Primakov's thinking— were replaced by more pragmatic means of asserting Russia's interests in global politics. This foreign policy transformation became possible due to a reshaped structure of domestic interest groups and their favored identity visions, as well as changes that had taken place in the international arena.

The overall record of Putin was rather positive and registered considerable progress in terms of meeting the foreign policy criteria of security, welfare, autonomy, and identity. The new course was encouraging in terms of address- ing its welfare dimension. Relative to the pre-1999 period, the country's economic and social standing improved considerably. Critics argued that this improvement reflected the increased world oil prices. This, however, was only one part of the story; the other part had to do with having the leader- ship ability to make the best of the favorable global conditions. Capitalizing on new economic opportunities, Putin managed to considerably improve relations with the United States, Europe, and the former Soviet states. Some examples of this include the energy summit in Houston, where Russia pledged to radically increase its oil supplies to the United States, and where it forged a joint venture with British Petroleum worth $6 billion. In 2003, Russia increased its oil production 11 percent and—in order to improve its bargaining position—it entered into a deal with Saudi Arabia. The five-year deal pledged cooperation between the Russian and Saudi energy sectors and in setting the international price of oil.[106] Renewed activism in winning energy and transportation markets in the former Soviet region added to the impression that the government was serious about economic modernization as its key foreign policy objective.

Table 3.14 summarizes the record of Putin's pragmatism.

The new foreign policy course also improved Russia's decision-making autonomy. Partly as a result of Russia's changed economic standing, its improved relations with Western nations did not come with strings attached. Russia was able to pay its debt obligations on time and was no longer in need

Table 3.14. The Record of Pragmatic Statism

Security	Remaining problems with terrorism
Welfare	Improved economic and social standing
Autonomy	No external assistance needed
Identity	Engaged Western and Statist dimensions of Russia's values

of additional external assistance. New engagement of the West on counterterrorism and energy issues did not mean that Russia's power to defend its own
perceived interests at home and in the region was to be seriously curtailed.

Putin's record in responding to Russia's security needs was weaker. The
president made the correct decision by supporting the US military operation
against the Taliban regime in Afghanistan. Also in order to fight terrorism,
Putin had been patiently assembling a coalition of the willing from the former
Soviet states. Working both bilaterally and multilaterally, he made progress in
pooling available military and intelligence resources in the region. However,
he was much less successful in defusing a key source of terrorism on his own
territory, in Chechnya. The improvement of the situation remained marginal,
with terrorist attacks continuing and the Russian public expressing reserva-
tions about the effectiveness of Putin's policies. In December 2003, one
poll registered as many as 68 percent expressing their frustration with the
situation.[107]

Finally, the record of Pragmatic Statism in addressing the Russian people's
identity needs was both positive and ambivalent. The new course was successful in engaging both the Westernist and the Statist components of Russian
national psychology and provided the space necessary for reformulating
Russia's national identity and moving beyond the post-Soviet identity crisis.
Yet that space was yet to be filled with some creatively defined national
idea capable of engaging some of the Russians' key cultural concerns. For
instance, polls consistently demonstrated that Russians supported the need to
maintain strong ties with the former Soviet republics. The state did not find
a way to respond to Russia's need to see itself as a civilization, not just as
a great power, if it wanted to defuse the appeal of hard-line Civilizationists.
Many Russians continued to feel the identity void.

The European and great power components of Putin's vision existed in
separation from one another. Ukraine's 2004 presidential elections showed,
among other things, the danger of separating the two. If Russia was going
to develop a viable civilizational identification, it should reconfirm its commitment to the cultural and institutional, rather than merely geopolitical,
objectives of its foreign policy. Russia's pragmatic Statist perspective was
therefore in danger of becoming a hostage of a narrowly defined and
state-driven modernization.

Partly because of not addressing the indicated identity issue, soon after his
reelection in March 2004, Putin was confronted with a series of new challenges. Most important among them were the rise of popular protests in the
wider region and the refusal of some European states to share Russia's vision
of history and the victory over fascism. While being dependent on recognition by the outside/Western world, Putin's vision of Russia as a normal great
power increasingly experienced tensions with that world.

As the country faced new challenges, the course came under criticism at home. Some Statists insisted that cooperation with the West was not paying off, and that Russia had to defend its interests more aggressively because its own survival was at stake. On the other side of the spectrum, liberal Westernizers argued the need to give up great power ambitions and pursue greater economic and political liberalization. In addition, the domestically questioned course had to be defended in the context of intensified efforts by Western nations, particularly the United States, to influence developments in the former Soviet region. The next chapter elaborates on these developments.

NOTES

1. Andrei Kozyrev, "Rossiya v novom mire," *Mezhdunarodnaya zhizn'* 3–4, (1992): 92.

2. Vladimir Putin, "Poslaniye Federal'nomu Sobraniyu Rossiyskoi Federatsiyi," Kremlin.ru, March 16, 2003.

3. Francis Fukuyama, "The End of History?," *National Interest* 16 (Summer 1989).

4. Timothy Garton Ash, *The Magic Lantern: The Revolution of '89 as Witnessed in Warsaw, Budapest, Berlin and Prague* (London: Vintage, 1989), 154.

5. The expression is that of US president Jimmy Carter's former national security adviser Zbigniew Brzezinski. See his book *The Grand Failure: The Birth and Death of Communism in the Twentieth Century* (New York: Charles Scribner's Sons, 1989).

6. William Pfaff, "Redefining World Power," *Foreign Affairs* 70, no. 1 (1991): 48.

7. Samuel Huntington, "The Clash of Civilizations?" *Foreign Affairs* 4, no. 72 (1993).

8. Leonid Gordon and Leonid Fridman, "Rossiya—velikaya derzhava vtorogo ranga," *Nezavisimaya gazeta*, April 4, 1995.

9. Richard Sakwa, *Russian Politics and Society*, 3rd ed. (London: Routledge, 2002), 294.

10. Some Statists linked the two events directly. See, for example, Aleksei Push-kov, "Otrezvlyayuschaya yasnost," *Nezavisimaya gazeta*, March 1999.

11. Vladimir Sogrin, "Zapadnyi liberalizm i rossiyskiye reformy," *Svobodnaya mysl'* 1 (1996): 32.

12. Philip Hanson, "Joining but Not Signing Up? Russia's Economic 'Integration' into Europe," *Russian and Eurasia Review* 2, no. 6 (March 18, 2003); Julien Vercuil, "Opening Russia? Contemporary Foreign Trade," *Russian and Eurasia Review* 2, no. 4 (February 18, 2003), www.jamestown.org.

13. Richard Rose, "How Floating Parties Frustrate Democratic Accountability," in *Contemporary Russian Politics*, ed. Archie Brown (Oxford: Oxford University Press, 2001), 221–22.

14. Andrei Kozyrev, *Preobrazheniye* (Moscow: Mezhdunarodnye otnosheniya, 1995), 16.

15. Kozyrev, "Rossiya v novom mire," 93.

16. As cited in George Breslauer, *Gorbachev and Yeltsin as Leaders* (Cambridge: Cambridge University Press, 2002), 157.

17. The terminology is that of Kozyrev. "Russia: A Chance for Survival," *Foreign Affairs* 71, no. 2 (1992): 9–10.

18. See, for example, Dmitri Furman, "Rossiiskiye demokraty i raspad soyuza," *Vek XX i mir* 1 (1992).

19. Boris Kapustin, "Rossiya i Zapad na puti k miru mirov," *Kentavr* 1, no. 2 (1993); Yuri Krasin, "O rossiyskikh natsional'nykh interesakh," *Svobodnaya mysl'* 3 (1996).

20. See, especially, Gennadi Zyuganov, *Drama vlasti* (Moscow: Paleya, 1993); *Rossiya i sovremennyi mir* (Moscow: "Obozrevatel," 1995); and *Geografiya pobedy* (Moscow, 1998).

21. Aleksandr Dugin, *Konservativnaya revolyutsiya* (Moscow: Arktogeya, 1994) and *Osnovy geopolitiki* (Moscow: Arktogeya, 1997).

22. Nikolai Fon Kreitor, "Stoletiye novogo mira," *Molodaya gvardiya* 6 (1998). See also Natalya Narochnitskaya, "Natsional'nyi interes Rossiyi," *Mezhdunarodnaya zhizn'* 3–4 (1992); Aleksandr Khatsankov, "Gorchakov—koshmar Kozyreva," *Den,'* August 8–14, 1992; El'giz Pozdnyakov, "Geopoliticheski kollaps i Rossiya," *Mezhdunarodnaya zhizn'* 8–9, 1992.

23. The argument is developed in Andranik Migranyan, "Podlinnye i mnimye orientiry vo vneshnei politike," *Rossiyskaya gazeta*, August 2, 1992.

24. See Kozyrev, "Rossiya v novom mire."

25. See, especially, "Strategiya dlya Rossiyi," *Nezavisimaya gazeta*, August 1992, and "Strategiya—2," *Nezavisimaya gazeta*, May 27, 1994. The term "Near Abroad," coined to refer to Russia's former Soviet periphery, was introduced in one of the first statements of the organization.

26. Zbigniew Brzezinski, "The Premature Partnership," *Foreign Affairs* 73, no. 1 (1994).

27. Andrei Kozyrev, "Partnership with the West: A Test of Strength," *Moscow News*, October 25, 1992.

28. Cited in Richter, "Russian Foreign Policy and the Politics of National Identity," in *The Sources of Russian Foreign Policy after the Cold War*, ed. Celeste A. Wallander (Boulder, CO: Westview Press, 1996), 86. After the December 1993 elections, even leaders of Gaidar's radically pro-Western Russia's Choice Party, among them Sergei Blagovolin and Boris Fedorov, acknowledged in private that it was a mistake on their part not to present themselves as a patriotic/nationalist group concerned about Russia's great power status. Astrid Tuminez, "Russian Nationalism and the National Interest in Russian Foreign Policy," in *The Sources of Russian Foreign Policy*, 65.

29. For elaboration, see especially Yevgeni Primakov, "Mezhdunarodniye otnosheniya nakanune XXI veka: Problemy, perspektivy," *Mezhdunarodnaya zhizn'* 10 (1996) and Yevgeni Primakov, "Rossiya v mirovoi politike," *Mezhdunarodnaya zhizn'* 5 (1998).

30. "Strategiya Rossiyi v XXI veke," *Nezavisimaya gazeta*, June 18, 1998.

31. "The Need for a New Ostpolitik," *Financial Times*, January 16, 1996.

32. Yevgeni Primakov, *Gody v bol'shoi politike* (Moscow: Sovershenno sekretno, 1999), 213, 217–21.

33. Primakov, presentation at the conference "Preobrazhennaya Rossiya," 104.

34. As cited in Primakov, "Rossiya v mirovoi politike." For a more extended analysis, see Flemming Splidsboel-Hansen, "Past and Future Meet: Aleksandr Gorchakov and Russian Foreign Policy," *Europe-Asia Studies* 54, no. 3 (2002).

35. National security concepts and foreign policy concepts are available in *Vneshnyaya politika i bezopasnost' sovremennoi Rossiyi*, ed. Tatyana Shakleyina (Moscow: ROSSPEN, 2002), 4:51–90, 110–11. For analysis, see Alla Kassianova, "Russia: Still Open to the West?," *Europe-Asia Studies* 6, no. 53 (2001).

36. Boris Yeltsin, "Mesto i rol' Rossiyi v period formiruyuschegosya mnogopolyarnogo mira," *Mezhdunarodnaya zhizn'* 6 (1998): 3.

37. For instance, Gorbachev's key foreign policy adviser, Georgi Shakhnazarov, prepared an analytical report on Russia's foreign priorities, in many respects sympathetic to Primakov's vision ("Vneshnepoiliticheskiye prioritety Rossiyi," *Politicheskaya mysl'* 1 [1998]).

38. For instance, the Ministry of Defense officials, such as General Leonid Ivashev, for quite some time dreamed of restoring Russia's superpower status ("Rossiya mozhet snova stat' sverkhderzhavoi," *Nezavisimaya gazeta*, March 7, 1995).

39. Yuri Fedorov, "Krizis vneshnei politiki Rossiyi," *Pro et Contra* 6, nos. 1–2 (2001).

40. Irina Kobrinskaya, "Pragmaticheski liberalizm vo vneshnei politike," *Otkrytaya politika* 7–8 (1997); Viktor Sheinis, "Rossiya i Yevropa: Interesy protiv mifov," *Nezavisimaya gazeta*, December 20, 2000.

41. Vladimir Putin, "Rossiya na rubezhe tysyacheletiy," *Nezavisimaya gazeta*, December 1999.

42. Putin, "Rossiya na rubezhe tysyacheletiy." In Putin's most revealing words, "If by democracy one means the dissolution of the state, then we do not need such democracy" (interview, *Washington Post*, September 26, 2003).

43. Peter Rutland, "Putin and the Oligarchs," in *Putin's Russia: Past Imperfect, Future Uncertain*, ed. Dale R. Herspring (Lanham, MD: Rowman & Littlefield, 2003), 148.

44. Dale R. Herspring, "Putin and the Armed Forces," in *Putin's Russia*, 170.

45. Putin, "Rossiya na rubezhe tysyacheletiy."

46. William Wohlforth, "Russia," in *Strategic Asia 2002–03: Asian Aftershocks*, ed. Richard J. Ellings and Aaron L. Friedberg (Washington, DC: The National Bureau of Asian Research, 2003), 199.

47. Grigori Yavlinski, "Druzhba na vremya ili soyuz navsegda?," *Obschaya gazeta*, January 24, 2002; Grigori Yavlinski, "Dver' v Yevropu nakhoditsya v Vashingtone," *Obschaya gazeta*, May 16, 2002.

48. Aleksei Kara-Murza, "Na perekrestke politiki i nauki," *Polis* 6 (2001).

49. Yevgeni Primakov, *Mir posle 11 sentyabrya* (Moscow: "Mysl,'" 2002), 106–7.

50. Sergei Kortunov, "Rossiysko-Amerikanskoye partnerstvo?," *Mezhdunarodnaya zhizn'* 4 (2002): 69.

51. See, for example, Aleksandr Panarin, "Ontologiya terrora," in *Geopolitika terrora* (Moscow: Arktogeya, 2002), 46; Aleksandr Prokhanov, "Ameriku potseloval angel smerti," *Zavtra*, September 18, 2001; Dugin, "Terakty 11 Sentyabrya: Ekonomicheski smysl," in *Geopolitika terrora*.

52. Sergey Ptichkin and Aleksei Chichkin, "From Where Russia Is Clearly Visible," *Rossiyskaya gazeta*, January 22, 2002; Evgeny Mikhilov, "The Art of Wiping Things Out," *Versty*, January 24, 2002 (as translated by *CDI Russia Weekly* 190, January 25, 2002).

53. A. Oslon, ed., *Amerika: Vzglyad iz Rossiyi* (Moscow: Institut Fonda "Obschestvennoye mneniye," 2001), 27. Another 64 percent of respondents perceived Washington's military activities in Afghanistan as dangerous for Russia (*Amerika: Vzglyad iz Rossiyi*, 124). At the same time, Russians continued to show strong support for Putin's decision to side with the West (*Amerika: Vzglyad iz Rossiyi*, 34, 124; "Rossiyani podderzhivayut sozdaniye soyuza RF i SshA v bor'be s mezhdunarodnym terrorizmom," *Nega-Set*, November 18, 2001).

54. The figure of $100 billion was calculated as the equivalent per capita value of aid to Eastern Europe from 1989 to 1991. Nigel Gould-Davies and Ngaire Woods, "Russia and the IMF," *International Affairs* 75, no. 1 (1999): 5.

55. Buszynski, *Russian Foreign Policy*, 57.

56. Robert H. Donaldson and Joseph L. Nogee, *The Foreign Policy of Russia: Changing Systems, Enduring Interests* (Armonk, NY: M. E. Sharpe, 2002), 193.

57. Peter Shearman, "Russian Policy toward the United States," in *Russian Foreign Policy since 1990*, ed. Peter Shearman (Boulder, CO: Westview Press, 1995), 121.

58. Yevgeni Bazhanov, "Russian Policy toward China," in *Russian Foreign Policy*, 161.

59. Bazhanov, "Russian Policy toward China," 170.

60. Shearman, "Russian Policy toward the United States," 129.

61. Vera Tolz, *Russia: Inventing the Nation* (Oxford: Arnold, 2001), 250.

62. Andrei V. Zagorski et al., *Posle raspada SSSR: Rossiya v novom mire* (Moscow: MGIMO, 1992), 6–11, 15, 17.

63. Alexander A. Pikayev, "The Russian Domestic Debate on Policy towards the 'Near Abroad,'" in *Peacekeeping and the Role of Russia in Eurasia*, ed. Lena Jonson and Clive Archer (Boulder, CO: Westview Press, 1996), 52.

64. David Kotz and Fred Weir, *Revolution from Above: The Demise of the Soviet System* (London: Routledge, 1997), 167.

65. Donaldson and Nogee, *The Foreign Policy of Russia*, 198.

66. In 1994, the rate of approval among Russians outside Russia ranged from 84 percent in Ukraine and Belarus, the two Slavic states, to about 50 percent in four central Asian states, with Kazakhstan falling in between these two poles ("Opinion Poll of the Newly Independent States," United States Information Agency, September 1994, 1).

67. Astrid Tuminez, "Russian Nationalism and the National Interest," in *The Sources of Russian Foreign Policy*, 59.

68. Wynne Russell, "Russian Relations with the 'Near Abroad,'" in *Russian Foreign Policy* (Boulder, CO: Westview Press, 1995), 65.

69. Russell, "Russian Relations with the 'Near Abroad,'" 65.

70. William Zimmerman, *The Russian People and Foreign Policy* (Princeton, NJ: Princeton University Press, 2002), 91.

71. For Western scholarship, see especially Peter Rutland, "Mission Impossible? The IMF and the Failure of the Market Transition in Russia," *Review of International Studies* 25, no. 5 (1999); Janine Wedel, *Collision and Collusion: The Strange Case of Western Aid to Eastern Europe, 1990–1997* (London: Palgrave, 1998); Peter Reddaway and Dmitri Glinski, *The Tragedy of Russia's Reforms: Market Bolshevism against Democracy* (Washington, DC: United States Institute of Peace, 2001).

72. For analysis of the decision to expand NATO and Russia's reaction to it, see James Goldgeier, *Not Whether, But When: The US Decision to Enlarge NATO* (Washington, DC: Brookings, 1999); and J. L. Black, *Russia Faces NATO Expansion: Bearing Gifts or Bearing Arms?* (Lanham, MD: Rowman & Littlefield, 2000), respectively.

73. As cited in Neil MacFarlane, "Realism and Russian Strategy after the Collapse of the USSR," in *Unipolar Politics*, eds. Ethan B. Kapstein and Michael Mastanduno (New York: Columbia University Press, 1999), 242.

74. As cited in Leonid Mlechin, *Ministry inostrannykh del: Romantiki i tsiniki* (Moscow: Tsentrpoligraf, 2001), 620.

75. I draw here on Robert O. Freedman, *Russian Policy toward the Middle East since the Collapse of the Soviet Union* (Seattle: The Henry M. Jackson School of International Studies, University of Washington, 2001), 34–40; and Donaldson and Nogee, *The Foreign Policy of Russia*, 301–05.

76. Allen Lynch, "Realism of Russian Foreign Policy," *Europe-Asia Studies* 53 (2001): 15, 28.

77. Oksana Antonenko, "Russia, NATO and European Security after Kosovo," *Survival* 41, no. 4 (1999/2000): 143.

78. Aleksei Pushkov, "Sindrom Chernomyrdina," *Nezavisimaya gazeta*, June 11, 1999.

79. Antonenko, "Russia, NATO and European Security," 134–36.

80. Freedman, *Russian Policy toward the Middle East*, 23.

81. Donaldson and Nogee, *The Foreign Policy of Russia*, 316.

82. "Vozroditsya li soyuz? Buduscheye postsovetskogo prostranstva," *NG-Stsenariyi*, May 23, 1996.

83. The poll data are from: Dimitri K. Simes, *After the Collapse* (New York: Simon & Schuster, 1999), 220; and Susan Birgerson, *After the Breakup of a Multi-Ethnic Empire* (New York: Praeger, 2002), 88.

84. Georgi Shakhnazarov et al., "Vneshnepoliticheskiye prioritety Rossiyi."

85. Graham Smith, *Post-Soviet States* (London: Arnold, 1999), chap. 6; Tolz, *Russia: Inventing the Nation*, chap. 8.

86. *Izvestiya* correspondent Stanislav Kondrashev, as quoted in Leonid Mlechin, *Ministry inostrannykh del*, 607.

87. William Zimmerman, *The Russian People and Foreign Policy* (Princeton, NJ: Princeton University Press, 2002), 91.

88. As cited in Dale R. Herspring and Peter Rutland, "Putin and Russian Foreign Policy," in *Putin's Russia*, 237.

89. Leon Aron, "Russian Oil and U.S. Security," *New York Times*, May 5, 2002.

90. Hanson, "Joining but Not Signing Up?"

91. Sergei Yastrzhembsky, "Russophobia Still Rampant," *New York Times*, April 24, 2002.

92. Stephen Foye, "The EU's Enlargement; Russia Plays Bridesmaid," *Eurasia Daily Monitor*, May 3, 2004, www.jamestown.org.

93. Associated Press, "Ex-defense Minister Accuses US of Seeking to Dominate Russia," June 19, 2003 (as cited by *CDI Russia Weekly* 262, June 2003).

94. Vladimir Putin, "Vystupleniye na soveschaniyi 'O perspektivakh razvitiya Dal'nego Vostoka i Zabaikalya,'" *Blagoveschensk*, July 21, 2000, www.kremlin.ru.

95. Wohlforth, "Russia," 201–2.

96. Marianna Belenkaya, "America's Iranian Policy and Russia's Interests," Russia's Information Agency, as cited by the *Center of Defense Information* 259, no. 6 (May 29, 2003), www.cdi.org/russia/259.cfm.

97. Vladimir Putin, "Vistupleniye Prezidenta na rasshirennom zasedaniyi s uchastiyem poslov Rossiyskoi Federatsiyi v MID Rossiyi," Kremlin.ru, July 12, 2002.

98. Boris Berezovski, "SNG: Ot razvala k sotrudnichestvu," *Nezavisimaya gazeta*, November 13, 1998.

99. *Strategiya dlya Rossiyi: Povestka dlya prezidenta—2000* (Moscow: Sovet po vneshnei i oboronnoi politike, 2000), www.svop.edu.

100. Alan Kasaiev, "Sovet Bezopasnosti Rossiyi reshil zakryt' SNG," *Nezavisimaya gazeta*, February 7, 2001.

101. Yekaterina Tesyemnikova, "Preimuschestva sodruzhestva dlya Rossiyi ochevidny," *Nezavisimaya gazeta*, August 2, 2001.

102. Igor' Glukhovski, "Mnogovektornaya integratsiya kak otvet novym vyzovam," *Nezavisimaya gazeta*, February 13, 2001.

103. Anatoli Chubais, "Missiya Rossiyi v XXI veke," *Nezavisimaya gazeta*, October 1, 2003.

104. Vladimir Socor, "Schroeder-Putin Gas Deal Undercuts Both New and Old EU Member Countries," *Eurasia Daily Monitor*, April 13, 2005, www.jamestown.org.

105. Sergei Rogov, *Yevraziyskaya strategiya dlya Rossiyi* (Moscow: Institut SshA i Kanady, 1998); also, Rogov, "Izolyatsiya ot integratsiyi," *NG-Dipkuryer*, December 7, 2000.

106. Stephen Blank, "Moscow's Cozy Saudi Connection," *Asia Times*, September 13, 2003.

107. The poll of VTSIOM, as cited in "Support for Putin's Policies Is Weak, But He Is Still Popular," *RFE/RL Newsline*, December 2, 2003.

4

Recovery and Assertiveness, 2005–2019

> Russia must not only preserve its geopolitical relevance—it must multiply it, it must generate demand among our neighbors and partners. I emphasize that this is in our own interest. This applies to our economy, culture, science and education, as well as our diplomacy, particularly the ability to mobilize collective actions at the international level. Last but not least it applies to our military might that guarantees Russia's security and independence.
>
> —Vladimir Putin, December 2012[1]

Soon after the color revolutions in the former Soviet region, Putin's Statist Pragmatism obtained a new dimension—assertiveness. Putin's speech at the Munich Conference on Security Policy in February of 2007 became a high point in Russia's new assertiveness and was extremely critical of US "unilateralism," yet it meant to preserve and deepen achievements of cooperation with the West. It sent a strong signal to the Western nations that in the Kremlin's perception, the course of Russia's integration with the West was in jeopardy because of highly destabilizing policies of the United States. Not satisfied with Western recognition of Russia's interests, the Kremlin had sought to defend them as it deemed appropriate. Russia had sought to capitalize on its economic recovery, energy competitiveness, and political stability, while breaking into international markets and protecting its political and security interests.

The assertive course in Russian foreign policy lasted until 2019. It was interrupted only for the period of Dmitri Medvedev's pragmatic effort to rebuild cooperation with Western nations during 2009–2011, following the war with Georgia in August 2008. Under Medvedev, the country's approach to the outside world was dictated by the need to modernize its domestic economy and to reach a new understanding with Western nations. Being seriously hit by the global financial crisis, Russia was keenly interested in developing economic and technological ties with the Western nations.

The return of Vladimir Putin as Russia's president in March 2012 signaled a return to assertiveness in relations with the West. Following interventions in Ukraine and Syria, Russia moved in another direction by demonstrating its power and "geopolitical relevance" abroad. Putin reached out to nationalist constituencies at home and sought to strengthen Russia's position in the former Soviet region. The crisis in Ukraine in 2022 resulted in part from attempts by Russia, the European Union, and the United States to pull Kyiv into their own areas of influence by further straining Russia's relations with the West. The Kremlin also sought to capitalize on new international opportunities by establishing stronger ties with non-Western countries. This chapter documents the three identified periods marked by Russia's overall desire to protect its foreign policy interest from the perceived pressures of Western nations.

GLOBAL AND DOMESTIC CHANGES

US Dominance and Global Instability

From 2005 to 2019, the earlier identified globalization of Western economic, political, and military policies resulted in growing instability in regions from the Middle East to Eurasia. The American invasion of Iraq betrayed the objective of democratizing the region by establishing a new pro-Western regime at its heart. Soon, it became apparent that the strategy of changing regimes and expanding liberty was not limited to the Middle East. President Bush's inaugural address in January 2005 made the spread of freedom and democracy the center of the United States' political strategy in the "war on terror," and his State of the Union speech in February continued the theme: "The attack on freedom in our world has reaffirmed our confidence in freedom's power to change the world."[2] The so-called Rose Revolution in Georgia in November 2003 replaced the old regime by popular protest over a rigged parliamentary election and emboldened Washington to apply the strategy in the former Soviet region as well. While the military option was excluded, the emphasis was still on providing opposition with relevant training and financial resources for challenging the old regimes in power.[3] The color revolutions then took place in Ukraine and Kyrgyzstan in 2004 and 2005, respectively.

The color revolutions that took place in Georgia, Ukraine, and Kyrgyzstan during 2003–2005 did not improve cooperation between Russia and Western countries in what had become a key international objective after September

11, 2001—fighting terrorism. Indeed, there was a connection between Washington's strategy of regime change and growing terrorist violence and political instability in the world. After the US invasion of Iraq, terrorism became more, not less, prevalent in the Middle East. Iraq was in a stage of civil war with hundreds of thousands of people killed and misplaced and millions leaving the country.[4] Afghanistan, recently considered a successful antiterrorist operation, also showed multiple signs of growing destabilization and was quickly turning into a new safe haven for terrorists and members of the overthrown Taliban regime. Yet Washington seemed determined to press ahead with its strategy and even showed signs of preparing to attack Iran unilaterally. A number of policymakers believed in "an attempt to revive the concept of spreading democracy in the Middle East by creating one new model state."[5] The United States pulled military forces into the Persian Gulf, including aircraft carriers, and it increased the number of troops in Iraq by 20,000. Washington also warned Tehran not to "meddle" in Iraq. In addition to perceiving Iran as building a nuclear bomb, Washington viewed it as a regime that harbored terrorists and obstructed US efforts to stabilize Iraq.

Both US unilateralism in foreign policy and global power decline contributed to instability in the world. The US military decline was evident in the growing proliferation of nuclear weapons and incidents of unsanctioned use of conventional weapons in non-Western regions. The United States failed in its efforts to successfully complete its military operations in Afghanistan and Iraq; to stabilize the Middle East; to impose its rules on Russia in Eurasia; and to maintain a viable international order. Its economic decline was obvious, with the rise of China and the Asia-Pacific region as new centers of the world's gravity. The global financial crisis affected Western economies more than it affected China's. Russia's oil-dependent economy was also hit hard (see below). The rising economies of China, India, Brazil, and others have challenged the dominant position of the West by establishing institutional venues, including annual meetings of BRICS (Brazil, Russia, India, China, and South Africa) and SCO (Shanghai Cooperation Organization), pooling financial resources and producing around 30 percent of the world's GDP.[6] The idea of Western-style democracy no longer commands the same attention in part because democracy promotion outside the West has been not infrequently accompanied by state weakness, lawlessness, and ethnic violence. In the meantime, observers have noted the intensification of processes of cultural reformulations and the rise of alternative soft power projects which develop both within and outside the legitimizing language of democracy.[7]

Overall, the unipolar moment known for dominance of the United States' values and interests in world affairs was challenged in a most fundamental way. Structurally, it is still the familiar world of American domination, with the country's superiority in military, political, economic, and cultural dimensions. But dynamically the world has been moving away from its West-centeredness,[8] even though the exact direction and result of the identified trajectory remains unclear.

This global instability has impacted the West itself. In 2016 Euro-skeptics won the referendum in Britain, leading to replacement of the government and initiation of the country's withdrawal from the EU. The voting reflected the continent's crisis of economy and migration. The migration crisis deepened the already-existing problem of Europe's coexistence with Muslim immigrants.[9]

In the United States, against expectations, liberal presidential candidate Hillary Clinton lost to maverick Donald Trump. The latter advocated more nationalist policies, such as introducing stronger restrictions on immigration and trade. He promised to put America first by withdrawing from expensive military commitments abroad and leaving the World Trade Organization. In his inaugural address, Trump pledged to be guided by the America First principle, "transferring power from Washington, DC [to] . . . the American People," and promising that "every decision on trade, on taxes, on immigration, on foreign affairs [would be] made to benefit American workers and American families."[10]

Other parts of the world were also entering economic and political uncertainty. Growing economic inequality and the decline of labor markets generated new protectionist sentiments, creating conditions for populism and fragmentation of the global economy.[11]

Western countries, however, have been determined to continue with their policies. With respect to Russia, the United States and the European Union were uncomfortable with Putin's return to power in 2012 and increased their criticism of Russia's domestic system and human rights record. Previously, members of the Obama administration rarely engaged in criticism of Russia under Medvedev, during 2009–2011, as the United States worked to strengthen relations with him at the expense of Putin.[12] Europeans, too, were hopeful that they would be able to rebuild their ties with Russia, although they were well aware that Medvedev's actions had Putin's full support.[13]

In addition to the shift of power to Putin, Washington found it difficult to accept new policies issued by the Kremlin. In particular, Western nations reacted critically to Putin's attempts to reassert power domestically. Western leaders voiced their disagreement with the Kremlin's handling of protesters following demonstrations that took place after fraudulent elections to State Duma in November 2011. The West also condemned corruption in Russia and imposed visa bans and asset freezes on those it linked to the case of Russian lawyer Sergei Magnitsky, who was arrested and died while in detention. In addition, US and EU leaders criticized Russia's policies of restricting the rights of minorities and opposition.

In the meantime, Russia and the West seriously diverged on foreign policy issues. The policy of reset initiated by President Obama during Medvedev's presidency helped to solve some important issues in the two countries' relations, yet failed to address the root causes of their disagreements (please see the analysis below). Increasingly, Western nations expected more cooperation from Russia, as the Kremlin expressed growing frustration with what it saw as insufficient cooperation on the part of the West. The two sides disagreed on Western plans regarding the Missile Defense System (MDS) in Europe, and policies in the Middle East and Eurasia. Russia proposed to build its MDS jointly, and was frustrated with the lack of progress in this area. The Kremlin's proposal of a new security treaty in Europe was not supported by Western partners. There were also growing disagreements over the issue of instability in Syria and the wider Middle Eastern region. In June 2013, Moscow and Washington also had to confront the problem caused by the defection of former CIA employee Edward Snowden to Russia, as the Kremlin refused to comply with the US demand to turn him over.[14]

Finally, Western leaders expressed concerns over the Kremlin's attempts to build the Eurasian Union. Even though Putin emphasized the open nature of the proposed union and laid out economic incentives for joining it,[15] American and European leaders perceived the idea as threatening. They were especially concerned about Ukraine being pulled into the Russia-centered union, and worked against it by presenting the proposed arrangement as anti-European, and offering Kyiv an opportunity to sign an Association Agreement with the European Union.

Following the revolutionary change of power in Ukraine and the Kremlin's annexation of Crimea and support for Donetsk and Luhansk, Western nations condemned Russia, imposed sanctions against the Russian economy, and moved to strengthen NATO's military readiness in Eastern Europe. Despite Trump's attempts to "get along" with Putin during 2016–2019, he was unable to increase the level of cooperation with Russia. In part due to domestic constraints, such as investigations of his potential "collusion" with the Kremlin, Trump continued the policy of political pressure and economic sanctions of his predecessor.

International conditions that affected Russia's foreign policy during the 2005–2019 period are summarized in table 4.1.

Table 4.1. Russia and International Conditions, 2005–2019

	2005–2008	2009–2011	2012–2019
International Conditions	Western political and military expansion	Global financial crisis	Western pressures and sanctions

Russia's Security Vulnerabilities

Because of US foreign policy and growing global instability, Russia became more vulnerable from a security standpoint. While the so-called color revolutions were strongly supported by Western nations, they have been viewed as destabilizing by Russia, and directed against the Kremlin's power and security. Georgia, Ukraine, and Kyrgyzstan failed to address the root causes of the revolutions, such as poor living conditions and unpopular leadership. In dealing with separatist South Ossetia, Tbilisi increasingly relied on force, while pressuring Russia out of the region. In addition, Georgia and Ukraine expressed their desire to join NATO, which added to Russia's sense of strategic insecurity. In the aftermath of the NATO summit in April 2008, President Putin stated, "We view the appearance of a powerful military bloc on our borders . . . as a direct threat to the security of our country. The claim that this process is not directed against Russia will not suffice. National security is not based on promises."[16] The public, too, reacted overwhelmingly negatively to the alliance's expansion. Seventy-four percent of Russians polled in March 2008 said that Ukraine's possible accession to NATO posed a threat to the national security of the Russian Federation, and 77 percent expressed a similar attitude toward Georgia's possible membership in the organization.[17]

Russia also felt vulnerable to the radicalization of Islam in response to the US style of fighting a war on terror. Although the situation in the Chechen Republic became more stable, North Ossetia, Ingushetia, Kabardino-Balkaria, and Dagestan were experiencing a growing number of terrorist attacks. Some of it, undoubtedly, could be attributed to Russia's own errors. The growing influence of radical Islamist ideologies, rising immigration from Muslim ex-Soviet republics, and attempts by some of Russia's authorities to address the problem by closing local mosques created a politically explosive environment. However, the other part had to do with the US style of fighting a war on terror that was increasingly perceived in the Muslim world as a war of civilizations. What began as a counterterrorist operation in Afghanistan with relatively broad international support has increasingly turned into a "war of civilizations," or a US crusade against Muslims and their style of living. Instead of engaging moderate Muslims, US policies tended to isolate them and give the cards to radicals. In a global world, these policies and transformations in the Middle East—from regime changes in Egypt, Tunisia, and Libya to rising instability in Syria—translated into greater support for Islamic radicals inside Russia.

Finally, Moscow feared a revolution inside Russia. In addition to growing instability in the region, the color revolutions added to the perception within the Kremlin that Washington's chief objective was in fact to change the regime in Russia. Although public support for a revolution was weak, the

Kremlin's political technologists took the threat seriously, knowing that less than 1 percent of the population was really involved in the recent capitals-centered color revolutions, and that influential elites in the United States maintained contacts with some radical organizations in Russia.

For instance, in April 2007, the US State Department issued a report highly critical of Russia's political system and pledging various forms of assistance to "democratic organizations" inside the country. In response, the Kremlin took a number of defensive steps. It trained its own youth organizations to defend what it saw as Russia's indigenous democracy, restricted activities of Western NGOs and radical opposition inside the country, and warned the United States against interference with Russia's domestic developments.

Following his return to the presidency in March 2012, Putin presented West-leaning protesters as unpatriotic and accused them of acting in concert with the United States. The fear of domestic protests continued to influence Putin's rule. A number of protesters were arrested on various charges, and the Kremlin submitted to the State Duma several laws restricting the activities of nongovernmental foreign-funded organizations, requiring state officials to renounce their foreign assets, denying the adoption of Russian children by US citizens, and others. These developments were greatly assisted by the United States' growing pressures on Russia that began with President Obama signing the Magnitsky Law, which introduced sanctions against Russian officials.

The Ukraine's Euromaidan Revolution in 2014 also brought with it alarming consequences for Russia. From the Kremlin's perspective, nationalist forces in Ukraine overthrew the legitimate government in Kyiv, jeopardizing Russia's military fleet in the Black Sea and the human rights of those gravitating toward the eastern neighbor. When Russia intervened in Crimea by sending additional troops to the region and then annexing the peninsula, Western countries imposed on Russia a series of economic sanctions, thereby playing into the Kremlin's already-formed fear of the West and strengthening the position of those internally and externally critical of Russia.

Economic and Political Strengths

Russia's economic and political conditions during 2005–2019, while mixed, pointed in the direction of the country's consolidation around its leadership. During 1999–2007, following the years of the post-Soviet depression, the economy caught up with the level of 1990 and continued to grow at an annual pace of about 7 percent (Russia's basic economic indicators are summarized in table 4.2). The overall size of the economy increased about six times in current dollars—from $200 billion to $1.3 trillion. Russia's per-capita GDP quadrupled to nearly $7,000, and about twenty million people were lifted out

Table 4.2. Russia's Basic Economic Indicators, 1999–2007 (% annual change)

	1998	1999	2000	2001	2002	2003	2004	2005	2006	2007
Real GDP growth	–5.3	6.3	10.0	5.1	4.3	7.7	7.2	6.4	6.7	7.3
Real wages	–10	–22	18	20	16	11	11	13	13	16
Budget surplus (% of GDP)	–5.3	0.5	3.5	3.0	1.4	1.7	4.5	8.1	8.5	5.5
Urals oil prices ($/ barrel)	12.0	17.0	27.0	23.0	24.0	27.0	34.0	50.0	61.0	69.0

Source: Peter Rutland, "Putin's Economic Record: Is the Oil Boom Sustainable?," *Europe-Asia Studies* 60, no. 6 (2008): 1052.

of poverty.[18] Russia's middle class at this time constituted about 25 percent of the population.[19]

From 2000 to 2005, the average Russian saw a 26 percent annual growth in income, relative to only a 10 percent rise in that of the average Chinese.[20] Direct foreign investments to the Russian economy skyrocketed, making it first in the world among developing economies.[21] Although much of the economic recovery was due to high oil prices, the government continued to work to reduce reliance on energy exports. In early 2008, for example, industrial production rose an annual 9.2 percent.[22] As a result, the number of Russians who thought that the chosen development course in Russia was correct was growing year on year.[23] The economic recovery provided conditions for Russia's active business promotion in Europe, which accounts for 50 percent of Russia's foreign trade. The Kremlin insisted on long-term contracts with Europeans and greater integration with European markets in order to avoid a repetition of the 1985–1986 scenario, when a sharp decline in energy prices contributed considerably to the breakup of the Soviet economy.

During 2008, Russia's economy was hit by the global financial crisis. The crisis ended an era of unprecedented growth which had lasted nine years (1999–2008), during which the economy not only caught up with 1990 levels, but continued to grow at an annual pace of about 7 percent. The global economic crisis revealed the tenuous nature of Russia's recovery and the remaining weaknesses of its power base. During the crisis, Russia, which is heavily dependent on energy, including exports, was hit particularly hard. Its GDP fell by around 9 percent in 2009, while China and India continued to grow, albeit at a slower pace. Russia had to spend a considerable portion of its reserves to bail out domestic enterprises, including noncompetitive ones, and to scale down its activist foreign policy in central Asia and the Caucasus.[24] The crisis revealed that while Russia had met some of its economic and security challenges, it had also perpetuated an insufficiently diversified economic structure and failed to address some serious gaps in its social infrastructure.

Although by 2011 the Russian economy had recovered from the financial crisis, the core economic problems—such as excessive dependence on exports of raw materials, corruption, and lack of rule of law—had not been addressed. Russia's economic competitiveness remained relatively low and the technological gap with the West, wide. Following the West's economic pressures, Russia had to urgently look for alternative foreign economic ties, reorienting its economy toward Asia and China. Putin's political and economic system centered on informal economic deals between the state and oligarchs, and Kremlin-controlled elections demonstrated their limitations.

However, the Russian state and society reached a new level of consolidation following the Euromaidan Revolution in Ukraine and the annexation of Crimea in March 2014. Russians felt united against the West and were not likely to yield to Western pressures, even as they were increasingly anxious about the decline of living standards and problems with the economy. The ineffectiveness of the economic system was revealed in the devaluation of the ruble in the fall of 2014, when Russian currency lost about 50 percent of its value due to the cumulative impact of declining oil prices and Western economic sanctions. By 2017, Russian living standards had been declining for four consecutive years, while the state continued to allocate money for defense purposes.[25]

On balance, despite the economic problems, Russians demonstrated political unity in the face of perceived Western pressures. This unity was further demonstrated during the country's presidential election in March 2018, with the official results of 77 percent support for Putin. This result exceeded many expectations, and confirmed that Russians overwhelming trusted Putin even as they favored more attention to economic development.[26] By supporting Putin, Russians voted not just for the president, but for a commander in chief who was capable of protecting the country from Western pressures and unfounded accusations.

Changes in Identity Coalitions

These global and domestic changes translated into changing positions of liberal and security-minded segments within the Russian political class. Those around Putin with security credentials are often referred as *siloviks*,[27] or those professionally concerned with defending the security of state from harmful domestic and foreign influences and favoring the preservation of a strong state and great power status. In practical terms, their preferences may translate into prioritizing state orders, increasing the defense budget, and suppressing pro-Western forces in the country.

Persistent security vulnerabilities strengthened the position of the security class. As a result, in the coalition of oligarchs and *siloviks*, the latter gained considerable prominence over the former. The security class did not become dominant, as some have suggested,[28] but it was affecting state decisions more than it had previously, and it gained a greater presence in commercial companies, especially energy-related companies. The state was not consolidated enough to isolate powerful security influences, yet it did not become a hostage to those influences. Liberals, such as Aleksei Kudrin and German Gref, stayed in the government and continued to make a case for more aggressive liberal economic policies. Members of the security class were unable to assert greater isolationism in economic matters by protecting large companies from international competition, or in politics, by forcing Putin to stay for the third presidential term.

Rather than staying for a third term, Putin designated Dmitri Medvedev—not known for his ties with members of the security class—as his successor. The power transition went generally smoothly. With Putin's support, Medvedev decisively defeated his three rivals—the Communist Party's Gennadi Zyuganov, Vladimir Zhirinovski of the Liberal Democratic Party, and the Democratic Party's Andrei Bogdanov—winning the overwhelming majority of the popular vote in the first round of voting. Although Western media and election-monitoring organizations were critical of the elections,[29] US and European governments preferred to work with the Kremlin and expressed cautious support for Medvedev. The elections improved the position of liberal-minded forces in Russia and testified yet again that Putin's state was not a hostage to ideologies of security-driven isolationism or liberal-minded openness, and was in charge when deciding between them.

The state has gradually reshaped the previously loose coalition of oligarchs and *siloviks* by acquiring a greater prominence in economic affairs, yet using it for keeping Russia open to international competition. Ever since most of the powerful oligarchs, such as Boris Berezovski, Vladimir Gusinski, and Mikhail Khodorkovski, were stripped of their economic empires, the state has consistently asserted itself in other key areas and become dominant in leading energy companies, such as Gazprom and Rosneft. It has renegotiated production-sharing agreements with Western companies in the most lucrative oil fields in Siberia and the Far East. In addition to the energy industry and military-industrial complex, the state announced plans to create "national champions," or state-supported companies, in the banking, aerospace, automobile, and heavy machinery industries. Yet the state has also argued that creation of such companies was necessary to position them for successful international competition.[30] Putin's strategy of a state-dominant capitalism recognized the vital need for foreign investments in order to continue high economic growth, particularly coming from Western nations.

The Ukraine crisis in 2014 further increased the power of *siloviks* in Putin's coalition. He made the Crimea decision in close consultation with security officials, thereby granting them an additional measure of policy influence. The Ukraine crisis, the Syria war, and elevated Western pressures on Russia following the election of US president Donald Trump served to heighten the perception of many Russians that they are under attack from the hostile West. Several rounds of Western sanctions against Russia convinced elites and society in general that this is indeed the case. Most Russians rallied behind Putin and did not want him to bow to foreign pressures. Many economic and security elites reached the conclusion that these sanctions revealed the "true" nature of the West, which was to fight and defeat Russia in a new Cold War.

The fact that Western governments held the Kremlin responsible for destabilizing the West also highlighted the power of Russia's *siloviks*. America and Europe, increasingly divided, were reaching out for external explanations of their instability, accusing Moscow of cyber interference in foreign elections; bribing potential allies abroad; and assassinating political opponents and former intelligence officers.

The incident with the poisoning of Russia's former intelligence officer Sergei Skripal in Salisbury, England, exacerbated Russia–West relations, yet largely confirmed the post-Crimean political consolidation inside Russia. On March 4, 2018, Skripal and his daughter were poisoned. They survived the attack and were released from the hospital in three weeks. As with the alleged cyber interference in the United States' presidential elections in November 2016, Russia denied any involvement, repudiating all charges made by Western governments, which accused the Kremlin of lying, and introduced additional sanctions against Russia.

The post-Crimean consolidation also served to further marginalize pro-Western critics who were often viewed and presented by state media as traitors of Russia. On February 27, 2015, a leading opposition politician, Boris Nemstov, was assassinated in central Moscow. Another member of a liberal political party and the governor of Kirov Oblast, Nikita Belykh, was arrested on corruption charges in July 2016. In late 2017, a similar arrest was made in the case of the economy minister, Alexei Ulyukayev, who was sentenced to eight years in prison on charges of demanding a $2 million bribe from a state official.

REDEFINED NATIONAL INTEREST

Responding to the above outlined conditions, the Russian state proposed its redefined perspectives on national interest, summarized in table 4.3. The following section provides details regarding content, as well as domestic, political, and intellectual reception.

Table 4.3. Russia's Perspectives on National Interest, 2005–2019

	Statist Assertiveness (Putin)	Alliances for Modernization (Medvedev)	State-Civilization (Putin)
What?	A great power in the West-centered world	A modernizing state	Distinct civilizational values
How?	Multilateralism among great powers Energy power Indigenous democracy	Exploiting economic opportunities with Western and non-Western powers Improving domestic institutions Remaining tough in defending security interests	Domestic consolidation Strategic cooperation with non-Western nations Pragmatic cooperation with the West

Putin's Assertiveness, 2005–2008

The Refined Statism and Assertiveness

The overall objectives of Russia's foreign policy stayed the same as previously outlined in Putin's early programmatic speech, "Russia at the Turn of the Millennium"—economic modernization, political stability, and enhancement of security.[31] Yet the context in which Russia had to act changed considerably, which meant modified methods of pursuing foreign policy objectives.

In his response to new challenges and security vulnerabilities, Putin sought to reaffirm Russia's commitment to European values. In his programmatic speech delivered to the Federation Council in March 2005, Putin declared that he saw Russia moving toward the same values that are shared by others in the European continent—"the ideals of freedom, human rights, justice and democracy."[32] In the former Soviet region, this translated into the doctrine of "continuing the civilizational role of the Russian nation in Eurasia." Responding to charges of "imperialism" toward post-Soviet nations in the wake of the color revolutions, Putin insisted that Russia seeks not the post-Soviet states' territory or natural resources, but the human dignity and quality of life of its citizens, whom it regards as its own cultural compatriots.

Putin was clear, however, that while moving in the same direction as Europeans—toward freedom and democracy—Russia will do so at its own pace and according to its own conditions. In the same speech, referring to the Western role in the color revolutions in Georgia and Ukraine, Putin insisted on Russia's right to "decide for itself the pace, terms and conditions of moving towards democracy," and he warned against attempts to destabilize the political system by "any unlawful methods of struggle."[33] The motive of noninterference in Russia's domestic developments from outside only became stronger over time, and in his addresses to the Federation Council in May

2006 and April 2007, Putin put an even greater emphasis on values of sovereignty and a strong national defense.[34]

Putin's supporters interpreted his vision of Russia's identity using the idea of "Euro-Eastern" civilization, which should be differentiated from the earlier discussed "West" and "Eurasia."[35] Intellectuals and political consultants, such as Gleb Pavlovski, articulated three components of the new civilizational idea. First, the countries of Euro-East, such as Russia, Ukraine, and Kazakhstan, shared with Europe the values of the market economy and a growing middle class. Second, because of their preoccupation with domestic economic and social modernization, the Euro-Eastern area had a special need for maintaining political stability. A growing middle class and political stability should not be viewed, however, as being in conflict with the development of democratic institutions. Rather, according to Pavlovski, each nation in the region should be given the right to experiment with its own democratic model that best fits its national and international conditions. According to Pavlovski, Kazakhstan, a country that was typically viewed as lacking democracy, was also in the process of finding its own model of democratic development.[36] Third, domestic transformation of the Euro-Eastern nations requires the preservation of political sovereignty and defense from attempts by outsiders to exploit internal resources of the nation or the region. Russia—by virtue of its size and capabilities—is in a special position to greatly contribute to providing the collective goods of security, sovereignty, and stability in the region.

The Kremlin's ideologists and theorists sympathetic to the official agenda developed concepts of "sovereign democracy" and "sovereign economy,"[37] insisting on the need for Russia to protect its path of development and natural resources. "Sovereign democracy" implied a desire to defend an internally determined path of political development.[38] "Sovereign economy" indicated that the state was determined to have an upper hand in deciding the conditions through which Western companies were to participate in Russia's economic development.

In the world of growing energy prices, the emphasis shifted from providing a macroeconomic discipline and tough fiscal policies toward a desire to capitalize on Russia's reserves of natural gas and oil. In addition, Russia insisted that a more assertive foreign policy would better protect its national security. Putin's speech at the Munich Conference on Security Policy,[39] with its strong criticism of US "unilateralism" in world politics, was especially noteworthy, serving as another reminder that Russia was not about to tolerate policies that it viewed as interfering with its sovereignty and security. The speech was delivered to a European audience, which was important, seeing that Putin's supporters had long argued that insistence on sovereignty and security was not inconsistent with European values. In their perspective, by upholding the values of sovereignty, Russia was in fact preserving the European values that

Europe itself could not always sustain when confronted with political pressures from the United States.[40]

Overall, a new foreign policy consensus emerged: An assertive style of achieving the objectives of development, stability, and security suited Russia well at the moment. The new Foreign Ministry report titled "A Review of the Russian Federation's Foreign Policy," commissioned by the Kremlin and released on March 27, 2007, further elaborated on the new face of Russia's Great Power Pragmatism. It indicated an important change in Russia's thinking since the 2000 Foreign Policy Concept. The report embraced the notion of multipolarity based on "a more equitable distribution of resources for influence and economic growth,"[41] which it said laid the foundation for a more self-confident and assertive Russia. The document presented Russia as ready to actively shape international relations by challenging the actions of others, particularly the United States, if they were "unilateral" and disrespectful of international law.

Increased toughness on the United States' "unipolar" actions, as indicated by the Kremlin's numerous public statements, did not mean to promote Russia's unilateralism or a crude accumulation of power. Rather, it meant to draw attention to critical challenges of the post–Cold War world, such as terrorism, weapons of mass destruction, poverty, and political instability. It also meant to convey Russia's desire to be more integrated with the Western economy, and for these reasons, it was hardly a return to Primakov's policy of balancing the United States. Although a chance of moving in Primakov's direction remained, the policy course stayed focused on strengthening economic relations with the world, especially Europe,[42] not on building a strong security alliance with China and India or tightening the CIS under the Kremlin's leadership.

Pro-Western Critics

Russia's liberal Westernizers criticized Putin for his insistence on advancing a great power status. In their mind, there existed only two fundamental paths—pro-Western or great power nationalistic. Accustomed to viewing reality in terms of dichotomies, they followed the line of some Western analysts, insisting that if Russia is not a Western-style democracy, then it must be an empire,[43] or if it is a great power, then it must be an anti-Western one. Despite Putin's efforts to integrate with Western nations economically and in terms of addressing common security threats, Westernizers charged that the Kremlin was becoming increasingly anti-Western in various aspects of its foreign policy. They blamed Putin for his lack of commitment to institutional integration with the West, and they insisted that Russia was becoming (1) increasingly imperialist toward its neighbors, (2) unnecessarily confrontational toward the

West, and (3) obsessed with restoring great power at the expense of domestic modernization needs.

For instance, Lilia Shevtsova of the Carnegie Moscow Center expressed a typical liberal view that the Kremlin had become obsessed with insecurity and control over economic assets, as the situation was growing increasingly unpredictable. Rather than building a pluralistic political system and improving relations with the West, she argued, "the Kremlin's policies have in fact become a tool for the elite, composed of representatives of energy companies and force structures, to pursue its own interests—and this in turn has led to a worsening in Russia's relations with the West and with the new independent states, including its closest allies."[44] Energy-dependent nations, such as Ukraine, Moldova, and even the loyal ally, Belarus, were now eager to escape Russia's embrace and look for alternative international ties. Members of the European Union, too, showed their reluctance to develop economic relations with Moscow. According to Shevtsova, the Kremlin had also abandoned domestic modernization in favor of becoming a petrostate that "transforms market relations into affairs of state, and economic resources into political tools."[45] For these reasons, liberals believed, a sharp decline in oil prices would do Russia good, as it would push it toward modernization and democratization.

Table 4.4 summarizes contending views on Assertive Statism.

Civilizationists

Civilizationists showed their ambivalence toward the new, more assertive foreign policy advanced by the Kremlin. On the one hand, a greater assertiveness is what they had been advocating since the 1990s, challenging Russia to restore its hegemony in the former Soviet region and strong ties with the Soviet allies (see chapter 3). On the other hand, the assertiveness they defended served entirely different purposes and was meant to support Russia's break with the West, not an appropriate place within the West-centered economic and political structures. For instance, Russian imperialists advocated a restoration of a "fortress Russia" able to resist powerful pressures from both Western and Eastern directions.[46]

A different group, the Eurasianists, advocated a close alliance with China or Iran in order for Russia to return to its "cultural roots" and defend itself against influences from the West, seen as the most dangerous.[47] According

Table 4.4. Great Power Assertiveness (GPA): Contending Views

Civilizationists:		Westernizers:
GPA is insufficient to achieve political and cultural independence	vs.	GPA provokes confrontation with the West

to Eurasianists, if Russia had indeed fully recovered as a great power, it did not need to seek the West's approval of its actions and intentions. Russia had to create energy cartels and exclusive military alliances, and push arrogant Americans out of Eurasia once and for all. As a member in the Eurasian coalition, Russia would grow much faster, thereby creating a meaningful counterbalance to the West. Eurasianists also frequently argued against Russia's preoccupation with ethno-nationalist ideas that were perceived as prone to violence and disruption of the region's ethno-religious balance. Although Eurasianists kept a relatively low profile, their influence in the Kremlin and Russia's media space grew. Their philosophy was often shared by Putin's powerful deputy head administrator, Igor Sechin, who was in control of the state-owned oil company Rosneft, the second largest in the country, and who had numerous allies in the media and political circles. Putin was not invulnerable to the group's pressures, and its members insisted on the president's third term, hoping to continue consolidating their influence in his shadow.

All groups within the Civilizationist school of thinking agreed that Putin's foreign policy was lacking a "civilizational mission" or an "image of a future." Their criticism of the Kremlin's ideology of a sovereign state was not a criticism of sovereignty as an outdated concept—something that a number of Westernizers were likely to agree with—but an argument that sovereignty itself must not be equated with state bureaucracy and its assets. Rather, Civilizationists argued, sovereignty is a tool of advancing a national sense of purpose, and before asserting its sovereignty Russia had to know first what it was, culturally and spiritually.[48] In their assessment, the Kremlin's policies of energy independence and raising prices for Russia's neighbors and "loyal allies," such as Armenia and Belarus, were harmful to Russia's status as spiritual leader and protector of the region.[49]

Medvedev's Pragmatism and Alliances for Modernization, 2009–2011

The Official Perspective

It took Russia's leadership some time to adjust its foreign policy perspective to the new global conditions. Until the fall of 2009, the country's officials refused to fully acknowledge the debilitating effects of the global financial crisis and continued to issue generally optimistic assessments. For example, the new National Security Strategy to the year 2020 provided a long list of potential threats to the country's security, but stated in its preamble confidence in the country's ability "to reliably prevent internal and external threats to national security and to dynamically develop the Russian Federation and to turn it into a leading power in terms of technological progress, people's quality of life and influence on global processes."[50]

As time was passing, Russia had begun to draw fundamental lessons from the crisis. In September 2009, Medvedev published the article "Go, Russia!" with a highly critical assessment of the country's domestic conditions. By pointing to "a primitive economy based on raw materials and endemic corruption," "semi-Soviet social sphere, fragile democracy, harmful demographic trends, and unstable Caucasus," the new president posed a rhetorical question: "If Russia cannot relieve itself from these burdens, can it really find its own path for the future?"[51] His proposed solutions included the modernization of the economic and the political system, technological changes, and strengthening the judiciary to fight corruption. In his address to the Federation Council in November 2009, Medvedev further insisted that the effectiveness of foreign policy must be "judged by a simple criterion: Does it improve living standards in our country?"[52] Finally, in his meeting with Russia's ambassadors in July 2010, he further highlighted the need to establish "modernization alliances" with the United States and other Western nations.[53]

Official documents, too, began to reflect the new vision. The Foreign Ministry document prepared for the president in February 2010 sought to strengthen Russia's economic position. By reflecting the realities of the global financial crisis, the document builds on Medvedev's notion of "modernization alliances" and provides detailed recommendations for attracting Western investments and creating favorable conditions for Russia's technological modernization.[54] (Table 4.3 summarizes the new vision of national interest in comparison with others.)

The new vision responded to the new realities without undermining the established foreign policy consensus in Russia. Such consensus assumes that the currently "unipolar" structure of the international system diminishes Russia's global influence and that its leadership must work to revive the country's status and remain tough in defending its national interest.[55] In addition, both Putin and Medvedev advocated essentially economic means for achieving Russia's international objectives. Both sought to position their country for successful competition in the world economy, including by capitalizing on Russia's rich energy reserves. Both were pragmatically focused on exploiting opportunities outside the West and building flexible coalitions with members of BRICS, members of SCO, and other non-Western countries to promote Russia's global interests. Finally, both were concerned that political changes in the Middle East and elsewhere might further complicate the already-painful global economic recovery.

National Reception

Medvedev's foreign policy vision was met with a mixed reaction at home. The group of Westernizers emerged hopeful that the new leader would move in the pro-Western direction. The initially skeptical members of the business community became increasingly supportive of the president's priorities, which included new incentives for investment from the private sector.[56] Critical of what they viewed as an excessively centralized and energy-oriented model of development, members of the business class supported Medvedev's emphasis on modernization as essential for the country's integration with the world economy and Western institutions. In particular, the Institute of Contemporary Development (INSOR), led by the head of Russia's Union of Industrialists and Entrepreneurs Igor' Yurgens, published a number of reports and statements supportive of Medvedev's domestic and foreign policy agenda. One such report described Russia's future aspirations in the twenty-first century, presenting the country as bound to the European Union by shared values, security interests, and visions of world order and a system of treaties on strategic partnerships in military, energy, political, and cultural areas.[57] Foreign policy analysts with ties to the West also supported Medvedev and encouraged him to go further in developing Russia's pro-Western orientation. For example, director of the Moscow Carnegie Center Dmitri Trenin argued that "Russia is not a distinct civilization or a world unto itself," and therefore "Russia's noninclusion into the European security architecture is a problem, while China's absence from the US-led system of security arrangements in Asia is not."[58]

More critical was the reaction from those groups within the political class who read Medvedev's policies as excessively pro-Western and detrimental to the nation's sovereignty. Those with strong ties to the defense and security establishment shared the Statist identity and demonstrated that their foreign policy priorities differed from those with commercial and political relations to the West. By highlighting Russia's obligations to preserve global strategic balance and influence in Europe, Eurasia, and other regions, these groups defended a more muscular and assertive foreign policy, and not the one "judged by a simple criterion: Does it improve living standards in our country?"

These groups' modernization priorities also differed from those of Medvedev. Those supported by Deputy Prime Minister Igor Sechin prioritized the development of the energy and military sectors, as opposed to the diversification highlighted by Medvedev. Importantly, Putin, too, was often sympathetic to the group's ideas.[59] The Middle Eastern changes had the effect of deepening fears that similar developments could take place inside Russia and destabilize the existing political structure. As the presidential election was approaching, foreign investors, too, were divided, with some showing signs of nervousness about political stability and leaving the country's markets.[60] Outside the Kremlin, the divide widened between successful professionals in large cities and those dependent on additional state assistance for survival during the economic crisis.

Table 4.5 summarizes contending views on Alliances for Modernization.

In September 2011, Putin responded to the growing divide by making public his decision to run for the presidency. Quite possibly, the decision reflected Putin's skepticism regarding his protégé's vision and ability to act on his perspectives regarding the country's future. On March 4, 2012, after running an aggressive and populist campaign, Putin was elected in the first round with an impressive 64 percent of the vote. The Medvedev project, therefore, remained half completed. The system was again stabilized on Putin's terms. However, the cities-based middle class, which was critical of Putin's system, grew restless and increasingly ready for political protest.

The elections to Duma on December 4, 2011, had amply demonstrated the public fatigue with the system, which worked to promote the ruling party, United Russia (UR), at the expense of other parties and movements. Even the official count recognized that UR had gained 49 percent of the vote by losing 15 percent of what it had obtained in 2007. In addition, the vote was widely contested across the country, especially in large cities. The new power structure assumed the need to incorporate Medvedev's supporters, to which Putin responded by appointing Medvedev prime minister.

State-Civilization and Renewed Assertiveness, 2012–2019

The situation of cultural ambivalence amid global uncertainty has stimulated a resurgence of civilizational thinking in non-Western cultures, including Russia. Several schools or perspectives have emerged to define their civilizational status and to determine its appropriate goals and international strategy.

State-Civilization

Putin's return to the Kremlin in 2012 meant a continuation of the effort to carve out a new role for Russia in the international system by the established position of Western nations. Partly in response to US criticism, since Putin's

Table 4.5. Alliances for Modernization (AM): Contending Views

Westernizers:	Statists:
AM should move further in the pro-Western direction	vs. AM is too pro-Western and not respectful of Russia's security and energy independence

return to presidency, Russia's foreign policy has obtained an ideological justification. Beginning with his election campaign, Putin has promoted the vision
of Russia as a culturally distinct power, committed to defending particular
values and principles relative to those of the West and other civilizations. In
July 2012, in his meeting with Russia's ambassadors, he called to actively
influence international relations by relying on the tools of lobbying and soft
power.[61] In his 2012 address to the Federation Council, Putin spoke of new
demographic and moral threats that must be overcome if the nation is to "be
preserved and reproduced."[62] He further stated that "[i]n the 21st century amid
a new balance of economic, civilizational and military forces Russia must be
a sovereign and influential country . . . We must be and remain Russia."

The 2013 Foreign Policy Concept developed the ideas of transition toward
a multipolar structure of the international system and the emergence of new
threats outside of those connected to nuclear weapons. The Concept began by
stating that "[t]he capabilities of the historically established West to dominate
the global economy and politics continue to decline" and "[t]he global potential of strength and growth is dispersing and shifting eastwards, particularly
towards the Asia Pacific region."[63] The document also emphasized global
economic competition, in which different "values and development models"
would be tested and "civilization identity" would obtain a new importance. In
this context civilization was understood to be a distinct cultural entity, not a
universal phenomenon. The 2016 Foreign Policy Concept further stressed the
importance of defending the country's cultural distinctiveness in the context
of new international challenges and attempts by the United States to preserve
global dominance. The document posited Russia's "right for a tough response
to unfriendly actions including by strengthening national defense and implementing symmetric and asymmetric measures."[64]

Inside the country, Putin's priorities included strengthening Russia's traditional values and articulating a new idea uniting Russian and non-Russian
nationalities. While proposing to unite the country around Russian values,
Putin argued for recognizing ethnic Russians as "the core (*sterzhen'*) that
binds the fabric" of Russia as a culture and a state.[65] Yet he also cautioned
against "the ideas of building a Russian 'national,' mono-ethnic state" as "the
shortest path to the destruction of the Russian people and the Russian state
system."[66]

Other themes developed by the president in his speeches included those
of a strong state capable of fighting "corruption" and "flaws of the law
enforcement system" as root causes of ethnic violence. Putin also pointed
to a "deficit of spiritual values" and recommended strengthening family and
schools as "the institutions that are the carriers of traditional values." In multiple statements, he further criticized what he saw as Europe's departure from
traditional religious and family values. In his 2013 address to the Federation

Council, Putin further positioned Russia as a "conservative" power committed to traditional values and principles of sovereignty, a multipolar balance of power, and respect for cultural/civilizational diversity in international relations.[67]

In 2014 Putin elaborated on his vision of conservatism, and justified the incorporation of Crimea in terms of consolidating Russia's centuries-old "civilizational and sacred significance."[68]

Domestic Reactions

Putin's civilizational turn resonated domestically. Global uncertainty and Western pressures had stimulated a resurgence of nationalist thinking in Russia. Pro-Western elites that had argued for modernization and integration with the West grew progressively weaker, while *siloviks* increased their influence on Putin. Some of them, such as the head of the state investigative committee, Alexander Bastrykin, favorably cited China's experience in resisting the influences of the West and proposed amending the country's constitution in order to introduce a new state ideology for surviving under the West's "hybrid" war against Russia in political, economic, information, and legal areas.[69] Officials referred to the notion of Russian civilization in their speeches and public writing.[70] A number of Orthodox priests, including Patriarch Kirill, endorsed the idea of Russia's religion-centered civilizational distinctiveness. Politicians from the relatively marginal to the well-established, such as the Communist Party leader Gennadi Zyuganov, regularly spoke on issues of Russia's national interest as tied to Eurasian geopolitics and self-sufficiency. Several clubs were established to promote the idea of Russia's distinct civilizational values.

Consistent with his Statist priorities, Putin used the ideas of civilization instrumentally, as a rhetorical tool for shaping Russia's values in the Kremlin's desired direction. These ideas assisted Putin in forging a greater loyalty among elites by serving as an additional source of legitimization and loyalty to the state. The language of national unity appeals to various elite strata, in particular Statists and supporters of Russia's cultural distinctiveness. It helps to deflect the domestic appeal of ethnic nationalism, to appear supportive of a dialogue with Islam, and to remain critical of Western human rights pressures at the same time. It also strengthens the Kremlin's bond with the masses by identifying the conservative majority sympathetic with the notion of Russia's distinct values, as opposed to the more cosmopolitan and West-leaning middle class.

Table 4.6 summarizes contending views on State-Civilization.

In the meantime, Russia continued to perceive the United States as the most important power in the international system and sought to normalize

Table 4.6. State-Civilization (SC): Contending Views

Westernizers:		Ethnic Nationalists:
SC implies confrontation with the West	vs.	SC is not sufficiently sensitive to needs of ethnic Russians

relations with it following the election of Donald Trump as the US president in November 2016. Putin stressed the pragmatic nature of bilateral relations and said that both presidents were motivated by their countries' interests, and not personal "chemistry."[71] During a press conference at the BRICS summit in China in September 2017, the Russian president famously quipped that Trump "is not my bride. I am not his bride, nor his groom. We are running our governments."[72]

Putin's perspective reflected Russia's complex internal perception of international realities. The Russian foreign policy community was still divided between those favoring the decline of liberal, US-centered globalization and Russia's international assertiveness and those cautioning against the fundamental disruption of the international system. The latter pointed to the limitations of Russia's power and to uncertainty regarding the contemporary world order transition. Unlike those pushing for change, the more pragmatic voices were skeptical that such change would result in a stable and secure global order.

For example, the Council on Foreign and Defense Policy, Russia's most influential think tank, concluded in its report that "the old West will not remain the leader," yet "the rapid shift of influence toward the 'new' centers of power observable over the last fifteen years will most likely slow down, while competition for power will increase."[73] Some Russian analysts proposed to draw lessons from the late-nineteenth-century rivalry of great powers that ended in World War I.

Timofei Bordachev argued that economic interdependence and nuclear deterrence notwithstanding, great power relations are likely to descend further toward military confrontation if lessons were not learned from the period of 1871–1914 in international relations.[74] Members of this group warned that during this period of international uncertainty, Russia should be wary of overextension and develop a strategy of internal concentration and reform.[75] Still others, such as Andrei Kortunov, argued that a viable alternative to US hegemony was still a Western liberal order, because it remained the one based on rationality, openness, and institutional norms.[76]

This divide was also evident in the Russian foreign policy community's assessment of Trump. During the United States' presidential elections, those favoring the decline of a US-centered order did not hide their preference for Trump's presidency and celebrated his victory in a hope for a grand bargain with America.[77] Others either did not have a preference or supported Hillary Clinton as a more predictable candidate than the highly impulsive Trump.[78] Subsequent developments complicated the world order debate inside Russia. In part, due to domestic constraints, such as investigations of his potential "collusion" with the Kremlin, Trump was unable to increase the level of cooperation with Russia. His supporters in Moscow no longer advised the Russian leadership to reach out to Trump in order to jointly negotiate a new global order. Instead, they advised leaders to continue building foreign relations with other countries in Asia, Europe, and the Middle East, thereby strengthening bargaining power for future negotiations with the United States.[79]

PUTIN'S ASSERTIVENESS, 2005–2008

Rivalry and Limited Relations with the West

The United States

Despite preserving cooperation with the United States following 9/11, tensions between the two countries grew dramatically, surrounding at least five issues—Iran, arms sales abroad, China, energy resources, and the expansion of American military infrastructure toward Russia's borders. On Iran, Russia was against putting additional pressure on the Middle Eastern nation, favoring continued negotiations. The Kremlin was not willing to support tough sanctions for two main reasons—its own interests, and fear of US unilateralism and the potential use of force. Russia wanted to find the right balance between pressuring the top leaders of Iran and not disrupting important ties between Russian and Iranian societies, and such an approach was sure to dictate a foreign policy that would differ from those adopted by the United States, the EU, and China. Second, Russia's leadership signaled that it was not optimistic about resolving the issue in the face of the US policy to continue with threats to use force, while abstaining from initiating any nuclear reductions.[80] The Kremlin's leadership did not want to be seen as responsible for moving the issue down the path toward military confrontation, and therefore participating in what it saw as another immoral act of aggression similar to those against Yugoslavia and Iraq.

An additional area of tension was Russia's sharply growing arms sales, including to regions of potential concern to the United States in the Middle East, China, and Latin America. In 2006 the sale of arms and military hardware was up 20 percent over 2005, for a total value of $6.5 billion.[81] Although the United States protested against sales to such US-unfriendly states as Iran, Syria, and Venezuela, Russia's response was that because those weapons systems were commercially important and of a defensive nature, by selling them, the Kremlin did not violate any international agreements; they were only doing what the United States was doing by selling its own weapons worldwide, including to areas that were of concern to Russia, such as Georgia and Azerbaijan.

Related to weapons sales was the issue of China, the single largest buyer of Russia's arms. Russia–China ties were of concern to the United States for a host of reasons, first and foremost geopolitical ones. Russia–China cooperation, particularly in addressing security issues in central Asia, was viewed in light of the two nations' growing ambitions to challenge American interests. For example, the Shanghai Cooperation Organization, established by Russia, China, and central Asian states, added India and Iran as its associate members, yet refused to consider such status for the United States.

Another issue was that of Russia's energy interests in the former Soviet region and Europe. Russia's energy strategy—increasing state share in energy companies, often at the expense of Western capital; building pipelines in all geographic directions; raising energy prices for its oil-and gas-dependent neighbors; moving to control transportation networks in the former USSR; and coordinating its activities with other energy producers—generated anxiety in the American political class. Its members, such as Senator John McCain and Vice President Dick Cheney, issued multiple statements that indicated their concerns about Russia's new "imperialism" and energy "blackmail." The United States built the alternative Baku-Ceyhan pipeline and worked hard to persuade potential investors and central Asian nations to build the Trans-Caspian route under the Caspian Sea, circumventing Russia. In May 2007, Putin secured a commitment from Kazakhstan, Turkmenistan, and Uzbekistan to increase exports of central Asian energy via Russia's pipelines, which only served to heighten US concerns. President Barack Obama's administration created the position of special envoy for Eurasian energy to support the United States' energy goals in the Eurasian region.

Finally, there was the issue of expanding American military infrastructure closer to Russia's borders, which was taking place within and outside NATO. The United States continued contacts with former Soviet states, such as Azerbaijan, Georgia, and Ukraine, who expressed their intent to join NATO. At the summit in Bucharest in April 2008, Russia, assisted by France and Germany, managed to block the issuing of Membership Action Plans (MAPs) to Georgia and Ukraine, and it further expressed a strong criticism of an OSCE/NATO-based security system in Europe, arguing against new "lines of division" between nations with a common history.[82]

In addition, Russia was "extremely disappointed" that the United States planned to deploy part of a missile defense system in the Czech Republic.[83] By then, the Kremlin had already tested new missiles capable of penetrating the missile defense system (MDS) and announced plans to reequip its new single-warhead intercontinental ballistic missile (ICBM) Topol-M (SS-27) with multiple warheads.[84] In early 2009, the United States signaled its willingness to reconsider the issue of the missile defense system in exchange for Russia's cooperation on Iran, but the Kremlin reacted with a counteroffer of not delivering short-range missiles (Iskander) if the United States abandoned its MDS plans.[85]

Energy Strategy and Relations with Europe

In relations with European countries, Russia's main focus was greater integration with the EU's economy, and it has concluded a number of important agreements to this effect. Russia's largest natural gas company, Gazprom, agreed to build a direct pipeline to Germany underneath the Baltic Sea. It also negotiated an agreement with Hungary to extend Russia's Blue Stream pipeline from Turkey to Hungary via Bulgaria and Romania. Another development was a planned oil pipeline to Bulgaria and Greece through the Black Sea, with Russia owning 50.5 percent and the other two countries 24.5 percent each.[86] Russia also managed to achieve greater integration with European economies by exchanging some companies' shares. Russia also made progress in political relations with the EU nations by developing a common understanding on solving the Middle Eastern conflict and the issue of Iran's nuclear program. Many Europeans shared the Kremlin's commitment to multilateralism and negotiations, rather than sanctions and force.

Still, the strategy of integration with European countries faced important obstacles. Economically, Russia and the EU disagreed on what defines economic security. The EU perceived Russia's energy disputes with former Soviet republics as a threat to its own interests, insisting that Russia ratify the Energy Charter. The charter had been signed by Boris Yeltsin during the 1990s and stipulated access of third parties to Russia's energy pipelines. The EU also saw the issue in terms of market diversification principles and wanted to have room for changing energy partners should such an opportunity present itself. However, Russia was an energy producer, not a consumer, and it wanted to sign long-term contracts with Europeans, resisting access to its pipelines. Given the significance of high energy prices for its economic development, Russia wanted to avoid a repetition of the 1985–1986 scenario, when a sharp decline in prices had undermined the Soviet economy. In addition, Russia was wary of European efforts to negotiate separate energy agreements with Azerbaijan, Turkey, and the countries of central Asia.

Other difficult issues with Europeans included the role of the OSCE in the former Soviet region and bilateral disputes with some Eastern European nations concerning, among other things, their decision to work with the United States in deploying elements of an antimissile system on their territory.

Russia saw the OSCE as deviating from its main mission of solving security conflicts and concentrating instead on pushing a particular version of democracy in the region. The Kremlin indicated to the organization that it would withdraw its financial contribution should the practice continue. Russia also took a hard line on the antimissile defense system, claiming that in response it was considering withdrawing from the Intermediate Nuclear Missile Treaty and aiming some of its missiles at Poland and the Czech Republic, the nations that agreed to host the system on their territory. In addition, Russia refused to yield to pressures from Eastern European states to acknowledge responsibility for their post–World War II occupation or transport energy to Western European countries through their territory. Russia–EU summits in Samara (May 2007), Khanty-Mansiysk (June 2008), and Khabarovsk (May 2009) failed to secure a "strategic partnership" pact or produce any substantive agreements.

The Non-Western Direction

Opposing the "War of Civilizations" in the Middle East

Russia demonstrated a renewed activism in the Middle East and the larger Muslim world. Aside from ambitious economic projects and weapons sales to India, Iran, Syria, and Palestine, the Kremlin encouraged an international conference on Iraq accompanied by phased American withdrawal from the country. In order to address growing suspicions of Iran's intent to obtain a nuclear bomb, it also encouraged Tehran to send its spent nuclear fuel to Russia. Acting independently from the UN-US-EU-Russia quartet, the Kremlin also opened a political dialogue with leaders of Hamas, who won the Palestinian elections but continued to refuse to renounce violence against Israel or recognize its right to exist as an independent state. In addition, Russia strongly condemned the publication in Denmark and some other European nations of cartoons satirizing the Prophet Muhammad as an "inadmissible" provocation against Muslims.

Russia's Middle East policies had roots in both global and domestic developments. Globally, the Kremlin was reevaluating its relations with the United States. Many of Russia's post–September 11, 2001, expectations had not materialized. Military cooperation in central Asia and Afghanistan had been replaced with rivalry over controlling security space and energy resources. Instead of rebuilding Afghanistan, the United States had launched a war in Iraq. The Kremlin no longer viewed Russia–US cooperation in central Asia and the Middle East as primarily beneficial, and it thought the US presence there invited terrorism rather than eradicated it. Russia's perception of the US role in the region as destructive corresponded with perceptions shared by many Muslims across the world, who viewed the US "war on terror" as a war on them.

For Russia's domestic well-being, the implications of the "war of civilizations" were fundamental. For a country with twenty million to twenty-five million Muslims, involvement in such a war would mean inviting fire to its own home. Russia's domestic intercultural ties were far from balanced. A growing influence of radical Islamist ideologies, rising immigration from Muslim ex-Soviet republics, and the poorly conceived actions of some of Russia's local authorities in failing to build ties with Muslims created a politically explosive environment. Although the situation in Chechnya was much more stable, Islamic radicals were spreading violence and extremist ideology across the larger Northern Caucasus.

Although Russia's Eastern initiatives were not anti-Western, they signaled that the "war of civilizations" between Western nations and Islam was intensifying, as well as an understanding that Russia had no business participating in that war. Just as it was a tragic mistake to get involved in World War I in 1914, Russia felt it would be tragic to have a fully hardened Western-Islamic front today and to see Russia joining it. Russia's willingness to engage Iran and Hamas was an effort to compensate for blunders of Western policies in the region, such as calls to boycott elections in Iran or clumsy attempts to pressure Palestinian voters, and to find a way out of a developing intercivilizational confrontation.

Implicitly, the new Kremlin initiatives also fully recognized that the threat of Islamic radicalism in Russia could not be successfully confronted without reaching out to the Muslim world. The notion of a dialogue with the Muslim world was strongly endorsed by Russia's political class. Russia called for an "intercivilizational alliance" and "compromise" involving countries in the Middle East. For example, in March 2008 President Putin sent a message to the Organization of the Islamic Conference meeting in Senegal in which he said that "deeper relations of friendship and cooperation with the Islamic world are Russia's strategic course" and that "we share concerns about the danger of the world splitting along religious and civilizational lines."[87]

Modernization and Security in Asia

Although Russia saw itself as a country of European identity, it sought to take advantage of its strategic proximity to Asia for the purpose of modernizing the economy. China and the Asia-Pacific region were important because of their potential for becoming a gateway for Russia's entrance into the global economy. With half of the population and one-fifth of global trade, the region was viewed by many as a success story of modernization/globalization. Rich in natural resources, Russia was poised to contribute to satisfying the region's growing demand for energy and modernizing its own domestic economy along the way. In addition, the region faced some long-standing security challenges, such as the nuclear ambitions of North Korea and China's relations with Taiwan.

Russia's first interest was in increasing its role in solving vital security issues in East Asia. For years, Russia's officials had argued for the development of a multilateral security framework both within and outside the region. The Kremlin insisted that security problems could only be solved through systematic coordination of state efforts, and not through the use of force by ad hoc coalitions. For instance, it developed the Shanghai Cooperation Organization (SCO) with China and four central Asian states, to address threats posed by terrorism and a security vacuum in the area. In East Asia, Moscow advocated multilateral solutions to the nuclear crisis with North Korea, and contributed considerably to creating the six-party format for dealing with the crisis.

Russia's most important priority remained economic modernization, and that required determination to win markets in arms and energy. China and India remained Russia's largest buyers, purchasing more than 90 percent of Russia's annual arms exports. Russia viewed itself as connected with Asia in an economically open region, in which Russia occupies an appropriately important role and reaps considerable economic, as well as political, benefits. Although its energy markets remained primarily in Europe and accounted for about 50 percent of its foreign trade, Russia continued to aggressively promote itself as an energy pipeline hub connecting Asia, Europe, and North America.

Russia's other priorities in the region include nuclear security and political stability. Seeking a non-nuclear status for North Korea, Moscow has worked to develop its ties with North Korea, and it has stayed engaged with Pyongyang during nuclear crises. Close relationships with North Korea helped Russia to increase its participation in security negotiations, and it was ultimately Pyongyang that demanded that Moscow join the six-party format. It was critical for Russia that changes in the region, such as reunification of the two Koreas, were orderly and not destabilizing in nature. On several occasions, Putin extended his support for unification of the two Koreas if it took place in an orderly fashion and on the basis of inter-Korean dialogue. Russian analysts considered a unified Korea a potential strategic partner, provided that the shape of unification was not overly determined by the United States. For these reasons, Russia has insisted on preserving special and evenhanded relations with both Koreas.

Assertiveness in Eurasia

The same commitment to economic development, political stability, and security delivered in assertive style was visible in Russia's foreign policy toward the former Soviet world.

"No More Energy Subsidies"

Consistent with the new vision, Russia moved to strengthen its energy position in world markets. Although many interpreted Gazprom's energy dispute with Ukraine in December 2005 as an attempt by the Kremlin to punish the new leadership of Ukraine for the Orange Revolution, the dispute also aimed to economically normalize relations with Kyiv by moving in the direction of establishing market-based prices for energy supplies. Moscow worked to reduce the amount of subsidies to the Ukrainian economy, and Kyiv, understandably, resisted the effort. Russia's decision reflected the Kremlin's long-articulated pragmatic modernization approach in the former Soviet region.

Russia's decision also reflected a policy adjustment in the post-Soviet world following the color revolutions. As Ukraine, Georgia, and Moldova moved to challenge Moscow by questioning the Russia-controlled CIS, the Kremlin was determined to secure economic gains in the region. As explained by Putin, "Over the last fifteen years Russia subsidized the Ukrainian economy by a sum that amounted to $3 to 5 billion each year," and "each year we raised the issue of whether we should change to the European regime for determining prices."[88] The fact that Russia's close allies in the region, such as Armenia and Belarus, were also presented with the same deal of tripled gas prices further indicated that the Kremlin's energy strategy reflected imperatives of economic modernization. In an energy dispute with Belarus during late 2006–early 2007, Russia's Gazprom canceled a preferential price, doubling it to $100 per 1,000 cubic meters and acquiring a 50 percent stake in the Belarusian state gas pipeline company, Beltransgaz. Russia imposed a new export duty on oil, increasing domestic revenue and reducing Belarus's chances of re-exporting Russian oil. The net gain from both deals for Russia, according to some calculations, amounted to around $4 billion, or over 2 percent of the overall budget.[89]

Importantly, the Kremlin also renegotiated price arrangements with the oil-and gas-rich Turkmenistan and Kazakhstan, leaving them with less incentive to sell to Europe and China.[90] With attractive prices and an energy transportation system in place, the Caspian states would be less likely to construct new pipelines that are favored by non-Russian nations. In addition, the autocratic regimes in central Asia appreciate that Russia does not aim to "democratize" them.

Russia's energy policy was pursued against objections from various directions. Western countries expressed concerns over the Kremlin's use of energy as a "political weapon" against its neighbors. Belarusian president Aleksandr Lukashenko accused Moscow of trying to incorporate his country into Russia.[91] At home, Russia's Civilizationists attacked Putin's policies as betraying the notion of "Slavic unity" and pushing Belarus into the arms of the "hostile" West.[92] Yet the Kremlin remained firm, insisting that its policies of ending energy subsidies were perfectly legitimate and indeed necessary for Russia to join the WTO and remain a reliable energy supplier to European markets. If anything, the story reaffirmed that Russia remained pragmatically focused on selfish considerations of national recovery, not empire.

In Search of Stability and Security

As Russia's economic recovery required preservation of the international status quo, the Kremlin sought to insulate the region from what it saw as politically destabilizing activities. It took different approaches to different parts of the region. In central Asia, the Kremlin chose to work independently from the West and in partnership with China to address a challenge of destabilization from local and foreign Islamic radicals. This was a departure from the original policy of working with the West and allowing US and NATO troops' presence in the central Asian states in order to launch a counterterrorist operation in Afghanistan. In Ukraine, Russia signaled a desire to move beyond the Orange Revolution and work with a broad range of political forces in the country.[93] In Georgia, the Kremlin took a hard-line approach, imposing sanctions, strengthening ties with separatist territories, and practicing containment toward Tbilisi. After President Mikhail Saakashvili's arrests of four of Russia's intelligence officers in September 2006, Moscow reacted with a heavy package of economic and political sanctions that stayed in place even after the officers had returned to Russia.

Even this hard-line approach did not work, and on August 8, 2008, Georgia attacked the South Ossetian capital of Tskhinvali in an attempt to restore control over the rebellious province. Georgian troops killed ten Russian peacekeepers and, by attacking the city with heavy artillery, Georgia inflicted heavy civilian casualties on South Ossetia. Russia responded with overwhelming force that included several armored battalions, airpower, and marines, defeating and destroying much of the Georgian military. Russia also recognized the independence of South Ossetia and Abkhazia and imposed areas of security control throughout Georgia. Despite Saakashvili's efforts to present his offensive as a response to Russia's aggression, sources as diverse as intelligence agencies, human rights organizations, the Georgian exiled leader Irakli Okruashvili, and various government analysts agreed that the aggression came from Tbilisi, not Moscow.[94]

Much of Russia's reaction can be explained by its perception of threat stemming from the expansion of NATO. The West's geopolitical advances into what Russia has traditionally viewed as its sphere of interests and the desire expressed by the postrevolutionary Georgia and Ukraine to join NATO exacerbated Russia's sense of vulnerability and isolation by the West. Following the NATO summit in Bucharest, Russia reiterated that it would do everything in its power to prevent expansion of the alliance and extension of its membership to Georgia and Ukraine.[95] The so-called frozen conflicts were merely leverage in the Kremlin's hands, and until the war in the Caucasus in August 2008, the Kremlin had planned to keep them frozen until NATO bore out its plans to continue its march to the East.

In the aftermath of the summit, to signal its dissatisfaction to Georgia, the Kremlin extended additional assistance to the secessionist South Ossetia and Abkhazia.[96] Some Russian analysts argued that if membership in NATO was most important to Georgia, then Tbilisi would be likely to obtain it at the cost of its territorial integrity.[97] South Ossetia and Abkhazia continued to oppose Georgia's membership in the Western alliance and to press for integrating with Russia. Such integration came a few steps closer after the United States' recognition of the independence of Kosovo and the Kremlin's recognition of South Ossetia and Abkhazia's independence in the wake of the Caucasus crisis. At the same time, Moscow expedited negotiations with Moldova over incorporation of Transdniestr, provided that Kishinev stayed a neutral state and did not join NATO.[98] Moscow was likely signaling that the "no NATO membership in exchange for territorial integrity" deal might still be possible with other republics outside Georgia, such as Ukraine and Azerbaijan.

Assessment and Challenges

The shift toward foreign policy assertiveness assisted Russia in defending its objectives. Apart from the conflict with Georgia, Russia did not experience any major threats to its security, from either terrorist attacks or elsewhere. While pressing for preserving and strengthening security ties with Western countries, Russia managed to sustain good relations with Iran and other Middle Eastern nations. The latter often had complicated relationships with the United States and the EU, and, no less importantly, had the potential to undermine Russia's security through funding religious extremist activities. The Kremlin's effort to reach out to the Muslim world by initiating contacts with its multilateral organizations and developing bilateral ties served Russia well. The overall situation improved in Chechnya, although terrorism in the

Caucasus remained an important issue. In the former USSR, Russia strengthened its security standing by maintaining evenhanded relations with other states in central Asia and the Caucasus. The exception was Georgia, against which the Kremlin applied sanctions and then military force.

Russia's foreign policy was also relatively successful in meeting the objective of economic development. The Kremlin's strategy of capitalizing on the country's energy reserves added revenue without alienating potential foreign investors. Russia's drastic decisions to cut energy supplies for some of its neighbors, as well as some other components of its energy strategy, raised concerns among Western countries and former Soviet republics, but on balance did not do any irreparable damage. More importantly, Russians themselves were strongly behind the course of foreign policy assertiveness. For example, in March 2007, 61 percent of respondents evaluated the Kremlin's international actions as well considered and well balanced. About 40 percent felt that another Cold War with the West was possible, while 48 percent did not think so.[99] Sixteen percent felt that the foreign policy course was too pro-Western for their taste, relative to only 8 percent who believed it was hard-line and uncompromising with regard to the West.[100]

Table 4.7 summarizes the record of Great Power Assertiveness.

Russia's challenge was to preserve the international status quo in order to continue with the vital program of domestic modernization. The country is strong in its growing international presence and energy power, yet it remains weak in such critical respects as population health, demographic dynamics, and the size of its middle class. Indicators of poverty, HIV infection, and demographic crisis were also alarming. Major economic disturbances, such as a world economic recession or a sharp decline in oil prices, are bound to complicate the process. The international financial crisis had made itself felt in Russia and continued to negatively affect its economic development.

Another danger was related to further destabilization of the Middle East and continued expansion of the Western military presence to Russia's borders. The withdrawal of US troops from Iraq without leaving an adequate security framework in place or a military confrontation with Iran would be sure to create a large flow of refugees, in which case the region would be further destabilized. The effects of such destabilization would likely be felt in the Caucasus and central Asia, and therefore, at least indirectly, in Russia. No less dangerous was NATO's continued desire to expand and American

Table 4.7. The Record of Great Power Assertiveness

Security	Remaining problems with terrorism in the Caucasus
Welfare	Improved economic and social standards
Autonomy	Increased ability to influence international affairs
Identity	Continued efforts to bridge Westernist and Statist values

attempts to deliver elements of an antimissile defense system in close proximity to Russia. These kinds of international disturbances provided ammunition to those inside Russia's political class who wanted to push foreign policy in a radically anti-Western direction.

MEDVEDEV'S PRAGMATISM, 2009–2011

"Reset" with the West

Improved Relations with the United States

Russia's ties with the United States began to improve soon after Washington's proclaimed desire to "reset" relations with Moscow and President Obama's trip to Russia in July 2009. The two sides were now cooperating in several areas. They signed and ultimately ratified the new START by replacing the old treaty of 1991. Signed in Prague on April 8, 2010, the new agreement further limited the number of strategic nuclear missiles to the level of 1,500, renewed a verification mechanism, and banned the deployment of strategic weapons outside the national territories.

Russia also cooperated with Western nations on Iran. The United States had earlier supported Russia's proposal to reprocess spent nuclear fuel outside Iran as a way for the country to continue with its nuclear program for peaceful purposes. However, Tehran refused to go along with the Russian proposal, and Moscow opted to support the United Nations' resolution on Iran. In addition, US–Russia relations notably improved in the area of stabilizing Afghanistan. Russia agreed to US military overflights and overland transportation of nonmilitary cargo. The two countries jointly raided several opium laboratories in Afghanistan, destroying more than two thousand pounds of heroin.[101] In March 2012, the Kremlin went so far as approving NATO use of an airport in Ulyanovsk as a transit point for moving soldiers and cargo to and from Afghanistan.[102]

Finally, Russia renewed a strong interest in developing economic relations with the United States. Medvedev stressed the importance of investments in the information technology sector. Russia also completed negotiations over its membership in the World Trade Organization—the end of the road that began in 1993. In addition, Russia's state oil company, Rosneft, struck a deal with ExxonMobil to explore and develop Russia's Arctic Basin,[103] the success of which depended on Moscow's commitment and approval by the US Congress.

The progress in relations with the United States did not overshadow a number of unresolved issues between the two countries. The Kremlin remained critical of the US proposal to develop an MDS jointly with the Europeans.

Russia was worried about being isolated from Western security developments
and viewed as potentially threatening the expansion of American military
infrastructure closer to Russia's borders, which had been taking place within
and outside NATO. Even after Obama's election, the United States continued
to develop programs of military cooperation with the former Soviet states
and remained supportive of their bids for NATO membership.[104] Russia
maintained its right to protect its interests in Georgia and elsewhere in the
former Soviet region, whereas the United States continued to demand that
the Kremlin withdraw its military from Northern Ossetia, Abkhazia, and
Moldova. The two sides also competed, rather than cooperated, on energy
transportation issues. As Russia worked to increase the exports of central
Asian energy via Russia's pipelines, the United States tried to persuade potential investors and former Soviet nations to build alternative transportation
routes, such as the trans-Caspian route under the Caspian Sea.

Outside Europe and Eurasia, Russia remained concerned about the United
States' foreign policy interventions, which became evident from Moscow's
decision to abstain from the UN Security Council (UNSC) resolution that
authorized air strikes against Libya.[105] The tensions between Russia and
Western nations became especially acute over a growing crisis in Syria. By
spring 2012, a military confrontation within the country between government
and opposition turned into a civil war, claiming many thousands of civilian
lives. The list of unresolved issues between the two countries also included
Russia's arms sales to non-Western countries, the Soviet-era Jackson-Vanik
amendment that blocked development of bilateral economic ties, and human
rights. In particular, against objections from the Russian government, the US
Congress considered a bill that would impose visa bans and asset freezes on
human rights violators in Russia. The bill was named after Russian accountant Sergei Magnitsky, who was defending a foreign firm but was arrested and
died while in detention.[106]

Security Relations with Europe

The attempts to "reset" US–Russia ties assisted the development of Russian
ties with European countries. Speaking in Berlin in June 2008, Russia's
president, Dmitri Medvedev, articulated a broad perspective on Europe
"from Vancouver to Vladivostok" and proposed a new all-European treaty
to establish a new security architecture by moving beyond NATO expansion
and the conflict over Kosovo.[107] He cited the need to strengthen international
law and urged moving beyond Atlanticism by developing an equal partnership between the European Union, the United States, and Russia. Medvedev
further suggested that, if the West and Russia were able to sign the Helsinki
Act of the Conference on Security and Cooperation in Europe in 1975, then

they would be in an even better position to negotiate a new security treaty after the end of the Cold War.

Moscow's intervention in Georgia's conflict with South Ossetia in August 2008 created new tensions in Russia–West relations, yet Medvedev saw the conflict as an opportunity to strengthen his case. According to him, the fact that neither NATO nor the OSCE was able to prevent the military confrontation indicated the need for an improved security framework in Europe. The two organizations, Medvedev argued, were important yet insufficient for filling the existing security vacuum. Comparing the significance of the Caucasus conflict to Russia to that of September 11, 2001, to the United States, Russia's president insisted that "We simply have to create a new security system, otherwise there will be no guarantees that someone like Saakashvili could not . . . try something similar to what happened in August."[108] In November 2009, Russia published its proposal for a new security treaty by pledging to legally restrict its unilateral use of force in exchange for European nations and the United States doing the same. The Kremlin presented the draft as the document that would "finally do away with the legacy of the Cold War."[109]

Still, the development of relations with European countries faced important obstacles. Despite sufficient backing at home, the idea of a new security pact did not receive the outside support Russia was looking for. Although some Western nations welcomed Russia's efforts to reach out to Europe, they offered only general support and remained wary of Medvedev's initiative. Germany and France responded by proposing to establish the EU-Russia Political and Security Committee as an institution to consult on strategic issues on the continent.[110] They agreed with the need to address the vacuum of European security, but did not find Russia's proposal satisfactory. NATO secretary-general Anders Fogh Rasmussen said he saw no need for the new legally binding security treaty "because we do have a framework already."[111] The United States was equally dismissive. US secretary of state Hillary Clinton found a new European treaty unnecessary—the position that Medvedev described as reflecting "a certain envy" among "our American partners."[112] Washington expressed full confidence in the NATO-centered security system in Europe and proposed that any revisions should be discussed in the OSCE context.[113] Finally, Eastern European nations were concerned that Russia's initiative was about recognizing Russia's sphere of interests and giving Moscow a veto over NATO's international operations. They shared the perspective of Georgia and viewed Russia as the most important threat to their security.[114] At the end of 2010 Medvedev expressed disappointment with the lack of international support and acknowledged that two and a half years of discussions had not led to any breakthrough. Citing the power of stereotypes, he said his initiative may have appeared ahead of its time and would have to wait before being considered in the future.[115]

Progress was also slow regarding Western plans for an MDS in Europe and the handling of the Middle Eastern crisis. Moscow threatened to develop new intercontinental ballistic missiles that could spark a new arms race. The Kremlin maintained that NATO's missile defense plans could undermine Russia's security as soon as 2020, when the system's fourth phase would be deployed. Russia also took issue with the West going after regime change and Libya's Muammar Gaddafi personally. Although Moscow had originally not vetoed the UNSC resolution on the use of force against him, it later criticized the implementation of the resolution and then vetoed a much weaker resolution on Syria. The problem lay in the divergent perception of interests by Russia and the West. Russia, through its initiatives—from merging the two missile defense systems to negotiating a new pan-European security treaty—demonstrated a desire to have strong cooperative relationships, whereas Western nations wanted more favors from Moscow—from allowing transit routes to Afghanistan to pressuring Iran into nuclear compliance and negotiating a political exit for Middle Eastern leaders.

China and the Middle East

Russia improved its standing in the non-Western world by participating in international coalitions, such as the SCO and BRIC (Brazil, Russia, India, and China), and fostering bilateral ties. Relations with China, Russia's largest neighbor, obtained a strategic dimension in the areas of commerce and regional security, and the two demonstrated an increased convergence in perceiving global priorities and proposing solutions to existing issues in world politics.

Turning to the Asia-Pacific Region

Considerations of economic modernization and security reinforced Russia's determination to develop ties with Asia and the Asia-Pacific region. In particular, the Asian and Pacific Economic Council (APEC) organization combines twenty-one countries and accounts for 55 percent of global GDP and 44 percent of global trade.[116] During the 2000s, Russia's trade share in that region increased from 16 percent to 24 percent—largely due to China—and continued to grow.[117] The region was also important in terms of meeting Russia's security interests in Siberia, East Asia, and the Korean peninsula.

Russian officials made clear their priority in building strong ties with the region. Medvedev chose China and central Asia as the first regions to visit. After being elected president, Putin visited China, among several other states. By September 2012, he had already hosted an APEC summit in Vladivostok, asserting Russia's status as "an intrinsic part of the Asia-Pacific region"[118] and offering new policies to strengthen his country's Pacific identity. Rather than viewing this priority as "a reorientation from West to East," the Kremlin saw it in terms of Russia's ability to develop a global capacity by strengthening relations with Asia. Russia's proposal to build a new Eurasian Union among the CIS states also fit this global design to become influential in connecting Europe and Asia. In Putin's words, the idea was to "become a bridge between the European Union and the Asia-Pacific region" by pursuing "closer integration of economic models, regulation and technical standards among the EU, APEC and the Eurasian Economic Union," which "would offer businesses the ability to operate seamlessly across a vast area."[119]

To facilitate such developments in Asia, Putin emphasized Russia's energy and transit potential. Given that Asia is resources-poor, Russia has much to offer and has worked toward this goal. For instance, in September 2010, Russia completed an oil pipeline connecting to northeastern China and also planned two gas pipelines.[120] Although Russia's sales of weapons and energy to China decreased, the two nations' economic and political interests were compatible, and it was certain their cooperation would continue to grow.

Russia also stressed the development of transportation logistics. One initiative includes unification of the Trans-Siberian and Trans-Korean railways, which Russia also views as a contribution to the security of the Korean Peninsula. The Kremlin has worked to promote trilateral cooperation with South Korea and North Korea. In August 2011, Moscow hosted a trip by North Korea's leader Kim Jong-il. Kim and then president Medvedev agreed to create a bilateral commission to investigate the possibility of constructing a trans-Korean pipeline.[121] Another logistical initiative is to utilize the Northern route to transport goods from Asia to Europe via the Arctic. The route is much shorter than via the Suez channel, although the route is open only four months per year.

In attempting to strengthen ties with the Asia-Pacific region, Russia is mainly motivated by considerations of developing Siberia and East Asia. After the Soviet disintegration, these parts of Russia became severely depressed, especially when compared with China's booming growth. With declining population and deteriorating infrastructure in Siberia and East Asia, Russia needs to secure foreign investments, especially from China, South Korea, and Japan. This explains why the Kremlin has not supported the United States' proposal to build a trans-Pacific free-trade zone. Russia views the proposed Trans-Pacific Partnership as potentially diverting trade and investments from Siberia and East Asia, should China choose to join it and move outside of APEC.[122]

Finally, in all economic initiatives, Russia is concerned for its sovereignty and security, especially in light of China's rise. By facilitating trans-Korean integration and investments in the East Asian region, Russia seeks to increase its cumulative power to offset China's growing influences. In preparation for the summit in Vladivostok, the Russian government invested around $9 billion in the city's infrastructure, with private investors contributing an additional $13 billion. Vladivostok is the home port of Russia's Pacific Fleet, which also suffered from the post-Soviet decline and needs new investments.[123] Moscow's decision to order heavy investments in the disputed Kuril Islands' defense and to send two new warships to patrol access to the Pacific Ocean may also reflect Russia's desire to strengthen its naval presence in the region.

Relations with the Middle East

In the Middle East, Russia has worked to develop relations across the region and sustain its influence on Iran, and it has considerably expanded ties with Turkey, Israel, and Afghanistan. Although Moscow failed to persuade Tehran to send its spent nuclear fuel to Russia, the Kremlin continued a dialogue with Iranian leaders. Russia sought to restrain Western leaders from military intervention or imposing additional sanctions on Iran, while welcoming negotiations. In Afghanistan, Russia attempted to introduce its own policy by appointing a presidential special representative for the country, fostering ties with its official leadership and establishing separate lines of communication to the Taliban leadership.[124]

Despite Russia's traditionally strong ties with Syria, Palestine, and other Arab states, the Kremlin also managed to deepen its relations with Israel. For example, the two sides signed the $100 million deal for Israel to provide Russia with unmanned aerial vehicles, thereby enabling Russian security forces to tighten surveillance over Georgia.[125] In addition, Turkey has emerged as especially important to Russia, with the two converging on perceptions of world order, developing ambitious energy plans, and cooperating on improving security in the Black Sea area. In May 2010, the two countries signed an agreement to carry Russian oil from the Black Sea to the Mediterranean. The two nations were also connected by important gas projects, such as a pipeline from Russia to Greece, Italy, and Israel, and from Russia to Southern Europe—both through Turkey or the Turkish sector of the Black Sea waters.[126]

Finally, the pragmatic orientation of Russia's leadership assisted it in making adjustments to the postrevolutionary realities in the Middle East. For example, the Kremlin sought to distance itself from the old leaders, such as Libya's Muammar Gaddafi, by not vetoing the UNSC resolution on the use of force against him.[127] At the same time, Russia was worried about the potential strengthening of extremist forces in the Middle East following revolutions in the region. Russia's officials continued to voice concern about the possible radicalization of Middle Eastern states. Acting jointly with China, Russia vetoed the United States and Europe–sponsored UNSC resolutions regarding Syria. Fearful that such resolutions would lead to a military intervention and regime change in Syria, as had happened in Libya, the Kremlin instead pushed for negotiations between Bashar al-Assad and the military opposition.

Russia's Middle East activism had roots in both global and domestic developments. Globally, the Kremlin was seeking to increase political influence and commercial gains. Domestically, Russia remained concerned about the potential reverberations of the Middle Eastern destabilization. A growing influence of radical Islamist ideologies, rising immigration from Muslim ex-Soviet republics, and insufficient state policy on the Northern Caucasus economic and political integration created an explosive environment. During 2010–2012, Russia was confronted with terrorist violence. Previously contained in Chechnya, terrorism spread throughout other parts of the region—Dagestan, Ingushetia, Kabardino-Balkaria, and North Ossetia. Since the October 2002 seizure of a Moscow movie theater, Chechen jihadists have worked to stage violent actions in Russia's capital. On March 29, 2010, two female suicide bombers trained by the Caucasus-centered Doku Umarov detonated their explosives inside a Metro train, killing 40 people and injuring many more. Another major attack came in March 2011, when a bomb detonated in the largest Moscow airport, Domodedovo, killing 36 and injuring 180 people. The Kremlin responded by outlining a new antiterrorism strategy for the region,[128] but the violence was far from curtailed. In August 2012, a female suicide bomber killed a leading moderate Muslim cleric in Dagestan, Sheikh Said Atsayev, who had been engaged in negotiations with radical Islamists.[129]

"Privileged Interests" in Eurasia

"Privileged Interests" and Regional Aspirations

In the former Soviet region Russia insisted on its own sphere of influence. The regional component of Russia's policy was supposed to reinforce the global one, moving Russia on the path toward becoming an independent center of power and influence in the world. Russia's foreign policy consensus assumed the importance of domination in the region by remaining "pragmatic" and avoiding the use of brute force in achieving its objectives. Although the Kremlin was unapologetic about using force against Georgia and recognizing the independence of South Ossetia and Abkhazia in August 2008, both Putin and Medvedev viewed regional dominance in terms of soft power, rather than direct control over Russia's neighbors' domestic and international priorities. They assumed that Russia had sufficient economic, diplomatic, institutional, and cultural capacity to regionally negotiate the preferred international postures of the former Soviet states. However, when soft power failed, the Kremlin was unapologetic about using force in Georgia and recognizing the independence of South Ossetia and Abkhazia in August 2008.

Medvedev's concept of "privileged interests" served to reinforce this thinking after the war with Georgia. Russia sought to downplay the use of force in the Caucasus and obtain international recognition of its regional vision. Immediately following the war, the president set out five principles in conducting foreign relations: the primacy of international law; multipolarity as a basis of global stability; nonconfrontational relations and active development of ties with Europe, the United States, and other nations; protection of Russia's citizens and business needs; and special ties with close neighbors.[130] It is the fifth principle that Medvedev articulated using the term "privileged interests." Following Russia's earlier expressed position,[131] the president sought to clarify that his country did not want an area of geopolitically exclusive influence. Rather, Medvedev was referring to a common historical experience, and spoke of "countries with which we have been living side by side for decades, centuries, now, and with which we share the same roots . . . countries where Russian is spoken, and that have a similar economic system and share much in terms of culture."[132]

Following the idea of strengthening Russia's ties with its neighbors, Putin proposed to build a new Eurasian Union among the CIS states.[133] Similar to Medvedev, Putin emphasized an open nature of the proposed union and laid out economic incentives for joining it, including increase in trade, common modernization projects, and improved standards of living.

Aiming at Low-Cost Political Stabilization

Following the outlined vision, Russia sought to strengthen its influence in the former Soviet region by relying on diplomatic, economic, and cultural tools. By capitalizing on high oil prices, it strengthened its presence in neighboring economies and contributed to reversing the color revolutions in Ukraine and Kyrgyzstan, which the Kremlin viewed as dangerous for Russia and destabilizing for the larger region. In both countries, anti-Kremlin governments were replaced with those in favor of stronger ties with Russia. Following a change in government, Russia negotiated new terms for its political influence. In Ukraine, the two sides agreed in April 2010 to extend the lease on Russia's Black Sea Fleet for twenty-five more years in exchange for the reduction of gas prices by 30 percent.[134] In 2011, Russia invited Ukraine to join the Customs Union, promising another major discount for gas prices.[135] The purpose of the latter was to close NATO's door for Ukraine and to keep it within the area of Russia's economic influence. The Customs Union was created in

2010 and includes Russia, Belarus, and Kazakhstan. In Kyrgyzstan, following the revolution that the Kremlin had helped to foment,[136] Russia sought to bring to power a pro-Russian coalition and establish a political system with a strong central authority.[137] In early November, the pro-Russian candidate, Almazbek Atambayev, was elected the new president in the first round of elections. Even in Georgia, the Kremlin was now finding a way to influence events without relying on force by developing ties with Georgian opposition to President Mikhail Saakashvili.[138]

The Kremlin also wanted to consolidate its military presence in the region. In Kyrgyzstan, Russia sought to create a new antiterrorism center under CSTO auspices in the southern part of the country.[139] In Tajikistan, Moscow negotiated redeployment of six thousand troops to patrol the border with Afghanistan in exchange for a promise to rearm the Tajik army. Finally, the Russia-controlled CSTO, which also includes Armenia, Belarus, Uzbekistan, Tajikistan, Kazakhstan, and Kyrgyzstan, amended its mission by pledging to defend its members from internal "unconstitutional disturbances." In an apparent response to Arab-like uprisings, the CSTO also conducted an ambitious military exercise by imitating the defeat of an attempted coup in Tajikistan.

Russia could not have preserved its influence in the region without its attempts to act globally and win at least some support for its policies from established powers in the West and rising non-Western powers. For example, the Kremlin would not have been as successful in its offensive against the United States' "unilateralism" were it not for France and Germany's tacit support, which had resulted from the three countries' opposition to the invasion of Iraq. Were the two Western European states to have supported NATO membership for Ukraine and Georgia, it would have taken longer for the color revolutions to run out of steam. In addition, Russia probably could not have been as successful in its war against Georgia were China to have taken a strong critical stance toward it. Although Beijing refused to endorse Russia's recognition of Abkhazia and South Ossetia's independence, the Chinese informally supported Russia during the crisis in the Caucasus, and the issue has not complicated the two nations' relations.[140]

The problem for Russia is that the non-Russian states in the region often perceive its policies as excessively selfish and its influence as hegemonic. For example, in order to balance against Russia's power, central Asian states increasingly seek to strengthen their ties with China and the United States. In June 2012, Uzbekistan went so far as to withdraw its membership in the CSTO—in part to signal its dissatisfaction with Russia. The perception of Russia as a hegemonic power partly explains why its increased influence has not translated into stability in the region. Evidence of instability included the tense atmosphere in the Caucasus following the war with Georgia, renewed terrorist attacks, the persistent failure of Western forces to stabilize Afghanistan, the inability of central Asian rulers to reign in local clans and drug lords, and the weakness of legitimately elected bodies of power in Moldova and Ukraine.

Kyrgyzstan was another example of instability in the region. When the second violent round of power struggles occurred in Kyrgyzstan in June 2010, the new interim government in Bishkek failed to gain control over the country, and the southern part—a stronghold of the ousted president Kurmanbek Bakiev—became de facto independent.[141] Yet the crisis elicited little serious response from key powers or international organizations in the region. Despite its perception as a hegemonic power, Russia was not eager to act single-handedly to stabilize and pacify the region. At best, the Kremlin wanted to defend its core interests in regional settings and address its economic interests.

Maximizing Economic Opportunities

Having reversed the color revolutions in Eurasia, Russia sought to gain economically from them. Not in the position to become the regional center, Russia instead emphasized "pragmatic" bilateral ties and issue-specific multilateral contacts. Energy remained its main card. In addition to gaining control over the most valuable assets abroad and increasing Russian shares in foreign companies, the Kremlin's objective was to strengthen its position in world markets.

In Ukraine, Russia was primarily interested in gaining control over energy infrastructure. In order to overcome the dependence on Ukrainian transit in transporting natural gas to European markets, the Kremlin developed a dual-track approach. It worked with Turkey and Southern European states in order to obtain their permission to build the Southern pipeline that would deliver Russian energy to Europe via the Black Sea by circumventing Ukraine. On the other hand, Moscow continued to pressure Kyiv to agree to a joint ownership of Naftogaz,[142] Ukraine's state-controlled gas company. The Kremlin wanted to avoid additional energy disputes with Ukraine similar to those in 2005 and 2006 by purchasing controlling stakes in Naftogaz. As articulated by Konstantin Kosachyev, chairman of the International Affairs Committee of the State Duma, the idea was for Ukraine and Russia to "become a single transit space between Europe and China, between European and Asian markets."[143] In 2011 Russia invited Ukraine to join the Customs Union, promising another major discount on gas prices. The Customs Union was created in 2010 and includes Russia, Belarus, and Kazakhstan. Ukrainian leaders declined the Customs Union offer, but indicated willingness to accommodate Russia in strengthening its presence in the Ukrainian economy.

In central Asia and the Caucasus, Russia sought to obtain valuable assets and renegotiate price arrangements with the oil-and gas-rich states, such as Azerbaijan, Turkmenistan, and Kazakhstan, leaving them with less incentive to sell to Europe and China. With attractive prices and an energy transportation system in place, the Caspian states would be less likely to construct new pipelines that are favored by non-Russian nations. In the energy-poor Kyrgyzstan, the Kremlin worked to gain controlling stakes in valuable companies, such as the enterprise that has supplied the United States' military base with energy and the Dustan torpedo plant on the shore of the country's mountain lake.[144]

Assessment

Under Medvedev's presidency the Kremlin preserved influence in a number of key areas. Following the difficult months after its military assertiveness in the Caucasus, Russia revived its relations with the Western nations. Not only had Russia preserved the existing level of ties with France, Germany, and other Western European nations, but Moscow had worked to strengthen these ties. European leaders reciprocated by proposing to establish the EU-Russia Political and Security Committee as an institution to consult on strategic issues on the continent. The United States' attempts to "reset" relations with Moscow further assisted the continuous development of Russian ties with Europe.

With respect to Asia and the Middle East, Russia has continued to develop economic and political ties across the two regions by prioritizing relations with China, Turkey, and Israel. The record on the Middle Eastern transformation is mixed. By rhetorically opposing the West's intervention in Libya and by diverging from the Western nations on Syria, Russia demonstrated its relevance and strengthened its prestige in international politics. On the other hand, regime changes in Libya and Syria damaged Russia's interests and desire to increase influence in the region.

In the former Soviet world, the Kremlin found new partners in the postrevolutionary governments of Ukraine and Kyrgyzstan. Uzbekistan's departure from the CSTO was a setback for Russia's efforts to stabilize central Asia, indicating the importance of new efforts to strengthen a collective security system in the region. In the economic area, Russia made some advancement in reviving the old Kremlin's initiative, the Customs Union. This became possible due to high oil prices and "pragmatic" economy-driven ties with the non-Russian states in the region.

The new course, which combined elements of Pragmatic Cooperation and assertiveness, was not fully consolidated at home and abroad. During 2011–2012, the course began to unravel in response to new domestic and international challenges. Russian elites remained divided on how to move forward, and the country's leadership showed sensitivity with respect to a possible rise of protest politics. Soon after Putin's inauguration as president, the State Duma passed several laws allowing for the election of regional governors and the registration of new political parties, but also strengthening control over activities of radical opposition politicians.[145] Russia's changed international environment included the West's continued international expansion and the rise of non-Western nations. The next chapter returns to these points.

Table 4.8 summarizes the record of Russia's international course through the summer of 2012.

CIVILIZATIONAL TURN AND NEW ASSERTIVENESS, 2012–2018

Russia's newly stated commitment to "conservative" values of national unity, sovereignty, and traditional family put it at odds with liberal Western priorities of minority rights, democratization, and the responsibility to protect people from abuses by their own governments. On major issues, Russia and Western nations had little to agree on. Russia's new assertive direction was to push for global changes based on the identified principles of sovereignty, diversity, and balance of power.

Civilizational Turn and New Rivalry with the West

Growing Conflicts with the United States

The developments since Putin's return to the presidency in 2012 revealed the extreme fragility of Russia's relations with the West. The value-based conflict served to exacerbate disagreements generated by different understanding of national interest. As the world power balance began to shift away from the West, the Kremlin was no longer motivated by the same vision of a normal great power articulated by Putin in the early 2000s, and now wanted to be recognized by the West as a civilization in its own right.

Table 4.8. The Record of Alliances for Modernization

Security	Remaining problems with terrorism in the Caucasus
	Instability in Afghanistan and the Middle East
	New tensions with NATO over MDS
Welfare	Economic decline and oil-based recovery
Autonomy	New vulnerability to international influences
Identity	Renewed efforts to engage the Westernist dimension of Russian values

Russia and the United States disagreed sharply on Russia's political system. The United States and other Western countries voiced their disagreement with the handling of protesters by the Kremlin and a Russian court's decision to sentence members of the punk band Pussy Riot to two years in jail for dancing near the altar of Russia's main cathedral. Another expression of US–Russia disagreement concerned the case of Magnitsky, whom Russia viewed as William Browder's accountant, charged with mass evasion of taxes, and whom the United States saw as an anticorruption fighter. The United States also expressed disappointment with Russia's new law against "propaganda of non-traditional sexual relations among minors" passed in June 2013. While 88 percent of Russians supported the law,[146] many human rights activists saw it as an "anti-gay law," leading them to call for a boycott of the Winter Olympics in Sochi.[147] The Kremlin continued to restrict the political space for radical pro-Western opposition, including by signing on May 23, 2015, a law giving prosecutors the power to shut down undesirable international organizations.[148] US and EU officials continued to be highly critical of the Kremlin's domestic policies and propaganda following the Ukraine crisis.[149]

In foreign relations, the two countries disagreed on Syria. Western nations supported the military opposition, whereas the Kremlin expressed concerns about instability in the country and the wider region after Bashar al-Assad, and strengthened ties with those within the Syrian opposition interested in working with Russia. As the United States accused Bashar al-Assad's regime of using chemical weapons against military opposition, Russian officials responded by rejecting such accusations and characterizing them as an effort to derail a planned peace conference on Syria.[150] The attempts at negotiations in Geneva in February 2014 proved unsuccessful in part due to the lack of a unified approach between the United States and Russia. Washington again raised the issue of regime change by refusing to recognize Assad, whereas Moscow insisted on negotiations between Syria's existing government and opposition. The situation began to change only in May 2015 when Secretary of State John Kerry arrived in Moscow to acknowledge the United States' "catastrophic errors" in handling the Middle East and to seek Russia's cooperation in isolating Islamic extremists in Syria and other parts of the region.[151] In late September 2015, Putin intervened in Syria by sending military aircraft to bomb terrorist organizations and support the Assad government. The decision in part reflected the Kremlin's desire to repair broken relations with the West.[152]

There was also no progress made on nuclear issues during this time. The United States indicated that it was interested in further nuclear reductions, but not in establishing the joint MDS preferred by Russia. President Obama wrote a long letter to the Kremlin explaining his interest in reducing strategic nuclear warheads in the United States by an additional one-third beyond the START treaty. Russia, however, did not want to consider any further cuts, viewing nuclear force as the basis of national defense and international stability. In the words of Russia's deputy foreign minister, Sergei Ryabkov, "Before discussing the necessity of a further reduction of nuclear weapons we need to arrive at an acceptable solution of the ABM [antiballistic missile] problem."[153] The other nuclear issue concerned the status of the Intermediate Nuclear Forces (INF) Treaty. US officials expressed multiple concerns with Russia's failure to comply with the treaty. In October 2018, Washington cited Moscow's violations as a key reason for considering withdrawal from the INF Treaty. Russia insisted that it was in full compliance and expressed its own fear that the United States' MDS may be used for deployment of nuclear missiles aimed at Russia.[154]

Other important disagreements included the issues of Snowden and Ukraine. In the eyes of the US political class, former CIA employee Edward Snowden, who defected to Russia in June 2013, was a traitor for making public the US government's surveillance activities over its citizens, initiated because of their importance in the fight against terrorism. Washington therefore expected Moscow to turn Snowden over to the United States. When Putin refused to comply and granted Snowden asylum, members of the American political class threatened a full range of retaliatory steps, while Obama expressed his disappointment with the decision and canceled a scheduled bilateral summit with Putin in Moscow.

In Ukraine, according to Putin, Western nations were behind the revolutionary change of power in 2014 without understanding their destabilizing consequences. In justifying his intervention in Crimea, Russia's president said that he acted on behalf of overthrown but still legitimate president of Ukraine, Viktor Yanukovich, and that the action was necessary to safeguard Russia's military fleet in the Black Sea and prevent violence and violation of human rights in the region by the "rampage of Nazi, nationalist, and anti-Semitic forces."[155] However, Western nations did not view themselves as meddling in Ukraine and imposed sanctions on what they saw as Russia's "imperialism" and violation of neighbors' sovereignty. European governments at first found sanctions to be unnecessary and potentially counterproductive,[156] but in April, following Russia's growing involvement in Ukraine and the downing of a Malaysian civilian airplane with 286 passengers on board, the EU, too, implemented sanctions against the Russian economy.

Following Donald Trump's election and subsequent inauguration as US president, the Kremlin did what it deemed necessary to improve relations with the United States. Putin chose not to reciprocate in response to Barack Obama's earlier decision to expel thirty-five Russian diplomats allegedly involved in spying and cyber interference with American elections. Instead, he wished Obama a "Happy New Year," and invited children of American Embassy staff in Moscow to celebrate the holiday in the Kremlin.

Two months after Trump's inauguration, Putin sent his envoy to the State Department to propose the full normalization of relations between their two countries.[157] The plan envisioned the restoration of diplomatic, military, and intelligence contacts and laid out a road map for moving in this direction. The road map included consultations on cyber issues with Russia's top cyber official, Andrei Krutskikh, in April of 2017, and special discussions on Afghanistan, Iran, Ukraine, and North Korea to take place in May. The expectation was that by the time of Putin and Trump's first meeting, top officials of both countries' executive branches would meet and discuss areas of mutual importance.[158] The Kremlin hoped that Trump's promises during the election campaign could be fulfilled.

Instead, relations between the two countries went into another crisis in April when the United States accused Assad of using chemical weapons against the opposition and bombed Syria's military base, which was partly exploited by Russia. The tough responses from Russia included a statement from the Ministry of Defense that promised to shoot down American missiles if similar cases took place. The incident destroyed Russia's domestic pro-Trump consensus and generated new fears of US pressures in the form of military encirclement and attempts to politically destabilize Putin's system.

In May Secretary of State Rex Tillerson traveled to Moscow in part to alleviate these fears, but the conflict only intensified. In July 2017, the US House of Representatives approved a package of new sanctions against Russia, alongside Iran and North Korea. The bill made it impossible for President Trump to ease sanctions without congressional approval.[159] The Kremlin reacted to the bill, as well as to an earlier decision by President Obama to expel Russia's diplomats accused of being responsible for intervening in the US elections in January 2017, by expelling hundreds of American diplomats. Russia also made only limited progress with the United States regarding Middle East, Ukraine, and other international issues.

The Kremlin drew its conclusions and, instead of proposing road maps for normalization, concentrated on addressing individual issues. When Putin and Trump met on the sidelines of G-20 in Hamburg in early July, they reached an understanding on the concrete issues of cybersecurity, Syria, Ukraine, and North Korea. In particular, they proposed to form a joint group to address cybersecurity, and initiated a cease-fire and establishment of de-escalation zones in Syria. A similar development took place in Helsinki in July 2018 when Putin and Trump made progress in further normalizing relations.

However, much of Putin and Trump's progress was invalidated by the United States' domestic political struggle between the president and the US Congress. Each meeting in 2017 and 2018 was accompanied by new rounds of sanctions against Russia for its actions in cybersecurity, Ukraine, and Syria, thereby complicating the bilateral dialogue. Under increased domestic pressures, Trump accepted tough measures and sanctions, even initiating some of his own. The Kremlin felt compelled to respond, thereby further worsening relations. For instance, in July 2017, the Kremlin ordered 750 members of the US Embassy staff to leave Russia, justifying it by saying that it restored "parity" in terms of the number of diplomats working in both countries. In response, on September 1 the United States ordered Russia to close its Consulate General in San Francisco within two days.

The United States also increased pressure on Russia regarding Ukraine and North Korea. Secretary of Defense James Mattis and the newly appointed State Department envoy on Ukraine, Kurt Volker, supported the idea of providing Kyiv with lethal weapons. Trump issued multiple threats to use force against North Korea if Russia and China failed to prevent Kim from developing a nuclear program and performing additional missile tests. Russia responded with a mixture of sticks and carrots with Ukraine. Putin made it clear that US supplies of lethal weapons for Kyiv would not alter the balance of power in the region. In addition, he proposed deployment of United Nations peacekeepers to prevent violations of the cease-fire in eastern Ukraine, and to provide the necessary conditions for implementing the Minsk-1 agreement, also known as the Minsk Protocol.

The Kremlin also sought to build alternative transportation routes for transporting Russian gas to Europe in the northern and southern directions. The northern direction included efforts to develop another Nord Stream line with Germany under the Baltic Sea, whereas in the South, Russia hoped to strengthen its transportation potential via Turkey.

On North Korea Russia cooperated with the United States by supporting the US-proposed sanctions in the UN Security Council. However, in exchange the Kremlin demanded that sanctions be considerably softened. Russia and China also indicated that they did not believe in sanctions as the solution to the issue.

Overall, Russia's relations with the United States entered a new territory. The Ukraine crisis and sanctions imposed by the West against the Russian economy made it impossible to implement another "reset" in bilateral relations. Trump and Putin's efforts notwithstanding, US–Russia relations remained frozen at the conflict stage, with the American political establishment blocking the White House's efforts to initiate a dialogue with the Kremlin. Fundamental world order preferences and power misperceptions divided the two sides.

Pragmatism and Assertiveness toward the European Union

Russia also continued to disagree with the European Union on multiple issues from energy to sanctions against the Russian economy and ways of building relations with Eastern European countries.[160] Overall, the Kremlin pursued a dual-track policy in relations with the EU, working pragmatically with incumbent governments while trying to develop informal ties with Euro-skeptics and critics of the liberal West. Moscow did not want to see the EU's disintegration, yet valued the ability to influence the Union's direction through special relationships with its individual members and Euro-skeptic political parties.[161]

For instance, Putin hosted Marine Le Pen before the French presidential elections in May 2017. However, soon after her loss and the victory of Emmanuel Macron, Putin traveled to Paris to discuss the improvement of bilateral relations. Russia also maintained relations with Angela Merkel, who was reelected for a fourth term as the country's chancellor, while working to influence German politics and elections. The year 2018 saw an increase in Russia's high-level diplomatic contacts with Germany and France following the two countries' growing disappointment in the United States' policies.[162] In the Balkans, Moscow strengthened ties with friendly Serbia, while trying to influence the internal politics in Montenegro in order to prevent it from joining NATO. In other parts of Europe, Russia strengthened relations with the conservative government of Hungary, but maintained semi-frozen ties with the pro-American Baltics and Poland.

Bilaterally, Russia had cultivated ties with Austria, Italy, Hungary, Slovakia, and Serbia. All of these states favored the relaxing or lifting of Western sanctions against the Russian economy; supported the Kremlin's energy projects, such as Nord Stream 2; and remained skeptical of the EU's liberal migration policies. Hungary, in particular, emerged as an important partner that deepened its dependence on Russia's energy supplies in 2017.[163]

In addition, Russia shares special Slavic and Orthodox Christian bonds with several southern European nations. For instance, it has been a tradition for Russian politicians to visit Orthodox monasteries and hold intellectual forums in Greece. Moscow also enjoys political leverage in those states that it views as pro-American and hostile to Russia.

Russia sought to influence Estonia and Latvia through the ethnic Russian minority population and targeted media campaigns, as well as cyber operations and economic tools. Moscow also sought to influence Moldova by cultivating relations with Moldovan president Igor Dodon, who was elected in November 2016 on the platform of improving ties with Russia. The Kremlin further exploited Serbian minorities to influence state decisions in Balkan states, such as Montenegro and Bosnia and Herzegovina.[164] Russian media outlets RT and Sputnik broadcast in major European states and members of NATO and EU. During 2015–2017, Russia sought to influence elections in France, Germany, the Netherlands, and others by strengthening ties with Russia-friendly political organizations and providing their favorable coverage in Russian media.[165]

In the Caucasus, Moscow's main partners were Armenia and Azerbaijan, both sensitive to Russia's great power aspirations and interests in the region. Relations with Georgia did not progress. Following the military conflict of August 2008, Tbilisi cut diplomatic relations with Russia and did not restore them despite the continued dialogue with Moscow.

The discussion within NATO and the US Ministry of Defense following the Ukraine crisis concerned the motives and tactics of Russia's military actions using the notion of "hybrid warfare"—Moscow's newly developed capacity to combine traditional military power with covert efforts to undermine an enemy government. Counteractions proposed by the Atlantic alliance's commanders ranged from building up defense capacity on Western borders to actively arming Kyiv and preparing to confront Russia should it choose to escalate the situation in Ukraine. Then supreme commander of NATO forces in Europe, General Philip Breedlove, advocated the latter approach, even lobbying in private to pressure President Barack Obama.[166] The Western defense approach prevailed.

In addition to consolidating the perception of Russia as a military threat, NATO pursued the movement of troops and military infrastructure, training exercises, defense spending, and acceptance of new members. Several summits by the alliance confirmed commitments to collective defenses; invited Chernogoria to join NATO; and approved the movement of troops to Poland and the Baltic states for an indefinite stay. The alliance also conducted massive military exercises in Eastern Europe annually.[167]

In Moscow, these developments accompanied by Western support for the Euromaidan Revolution in Ukraine and sanctions imposed against the Russian economy consolidated the perception that the West wanted to punish and, possibly, attack Russia for standing firm in defending its national interest. In the words of the Security Council's secretary, Nikolai Patrushev, "the assurances of some Western leaders that NATO is a defensive alliance serve only to cover the alliance's aggressive nature."[168] Elsewhere, Patrushev also stated that NATO and the United States were considering a dismemberment of Russia's territory in order to achieve their goals of global domination.[169] According to Russia's NATO representative Alexander Grushko, the alliance's decision to station its troops in the Baltics on a rotating basis was merely a way to stay there permanently in violation of previous agreements,[170] and such military expansion served the purpose of consolidating the Russian threat in order to control the European continent.[171]

Lack of Progress on Ukraine

The Ukraine crisis ended Russia's ambitions to build a new Eurasian Union with Ukraine as one of its members. In October 2011, Putin proposed building a new Eurasian Union among the CIS states, and laid out the economic incentives for joining it, including an increase in trade, common modernization projects, and improved standards of living.[172] In December 2014, speaking at the Valdai forum of international experts, Putin further stated that "Eurasian integration is a chance for the entire post-Soviet space to become an independent center for global development, rather than remaining on the outskirts of Europe and Asia."[173] In the following year, Russia also invited Ukraine to join a Customs Union, promising a major discount for gas prices. Armenia and Kyrgyzstan were also being considered for membership in the Eurasian Union. By capitalizing on high oil prices, the Kremlin hoped to reverse the pro-Western revolutions in Ukraine and Kyrgyzstan by supporting those governments in favor of stronger ties with Russia.

However, Moscow's regional initiatives were met with opposition from those outside the former Soviet region who perceived the Kremlin's promoted values as threatening. In addition, there was evidence of instability in the region, which included the tense atmosphere in the Caucasus following the war with Georgia; renewed terrorist attacks; the persistent failure of Western forces to stabilize Afghanistan; the inability of central Asian rulers to rein in local clans and drug lords; and the weakness of bodies of power in Moldova and Ukraine.

The Ukrainian Euromaidan Revolution served as a powerful testament that Russia's influence had not translated into stability in the region. In November 2013, following President Viktor Yanukovich's decision not to sign an Association Agreement with the European Union, mass protests took place in Kyiv, pressuring Yanukovich to reverse his decision. Russia and the European Union pulled Ukraine in different directions by promising benefits from joining their political-economy arrangements. With the Ukrainian economy in recession, Yanukovich declined the EU offer because Putin gave Ukraine a major discount in energy prices and pledged $15 billion in aid.

In the meantime, the Ukrainian protest was gathering momentum and reached unprecedented proportions. The opposition was critical of Yanukovich's policies at home and favored the country's pro-European development. On February 21, 2014, the compromise agreement between the president and the opposition, brokered by the European Union, collapsed. For unknown reasons, Yanukovich left office and moved to the east of Ukraine, and then to Russia.

Since the revolution and removal of the president from power, the situation in Ukraine continued to worsen, with Russia and the Western nations providing support and assistance for different sides of the conflict. Residents east and south of Ukraine did not trust Kyiv's rule and demanded more autonomy. Assisted by Russia, activists in several key regions (Donetsk, Luhansk, Nikolayev, Khar'kiv, and Odessa) refused to cooperate with the central government, while the latter launched "anti-terrorist" operations against the protesters, thereby exacerbating tensions. Russia blamed Western governments for the collapse of the compromise agreement, and demanded that Kyiv refrain from using force and initiate new constitutional changes; guarantee the protection of Russian speakers; and conduct decentralization reform in the country. Russia also annexed Crimea, provided various forms of assistance for protesters in eastern Ukraine, amassed troops on Ukraine's border, and raised prices for natural gas deliveries to Kyiv.[174]

As violence and instability in the eastern and southern parts of Ukraine proliferated, attempts to negotiate peace brought limited results. The Geneva Accord negotiated on April 17, 2014, did not hold, as radicals on both sides refused to abide by it. On May 2, forty people were burned alive in Odessa. That summer saw especially intense fighting between the eastern rebels and the Ukrainian army. A new military escalation in eastern Ukraine in August resulted in Kyiv's defeat, and a new cease-fire agreement was negotiated in Minsk on September 3, 2014. However, in October of the same year, heavy fighting resumed, with thousands of people killed and over a million refugees fleeing the eastern part of the country. On February 11, 2015, the leaders of Ukraine, Russia, France, and Germany, along with the East's representatives, met to formulate new conditions for peace in the Minsk-II agreement. The conditions included: the removal of heavy weapons by the fighting sides; amnesty and exchange of prisoners; decentralization reform and passing of the law on self-governance in Donetsk and Luhansk; restoration of pensions and services for residents of the East by Kyiv; and control of the border with Russia.[175]

The reality, again, proved different. Although the fighting was not as intense as it had been before the agreement, the violence did not stop, and the two sides failed to implement the signed conditions. Rather than working in concert, Russian and Western powers blamed each other for not putting sufficient pressure on their patrons and engaged in mutual sanctions against each other's economies. Despite the formal peace, the situation remained highly unstable.

By the early summer, many analysts speculated that full war could resume at any moment. The position by the leading powers, as well as Ukraine's deep cultural divide between West, Center, and the East–South, continued to challenge the government's job of building a nation. In addition, the post-Soviet years had led to the degradation of the economy, with the superrich controlling its various parts and the majority of the population living in poverty, with little prospect to improve its living standards.

The new issue in Russia–Ukraine relations concerned Kyiv's decision to establish independence (or autocephaly) of Ukrainian churches from Moscow's Patriarchate. The decision undermined the canonical Ukrainian Orthodox Church's ties to Russia.[176] Politically the decision assisted incumbent president Pyotr Poroshenko in presenting himself as a nation-builder, standing firm against hostile influences from Russia. The Moscow Patriarchate called the decision an "illegal intrusion" into its "canonical territory,"[177] while the Kremlin promised to honor the interests of the faithful in Ukraine.

Turning to the East and "Greater Eurasia"

The Idea of Cooperation with the Non-West

Russia's newly discovered civilizational identity assumed the need to protect it from the West's pressures by developing relations with the non-West. In one of his presidential addresses, Putin defended the preservation of a "new balance of economic, civilizational and military forces" in global politics."[178] Consistent with such a worldview, Putin not only continued bilateral pressures on Ukraine and other former Soviet states in attempting to build upon Russia's influence in Eurasia, but also worked on strengthening its relations with China, Iran, and India, and to exploit non-Western institutional vehicles, such as BRICS and SCO. In the summer of 2015, Russia hosted summits of both organizations in the city of Ufa. The BRICS members pledged $100 billion as a reserve currency pool and additional resources for development projects,[179] while the SCO began the process of admitting India and Pakistan as members.

The positions of Russia and non-Western nations on various international issues were growing increasingly closer. BRICS countries did not publicly condemn Russia's incorporation of Crimea; did not join Western sanctions; and did not support the campaign to isolate Russia politically. According to the Russian Foreign Ministry, a "top priority" for Russia's presidency in BRICS was to transform the assembly into "a full-scale mechanism of strategic interaction on key issues of global policy and economics."[180] Other agenda items included plans to strengthen strategic stability and international information security, reinforce the nonproliferation regime, and combat international terrorism.[181]

In comparison with the West, non-Western nations largely shared Russia's values and priorities. China, India, Brazil, and the Middle Eastern nations had never been critical of human rights violations or the domestic political system in Russia. On the Middle East and Syria, Russia frequently acted jointly with

China by vetoing Syria resolutions introduced in the UNSC by the Western nations. Moscow and Beijing were concerned that such resolutions would pave the way for a military intervention and regime change in Syria, as had happened in Libya. By building on non-Western resentment toward US hegemony and military interventions, Putin strengthened his global reputation as an advocate for sovereignty, national unity, and cultural values. While meeting with Barack Obama during the G-20 summit in St. Petersburg, Putin obtained the support of most non-Western leaders present for his position on Assad and the Middle East. In addition, the Kremlin was able to take advantage of the Snowden affair. By granting Snowden asylum, Moscow again positioned itself as a defender of national sovereignty and a protector against global interferences from hegemonic power.

Strengthening "Greater Eurasia" in Partnership with China

Relations with China, Russia's largest neighbor, obtained a strategic dimension, as the two nations demonstrated an increased convergence in global priorities and solutions to existing issues in world politics. Although Beijing did not recognize Russia's annexation of Crimea, the two nations had multiple complementary interests in the areas of commerce and regional security. Their energy-related ties continued to progress. In May 2014, Putin traveled to Beijing to sign a $400 billion agreement to export almost 40 billion cubic meters (bcm) of gas annually to China, thereby further diversifying Russia's trade away from Europe. In November 2014, Russia signed another massive gas deal by pledging to supply China with an additional 30 bcm, starting in 2019.[182]

Other important agreements were signed in Moscow in May 2015, on the eve of a military parade on the Red Square marking the anniversary of the end of World War II. The parade also featured China's president Xi Jinping and Putin presiding over the ceremony in the front row, observing the marching of Russian, Chinese, and Indian soldiers. Western leaders were invited but chose not to attend due to their disagreement with the Kremlin over Ukraine.[183]

Russia's main priority, however, remained that of Eurasia's regionalism. Moscow's vision of "Greater Eurasia" included China and Europe but excluded the United States. At the International Economic Forum in St. Petersburg in June 2016 Putin articulated the perspective of creating various economic agreements between the Eurasian Economic Union (EAEU), China, member states of the SCO and ASEAN, as well as the EU.[184] The Kremlin anticipated several policies to consolidate Russia's place in Eurasia as that of a great power, such as strengthening relations within the EAEU, developing ties with neighbors through the CSTO and bilaterally, and proposing wider projects with China, European countries, Turkey, and Iran.

China was especially active in promoting its vision for the development of Eurasia and offering its support in building the region. Increasingly, Beijing acted on its own economic ambitions by inviting former Soviet states to join a larger China-centered trade and transportation arrangement, titled the Silk Road Economic Belt.[185] In this scheme the Eurasian Union would become an integrated part of an economic and transportation project advanced by China. On May 8, 2015, the vision obtained major support with an endorsement by leaders of Russia and China. During President Xi Jinping's visit to Moscow, the two nations signed an agreement on cooperation between the Eurasian Union and the Silk Road.[186] Among the objectives were the establishment of a network of land and sea routes to connect the western regions of China with the main markets of Central Asia and Europe via the territories of Kazakhstan and Russia.[187]

The new vision and practice of the Russia-initiated Eurasian Union and the China-advocated Silk Road's convergence encouraged those who viewed the two nations' cooperation in terms of being a valuable alternative to the European Union.[188] The fact that the United States and the European Union had worked to keep Ukraine away from the Russia-dominant Eurasian Union may have contributed to the Kremlin's motivation to develop Russia's own civilizational ideology. The West's sanctions against the Russian economy in response to the Kremlin's annexation of Crimea and support for eastern fighters in the Ukrainian civil war served to strengthen Russia's reorientation away from Western nations and toward China.[189] Such foreign pressures also emboldened those defending the objective of Russia's development in isolation from Europe.[190] Although China's system of values is distinct from that of Russia, the two systems were seen as potentially compatible, especially relative to the West's system.[191] Therefore, the cultural pillar was seen as possibly strengthening the rapidly progressing economic and political partnership between the two nations.

China was also an essential partner in bringing jobs and investments to Russia's non-European regions, especially Siberia and the Far East. To offset a potentially excessive dependence on one partner, the Kremlin continued earlier developed policies of building relations with non-Chinese countries and strengthening regional integration in Asia. In 2014, Moscow wrote off $10 billion of North Korean debt on the condition of building a gas pipe and rail link into the south.[192] Russia also increased diplomatic contacts with Japan in order to eventually solve the territorial issue and begin a new era of economic relations with the eastern power. In the fall of 2013, Putin had visited Japan to make progress on the issue, and had signed a number of investment and trade agreements. Moscow also increased its level of participation in regional arrangements and forums, such as the APEC summits in June 2012 and November 2014. In May 2015, Russia and other members of the Eurasian Union signed a free trade agreement with Vietnam, pledging a reduction of tariffs from 10 percent to 1 percent.[193]

Russia's stagnating economy made it difficult to make progress in strengthening ties within the EAEU. GDP growth was negative during 2015 and 2016, and grew by less than 2 percent in 2017. Trade among members of the union also declined, reflecting its poor performance. Intraregional trade, which stood at $65 billion in 2012 and 2013, shrank by some 40 percent in 2016, to $42.5 billion.[194] The situation improved in 2016–2017. As the Russian economic slowdown bottomed up and was reversed, trade and investments within the EAEU began to recover. According to the Eurasian Development Bank, after three consecutive years of decline, investments increased by 16 percent in 2016, reflecting Russia's contribution of over 78 percent of the stock in the Union member states.[195]

Despite the economic slowdown, the Kremlin managed to strengthen its bilateral relations with those neighboring countries interested in such relations. Following a change of power in Uzbekistan in 2016, Russia improved ties with the country's new leader, Shavkat Mirziyoyev. In 2017, the newly elected leader of Kyrgyzstan made his first foreign trip to Russia to proclaim continuity of strategic relations between the two countries. In October 2017, Putin also visited Turkmenistan, concluding important economic agreements in the country. In all of these cases, Russia sought to position itself as a security provider and a means to reduce China's influence in the region.[196] Turkmenistan, in particular, was supplying China with natural gas, but sought to transport some of its ample reserves through Russian pipelines to Europe.

Russia and China reached an understanding on Central Asia. As described by analysts of their relations, "Moscow and Beijing found ways to divide their influences, with China dominating the energy realm and Russia the security realm."[197] Russia's power in Central Asia was primarily, though not exclusively, based on military capabilities. The Kremlin had worked on consolidating its military presence in the former Soviet region since the mid-2000s, and possessed important military and geopolitical advantages. On the other hand, the power of China in the region was largely economic and based on its ability to finance important regional projects and offset various threats to central Asian economies.

While Russia had maintained an ambition to preserve its economic influence in the region, it found it was increasingly unable to compete with Beijing and had learned to accept China's lead in exchange for Beijing's recognition of Russia's military and political dominance in the former Soviet region. In the meantime, Chinese military attention was directed less at central Asia than the regions of East Asia and Asia Pacific. In the central Asian region, Beijing deployed no troops and expressed no desire to lease any military facilities.[198] Therefore, from a military standpoint, Russia remained the regionally dominant power. This was acceptable to Beijing, which has focused on fighting local threats of terrorism and separatism.

Russia–China coordination should not be viewed as a state of stagnation in central Asia. Contemporary reform agenda in Uzbekistan is a case in point. Since the election of Mirziyoyev, the country's president, Uzbekistan has moved in the direction of controlled economic change, media freedom, and international openness.[199] Against the common expectations of Western analysts, "it was precisely Western disengagement that opened the door for change," with Russia and China both favoring it.[200]

Overall, the Russia–China division of power and its success in central Asia has served as a model for potential solutions to other problems in Asia, such as North Korea's nuclear ambitions, economic development, the security of the greater region, and future Korean unification. Increasingly these solutions were being found without the United States' involvement and at the expense of US global interests. In all prominent political and security issues in Asia, Moscow acting jointly with Beijing was able to advance Russia's objectives of preserving great power status and delivering stability on Russia's, not America's, terms. The Kremlin fostered negotiations with North Korea, developed special relations in central Asia, and pushed the resolution of issues in Afghanistan and counterterrorism toward the SCO framework. It also made progress in attracting Asian investors despite the United States' insistence on Asian nations continuing to impose sanctions against Russia. As American presence in the region shrinks, the room for United States–Russia rivalry in the region also declines.

As a result of Russia's stagnating economy and relations within the EAEU, Moscow's overall ties with Asia remained heavily centered on China, while Moscow's attempts to diversify these relations by strengthening ties with Japan and others did not bring impressive results. The pivot to China resulted in growing trade and military ties. Bilateral trade in 2017 increased by 25 percent relative to the previous year, though it had yet to reach the level of 2013.[201] In addition, the revitalization of the EEU increasingly meant working in partnership with China, including the China-centered trade and transportation arrangements with the Economic Belt of Great Silk Road.

Rebuilding Influence in the Middle East

Partly in order to compensate for its internal economic weakness and partly to realign with the quickly changing international political economy, Russia has sought to actively participate in transregional projects. In addition to developing ties with China and working to preserve energy relations with European countries, the Kremlin has also tried to build relations with Iran, Turkey, and other countries in the Middle East. The fact that Russia and China had similar perspectives on international crises, including those in the Middle East and East Asia, assisted the Kremlin with developing influence in the regions. Both Russia and China supported Assad in his fight with militant opposition and terrorism, although Beijing refrained from providing military assistance and tended to abstain from, rather than vetoing, the US-sponsored resolutions on Syria in the United Nations' Security Council. Russia and China's positions on handling North Korea's nuclear ambitions were also aligned, and markedly different from the tough, threatening tone assumed by the United States.

In 2014, following Western attempts to impose sanctions on Russia over its annexation of Crimea and its position on the Ukraine crisis, Moscow and Tehran increased their level of economic relations. In particular, they discussed an energy deal worth $10 billion that would involve a barter trade of oil in exchange for building electricity stations in Iran.[202] As the United States intensified its diplomacy to ensure Iran's compliance with the nuclear nonproliferation treaty, the Kremlin was supportive of the diplomacy, but had its own priorities in mind. Among them were the strengthening of bilateral commercial and political ties with Tehran and its membership in non-Western institutions, such as the SCO. In April 2015, to further revitalize relations with Iran, Putin removed the ban for delivering the S-300 (advanced military system for air defense). Previously, Russia had signed but then canceled the delivery agreement.[203]

Outside Iran, Russia focused on regional stability by encouraging negotiations between Syria's Assad and moderate elements of opposition. Here, too, Russia worked jointly with its non-Western partners. The BRICS summits supported negotiations in Syria, such as those that started in Geneva in February 2014. In addition, with the continued destabilization of Syria and Iraq by Islamic radicals, the focus of Russia and other powers was on shifting to counter the region-wide threats posed by the self-proclaimed Islamic State (IS). By early 2015, the IS had emerged as the leading force in the area, with the capacity to topple Assad and secure important territorial gains in Iraq. In particular, IS militants conquered western Iraq and eastern Syria, claiming to control a territory that contained six and half million residents.[204] In June 2014, they took control of Mosul, Iraq's second-largest city, and in May 2015, they seized the ancient and UNESCO-protected town of Palmyra in Syria. To contain and defeat the IS, Russia consulted both Western and non-Western nations, especially Iran.

Moscow continued to strengthen economic and political relations with Tehran, in part for the purpose of jointly assisting stabilization in Syria and Iraq. Increasingly, Moscow was also reviving strong ties with Egypt,[205] and, disagreements on Syria and Iran notwithstanding, sought to strengthen relations with Saudi Arabia.[206]

Another important partner of Russia in the Middle East was Turkey. Although the two nations supported different sides in the Syrian conflict, they were both critical of the Western role in the region and shared a desire to stabilize it with local powers. Russian–Turkish relations were also made easier by the shared values of a civilizational identity and a strong modernizing state able to overcome pressures from domestic and foreign influences.[207] In addition to similar values, their interests were also compatible. In particular, Moscow and Istanbul continued to cooperate on energy issues. As Russia sought to circumvent Ukraine in developing an alternative transportation route to European markets, Turkey wanted to position itself as a major energy hub. In January 2015, Putin traveled to Istanbul to propose the building of a gas pipeline to Europe's borders, through Turkish territory. The European Union objected to the development in part because of the need to build the required infrastructure.[208] Previously, due to disagreements with Ukraine, Russia had cut gas supplies for European customers to pressure Kyiv into paying negotiated fees.

Due to military successes and engagement in negotiations with all relevant actors in the Middle East, the Kremlin strengthened its ties even with leading critics of Assad, such as Saudi Arabia, Turkey, and Egypt. In October 2017, the King Salman of Saudi Arabia visited Russia to build on an earlier agreement limiting oil production, to sign economic and military agreements, and to signal a new political understanding of the region's realities that was not based on Assad's departure.[209] Since then Moscow has continued its energy production with this most important oil-producing state.[210]

Putin also traveled to Tehran to discuss jointly with Azerbaijan, among other projects, the idea of developing an economic corridor to the Arabian Sea and the Indian Ocean. If developed, the project could save costs in transporting goods from the Middle East, India, and other countries of South Asia. In the long term, the project could become the necessary complement to Russia's limited participation in China's Silk Road.[211] Although Turkey remained a difficult partner for the Kremlin, Russia continued to develop relations and negotiate the possible construction of an additional natural gas pipeline through Turkish territory to European markets. The Kremlin also continued to foster military and energy ties with Egypt.

Has the New Assertiveness Paid Off?

Following the ongoing state of international instability, the Kremlin continued with its policy of asserting Russia's status as an independent great power, while seeking partners for its course among both Western and non-Western politicians. In the West, Moscow sought to connect with those skeptical of the values of liberal globalization and sympathetic with Russia's insistence on the protection of conservative values and national interest. Outside the West, Russia worked to strengthen its reputation as a global security provider, and advocated building new global economic and political institutions alternative to those centered on the West.

Results of the policy were mixed. The Kremlin strengthened Russia's national security by choosing to fight terrorism in the Middle East; developing and testing new weapons systems; and demonstrating resolve in deterring NATO from further expansion in the eastern direction. Russia also made progress in strengthening its autonomy and its reputation as a great power, particularly through demonstrating its importance in ending the military conflict in Syria. Furthermore, the Kremlin continued to make progress in building ties with Asian, Middle Eastern, and Latin American partners outside the West. In addition, Russia partly preserved the identity connection with the West and Western political circles by employing the idea of conservative values.

Still, the selected "conservative" foreign policy course had serious limitations. While based on the assumption of a global transition of power from the West to the non-West, Russia's strategy often lacked specifics regarding this transition toward a new international system. These specifics concerned relations and cooperation with the United States and European countries; participation in developing alternative geoeconomic projects with China, Turkey, Iran, and other non-Western countries; and how to conduct Russia's domestic economic and political reforms.

First, Russia's foreign policy was partly based on an incorrect reading of the United States' position and intentions in the international system. The Kremlin assumed that America's material capabilities were on the decline, and that Trump would begin to reorient the country's foreign policy toward Russia by lifting sanctions and cooperating with Moscow on various international issues. However, Trump was largely incapable of acting because of opposition to his policy from the political establishment and several investigations launched against him by Congress and special investigator Robert Mueller. Trump also demonstrated that he had plans for the United States to remain the superpower in the international system. The US economy continued to grow, and the United States preserved the capacity to strongly influence global and regional political developments.

Second, non-Western countries such as China, India, and others were not as proactive in building foundations for an alternative international system, and remained interested in building economic and political relations with the United States and other Western countries.

Third, Russia's foreign policy rested on weak economic foundations, overestimating the country's capacity to challenge the West-centered international order. In response to the collapse of energy prices in 2015, Western economic

Table 4.9. The Record of State-Civilization

Security	Confrontation with the West and Ukraine
Welfare	Economic crisis
Autonomy	New vulnerability to international influences
Identity	Undermined Westernist dimension of Russia's identity

sanctions, and the absence of domestic reforms, the Russian economy was underperforming. Instead of becoming a part of a vibrant non-Western alternative system, Russia was stagnating and experiencing difficulties. Russian living standards had been declining while the state continued to generously fund its military and limit investments in education and health. Russia relied on asymmetrical forms of geopolitical activism in order to demonstrate its global relevance and great power status.

Table 4.9 provides a tentative summary assessment of Russia's "civilizational" foreign policy.

NOTES

1. Vladimir Putin, Annual Address to the Federal Assembly, Moscow, the Kremlin, December 12, 2012, Kremlin.ru.

2. As quoted in Anatol Lieven, "Bush's Choice: Messianism or Pragmatism," OpenDemocracy.net, February 22, 2005.

3. For some evidence of and discourse on such strategic calculations, see, for example, Stephen Blank, "Georgia: A Study in Democracy Exportation," *Asia Times*, December 6, 2003, atimes.com; Graeme P. Herd, "Colorful Revolutions and the CIS," *Problems of Post-Communism* 52, no. 2 (2005).

4. Charles Recknagel, "Iraq: U.S. Plans to Take in 7,000 Refugees," *RFE/RL Research Report*, February 15, 2007, www.rferl.org.

5. Seymour M. Hersh, "The Next Act," *New Yorker*, November 27, 2006.

6. "BRICS pomeryayetsya siloi s MVF," Editorial, *Nezavisimaya gazeta*, 02.04.2015.

7. For example, despite their differences from the West, both Russia and China present their grand visions as consistent with the idea of democracy. Islamists, however, promote the Islamic caliphate and do not hide their despisement for secular democratic ideals.

8. I follow here a conventional institutional definition of the West as an area that includes the United States and European nations. These nations share pluralistic political institutions, a market economy, and the basic geopolitical objectives of advancing their values and institutions across the globe and defeating their ideological and politico-economic opponents.

10. Donald Trump, Inaugural Address, January 20, 2017, https://www.whitehouse.gov/inaugural-address.

11. Rawi Abdelal and Igor Makarov, *The Fragmentation of the Global Economy and U.S.–Russia Relations* (Cambridge: Working Group on the Future of U.S.–Russia Relations, Working Group Paper 8, 2017).

12. Paul J. Saunders, "Another Setback for the Reset," *The National Interest*, March 6, 2012, http://nationalinterest.org.

13. As three European analysts concluded about the Russian discourse, "Although there is a lively debate between different factions around the Kremlin . . . it is important to understand that this is a competition within the wider 'Putin consensus,' " Ivan Krastev, Mark Leonard, and Andrew Wilson, eds., *What Does Russia Think?* (London: European Council on Foreign Relations, 2009).

14. For background, see Cory Welt, "What the Snowden Affair Says about U.S.–Russian Relations," *The Center for American Progress*, July 17, 2013.

15. Vladimir Putin, "The New Integration Project for Eurasia," *Izvestia*, October 3, 2011.

16. Vladimir Putin, "Press Statement and Answers to Journalists' Questions Following a Meeting of the Russia-NATO Council," Bucharest, April 4, 2008, Kremlin.ru.

17. "Poll Shows Russians See NATO Membership for Ukraine, Georgia as Threat," *Interfax*, April 1, 2008.

18. "Russia's Economy under Vladimir Putin: Achievements and Failures," *RIA Novosti*, March 1, 2008.

19. "Middle Class Grows Atop," *Kommersant*, February 27, 2008.

20. Andrea Crandall, "Invest in China? Invest in Russia," *Johnson's Russia List* 22, April 19, 2006, www.cdi.org/russia/johnson.

21. "Russia Is Most Attractive Emerging Economy for Investors," *Kommersant*, February 14, 2008.

22. Paul Abelsky, "Russia Industrial Output Rises 9.2%, Nine-Month High," *Bloomberg*, May 20, 2008.

23. "Russians Think Chosen Development Course Correct—Poll," *Interfax*, June 18, 2008.

24. Jeffrey Mankoff, "Internal and External Impact of Russia's Economic Crisis," *Proliferation Papers* 48, March 2010.

25. The defense budget was at the level of 5.3 percent of GDP (*Nezavisimaya gazeta*, November 15, 2017).

26. Ol'ga Solovyeva, "Rossiyane soetuyut vlastyam zanyat'sya ekonomikoi," *Nezavisimaya gazeta*, February 16, 2018.

27. From the Russian *sila*, or "power."

28. Both Russian and Western analysts speculated that the security class became omnipresent in policymaking. See, for example, O. Kryshtanovskaya and S. White, "Putin's Militocracy," *Post-Soviet Affairs* 19, no. 4 (2003); Daniel Treisman, "Putin's Silovarchs," *Orbis*, Winter 2007.

29. See, for example, "A Potemkin Election," editorial, *Washington Post*, January 30, 2008; "Kicking Democracy's Corpse in Russia," *New York Times*, editorial, January 30, 2008; Alvaro Vargas Llosa, "Eternal Putin," *New Republic*, March 5, 2008; "Putin's Mini-Me (or Not?)," *New York Times*, editorial, March 4, 2008.

30. Dmitri Medvedev, "Dlya protsvetaniya vsekh nado uchityvat' interesy kazhdogo," *Ekspert* 28 (522), July 24, 2006, expert.ru.

31. Vladimir Putin, "Rossiya na rubezhe tysyacheletiy," *Nezavisimaya gazeta*, December 1999.

32. Vladimir Putin, "Poslaniye Federal'nomu Sobraniyu Rossiyskoy Federatsiyi," March 2005, Kremlin.ru.

33. Putin, "Poslaniye."

34. Vladimir Putin, "Poslaniye Federal'nomu Sobraniyu Rossiyskoy Federatsiyi," May 10, 2006, April 26, 2007, Kremlin.ru.

35. For development of this comparison, see Andrei P. Tsygankov, "Finding a Civilizational Idea: 'West,' 'Eurasia' and 'Euro-East' in Russia's Foreign Policy," *Geopolitics*, 12, no. 3 (2007).

36. Gleb Pavlovski, "O politike Rossiyi na postsovetskom prostranstve," America-Russia.net, April 28, 2005; "Zapad—eto antiyevropeyskoye ponyatiye," *Izvestiya*, July 14, 2006.

37. Vladislav Surkov, "Suverenitet—eto politicheski sinonim konkurentnospo sobnosti," *Moscow News*, March 3, 2006; Aleksandr Tsipko, "Obratno puti net," *Literaturnaya Gazeta* 19 (May 2006).

38. Not all in the Kremlin shared the concept of "sovereign democracy." For a different view, see Medvedev, "Dlya protsvetaniya vsekh nado uchityvat' interesy kazhdogo."

39. Vladimir Putin, "Munich Conference on Security Policy," February 10, 2007.

40. Vlad Sobel, "A Resurgent Russia, or Triumphalist West?," *Johnson's Russia List* 249, November 6, 2006. In an attempt to emphasize Europe's independence, Pavlovski has criticized the concept of "West," viewing it as "anti-European" and only relevant for understanding the Cold War ("Zapad—eto antiyevropeyskoye ponyatiye").

41. "Obzor vneshnei politiki Rossiyskoi federatsiyi," March 27, 2007, www.mid.ru.

42. Putin's special representative to the European Union, Sergei Yastrzhembsky, suggested that Putin's Munich speech was a "cold shower [and not a return] to a Cold War." Yastrzhembsky added that Putin's remarks were aimed primarily at a European public, and also sought to draw attention to a variety of world issues. Pointing out that Putin challenged the concept of what he called a US-dominated "unipolar world," the aide said that an unspecified recent poll showed that at least 60 percent of German respondents agreed with Putin's remarks (RFE/RL Newsline, February 23, 2007). In a different interview, Yastrzhembsky drew attention to Russia's desire to integrate with Europe economically. "The Russian business elite wants to go into a massive investment offensive, shall I say, in the best meaning of this word, in the European market. One of the goals of the state is to create conditions for such activities of Russian entrepreneurs" (press conference with presidential aide Sergei Yastrzhembsky on RF–EU relations, January 30, 2007, www.fednews.ru).

43. For an early statement of this viewpoint, see Zbigniew Brzezinski, "The Premature Partnership," *Foreign Affairs* 73, no. 2 (March/April 1994).

44. Lilia Shevstova, "Rossiya-2007: Vlast' gotova k samovosproizvodstvu, ili ob opredelennosti neopredelennosti," Carnegie Moscow Center Briefing 1, January 2007, www.carnegie.ru.

45. Ibid. For similar statements by Russian liberals, see Vladimir Milov, "Bratya imperialisty," *Vedomosti*, February 7, 2007; Grigori Yavlinski, "Present-Day Russia in an Autocracy," *Gazeta*, March 16–18, 2007, www.gazeta.ru.

46. Mikhail Yuryev, *Tretya imperiya* (St. Petersburg, Russia: Limbus Press, 2007).

47. Den'ga Khalidov, "Myunkhen: rasstavaniye s illuziyami," *Russki zhurnal*, February 27, 2007, www.russ.ru.

48. Oleg Matveychev, "Dukhovkyi suverenitet," *Russki zhurnal*, February 17, 2006, www.russ.ru.

49. Aleksandr Prokhanov, "Belarus, ty prava!," *Zavtra* 3 (687), January 17, 2007.

50. *Interfax-AVN*, May 13, 2009. The full Russian text of the strategy is published on the website of the Russian Security Council at the address www.scrf.gov.ru.

51. Dmitri Medvedev, "Go Russia!" Kremlin.ru, September 10, 2009.

52. Dmitri Medvedev, address to the Federation Council of the Russian Federation, Kremlin.ru, November 12, 2009.

53. Dmitri Medvedev, speech at meeting with Russian ambassadors and permanent representatives in international organizations, Kremlin.ru, July 12, 2010.

54. *Programma effektivnogo ispol'zovaniya vneshnepoliticheskikh faktorov v tselyakh dolgosrochnogo razvitiya Rossiyskoi Federatsiyi* (Program of Effective Use of Foreign Policy Factors to Assist Long-Term Development of the Russian Federation), February 10, 2010, www.runewsweek.ru/country/34184.

55. For a more detailed description of Russia's global strategy, see Andrei P. Tsygankov, "Preserving Influence in a Changing World: Russia's Grand Strategy," *Problems of Post-Communism* 58, no. 1 (2011).

56. See, for example, Medvedev's speech in Magnitogorsk, which stressed the need to improve the business climate (Dmitri Medvedev, meeting of the Commission for Modernization and Technological Development of Russia's Economy, Magnitogorsk, March 30, 2011, eng.kremlin.ru/news/1981).

57. *Rossiya XXI veka* (Moscow: Institut sovremennogo razvitiya, 2010), 44–45.

58. Dmitri Trenin, "Blowing Both Hot and Cold," *Moscow Times*, March 24, 2009.

59. Vladimir Putin, speech at meeting with deputies of State Duma, April 20, 2011, premier.gov.ru/events/news/14898/.

60. Tai Adelaja, "Competitive Constraints: A New Report Says Russia Is Losing the Global Battle for the Hearts and Minds of Investors," *Russia Profile*, September 8, 2011.

61. Vladimir Putin, "Meeting with the Russian Federation Ambassadors," Moscow, Foreign Ministry, July 9, 2012.

62. Vladimir Putin, "Poslaniye Prezidenta Federal'nomu Sobraniyu Rossiyskoy Federatsii," December 15, 2012, http://president.kremlin.ru.

63. Foreign Policy Concept of the Russian Federation, Kremlin.ru, February 18, 2013.

64. Foreign Policy Concept of the Russian Federation," Kremlin.ru, November 30, 2016.

65. Vladimir Putin, "Samoopredeleniye russkogo naroda—eto polietnicheskaya tsivilizatsiya, skreplennaya russkim kul'turnym yadrom," *Nezavisimaya gazeta*, January 23, 2012.

66. Putin, "Samoopredeleniye russkogo naroda." Along these lines, the new official nationalities strategy, until the year 2025, signed by Putin in December 2012 reintroduced Russia as a "unique socio-cultural civilization entity formed of the multi-people Russian nation," and, under pressure from Muslim constituencies, removed the reference to ethnic Russians as the core of the state (*Kommersant*, December 19, 2012).

67. Vladimir Putin, "Poslaniye Prezidenta Federal'nomu Sobraniyu Rossiyskoy Federatsii," December 13, 2013, http://president.kremlin.ru.

68. Vladimir Putin, "Poslaniye Prezidenta Federal'nomu Sobraniyu Rossiyskoy Federatsii," December, 2014, http://president.kremlin.ru.

69. Alexander Bastrykin, "Pora postavit' deystvennyi zaslon informatsionnoi voine," *Kommersant*, April 18, 2018, https://www.kommersant.ru/doc/2961578; see also, "Alexander Bastrykin prizval zakonodatel'no zakrepit' natsional'nuyu ideyu Rossiyi," *Kommersant*, May 26, 2016, https://www.kommersant.ru/doc/2996728.

70. Vladimir Yakunin, "Dialog tsivilizatsiy dlya postroyeniya mirnykh i inkluzivnykh obshchestv," *Polis* 5 (131), 2012; Vladimir Yakunin, "Politicheskaya tektonika sovremennogo mira," *Polis* 4 (136), 2013.

71. Andrew Roth, "Trump 'is not my bride': Putin wades into diplomatic row with U.S.," *Washington Post*, September 5, 2017.

72. Ibid.

73. *Strategiya dlya Rossiyi: Tezisy Soveta po vneshnei I oboronnoi politike*. Moscow: Sovet po vneshnei I oboronnoi politike, May 2016, thesis 2.3.1.

74. Timofei Bordachev, "Pushki aprelya," *Russia in Global Affairs*, July 3, 2017.

75. Aleksei Miller and Fyodor Lukyanov, "Otstranennost' vmesto konfrontatsiyi," *Russia in Global Affairs,* November 27, 2016; Boris Mezhuyev, " 'Ostrov Rossiya' i rossiyskaya politika identichnosti," *Russia in Global Affairs*, April 5, 2017.

76. Andrei Kortunov, "Neizbezhnost' strannogo mira," July 15, 2016, http://old.russiancouncil.ru/inner/?id_4=7930#top-content.

77. See, for example, Dmitry Drobnitsky, "Zapad—eto dve tsivilizatsiyi, a ne odna," July 12, 2017, https://www.politanalitika.ru/v-polose-mnenij/zapad-eto-dve-tsivilizatsii-a-ne-odna/; Ruslan Ostashko, "Zakat epokhi globalizatsiyi," *Natsional'naya oborona* 10 (2017).

78. Andrei Kortunov, "Rossiya proshchayetsya s Obamoi," *Valdai Club*, October 5, 2016.

79. Fyodor Lukyanov, "Opasnost' bolshoi sdelki," Gazeta.ru, February 9, 2017; Alexander Vysotsky, "Vremya dlya taym-auta," *Russia in Global Affairs*, August 28, 2018.

80. "Moscow Warns U.S. Iran Policy May Spark 'Clash of Civilizations,' " *RIA Novosti*, March 27, 2007.

81. "Russian Arms Business Breaks New Records," RFE/RL Newsline, March 22, 2007.

82. "Medvedev Doubts Effectiveness of OSCE/NATO-Based Security System," ITAR-TASS, June 11, 2008; Dmitry Rogozin, "Global Security and Propaganda," *International Herald Tribune*, July 1, 2008.

83. Henry Meyer and Sebastian Alison, "Medvedev Says Russia to Respond to U.S. Missile Deal," *Bloomberg*, July 9, 2008.

84. "Russia to Re-equip Its New Mobile ICBMs with Multiple Warheads," *RIA Novosti*, December 15, 2007.

85. "Iskander Plans if U.S. Scraps Missile Shield," *RIA Novosti*, March 3, 2009.

86. Andrew E. Kramer, "New Pipeline Will Bypass the Bosporus but Involve Russia," *New York Times*, March 16, 2007.

87. "Putin Wants 'Deeper Friendship' with Islamic World," RFE/RL Newsline, March 14, 2008.

88. Vladimir Putin, transcript of meeting with the leaders of the news agencies of G-8 member countries, June 2, 2006, Novo-Ogaryovo, Kremlin.ru.

89. Andrei P. Tsygankov, "The Test of Belarus," *Johnson's Russia List* 14, January 19, 2007.

90. Max Delany, "Energy Ties Take Medvedev Eastward," *Moscow Times*, July 2, 2008.

91. "Belarusian President Rejects Russia's 'Imperial' Approach," RFE/RL Newsline, February 6, 2007.

92. Prokhanov, "Belarus,' ty prava!"

93. However, in August 2009, President Medvedev delayed sending a new Russian ambassador to Ukraine, blaming Ukrainian president Viktor Yushchenko for conducting anti-Russian policies. Medvedev's letter to the Ukrainian president was widely interpreted as Russia's attempt to influence Ukrainian presidential elections by undermining the position of Yushchenko and his political supporters (for Medvedev's letter, see Dmitri Medvedev, address to the President of Ukraine Victor Yushchenko, Kremlin.ru, August 11, 2009).

94. See, for example, "A Month after the War: Violations of Human Rights and Norms of Humanitarian Law in the Conflict Zone in South Ossetia," special press release by Memorial Human Rights Center, September 16, 2008; Brian Rohan, "Saakashvili 'Planned S. Ossetia Invasion': Ex-Minister," Reuters, September 15, 2008; "Did Saakashvili Lie?," *Der Spiegel*, September 15, 2008.

95. "Russia Again Vows to Block NATO Enlargement," RFE/RL Newsline, April 9, 2008.

96. C. J. Chivers, "Russia Expands Support for Breakaway Regions in Georgia," *New York Times*, April 17, 2008.

97. Anatoly Tsyganok, "On the Consequences of Georgia's NATO Entry," Fondsk.ru, January 2, 2008, www.fondsk.ru/article.php?id=1148.

98. "Moldovan President, Transdniester Leader Hold Landmark Talks," RFE/ RL Newsline, April 14, 2008.

99. "Poll Suggests Russians Favor Tough Foreign Policy," RFE/RL Newsline, March 14, 2007.

100. Leonti Byzov, "Narodnyye imperialisty," *Vremya Novostei*, March 13, 2007.

101. Michael Schwartz, "Russia Joins Drug Raid in Afghanistan, Marking Advance in Relations with U.S.," *New York Times*, October 29, 2011.

102. "NATO Base in Russia 'Pragmatic Decision'—Analysts," *RIA Novosti*, March 21, 2012.

103. Roland Nash, "Rosneft and Exxon—a Big Deal," *Business New Europe*, September 7, 2011, www.bne.eu.

104. Arshad Mohammed, "Hillary Clinton Tells Ukraine Door to NATO Open," Reuters, July 2, 2010; Yuri Paniyev, "NATO prosit Moskvu pomoch' Afghani-stanu," *Nezavisimaya gazeta*, May 23, 2012; Geogri Dvali, "SshA moderniziruyut PVO Gruziyi," *Kommersant*, June 15, 2012.

105. Indeed, Putin criticized the resolution as "defective and flawed" and resembling "medieval calls for crusades." Medvedev rebuked Putin's criticism (Alexei Anishchuk, "Russia's Medvedev Raps Putin's Libya 'Crusade' Jibe," Reuters, March 21, 2011).

106. For further discussion, see Cory Welt, "Russia, Trade, and Human Rights: Thinking through U.S. Policies," *American Progress*, April 30, 2012, www.americanprogress.org/issues/2012/04/us_russia_magnitsky.html.

107. Dmitri Medvedev, speech in Berlin, *Izvestiya*, June 6, 2008.

108. Dmitri Medvedev, meeting with the participants in the International Club Valdai, Moscow, Kremlin.ru, September 12, 2008; Dmitri Medvedev, interview of the president to the Spanish media, Kremlin.ru, March 1, 2009.

109. Conor Humphries, "Russia Drafts 'Post–Cold War' East-West Security Pact," Reuters, November 29, 2009.

110. Judy Dempsey, "Russia Wants to Formalize Relation with E.U.," *New York Times*, October 18, 2010.

111. Robert Bridge, "Moscow Looking for European 'Re-think' at Munich Security Conference," *Russia Today*, October 21, 2010, www.russiatoday.com.

112. "Europe Will Need European Security Treaty Sooner or Later—Medvedev," *RIA Novosti*, December 1, 2010.

113. For a more detailed analysis of the United States' position from a conservative perspective, see Sally McNamara, "Russia's Proposed New European Security Treaty: A Non-Starter for the U.S. and Europe," Heritage Foundation, Backgrounder 2463, September 16, 2010.

114. For documentation that the Baltics and Poland wanted NATO to develop secret contingency plans in response to the war in the Caucasus, see Ivo Daalder, "Action Request: Baltic Contingency Planning," October 18, 2009, wikileaks.ch/cable/2009/10/09USNATO464.html.

115. *RIA Novosti*, December 1, 2010.

116. Alexey Eremenko, "Russia's APEC Integration 'Just Beginning,' " *RIA Novosti*, September 2, 2012.

117. Sergei Strokan, "Strana voskhodyashchego Vostoka," *Kommersant*, September 25, 2012.

118. Vladimir Putin, "An Asia-Pacific Growth Agenda," *Wall Street Journal*, September 6, 2012.

119. Putin, "An Asia-Pacific Growth Agenda."

120. Gillian Wong, "Russia Wants to Supply All of China's Gas Needs," Associated Press, September 27, 2010.

121. Russia pledged an annual supply of 10 billion cubic meters of gas for the projected pipeline, two-thirds of which would go through North Korea (Khristina Narizhnaya, "Kim Endorses Trans-Korean Pipeline," *Moscow Times*, August 25, 2011).

122. Ben Aris, "Russia Looks East for Business; Cool on US-led Asia Trade Group," *Business New Europe*, August 30, 2012.

123. Vlad Sobell, "Russia and APEC: Increased Cooperation Will Aid Russia's Modernization," us-russia.org, September 4, 2012.

124. M. K. Bhadrakumar, "Mullah Omar Gets a Russian Visitor," *Asia Times*, March 23, 2011.

125. M. K. Bhadrakumar, "Israel Joins Russian Ballet School," *Asia Times*, September 11, 2011.

126. Anna Smolchenko, "Medvedev Hails 'Strategic' Turkey Ties," Agence France-Presse, May 12, 2010.

127. The Kremlin also recalled Russia's Libya ambassador for criticizing Moscow's decision ("Former Russian Ambassador to Libya Chamov on Dismissal, Situation There, UN Vote," *Zavtra*, March 30, 2011, www.zavtra.ru).

128. "Medvedev Outlines Anti-Terrorism Strategy for North Caucasus," *RIA Novosti*, April 1, 2010.

129. James Brooke, " 'Civil War' among Muslims Shakes Russia's South," *Voice of America*, August 30, 2012.

130. Paul Reynolds, "New Russian World Order: The Five Principles," BBC News, September 2, 2008.

131. For example, see Putin's insistence that Russia seeks not the post-Soviet states' territory or natural resources, but the human dignity and the quality of life of their citizens, whom it regards as its own cultural compatriots (Vladimir Putin, address to the Federation Council of the Russian Federation, March 2005, Kremlin.ru).

132. Dmitri Medvedev, meeting with members of the Council on Foreign Relations, Washington, DC, November 15, 2008, Kremlin.ru.

133. Vladimir Putin, "The New Integration Project for Eurasia," *Izvestia*, October 3, 2011.

134. Lyubov Pronina, "Russia Gas Deal Shuts NATO Door for Ukraine, Opens Asset Access," *Bloomberg*, April 23, 2010.

135. *Kommersant*, April 7, 2011.

136. Philip P. Pan, "Russia Helped Fuel Unrest in Kyrgyzstan," *Washington Post*, April 12, 2010. One element of Russia's pressures concerned export duties for gasoline and diesel fuel. By shifting from selling fuel duty-free to raising duties for dependent neighbors, the Kremlin could achieve impressive results. In the second half of 2010, Russia also tried the approach in Tajikistan by seeking its permission to install a military base there. Russia supplies 93 percent of the country's petroleum products ("Russia Ends Fuel Duties for Kyrgyz, Raises Them for Tajiks," CentralAsiaOnline.com, March 25, 2011).

137. Steve Gutterman, "Russia, U.S. at Odds on Kyrgyzstan's Future," Reuters, October 6, 2010.

138. Yuri Simonyan, "Nino Burdzhanadze obyavili 'predatelem Guziyi'" (Nino Burdzhanadze is pronounced a traitor of Georgia), *Nezavisimaya gazeta*, April 3, 2010.

139. Bruce Pannier, "Russia's Star on Rise Again in Kyrgyzstan," RFE/RL Newsline, April 8, 2011.

140. As Elizabeth Wishnick writes, "Prior to the recognition [of Abkhazia and South Ossetia's independence], Chinese media coverage largely echoed Russian positions, and, even afterwards, Chinese experts sympathized with Russian opposition to NATO's expansion" (Elizabeth Wishnick, *Russia, China, and the United States in Central Asia* [Carlisle, PA: Strategic Studies Institute, US Army War College, February 2009], 41).

141. Andrew Higgins, "In Central Asia, a New Headache for U.S. Policy," *Washington Post*, September 1, 2010.

142. Tatyana Ivzhenko, "Ukrayina i Rossiya mogut izmenit' gazovo-flotski dogovor," *Nezavisimaya gazeta*, March 15, 2011.

143. "Moscow to Counteract 'Anti-Russian' Form of Ukraine's Integration with EU," *Interfax*, March 4, 2011.

144. Aleksandr Gabuyev, "Rossiysko-kirgizskiye otnosheniya smazali i zapravili," *Kommersant*, March 22, 2011.

145. Darya Garmonenko, "Pod silovym kolpakom," *Nezavisimaya gazeta*, July 3, 2012; Aleksandra Samarina, "Novyi ritm possiyskoi politiki," *Nezavisimaya gazeta*, August 14, 2012.

146. "Moscow Dismisses Western Criticism of Gay Propaganda Law," *RIA Novosti*, August 7, 2013.

147. President Obama, too, publicly spoke against the new legislation and declared that he has "no patience for countries that try to treat gays, lesbians or transgender persons in ways that intimidate them or are harmful to them" (Christi Parsons, "Obama Criticizes Russia's New Anti-Gay Law in Leno Interview," *Los Angeles Times*, August 7, 2013).

148. On May 23, 2015, Putin signed a law giving prosecutors the power to shut down undesirable international organizations ("Putin Signs Russian Law to Shut [Down] 'Undesirable' Organizations," Associated Press, May 23, 2015).

149. For example, see Assistant Secretary of State for Democracy, Human Rights, and Labor Tom Malinowski's interview in Russian newspaper *Kommersant* on March 3, 2015, "Vesti dielo stalo ochen' slozhno," http://www.kommersant.ru/doc/2678676.

150. Fred Weir, "Chemical Weapons in Syria: How Russia Views the Debate," *Christian Science Monitor*, August 22, 2013.

151. Andrei Kolesnikov, "Na poltona blizhe," *Kommersant*, May 12, 2015, http://www.kommersant.ru/doc/2725130.

152. For further discussion, see Pavel Koshkin, "Is There Any Way to Reconcile the Interests of the US, Russia in Syria?" *Russia Direct*, October 5, 2015; Andrei Tsygankov, "The Kremlin's Syria Gamble Is Risky, But Could Have a Big Payoff," *Russia Direct*, October 3, 2015.

153. Sergei L. Loiko, "Russia Reacts Coolly to Obama's Nuclear Proposals," *Los Angeles Times*, June 19, 2013.

154. "US Missile Defense System in Europe May Ruin INF Treaty, Warns Russian Foreign Ministry," TASS, September 25, 2018.

155. Vladimir Putin's Press Conference, Kremlin.ru, March 4, 2014, http://eng.kremlin.ru/news/6763.

156. Kirill Belyaninov, "Yevropa ne prisoyedinilas' k SshA," *Kommersant*, March 5, 2014.

157. John Hudson, "Russia Sought a Broad Reset with Trump, Secret Document Shows," *Buzzfeed.com*, September 12, 2017.

158. Ibid.

159. Mike DeBonis and Karoun Demirjian, "House Passes Russia Sanctions Bill, Setting Up Veto Dilemma for Trump," *Washington Post*, July 25, 2017.

160. Philipp Casula, "Russia's and Europe's Borderlands," *Problems of Post-Communism* 61, 6, 2014; Hiski Haukkala, "From Cooperative to Contested Europe? The Conflict in Ukraine as a Culmination of a Long-Term Crisis in EU–Russia Relations," *Journal of Contemporary European Studies* 23, 1 (2015).

161. Tuomas Forsberg and Hiski Haukkala, "The European Union," in *The Routledge Handbook of Russian Foreign Policy*, edited by Andrei P. Tsygankov (London: Routledge, 2018).

162. Speeches by Maas and Macron in August 2018.

163. Paul Stronski and Richard Sokolsky, "The Return of Global Russia," Carnegie Endowment for International Peace, December 14, 2017.

164. Ibid. For a detailed review of Russia's Balkan priorities and actions, see Dimtar Bechev, *Rival Power: Russia in Southeast Europe* (New Haven: Yale University Press, 2017).

165. Lucan Ahmad Way and Adam Casey, "Russian Foreign Election Interventions Since 1991," *PONARS Eurasia Policy* Memo No. 520, March 2018.

166. Lee Fang and Zaid Jilani, "Hacked Emails Reveal NATO General Plotting Against Obama on Russia Policy," *Intercept*, July 1 2016.

167. In June 2016, the alliance held a simulated defense against Russia known as Anakonda, the largest military exercise since the end of the Cold War involving some 31,000 troops and thousands of combat vehicles from twenty-four countries; Michael T. Klare, "The United States and NATO Are Preparing for a Major War With Russia," *Nation*, July 7, 2016.

168. Nikolai Patrushev, "Vyzov prinyat," *Rossiyskaya gazeta*, December 22, 2015.

169. Nikolai Patrushev, "Mirovoiye soobshchestvo dolzhno skazat' nam spasibo za Krym," *MK*, January 26, 2016.

170. Alexander Grushko, "Rossiya ne ostavit bez otveta usileniye NATO," *Izvestia*, June 16, 2016. The 1997 Russia-NATO Founding Act prohibits the deployment of substantial military forces in Eastern Europe on a permanent basis. Russia interprets 3,000 to 5,000 troops to be "substantial," while NATO officials disagree (Yelena Chernenko, "Ekspressivnyye plany NATO," *Kommersant*, September 6, 2014).

171. Alexander Grushko, "Bez strashilki o Rossiyi NATO ne uderzhat' kontrol' za ES," March 25, 2016, http://www.vestifinance.ru/videos/26759.

172. Vladimir Putin, "The New Integration Project for Eurasia," *Izvestia*, October 3, 2011.

173. Vladimir Putin, "Meeting of the Valdai International Discussion Club," September 19, 2013.

174. For details, see Tsygankov, "Vladimir Putin's Last Stand: The Sources of Russia's Ukraine Policy," *Post-Soviet Affairs* 31, 4 (2015).

175. "The Minsk Ceasefire Deal, Point by Point," *Russia Today*, February 12, 2015.

176. Nicolai N. Petro, "Russian-Ukrainian Church Turmoil Driven by Political Ambitions," *Russia Matters*, October 19, 2018.

177. Ibid.

178. Putin further insisted on the preservation of a "new balance of economic, civilizational and military forces" and instructed the government to pay more attention to the development of patriotic and military education. See his Annual Address to the Federal Assembly, Moscow, the Kremlin, December 12, 2012, Kremlin.ru.

179. Katya Golubkova, "New BRICS Bank to Look at Local, International Borrowing," Reuters, July 9, 2015.

180. Aleksey Nikolsky, "Russia Charts New Course for BRICS Nations as Presidency Begins," Tass, April 1, 2015.

181. Ibid.

182. Aleksey Nikolsky, "Russia-China Gas Deal Requires Moscow's Reconciliation with US, EU," *Sputnik*, November 10, 2014.

183. Vladimir Soldatkin and Timothy Heritage, "Russia and China Deepen Ties with New Economic Deals," Reuters, May 8, 2015.

184. Marcin Kaczmarski and Witold Rodkiewicz, "Russia's Greater Eurasia and China's New Silk Road: Adaptation Instead of Competition," *OSW Commentary*, July 27, 2016.

185. Yuri Tavrovsky, "Pekin sobirayet gory i morya," *Nezavisimiaya gazeta*, November 15, 2013.

186. "Rossiya i Kitai podpisali dogovor o 'Shelkovom puti,'" BBC, May 8, 2015.

187. For detailed proposals by Russian experts of Russia–China cooperation in Eurasia, see the Valdai Club's Report, "Toward the Great Ocean—3: Creating Central Eurasia (Moscow, June 2015).

188. Alexander Lukin, "What the Kremlin Is Thinking: Putin's Vision for Eurasia," *Foreign Affairs*, July–August, 2014.

189. Dmitry Trenin, *From Greater Europe to Greater Asia? The Sino-Russian Entente* (Washington, DC: The Carnegie Endowment for International Peace, 2015).

190. Sergei Glazyev, "Moment istiny: Rossiya i sanktsiyi Zapada," Moscow: the Izborsky Club, 26 June, 2014.

191. Gilbert Rozman, *The Sino-Russian Challenge to the World Order: National Identities, Bilateral Relations, and East versus West in the 2010s* (Stanford: Stanford University Press, 2014).

192. Chris Weafer, "Russia Needs to Pivot East and West," *Moscow Times*, May 8, 2014.

193. Tatyana Yedovina, "K Evraez prisoyedinili vyetnamsky rynok," *Kommersant*, May 30, 2015.

194. Mikhail Molchanov, "The Eurasian Economic Union," in *The Routledge Handbook of Russian Foreign Policy* (London: Routledge, 2018).

195. Clare Nuttell, "Investment Revives within Eurasian Economic Union After 3-year Decline," *Intellnews*, October 17, 2017.

196. Andrej Krickovic and Mikhail Breatersky, "Benevolent Hegemon, Neighborhood Bully, or Regional Security Provider?," *Eurasian Geography and Economics* 57, 2 (2016).

197. Marcin Kaczmarski, "The Asymmetric Partnership? Russia's Turn to China," *International Politics* (2016), 2.

198. Ibid., 12.

199. Edward Schatz, "How Western Disengagement Enabled Uzbekistan's 'Spring' and How to Keep It Going," *Ponars*, Policy Memo 531, June 2018.

200. Ibid.

201. Olga Solovyeva, "Tovarooborot s Kitayem vyros na chetvert,'" *Nezavisimiaya gazeta,* August 9, 2017.

202. Yeveniya Novikova, "Moskva i Tegeran soprotivlyayutsya sanktsiyam," *Nezavisimaya gazeta*, April 30, 2014.

203. For details of Russian–Iranian relations, see Nikolay Kozhanov, "Understanding the Revitalization of Russian-Iranian Relations," Moscow Carnegie Center, May 5, 2015.

204. Zachary Laub and Jonathan Masters, "The Islamic State," Council on Foreign Relations, May 18, 2015.

205. Yelena Suponina, "Kak Yegipet opyat' stal luchshim drugom Rossiyi na Blizhnem Vostoke," *Nezavisimaya gazeta*, June 10, 2015.

206. Simeon Kerr and Kathrin Hille, "Saudi Defence Minister to Meet Vladimir Putin for Talks on Syria," *Financial Times*, June 17, 2015.

207. P. Bilgin and A. Bilgiç, "Turkey's 'New' Foreign Policy toward Eurasia," *Eurasian Geography and Economics* 52, 2 (2011).

208. Ben Aris, "The Riga Summit of Disappointment," *Business New Europe*, May 21, 2015.

209. Yury Barmin, "What's Behind the Saudi King's Historic Visit to Russia," *Moscow Times*, October 4, 2017.

210. Will Kennedy, Elena Mazneva, and Wael Mahdi, "Russia–Saudi Plans for Super-OPEC Could Reshape Global Oil Order," *Bloomberg*, June 22, 2018.

211. Konstantin Truyevtsev, "Rossiya-Azerbaijan-Iran," *Valdai Club*, November 2, 2017.

5

From Assertiveness to Isolation? 2019–2022

[W]e behave in an extremely restrained manner . . . Often, we prefer not to respond at all, to not just unfriendly moves, but even to outright rudeness. We want to maintain good relations with everyone who participates in the international dialogue. . . . We really do not want to burn bridges. But if someone mistakes our good intentions for indifference or weakness and intends to burn or even blow up these bridges, they must know that Russia's response will be asymmetrical, swift, and tough.

—Vladimir Putin, April 2021[1]

A new set of domestic and international pressures on Russia, such as economic weakness and global instability, challenged the adopted policy of assertiveness. Conditions have emerged for a possible adjustment of Russian foreign policy in the direction of becoming more defensive and driven by internal needs. Historically, Russia has seen such a course as one of internal concentration, which it has followed under two essential conditions—domestic weakness, or vulnerability to external pressures and international multipolarity. While the former is the rationale for a more moderate foreign policy, following the latter provides an opportunity not to yield to external pressures by allowing sufficient space for maneuvering.

Russian policymakers found themselves facing the choice of continuing with assertiveness or adopting steps that would strengthen the economy and the state while avoiding excessive international commitments and limiting foreign engagement to the protection of core national interests. The departure of the international system from the US-centered unipolar structure to a more complex and multipolar one has provided an additional opportunity for pursuing the new moderate course.

However, the chosen course of action was to continue many of the assertive policies described in the previous chapter. During this new period, Russia has not developed a coherent strategy of internal concentration. Instead, it has escalated tensions with the West to the level of confrontation. The military intervention in Ukraine in February 2022 became the culmination of the Russia–West conflict. Moscow acted on the perception of Western decline and Russia's increased military strength. Despite the country's internal vulnerabilities, influential groups within the political class assumed that Russia had the opportunity to assert its interests in Europe and Eurasia. The increased tensions with the West have led to the latter's heightened efforts to isolate Russia from global economic and political relations, thereby treating Moscow as it once did during the Cold War. In relations with non-Western countries, Russia's leadership has displayed greater flexibility, trying to take advantage of growing opportunities in the increasingly post-Western world.

GLOBAL INSTABILITY AND DOMESTIC RESPONSE

Power Transition and Global Instability

Several international developments have served to increase the sense of global instability in Russian foreign policy establishment. These developments have had to do with power transition in the international system and the rise of globally significant issues that required urgent attention by all the major participants in the international system.

With respect to the power transition dimension, the most important developments concerned elections in the United States and the return to Washington of liberally minded elites in charge of American foreign policy. The newly elected president Joe Biden made it clear that he aimed to revive the US-centered international system based on liberal ideas. In one of his articles, he argued, "We must once more harness that power and rally the free world to meet the challenges facing the world today. It falls to the United States to lead the way. No other nation has that capacity. No other nation is built on that idea. We have to champion liberty and democracy."[2]

At the same time, the United States faced important problems at home and abroad. Domestically, it had to address the challenge of reviving the economy following the coronavirus pandemic, racial justice issues, migration, and the political polarization that had previously helped to elect Donald Trump. Biden's election in 2020 ended the chaotic years associated with the previous presidency yet presented the country with new challenges. Trump remained popular within the Republican Party. Without major successes at home, the country's political and social divides were set to continue making it difficult to conduct a foreign policy aimed at preserving global leadership.

Externally, China emerged as the most important challenger to the United States' global ambitions. Beijing succeeded in managing the COVID-19 crisis, demonstrated its ability for continued economic growth even throughout the pandemic, and did not yield to pressures to renegotiate bilateral trade on terms favored by the United States. As Biden signaled his plans to confront China as the United States' most important competitor, observers began to discuss the possibility of a Cold War between the two countries.[3] Whether or not one accepts the argument, the tensions between these two global powers promises continued instability and difficult choices for all of those not directly involved in bilateral disputes for years to come.

The emergence of these new global issues served to exacerbate the instability related to international power transition. The COVID-19 crisis turned the countries' attention to their health-care systems and social safety nets. Challenged externally and internally, states reacted by closing their national borders to protect their citizens from the deadly virus. However, such unilateral actions could not offer global solutions, further increasing the sense of international uncertainty. Another challenge emerged from changes in global climate, evident in sharp fluctuations of temperature and an increased number of fires during the summer months. Climate change created additional economic and demographic pressures, demanding the attention of all major states in the international system. Other global issues concerned the security of cyberspace and outer space and freedom of navigation, as well as transportation of vital sources of energy in the Arctic and other areas.

The combination of power transition and global issues increased the potential for international instability and security competition across the world. The growing prospect of such competition, especially among great powers, meant new arms races and the militarization of areas traditionally not affected, including explorations in outer space and geographically remote areas such as the Arctic and Antarctic. The new environment of instability pressed other states to make difficult choices and allocate additional funds for defense. In this environment, those willing to take risks in the Middle East, Eurasia, Europe, and elsewhere have contributed to the destabilization of the international system. In the absence of a strong global security framework, the world was becoming a more dangerous place.

Russia's Internal Challenges and State Response

The described developments increased Russia's perceived vulnerability to external and global pressures, prompting the country's leadership to search for new sources of unity and stabilization at home.

The new vulnerabilities concerned Russia's health-care system, economy, and political system. The COVID-19 pandemic revealed problems with national demographics and health-care institutions. Although Russian scientists developed internationally recognized vaccines for fighting the virus, the national statistics of rising infections and mortality demonstrated the magnitude of the issue. During 2020, life expectancy in the country declined by 1.8 years, while the overall mortality increased by 20 percent, including among people under the age of sixty.[4] The related problem was with the underperforming economy. Russia's living standards have been declining since 2015, and the size of Russia's GDP has declined at a constant rate.[5] If measured as GDP per capita in current US dollars, then it has declined by approximately one-third since 2013.[6] The decline of oil prices in 2015, the insufficiently diversified economy,[7] and the pandemic all contributed to the indicated vulnerabilities.

Although the political system established in Russia during Putin's years in office served to provide stability, it was increasingly at the expense of economic and social dynamism. In such a system, the state mediates between powerful economic and security interests, while being unable to formulate and impose overarching rules of behavior in the interests of the larger society. In practice, Putin's power is insufficient to propose and carry out widespread social reform. During the pandemic, Putin delegated parts of the decision-making power to regional governors, while relying on conservative tools to regulate the economy. Under the lobbyism of big business, oligarchs received greater support from the state than other social groups.[8] The insufficiently diversified economy was stable yet without important incentives to grow.

In April 2021, Putin delivered an address to the Federation Council, in which he articulated several urgent and long-term policies.[9] He encouraged Russian citizens to be vaccinated against the coronavirus pandemic. In the area of the economy, Putin promised to contain rising prices for food; to stimulate tourism; to encourage the growth of small and medium-size businesses; and to provide financial assistance to low-income and single-parent families, with a separate payment for each child. He also promised a technological overhaul of the health-care system, and to initiate measures to protect the country against environmental crises by creating a system of control over carbon emissions. Putin further formulated some medium-and long-term objectives, such as increasing the average life expectancy from seventy-one to seventy-eight years by 2030, and lowering greenhouse gas emissions below those within the European Union by 2050. In foreign affairs, the Russian president stressed the importance of a strong defense, and promised a tough, asymmetric response if Russia's interests and "red lines" were not recognized. In one of his speeches, Putin also called on foreign powers to respect Russia's national values and traditions while refraining from interference in the internal affairs of other states.[10]

State Concentration of Power

Although the Russian state felt the urgent need to respond to the revealed social, economic, and political vulnerabilities, the chosen policy response was stronger on power concentration than on stimulating internal economic and social development. In the absence of a long-term strategy, the Kremlin proposed steps to unify society and stabilize the system where possible, while providing powerful interest groups with greater latitude and flexibility. In 2020, Putin extended his term in office until 2036 by initiating a constitutional amendment. The state cracked down on the system's opponents by arresting Aleksei Navalny, the leader of a radical opposition group, and passing a law to ban his political movement as an "extremist organization."[11] While the potential for political protest in the system remained significant, there was also considerable support for the authorities and disapproval for Navalny.[12] In foreign affairs, the Kremlin stressed the importance of asymmetrical yet formidable power to offset potential pressures by external/Western nations.

In addition, as the potential for political protest grew, Putin seemed to have accepted the autonomy of Russian security services.[13] Judging by various incidents, including a possible attempt to poison Navalny, the security services increasingly relied on intimidation when dealing with perceived domestic and foreign enemies of the state. In terms of foreign relations, Russian intelligence agents were reportedly involved in assassination attempts and other special operations. Western governments sought to react accordingly with what they assessed as the Kremlin-ordered operations of security services. For instance, in April 2021, the Czech Republic expelled eighteen Russian diplomats over suspicion of members of the Russian intelligence service being involved in the explosion of a military storage facility in 2014. Several European governments, such as those of the Baltic States and Bulgaria, also expelled several Russian diplomats out of solidarity with the Czech Republic.

Most of the Russian political class has been supportive of Putin's message and proposed steps to address the country's vulnerabilities. The elections to the State Duma in September 2021 brought victory to the pro-Kremlin party, the United Russia, which was to form the parliamentary majority and control the most important committees. For the time being, the global instability seems to have brought together different elite groups with diverse economic and political preferences on the grounds of protecting the country. The need to resist Western pressures was often the definition of such protection. Even the so-called liberals within the system have become highly critical of the West for its policies with respect to Russia. For instance, former president and prime minister Dmitri Medvedev went so far as to compare the current global situation with the Cuban Missile Crisis. He assigned the blame for this mainly to the United States, for its withdrawal from important international treaties, and for replacing dialogue with pressures against Russia and China.[14] The so-called *siloviks* within the system grew especially influential and offered a similar critique of the United States and Western countries. The head of the Security Council, Nikolai Patrushev, elaborated on Medvedev's argument by identifying US global policies as being responsible for the growing instability across the world and the decline of trust in relations with Russia.[15]

In the meantime, Russia's military, nuclear, and cyber capabilities have increased, emboldening the security-minded elites to rely on coercion in foreign policy. Russia has reformed its military in response to the United States' decision to withdraw from the ABM Treaty and Russia's sluggish performance during its five-day conflict with Georgia in 2008. The country has developed new, hypersonic weapons capable of penetrating the MDS; obtained new combat experience in Syria; and trained new rapid reaction units for operating in the former Soviet region.

Russia's political system and foreign policy are not likely to undergo fundamental changes anytime soon. Protests have been taking place for a long time, and the support for Navalny by some segments of the population did not constitute a major threat to stability. The opposition to the war in Ukraine was also not sufficient to challenge the foundations of Putin's systems. Even if Putin decides to step down as leader, there is likely to be considerable continuity in the functioning of both the country's foreign policy and its domestic political system.

PERSPECTIVES ON NATIONAL INTEREST: ASSERTIVE OR DEFENSIVE FOREIGN POLICY?

The post-2019 period has been distinct with respect to Russian foreign policy discussions. Following the mid-2000s, Russia tried to cooperate with Western nations on mutually acceptable terms, or it asserted its interests unilaterally. The former attempts included Dmitri Medvedev's policies during 2009–2010 and Putin's efforts to improve relations with Trump during 2017–2018. During these periods, Russia's foreign policy disagreements included mainly those between supporters of cooperation and assertiveness with those voices of defensiveness and limited engagement, with the latter being relatively marginalized. Following 2019, the nation's international discourse has shifted with the growing influence of those who argue for the need to have a more limited foreign policy. Increasingly, Russian experts have begun to stress the need to direct the country's attention away from the West, maneuvering between major centers of global power while searching for new international opportunities, focusing on domestic recovery, and containing only those foreign actions that threaten Russia's core interests.

Advocates of a Defensive Foreign Policy

The discourse of a new defensive foreign policy for the purpose of concentrating on domestic development rose to prominence in 2017–2018 in response to Trump's inability to rebuild relations with Russia due to opposition from the American liberal establishment in Congress, the media, and the intelligence community.[16] The discourse grew stronger in the context of the COVID-19 pandemic, the presidential elections in 2020, and the new US–China rivalry.

Russian voices favoring pragmatism in relations with the United States became louder. Even some of those formerly supportive of assertiveness now shifted toward defensiveness. Since 2015, in a series of published reports, the mainstream foreign policy think tank Valdai Club and its organizers have advanced the pragmatic position of gaining distance from America and the West. In their assessment, the world is undergoing a major transformation with the outcomes uncertain, and this requires a prioritization of self-help by the main international actors.[17] In 2020, these analysts further highlighted the importance of national unity and state strength in the face of international instability.[18] Russian moderate media also cautioned against the country's engagement in another round of confrontations with the West.[19]

Those favoring Russia's conservative development also supported the course of defensive foreign policy. Some of them advocated a focus on regional development with clearly delineated "civilizational" borders between Russia and the West.[20] According to this perspective, Russia needed to draw political borders in Eurasia along the lines of a cultural/civilizational division with Western nations. The world was moving away from globalization toward regionalization, and Russia would need to firm up its presence in Eurasia for both domestic and international reasons. The argument opened up a space for defending formal incorporation by Russia of those former Soviet territories culturally gravitating toward Russia, although some of its supporters argued against such incorporation by non-Russian states. They cautioned against Russia's annexation of eastern Ukraine while insisting on doing everything in Russia's power to protect the territory from being reunited with Kyiv.[21]

Even some of the former advocates of an assertive, muscular foreign policy in relations with the West had changed their views and now advocated a more inward-focused international strategy. A good example is the intellectual evolution of the former dean of the Faculty of World Economy and International Affairs at Moscow's Higher School of Economics, Sergei Karaganov. Since

2019, he has stopped promoting an assertive or "victorious" global policy to make the West change its views on Russia and has begun to advocate a "neo-isolationist" policy in the interests of national development. He has cautioned against unwarranted interventions, not only in remote regions such as Latin America, but also in Ukraine and Eastern Europe, as potentially "too costly."[22] He has also advocated a strong, "authoritarian" type of government as a way to address Russia's domestic problems under foreign instability.[23] Following Biden's attempts to engage in dialogue with Putin, other analysts argued that the purpose of relations with the United States should be restricted to "manageable confrontation."[24]

Supporters of Assertive Foreign Policy

Most supporters of a defensive foreign policy have argued for a firm response to perceived Western encroachment on Russia's interests and, if necessary, building stronger military ties with China. This defensive policy does not mean disengagement from international affairs, and is not comparable to the nineteenth-century concentration on domestic affairs,[25] as increasing globalization requires Russia's constant attention to foreign policy.

Supporters of assertive foreign policy took the latter line of reasoning to the next level. In their view, if Russia was to protect its sovereignty and core interests, it had no choice but to counterbalance the United States' actions globally. Within the mainstream, influential experts and politicians, such as member of the Federation Council, Aleksei Pushkov; member of the State Duma, Vyacheslav Nikonov; and others have advocated a globally assertive foreign policy for containing an "aggressive" America.[26] In the above-mentioned interview, secretary of the Security Council Nikolai Patrushev stressed the "diminishing space" for cooperation with the United States and the need to prevent the West's economic, political, ideological, and military actions aimed at undermining the national sovereignty of Russia.[27] Members of the political class and media circles have argued for a decisive response to Ukrainian and NATO's activities in the Black Sea, as well as the European Union's sanctions and criticisms of Russia.

The belief in global containment of the West had its roots in the period of Soviet confrontation with Western countries formed on the assumption that no other policy would adequately protect Russia's national interests.[28] Many Soviet officials viewed the policy as necessary for surviving as a sovereign power under the West's "expansionist" foreign policy. To the extent that Russia intervened in the affairs of foreign nations, including by interfering in Western elections and domestic politics, such actions continued the tradition of assertiveness.

MINIMIZING RELATIONS WITH THE WEST

The proposed defensive direction of Russia's foreign policy was meant to limit relations with Western nations to those of absolute necessity while developing ties with countries outside the West. However, according to those in favor of assertiveness, such outcomes could only be accomplished by keeping pressures on the West high. Putin did not hide his intention to create "tensions" in relations with Western states in the NATO coalition.[29]

Continued Rivalry with the Liberal United States

Russia began to limit its relations with the United States under Donald Trump's presidency. The new policy of gaining distance from the United States reflected the Kremlin's perception of the two countries' different interests in the international system, rather than that of different political systems. The Russian leadership preferred a multipolar world and maintaining relations with the United States from a position of equality, whereas Trump wanted to preserve America as the only superpower.[30] He viewed Russia as a potential junior partner in a global competition with China, the main perceived rival. While cherishing relations with China, the Kremlin did not perceive Trump as an existential threat because the latter never expressed any interest in global democracy promotion and regime change.

Liberal America was a different matter. The US foreign policy interventions in Yugoslavia, Iraq, and elsewhere, the experience of the color revolutions in Eurasia, and the many years of Western criticism of Russia as a corrupt autocracy disrespectful of human rights and political opposition had taught the Kremlin to prioritize sovereignty in international relations. Even though Russia's relations with Trump did not develop in any meaningful way, the Kremlin preferred for him to remain president after the 2020 elections in the United States. Following Joe Biden's victory in November and Trump's refusal to concede, Putin waited to congratulate Biden until the Electoral College vote in December. During the annual press conference on December 20, 2020, Putin further expressed hope for cooperation with Biden, while attributing problems in bilateral relations to the United States' domestically polarizing politics. Putin further responded to the storm of the Capitol by Trump's sympathizers on January 6, 2021, by comparing them to Russia's radical opposition and cautioning against destabilization in politics.[31]

However, if Putin had hoped to improve relations with the United States, he was soon disappointed. In January 2021, Biden called the Russian president to inform him of America's willingness to extend the expiring START treaty for another five years, but Biden also warned Putin of new sanctions to come against Russia. US intelligence services had determined that Russia was likely behind not only election interference but also hacking the computer company SolarWinds. Putin reciprocated on the START treaty by quickly signing it into law, but in March 2021, he faced American sanctions against several Russian companies and Russian sovereign debt.[32] In addition, in a public interview, Biden made it clear that he considered Putin a "killer"—a likely reference to the attempted poisoning of Aleksei Navalny in September 2020.[33] Biden further warned Putin against intervention in Ukraine and promised Kyiv unspecified assistance should the intervention occur.

Russia responded to the new crisis by recalling its ambassador in Washington to Moscow for consultations; imposing a series of sanctions against the United States; and "recommending" that US Ambassador John Sullivan leave Russia for consultations in his own country. The imposed American sanctions included, among others, the requirement to cut diplomatic personnel in the US Embassy and to stop the hiring of Russian nationals by the Embassy. As of April 2021, the United States announced that it lacked sufficient personnel to issue visas for Russians planning to travel to America.

In addition to sanctions, Russia staged new military exercises in the Black Sea, closed the Kerch Bridge in the Azov Sea, and amassed many troops on the border with Ukraine. The Kremlin's reaction was partly a response to Ukraine's own movement of military units and stated intent to "liberate" Crimea, and partly a demonstration of Russia's force and determination to NATO and the United States. In April 2021, following several tense weeks, Biden called on Putin to de-escalate the situation, inviting him to a summit meeting to discuss a "wide range of issues."

Some de-escalation indeed took place. On June 15, 2021, the leaders of the United States and Russia met in Switzerland. The two sides agreed to have regular contact and to establish working groups to address the issues of nuclear and cyber security. In the following month, Biden also indicated his lack of support for sanctioning the Russian-German pipeline, the Nord Stream 2, referring to it as "nearly completed." In addition, the US president did not support Ukraine's bid to join NATO, and indicated this during President Volodymyr Zelensky's visit to Washington, DC, in August 2021. In October 2021, prominent US officials—such as Under Secretary of State Victoria Nuland and CIA director William Burns—made separate trips to Moscow to discuss international issues of mutual importance.

Russia and America cautiously engaged in cooperation over various global issues during this period. In addition to extending the START treaty, Russia participated in the US-organized global climate summit on April 22, 2021, by opening a space for future environmental cooperation. Other potential areas of cooperation included Iran's nuclear deal, Arctic security, cybersecurity, counterterrorism, and vaccination during the coronavirus pandemic.

In particular, the two sides registered progress in reaching an understanding regarding issues of cybersecurity. In October 2021, the United States and Russia jointly sponsored the United Nations resolution about the responsible behavior of states in cyberspace, and took joint actions against those acting as cyber aggressors.[34] More than fifty states supported the UN resolution.

However, the main sources of bilateral tension remained unaddressed. As the two sides did not recognize each other's desired role in the international system, rivalry prevailed over cooperation, which was limited, and the two nations remained critical and suspicious of each other's intentions. United States officials clearly stated that they mainly needed "stability and predictability" of bilateral relations with Russia. The Kremlin interpreted the US position as reflecting Washington's prioritization of global competition with China. At the same time, Russia remained resentful of American sanctions and the US perception of Russia as a national security threat. While NATO increased military training near Russia, including the Black Sea area, the Kremlin continued to strengthen what it viewed as a protection of national sovereignty against potentially threatening foreign actions. It conducted regular military exercises on the western borders and banned Navalny's political movement inside Russia, viewing the movement as a fifth column meant to destabilize the country. Putin further stated that he would draw "red lines" as he deemed appropriate. Russian authorities signaled that if Washington chose a cyberattack against critical infrastructure in Russia or provided essential military support for Ukraine, then Moscow would not hesitate to counterattack. On issues vital to Russia's security, the Kremlin preferred cooperation with China.

Bilateralization of Relations with Europe

A similar dynamic characterized Russia's relations with European nations. Here, too, rivalry prevailed over cooperation, with the escalating tendency of the two sides to disagree. Russia reacted by defending its perceived core interests and continuing to diversify its economic and political ties away from Europe. As a result, for the first time since the Cold War, Russia's foreign exports in 2020 were conducted in US dollars, with euros amounting to less than 50 percent of the total.[35] The Kremlin also sought to limit involvement in European affairs as a way of concentrating on domestic politics and other international directions.

Following the election of Joe Biden as the US president in November 2020, European leaders expected to revive transatlantic relations and forge greater unity in the face of difficult relations with Russia. Donald Trump's America First approach and his unwillingness to confront Russia except on issues of commercial importance greatly damaged transatlantic relations. For instance,

Trump opposed Russia's construction of the Nord Stream 2 pipelines to Germany while promoting US energy sales to European markets. By contrast, Biden's vision aligned better with those of European nations because it stressed human rights, the unity of NATO, and opposition to Russia on issues ranging from elections in Belarus to interference in Ukrainian and Central European politics. While critical of the Nord Stream 2 as increasing dependence on Russia, Biden did not want to strain relations with Europeans, and refrained from imposing any sanctions against those involved in constructing the pipeline.

Partly because of revived transatlantic unity, European leaders increased pressure on Russia on these issues. Russia responded by hardening its approach and further highlighting differences in the two sides' worldview and perceptions. European leaders continued to visit Moscow yet failed to make any progress in bridging these differences. For instance, in February 2021, the head of EU foreign policy, Josep Borrell, traveled to Russia to criticize it for jailing Navalny and to address other issues related to the country's political system. Russian officials refused to discuss these matters with Borrell, and to reinforce their point, Moscow embarrassed the EU official by announcing its decision to expel two European diplomats while he was attending an official meeting.[36] Russian Foreign Minister Sergei Lavrov followed up on the European visit by warning that Russia could decide to cease communications with EU officials and conduct relations with the continent's countries strictly on a bilateral basis.

In April 2021, Russia's relations with Europe reached a new low not only due to the crisis over Ukraine, but also because of the new diplomatic scandal over the activities of Russian security services in the Czech Republic and Bulgaria. Both countries had expelled Russia's diplomats over suspicion of their roles in an explosion of stored weapons and military ammunition in a Czech village. In addition, the European Parliament followed its discussion of relations with Russia by recommending that the EU change the country's economy from the SWIFT payment system, and that they stop purchasing Russia's energy should the Kremlin conduct a military intervention in Ukraine.

Russia reacted symmetrically by demonstrating its determination to protect its sovereignty and perceived core interests. Moscow expelled a larger number of Czech diplomats from the country. The Russian Foreign Ministry also included the Czech Republic in its list of "unfriendly" governments by banning it from hiring Russian nationals. The Kremlin also imposed sanctions against top-level European officials, including the head of the European Parliament, by banning their entry into the country. Russia's experts, such as the head of the Carnegie Moscow Center, Dmitri Trenin, argued that the Kremlin would no longer tolerate any foreign interference in its internal affairs, and that Russia's continued membership in the Council of Europe and its parliamentary assembly were "no longer to be taken for granted."[37]

In the fall of 2021, European crises with energy and migrants further affected Russia–EU relations. An energy crisis developed as prices for natural gas increased several times in response to new demands and the EU's decision to be guided by markets, rather than long-term contracts with Russia and other exporters. The second crisis was more political in nature and involved the decision by Belarusian authorities to encourage migrants from the Middle East to move to Poland, Germany, and other countries within the EU, through Belarus's territory. Minsk responded to European sanctions and criticism of Belarus's fraudulent presidential elections of August 2020. In November 2021, several thousands of migrants from Iraq, Syria, and other countries concentrated on the Belarus–Poland border only to be blocked from entry by Polish authorities.

These crises revealed the tendency among some European politicians to blame "autocratic" Putin for undermining the unity and democracy within the EU. The Kremlin, however, refrained from engaging in openly confrontational behavior. Putin used the energy crisis to promote the Nord Stream 2, but also instructed Gazprom to increase supplies, which helped to reduce demands and prices on European markets. Regarding the migration crisis, Russia supported Belarus but also sought to de-escalate the situation by encouraging a direct dialogue between Minsk and the EU.

The overall space for Russian–European cooperation had shrunk considerably and was now limited to energy supplies and dialogue over the preservation of political stability. Even on the climate change issue, little effort was made to develop cooperation. Some Russian experts proposed to move in this direction,[38] but neither side was prepared for a serious discussion. In the meantime, the potential for disagreement continued to grow. While EU leaders were framing the issue in terms of new carbon regulations for industries, Russia did not fully endorse the recommendations of the UN Climate Conference in Glasgow, instead formulating its own plan for addressing the issue. The plan included not only the reduction of emissions, but also a greater reliance on forest absorption of greenhouse gases,[39] allowing continued, albeit more limited, reliance on traditional energy sources.[40]

CONFRONTATION WITH THE WEST OVER SECURITY AND THE INVASION OF UKRAINE

Russia and the West continue to mistrust one another while developing their military capabilities and believing in dialogue from a position of strength. In this context, Russia confronted the Western nations by insisting on guarantees to its national security.

Russia's Demands and the Western Response

On December 17, 2021, Russia revealed new diplomatic initiatives to ensure guarantees for national security. Moscow demanded that NATO expansion be stopped and meaningful measures be taken to prevent military escalation in Europe. The Kremlin raised the bar to the highest level by insisting on written assurances from the United States and NATO that the alliance would end the process of admitting new members, withdraw its military presence to pre-1997 levels, and cease military cooperation with the states neighboring Russia.

Simultaneously, Russia expected Western leaders to pressure Ukraine to implement the Minsk-II agreement in its original format by engaging in direct negotiations with leaders of separatist territories and eventually granting the Donbas regional autonomy. The Kremlin also wanted Kyiv to renounce its claims to NATO membership and commit to military neutrality.

The Kremlin felt threatened by the Western alliance and its increased activities in the Black Sea, the Baltics, and the region as a whole. Russia had warned that it would use military and "military-technical" measures if its proposals were ignored. It had indicated that it was prepared to act in Ukraine and elsewhere to prevent further NATO expansion and allocation of the alliance's military infrastructure in close proximity to Russia. Emboldened by its perceived military strength and the West's decline, the Kremlin was not afraid of escalation and was prepared to take major steps to defend its interests. In his press conference in December 2021, Putin insisted that the West must provide guarantees of security to Russia "immediately, right now, instead of talking about it for decades." Warnings by advocates of a more cautious foreign policy were left unheeded.

Following years of conflict after the Cold War, the Kremlin did not expect to agree with the West on important economic and political issues. However, Moscow had hoped to develop a greater sense of security in the midst of what it saw as the West's relentless global expansion. Russia's relations with NATO became especially tense in part because the alliance expedited its support for Kyiv while moving some of its units closer to Russia and Ukraine. In particular, NATO moved four battalions to Poland and the Baltic States. In August 2020, the United States had also redeployed its troops from Germany to Poland by increasing their size in the country to about 5,500.[41]

Military Intervention in Ukraine

In November 2021, Putin referred to "tensions" with NATO on the western border as having a deterrent effect and proposed to preserve them to prevent a military conflict.[42] In order to do so, Russia again concentrated a large number of troops on the border with Ukraine, prompting widespread speculations that the Kremlin was preparing to invade the country.

Having gone through two months of diplomacy, Putin concluded that the West was not interested in engaging with Russia on the issue of security guarantees. The United States indicated that it was prepared to negotiate regarding matters of military transparency and verification. President Biden also said that Ukraine would not be qualified to join NATO anytime soon, and that the United States had no plans to build offensive capabilities in Ukraine. Foreign Minister Sergei Lavrov planned to press the West politically on NATO non-expansion as consistent with the principles of indivisible security in Europe. To Putin, however, Western offers did not amount to the security guarantees he was seeking, but rather promises and assurances that could be easily broken.

On February 24, 2022, following several days of intense shelling in the Donbas region and Russia's recognition of the independence of two break-away territories in eastern Ukraine, the Kremlin began its "special military operation" against Kyiv, the most significant conventional warfare operation in Europe since World War II. Putin justified the war on the grounds of protecting the security of Russia and the people of the Donbas from NATO and Ukraine's growing militarism, as well as the "Nazism" of Ukrainian ruling elites. During the first month of the invasion, the Russian army surrounded the main Ukrainian cities, with reported mass casualties and a million Ukrainian refugees traveling to European nations.

Western nations responded by issuing the toughest sanctions yet against the Russian economy. The sanctions included but were not limited to financial restrictions for the main banks, a freeze of foreign currency reserves, sectoral bans for the defense industry, and personal sanctions for the country's oligarchs (or wealthiest businessmen) and many politicians, including Vladimir Putin. The West also sanctioned the Russia-built natural gas pipeline with Germany, Nord Stream 2. However, most of the indicated steps were to make a difference in the medium term, thereby allowing Moscow to continue with the military operation. Western military aid for Ukraine also did not make a major difference. Russian–Ukrainian negotiations resulted in an agreement to create humanitarian corridors to evacuate civilians, but not a cease-fire.[43]

The main responsibility for the military conflict lies with Putin, while Ukraine and its Western allies have greatly contributed to the escalation and to Russia's growing perception of insecurity.[44] Each of them thought it was making defensive preparations while increasing the other side's feeling of insecurity—a situation referred to in international relations theory as a "security dilemma." Western leaders were reluctant to negotiate regarding Russia's main demands, or to pressure Kyiv to implement the Minsk-II agreement. They also failed to build a direct dialogue with Putin and correctly read his warnings by expecting to conduct negotiations about European security from a position of dominance. According to Jack Matlock, former US ambassador to the Soviet Union, the war was both predictable and avoidable.[45]

As for Ukraine, it refused to fully accept the people of Donbas, stalled on the Minsk-II agreement, and passed multiple national restrictions on the Russian language. It also concentrated a large number of troops near the Donbas, named Russia as their main military threat,[46] and encouraged radical paramilitary groups, including some neo-fascist militias, to fight Russian-backed separatists in the Donbas.

PARTNERSHIP WITH NON-WESTERN POWERS

During 2020–2021, Russia made progress in developing relations outside the West—in part, to offset Western economic and political pressures, but also increasingly because of the perceived importance of building foundations for a new, multipolar world order. While having political, economic, and military ties with other countries/regions, including Africa and Latin America, Russia's most important foreign relations have concerned Asia, the Middle East, and Eurasia. This section concentrates on these three directions.

The China-Centeredness of Asia Ties

China remained Russia's main partner outside the West. In economic relations, Russia–China ties exceeded the level of $100 billion in mutual trade conducted increasingly in local currencies. Russia continued to sell arms and energy to their eastern neighbor, and even considered a joint strategy to overcome Western sanctions.[47] During this period, more than 70 percent of Russians held favorable attitudes toward China.

Russia–China relations continued to grow in political and military areas. The two countries conducted regular military exercises and held largely compatible views on international security threats. In 2019, Putin announced Russia would assist China in air defense. In January 2021, foreign ministers of the two countries passed a declaration about reaching a new "level of strategic mutual trust" in bilateral relations. Although the two sides have not entered into a formal military alliance, many Russian experts favor such an alliance, referring to the countries' relations as an "entente,"[48] an arrangement that indicates all levels of military cooperation except the NATO-like commitment to defending each other from an outside attack.

Experts have noted various areas of Russia–China tensions as stemming from different interests in the Arctic, the Beijing-initiated Silk Road project, the asymmetrical structure of mutual trade, and other issues.[49] They have also noted Russia's largely unsuccessful efforts to diversify its relations with China by developing alternative ties in Asia and elsewhere. Although Russia–South Korea cooperation has remained strong, Moscow's ties with India have stagnated and even declined as Russia has sought to rebuild relations with Pakistan. In addition, Russia did not invite India to participate in negotiations over Afghanistan in Moscow. The Kremlin revived relations with India by signing a number of new agreements during Putin's official visit to New Delhi in December 2021.

Seeking Consolidation in the Middle East

In the Middle East, Russia sought to consolidate its gains in relations with Syria, Turkey, and Iran while expanding their circle of potential partners.

In Syria, Moscow continued to seek a diplomatic formula for a postwar reconstruction that would be acceptable for all involved parties—President Bashir Assad, Iran, Turkey, and Saudi Arabia. Russia also aspired to an agreement with Turkey regarding security in the strategically important province of Aleppo, which was not under Assad's control. Reaching and implementing such an agreement was difficult because of Turkey's interest in exercising a decisive influence in the province. In October 2021, Turkey's president visited Vladimir Putin to address the issue, but failed to reach an understanding with him. In particular, the two sides disagreed on how to stabilize the situation in Idlib, Syria's largest province not controlled by Damascus.[50]

Turkey remained a difficult partner in other issues as well. It harbored ambitions for geopolitical influence in the Black Sea area, including Crimea. President Recep Tayyip Erdogan was interested in resources that were in close proximity to Cyprus. He was also considering supplementing the Turkish Straits by building another channel for connecting the Black Sea and the Mediterranean. Erdogan's position on Crimea and the Donbas was pro-Ukrainian. He met with Ukrainian president Volodymyr Zelensky on several occasions, expressing concerns over the Turkic-speaking Crimean Tatars and promising to increase military supplies, especially drones for the Ukrainian army. The issue of drones emerged as important following Istanbul's military assistance in Azerbaijan's war with Armenia over Nagorno-Karabakh in the fall of 2021. Azerbaijan won by gaining control over a large part of Nagorno-Karabakh, with Russia negotiating a cease-fire and the presence of peacekeepers in the region. To those in Ukraine aiming to seize control over Donbas and Crimea, the analogy with the Caucasus seemed applicable.[51] The situation in Donbas remained tense and ultimately resulted in Russia's military intervention in Ukraine.

Russia also continued to cultivate relations with Iran by discussing ways to develop economic ties outside of US sanctions, including via arrangements supported by European countries. Moscow was supportive of Tehran's approach to resuming the nuclear deal broken by President Trump in exchange for lifting most of the American sanctions. Moscow also worked with the Biden administration to bring Iran back into compliance with the nuclear deal known as the Joint Comprehensive Plan of Action. Russia and Iran's views with respect to Syria were not identical, yet shared important similarities in terms of support for Assad's regime and the country's territorial integrity.[52]

In addition to these three important relations, Russia sought to develop ties with the Gulf States while preserving strong relations with Israel. In March 2021, Foreign Minister Sergei Lavrov visited the United Arab Emirates, Saudi Arabia, and Qatar, capitalizing on new opportunities in the region. These opportunities were both political, related to the change in the US administration, and commercial in nature. The latter involved the possible construction of nuclear energy plants and sales of air-defense systems. Significantly, the UAE supported Moscow's effort to promote the gradual return of Syrian refugees, and the return of Syria to the Arab League, while expressing criticism of US-imposed sanctions against Damascus.[53]

The Eurasian Direction

Eurasia has been Russia's focus outside the West. Moscow no longer views the Eurasian region as predominantly former Soviet space, as it did during the years following the dissolution of the Soviet state, but rather as the geographic area that includes parts of Asia, the Middle East, and Europe. Institutionally, Russia sought to organize the region in partnership with China, Kazakhstan, and other states using the framework of the Shanghai Cooperation Organization (SCO), the Collective Security Treaty Organization (CSTO), and the Eurasian Economic Union (EAEU).

In the former Soviet region, Russia acted through the EAEU and the CSTO. The former organization remained essential for facilitating economic relations among Russia, Kazakhstan, Armenia, and Kyrgyzstan. Tajikistan, too, was considering membership in the organization. To Russia, strong ties with the country were essential for political reasons, as well—in part, because of the uncertain security situation resulting from the potential withdrawal of the US military from Afghanistan. Outside multilateral institutions, Russia's priorities in Central Asia included strengthening relations with a major state in the region, Uzbekistan. In April 2021, the two countries signed several economic and political agreements, including one that promised strategic military cooperation until 2025. In 2020, Russia became Uzbekistan's second-largest trade partner by increasing its exports to the country by 19.2 percent relative to the previous year.[54] In early 2022, Russia assisted Kazakhstan by leading the CSTO mission to defend the country from internal destabilization.[55]

In the area of political and military relations, Russia improved cooperation with Belarus by capitalizing on the latter's strained ties with the West over the fraudulent election of Aleksandr Lukashenko in August 2020 and his violent suppression of popular protests. In November 2021, the two countries' leaders signed key agreements promising further integration of their union in areas of finance, taxation, free movement of labor, and political institutions. The two sides also agreed to strengthen military cooperation in the face of potential "Western aggression" by establishing a joint training center and air-defense systems in western Belarus. Moscow and Minsk also cooperated during Russia's military intervention in Ukraine.

In the Caucasus, Moscow deployed its peacekeepers in the Nagorno-Karabakh area following the Armenia–Azerbaijan war in 2020, thereby cementing Russia's military presence in the area. Russia's role in negotiating the end of that war made clear its central role in the larger region. While tolerating the increased influence of Azerbaijan and Turkey, Russia helped to restrain them by stressing its own status as an honest broker. Moscow made it clear that it would not side with Armenia, its military ally within the CSTO, if Azerbaijan refrains from attacking the Armenian territory proper.

Overall, the former Soviet states remained fragile and fraught with instability. In addition to the instability in the Caucasus, the ongoing conflict in Ukraine, and the new wave of political protests in Belarus, there were signs of instability in Moldova and Central Asia. Internally weak institutions and economies faced potentially violent border disputes, such as those between Kyrgyzstan and Tajikistan in April 2021 and Armenia and Azerbaijan in May 2021. Russia preserved the role of mediator while prioritizing peace and security in the region.[56]

Within larger Eurasia, Moscow's priorities included those of working with China, Turkey, India, Iran, and others within the SCO framework. Here, the challenge was to harmonize the divergent interests of all involved actors while strengthening Russia's own role. Following the withdrawal of the US military from Afghanistan and the emergence of the Taliban regime in the country, Russia and China did not welcome the idea of America's extended presence in the region, and sought to address the issue of regional stability through the Shanghai Cooperation Organization. However, Moscow's and Beijing's priorities differed.[57] Russia also sought to increase its presence in Chinese geoeconomic schemes, while Beijing had its own priorities in mind and allocated only 15 percent of its Silk Road transportation routes to go through the territory of Russia.[58] Other states in the region also did not fully share Russia's interests.[59]

TENTATIVE RECORD

Overall, Russia's briefly entertained course of defensive foreign policy did not survive. The continued assertiveness in relations with the West escalated into a confrontation over security in Europe and Ukraine. The military intervention in Ukraine served to severely worsen these relations by limiting Russia's options for economic and political development in the global world. The assertive course has been accompanied by the centralization of Putin's political system at home. The system may last until 2036, as indicated by recent constitutional changes. Even if Putin resigns, his state system is likely to remain in place. The global transition will continue to be destabilizing, discouraging wide-ranging international cooperation and making it difficult to expect serious domestic reforms.

If Russia continues to be isolated from the West, then foreign incentives for the country's development must come from relations with non-Western nations. In the increasingly multipolar world and under the conditions of growing US–China competition, Russia potentially will obtain new opportunities for diversifying international ties. However, exploiting such opportunities requires not only political skills, but also strong internal political and economic institutions, and improvement of relations with Western nations.

This suggests the need for Russia and the West to find a way to reduce tensions and negotiate a mutually acceptable security agreement. Moscow may yet concentrate on issues of domestic and regional development as prescribed by supporters of defensive foreign policy, but not until it obtains clear security guarantees in its relations with the West. If such security is not challenged, the country may normalize ties with Western nations while expanding economic, political, and military relations with China, India, Turkey, Iran, and others. In relations with these nations, Russia does not feel that its security is threatened, and is ready to develop multiple projects to build a post-Western world order on a multipolar and multilateral foundation.

Russia's foreign policy may then recall those historical periods when Moscow was less active in European affairs while trying to rebuild domestic foundations for a return to world politics. In addition to Alexander II's policy of concentration following the Crimean War in the mid-nineteenth century, such periods of isolation from the West included Ivan III's anti-Catholicism and Eurasian expansion in the fifteenth century; the recovery from the *Smuta* (Time of Troubles), which lasted until the mid-seventeenth century; and

Catherine the Great's withdrawal from the Seven Years War in the eighteenth century. Each of these periods allowed Russia to deal with various nation-building issues, including problems of territorial unity, economy, finance, and demography.

NOTES

1. Vladimir Putin, Presidential Address to the Federal Assembly, April 21, 2021, Kremlin.ru, http://en.kremlin.ru/events/president/news/65418.

2. Joseph Biden, "Why America Must Lead," *Foreign Affairs*, 2020.

3. Robert D. Kaplan, "Kennan's Containment Strategy: A Consensus on What Not to Do," *The National Interest*, April 24, 2021. For a critical view, see Thomas J. Christensen, "There Will Not Be a New Cold War. The Limits of U.S.–Chinese Competition," *Foreign Affairs*, March 24, 2021.

4. Yevgeni Andreyev, "V Rossiyi ot koronavirusa umirali sravnitel'no molodyye lyudi," *Kommersant*, April 27, 2021.

5. "Claim in 2021: Russia's GDP per capita is 30 percent lower than in 2013," *Russia Matters,* August 25, 2021, https://russiamatters.org/analysis/fact-check-has -russias-gdp-capita-really-dropped-30-2013.

6. Ibid.

7. In 2020, hydrocarbons accounted for over 60 percent of exports, and some 40 percent of government revenues (Ibid.).

8. Stephen Crowley, "Global Cities versus Russian Rustbelt Realities," *PONARS Eurasia*, May 2020.

9. Putin, Presidential Address to the Federal Assembly, April 21, 2021.

10. Vladimir Putin, Participation in the Plenary Session of the Valdai Forum, Moscow, The Kremlin, October 21, 2021.

11. Leonid Ragozin, "What Is Next for Aleksey Navalny's Movement," Al Jazeera, April 22, 2021.

12. During the period of 2011–2020, public awareness of Navalny has grown from 6 percent to 20 percent, but the disapproval rate also increased from 35 percent to 50 percent, https://www.levada.ru/en/2020/11/02/alexey-navalny/.

13. Tatyana Stanovaya, "Zhizn' pri kollektivnom Putine," *Carnegie Moscow Center*, December 31, 2020.

14. Dmitry Medvedev, "Nevyuchennyye uroki istoriyi," *RIA Novosti*, April 23, 2021.

15. Nikolai Patrushev, "Verim delam, a ne slovam," *Argumenty i fakty*, April 30, 2021.

16. Andrei P. Tsygankov, *Russia and America* (Cambridge: Polity, 2019).

17. *New Rules or No Rules?* (Valdai Forum, March 2015); *War and Peace in the 21st Century* (Valdai Forum, September 2016); *Global Report and Global Order* (Valdai Forum, February 22, 2017); *Living in a Crumbling World* (Valdai Forum, October

15, 2018); *Time to Grow Up, or the Case for Anarchy* (Valdai Forum, September 30, 2019); *Staying Sane in a Crumbling World* (Valdai Forum, May 14, 2020).

18. For an analysis of Russian foreign policy discourse, see Tsygankov, "The Revisionist Moment," *Problems of Post-Communism* (2020).

19. Konstantin Remchukov, "V interesakh Rossii ne dat' vtyanut' sebya v konfronatsiyu s Zapadom," *Nezavisimaya gazeta*, August 12, 2021.

20. Boris Mezuyev, " 'Ostrov Rossiya' i rossiyskaya politika identichnosti," *Rossiya v global'noi politike* 6 (2019).

21. Ibid.

22. See, for example, his comments on the TV program *Bol'shaya igra* on January 25, 2019, and on the TV program *Pravo Znat'* on March 21, 2021.

23. Sergei Karaganov, "Ochistitel'nyi krizis," *Rossiya v global'noi politike* 19, 1 (2021), 13.

24. Dmitry Suslov, "Stabil'no, no khrupko," *Izvestia*, June 16, 2021. Others favored a "limited engagement" with the West (Dmitry Trenin, "Rossiya budet nakhodit'sya v sostoyaniyi konfrontatsiyi," *Kommersant*, June 3, 2021).

25. Timofei Bordachev, "Geopolitika vybora," *Vzglyad*, May 21, 2021.

26. For example, see comments on the TV program *Bol'shaya igra* in April 2021.

27. Patrushev, "Verim delam, a ne slovam."

28. For details, see Andrei P Tsygankov, *Russian Realism: Defending "Derzhava" in International Relations* (London: Routledge, 2022).

29. Vladimir Putin, Participation in the Expanded Meeting of the Foreign Ministry Board, Moscow, The Kremlin, November 18, 2021, http://en.kremlin.ru/events/president/news/67123.

30. Tsygankov, *Russia and America*, chap. 3.

31. https://www.rbc.ru/politics/25/01/2021/600ebb669a79470a77ca2767.

32. Trevor Hunnicutt, Arshad Mohammed, and Andrew Osborn, "U.S. Imposes Wide Array of Sanctions on Russia for 'Malign' Actions," Reuters, April 15, 2021.

33. Dan Mangan, "Biden Believes Putin Is a Killer, Vows Russian Leader 'Will Pay a Price' for Trying to Help Trump Win the Election," CNBC, March 17, 2021.

34. Anton Troianovski and David E. Sanger, "Rivals on World Stage, Russia and U.S. Quietly Seek Areas of Accord," *New York Times*, November 1, 2021.

35. "Putin's Bid to Ditch Dollar Picks Up as Exports Move to Euro," *Bloomberg*, April 26, 2021.

36. Dmitry Drize, "Yevrosoyuzu kak sleduyet vrezali po shcheke," *Kommersant*, February 9, 2021.

37. Dmitri Trenin, "Carnegie Moscow Center, February 18, 2021," *Carnegie Moscow Center*, February 18, 2021.

38. Igor' Makarov, "Kakuyu al'ternativu Rossiya mozhet predlozhit' Yevropeiskomu zelenomu kursu," *Profil*, May 14, 2021.

39. Anastasia Likhacheva, "A Greener Russia? Moscow's Agenda at the COP26 Climate Summit," *Carnegie Moscow Center*, November 9, 2021.

40. Dmitri Trenin, "After COP26: Russia's Path to the Global Green Future," *Carnegie Moscow Center*, November 16, 2021.

41. Jonathan Marcus, "Pompeo Signs Deal to Redeploy Troops from Germany to Poland," BBC, August 15.

42. Putin, Participation in the Expanded Meeting of the Foreign Ministry Board.

43. "Ukraine Says Talks with Russia Agreed on Humanitarian Corridors," Reuters, March 3, 2022.

44. Andrei P Tsygankov, "The Russia–Ukraine War: Why the Hawks Prevailed," *Canadian Dimension*, February 27, 2022.

45. https://usrussiaaccord.org/acura-viewpoint-jack-f-matlock-jr-todays-crisis-over -ukraine/.

46. https://www.reuters.com/article/us-ukraine-crisis-poroshenko -idUSKCN0RO28F20150924.

47. "China Ropes in Russia to Push Back against Western Sanctions," *Nikkei Asia*, March 23, 2021.

48. Artyom Lukin, "The Russia–China Entente and its Future," *International Politics* (2020); Dmitri Trenin, "China–Russia Relationship Model for Major Powers," *Global Times*, July 15, 2020.

49. Igor Denisov and Alexander Lukin, "Russia's China Policy: Growing Asymmetries and Hedging Options," *Russian Politics*, November 2021.

50. Bobby Ghosh, "Erdogan Says Bye-Bye Biden But Is Putin a Keeper?," *Bloomberg*, October 4, 2021.

51. Nicolai N. Petro, "Why the US Should Rethink Its Russia-centric Ukraine Policy," *Russia Matters*, September 9, 2021.

52. Iran's own position was not uniform. In April 2021, an Iranian foreign minister revealed that in his assessment, Russia's position with respect to Syria was closer to that of Iranian hard-liners such as General Suleimani, who was later killed by the United States while visiting Iraq (*Kommersant*, April 26, 2021).

53. Kirill Semenov, "Russian Foreign Minister's Visit Aimed at Challenging US Influence in Gulf," *Al-Monitor*, March 19, 2021.

54. Viktoriya Panfilova, "Moskva ukreplyayet positsiyi v Tsentral'noi Azii," *Nezavisimaya gazeta*, March 2, 2021.

55. "CSTO Peacekeepers Accomplished Mission in Kazakhstan, Time to Return Home—Putin," Tass, January 13, 2022.

56. Timofei Bordachev, "Ispytaniye svobodoi," *The Valdai Club*, March 22, 2021.

57. Elizabeth Wishnik, "The Collapse of the Afghan Government Provides a Challenge for China and Russia, Not a Windfall," *Ponars*, November 1, 2021.

58. Ankur Shah, "Russia Loosens Its Belt," *Foreign Policy*, July 16, 2020.

59. For analysis of diverse state interests in the region, see Moritz Pieper, *The Making of Eurasia: Competition and Cooperation between China's Belt and Road Initiative and Russia* (London: Bloomsbury, 2021).

6

Conclusions and Lessons

All healthy human action . . . must establish a balance between utopia and reality, between free will and determinism.

—E. H. Carr[1]

This final chapter summarizes the approach taken in this book to understanding change and continuity in Russian foreign policy. It also suggests several lessons that Russian and Western policymakers can learn from the past thirty years of their interaction if they wish to improve their communication and security in the world. If Russia and the West are to jointly address the pressing issues of the twenty-first century, learning these lessons is essential.

CHANGE AND CONTINUITY IN RUSSIA'S FOREIGN POLICY

Seven Visions of National Interest

Despite what realists and liberals often assume, nations rarely have once and forever established visions of their fundamental external interests. More typically, a country's national interest fluctuates with changes in the domestic and international political scene. This book identifies seven distinct visions of national interest that Russia has developed and pursued throughout the past thirty years.

Mikhail Gorbachev's vision of New Thinking was part of his perestroika project, which meant to revive socialist values at home and achieve a fundamentally new level of cooperation abroad. New Thinking saw the world as socially diverse and yet united by common human values, as well as by fundamental threats. In particular, the new leadership pointed to threats of nuclear catastrophe, ecological devastation, and poverty. The country's national interest was to be pursued in close coordination with other members of global society, and, for the Soviet Union, this meant the need to give up the old ideological vision and to acknowledge positive contributions by the West to the world's development.

Despite growing resistance from various domestic opponents, the leader of New Thinking acted consistently with his beliefs. He made disproportionately large cuts in conventional and nuclear arsenals and proposed to eliminate all nuclear weapons by 2000. He also withdrew from Afghanistan and other third world countries. Furthermore, Gorbachev abandoned the "Brezhnev doctrine" of limited sovereignty in Eastern Europe and made it possible to tear down the Berlin Wall. Finally, the new Soviet leader committed himself to the idea of principally reforming the United Nations and supporting it with greater resources, so the organization would be capable of meeting new world challenges. At home, Gorbachev—admittedly, belatedly—recognized the need to give up the old imperial principles of maintaining Soviet unity, and he offered a vision that combined elements of federation and confederation. The new union treaty was to be renegotiated and approved through a people's referendum.

For various domestic and international reasons, the New Thinking vision could not be sustained and was soon replaced by the idea of Integration with the West. The new domestic coalition undermined Gorbachev's standing by insisting that Russia had been a country with a suppressed Western identity and that it now had to give up its socialist system in favor of Western-style market democracy. Unlike New Thinkers, who sought to engage the West by developing the notions of global threats and common responsibility for their emergence, the new Russian leaders—Boris Yeltsin and his foreign minister, Andrei Kozyrev—saw no major flaws in the West. They planned to rapidly gain membership in Western international organizations and to minimize relationships with the former Soviet states. These steps were meant to bring Russia to the front-rank status of advanced European countries and the United States. Opposition to the course of Integration with the West was formidable, and the course began to unravel soon after attempts at its implementation.

When a leading critic of this course, Yevgeni Primakov, was appointed as the new foreign minister, the vision of national interest changed yet again. By selecting him, Yeltsin, to a degree, committed himself to a new perception of external threats and foreign policy objectives. Rather than proposing modernization and Westernization as Russia's key national priorities, Primakov pointed to the dangers of a concentration of world power associated with the unipolar status of the United States. A realist rather than an economic liberal, Primakov proposed the vision of Great Power Balancing for the purpose of gradually turning the existing unipolar world into a multipolar one. In particular, the new minister sought to prevent—or at least, to slow down—the announced expansion of NATO toward Russia's western borders. The vision required integration of the former Soviet region under Russian leadership and seeking assistance from other powerful states, such as China and India, in order to balance American hegemony.

Many of Primakov's initiatives remained on paper only, and that contributed to the replacement of his vision with a new one. Vladimir Putin drew attention to the world's instabilities, such as terrorism, as well as some new economic opportunities. Unlike Primakov, and similar to Gorbachev, Putin saw the need to engage the West in an ambitious joint project. However, unlike Gorbachev and Kozyrev, Putin visualized Russia as a great power and sought Western recognition of this. Putin redefined national interest as that of the Pragmatic Cooperation of great power. Rather than balancing the United States' power, the key objective was now pronounced as an economic modernization for the sake of preserving the great power status.

In attempting to reengage the West, Putin showed himself to be extremely active in developing relations with the United States, particularly after the September 11, 2001, terrorist attacks on that country. He offered far-reaching intelligence cooperation and proposed new ways to develop Russian–US energy ties. Putin was even more energetic when it came to activating economic and political ties with Europe. In some areas, such as visa relations with European countries, the president demonstrated his readiness to go much further than European leaders themselves. Yet Putin was no Gorbachev; his activism was pragmatic, and driven by calculations of state power. On issues where Russian state sovereignty was at stake, he was firm in limiting cooperation with foreign nations. Thus, despite his support of US actions in Afghanistan, Putin sided with a number of European nations in condemning American intervention in Iraq without a United Nations mandate. And in his relations with Europe, he placed the emphasis on economic and energy cooperation while restricting cooperation on security issues, such as in Chechnya, or with peacemaking activities in the former Soviet region. In this, as in actively pursuing commercial sales of weapons abroad, Putin continued the traditions of Primakov's diplomacy.

In the former Soviet Union, the vision of Pragmatic Cooperation implied an abandonment of Primakov's integration project in favor of less costly and mutually advantageous bilateral relations. In reestablishing bilateral ties consistent with his belief in economic modernization, Putin reasserted control over many of the ex-republics' strategic property and transportation, particularly electricity and energy pipeline facilities. He concluded a number of partnership and strategic partnership agreements in the Caucasus and central Asia, as well as with Ukraine and Belarus. The Russian leader also strengthened Russia's military presence in central Asia and the Caucasus by signing appropriate bilateral and multilateral agreements. Finally, Putin promoted new energy and transportation projects to further implement his vision of geoeconomic and state-driven modernization.

Around 2005, Putin's vision changed in the direction of assertiveness. The Kremlin no longer believed in defensive cooperation with Western nations and insisted on the greater acceptance of Russia's interests. Russia's leadership sharply criticized what it viewed as the United States' "unilateralism" in world politics, and pursued more independent economic and security policies in the world. Following Putin's speech at the Munich Conference on Security Policy, held on February 10, 2007, the Kremlin was busy signaling its frustration with its inability to develop more equitable relations with the United States. Russia felt humiliated that it had had to swallow the war in the Balkans; two rounds of NATO expansion; the US withdrawal from the ABM Treaty; the US military presence in central Asia; the US invasion of Iraq; and US plans to deploy elements of nuclear missile defense in Eastern Europe. In the wake of the Russia–Georgia conflict, Dmitri Medvedev stated, "[W]e will not tolerate any more humiliation, and we are not joking."[2]

However, after 2009, Russia's rhetoric began to change. In response to the global financial crisis, Medvedev declared that Russia needed to explore new opportunities for development and to build new international alliances for modernization. In the post-Western world, this translated into Russia's efforts to improve ties with the West, while strengthening relations with fellow BRICS countries (Brazil, Russia, India, China, South Africa). In the former Soviet region, the Kremlin's emphasis shifted toward initiating new projections of regional integration, such as the Eurasian Union.

The return of Putin to the presidency was accompanied by the vision of state-civilization and a new stress on assertiveness in relations with the United States and the European Union. Russia again was insisting on the West's recognition of its values and interests across the world. In Europe, Russia wanted a stronger role in defining its security framework and a greater share in economic projects. In Eurasia, the Kremlin initiated an ambitious idea of regional integration under the umbrella of the Eurasian Union by inviting several former Soviet states to join the union. In the Middle East, Russia fought against what it saw as a Western destabilization scheme behind the Arab Spring events. Instead of regime change, Moscow was committed to propping up existing governments, such as the one led by Bashar al-Assad in Syria. In Asia, Russia sought to pool its resources with China in order to challenge the West-centered world. The Kremlin also contributed to the development of alternative international organizations such as the Shanghai Cooperation Organization (SCO) and BRICS, with the idea of taking advantage of new international opportunities outside the West. Finally, Russia reacted harshly to Western criticisms of its human rights record by insisting on Russia's own "civilizational" status and system of values.

The election of Donald Trump as US president, while initially generating in the Kremlin expectations of cooperation with the West, resulted yet again in the resumption of Russia's assertiveness in response to what it perceived as unfair pressures exerted by the United States. The Kremlin remained assertive in some areas while developing a more defensive posture in others. Russia continued to insist on equal treatment as a major power and as a contributor to international stability, but wanted to gain distance from Western nations. Russian leadership indicated that it no longer wanted to integrate with the West or be recognized as sharing Western values. Instead, Russia felt deeply insecure and demanded from the United States and NATO guarantees for Russia's security. In 2022, in response to perceived disrespect of its security interests in Europe and Ukraine, Russia launched a military intervention in Ukraine.

Table 6.1 summarizes Russia's seven visions of the world and national interest.

Understanding National-Interest Formation

Liberal and realist theories of international relations are too simplistic for understanding the described process and outcomes of national-interest formation. Each of them emphasizes either modernization or the need to maintain power as shaping foreign policy choices. Yet in reality, both of these forces figure prominently in how nations determine their interests. In order to understand the formation of Russia's national interest, this book employs a complex framework that incorporates both types of influence.

Table 6.1. Russia's Seven Visions of the World and National Interest

	Perceived World	*National Interest*
GORBACHEV	Cold War crisis	New Thinking and cross-cultural dialogue
YELTSIN/KOZYREV	Western institutional dominance	Integration with the West
PRIMAKOV	US power hegemony	Balancing against the United States
PUTIN I	Terrorism and economic competition	Pragmatic Cooperation with the West
PUTIN II	US unilateralism	Assertiveness
MEDVEDEV	Opportunities for economic development	Alliances for Modernization
PUTIN III	Competition between West and non-West	Promotion of Russia as a civilization Asymmetric assertiveness

In the first chapter, I hypothesized that the vision of national interest is a product of the nation's interaction with the world, and Russia's strategic choices can be viewed as reactions to the behavior of Western powers. At least since Peter the Great, the West has played a special role in Russian development, and much of the country's international behavior has meant efforts of the Russian Self to win recognition by its significant Other. Western actions are contested domestically, and local conditions are no less important in shaping a dominant vision of national identity and foreign policy. A closer analysis of Russia's foreign policy developments throughout the book has revealed three local factors that clarify the process of Russian interpretation of Western actions. These three—national tradition, current concerns, and state capacity—specify, rather than distort, the general causal mechanism of national-interest formation.

Gorbachev's New Thinking originated, in part, from the hostilities of the Cold War and unrealized opportunities presented by the brief period of détente. In contrast to the realists' emphasis on the West's economic and military strength, Gorbachev responded to the social democratic ideas of détente's European supporters and the domestic tradition of reform social-ism, which was associated with the late Lenin, Bukharin, and Khrushchev. In putting forth his vision, the leader of New Thinking was hoping to garner and maintain sufficient support to continue with his course among elites and within the broader society. It is no accident that his project contained ele-ments of Westernism, Statism, and Civilizationism—the three main schools of foreign policy thinking in the Soviet Union.

Yet the task of keeping the unstable coalition together proved to be unten-able. Soon, conservative Civilizationists and Statists, on the one hand, and radical Westernizers, on the other, were attacking New Thinking. The conser-vative and radical opponents wanted principally different—in fact, mutually exclusive—outcomes, and Gorbachev would have made progress only if he were to deliver on his promises to improve people's lives. Instead, busy per-suading the West of the authenticity of his intentions and not getting as much as he expected in return, the leader of perestroika was rapidly losing initiative and support at home. The perception was strengthening that Russians were living through an unavoidable political disintegration and economic deterio-ration, and this served to radicalize society and improve the political standing of Gorbachev's opponents.

After 1989, it was the vision of radical Westernizers, expressed by Boris Yeltsin, that received growing social recognition. The Westernist opposition skillfully exploited newly emerging opportunities to challenge the ruling center. Unlike Gorbachev, Yeltsin was elected president of Russia by popular vote, and he continued to argue that economic deterioration could be stopped only by radical Western-style reforms. Yeltsin also entered a coalition with other republican nationalists and insisted that the efforts to preserve the union were doomed.

However, the new Westernist coalition was hardly a stable one. It consisted of pragmatic members of the former Communist *nomenklatura*, such as Yeltsin himself, and idealistic liberal reformers, such as Yegor Gaidar and Andrei Kozyrev. The new ruling coalition, therefore, tried to synthesize the influences of Westernizers and former Soviet Statists, but the majority of the elites—military industrialists, the army, and the security services—were still excluded. The challenge that came from that majority was formidable, and the Westernist foreign policy course soon began to fade under powerful attacks from both Statists and conservative Civilizationists.

The opposition took advantage of the attitude the Western nations had adopted toward the new Russia. Despite some considerable financial assistance given to the new Russian government, the West was clearly not eager to integrate Russia into its midst. NATO's decision to expand brushed aside Russia's hopes for transforming the alliance into a nonmilitary one, or for being admitted as a full member of the organization. NATO's expansion also provided the anti-Western opposition with the required ammunition to construct an image of an external threat and question the objectives of the new government. Along with the failure of the West-recommended liberal economic reforms, NATO expansion strengthened domestic Statists who advanced a different concept of national interest.

The new foreign minister, Yevgeni Primakov, articulated the new vision of Great Power Balancing and attempted to put it into practice. Working with the much less cooperative West, he sought to consolidate Russia's position as a great power and to re-situate it at the center of the former Soviet region. The new minister—who subsequently became prime minister—also attempted to limit the power of the oligarchs in Russian economic and political life. The new course was not successful in delivering improved social and economic standards, and it unnecessarily alienated pro-Western forces, pushing them into opposition. The course was also quite expensive because it sought to restore the ties among former Soviet republics primarily through subsidies by the Russian state. The vision therefore was not attractive to Russian business elites, and it also had little appeal to some isolationist-minded nationalists, who were formerly supportive members of Primakov's coalition.

As a result, when Yeltsin appointed Vladimir Putin prime minister and, subsequently, acting president, the new leader had a considerably different coalition of support behind him. In particular, he drew support from pro-Western commercial groups, formerly neglected by Primakov, and from state-oriented security services. Changed international conditions and Western attitudes assisted the new leadership in keeping the coalition together. Both the Russian economic recovery and the renewed threat of international terrorism made Russia important in the eyes of Western leaders. Russia's energy supplies were becoming critical in European economies, and Russian intelligence was now available to assist in American efforts to crush terrorism in Afghanistan and other areas of central Asia.

At home, Putin's vision resonated with the need to stabilize the economy and defeat terrorism in the Caucasus. Although the war in Chechnya had its own unique characteristics, many Russians saw parallels between the Chechen rebels and Al Qaeda. So did the Western leaders, who softened their rhetoric regarding Russian violations of human rights in Chechnya and acknowledged the significance of Russia in fighting the threat of international terrorism. As a result, Putin was able to restore the state ability to govern, initiate far-reaching military reform, and centralize governing institutions. Medvedev preserved Putin's institutional legacy while working to make political and economic institutions more inclusive of Russia's increasingly active society.

Putin and Medvedev's approval ratings remained high as they each adopted the more assertive and cooperative vision, respectively. The West, too, has had an important role to play. While George W. Bush's global regime change strategy worked to shape Putin's assertiveness, Barack Obama's effort to "reset" relations with Russia made it possible for Medvedev to formulate his notion of alliances for modernization. As Russia continues to be influenced by Western ideas and practices, Western policymakers and public opinion leaders ought to be sensitive to the perception of these influences in Russia. A better appreciation of Russia's cultural distinctness and foreign policy concerns may encourage Putin and his successors to move further toward long-term cooperation with Europe and the United States. On the other hand, a more unilateral and isolationist approach is more likely to push the new regime in the direction of suppressing opposition at home.

Finally, both renewed Western pressures and Russia's domestic vulnerabilities help to explain Putin's transformation toward "civilizational" and West-assertive foreign policy. In his perception, the United States and the European Union failed to address Russia's concerns under Medvedev but remained determined to preserve the West-centered world. As new, non-Western powers rose to prominence, Russia sought to position itself as an independent cultural and political center in a multipolar and multicivilizational world. The new course was reminiscent of Primakov's Great Power Balancing, but took place in a changing international environment. The world was transitioning from being US-centered, and Russia was aiming to capitalize on new economic and political opportunities outside the West. Russia also concentrated on ensuring its security from the expansion of NATO and Western military infrastructure in Europe. In 2022, in part due to Putin's character and the way he perceives threats, such policy focus resulted in greatly exacerbated tensions with the West, Russia's military intervention in Ukraine, and increased isolation from the international economy.

Such were some of the key foreign policy challenges confronted by the Russian leaders. Each of the leaders sought to creatively respond to various external developments, particularly those initiated in the West. Some, like Gorbachev, Kozyrev, and, to a lesser extent, Medvedev, wanted to engage the West in essentially liberal projects and to demonstrate their willingness to bring Russia into the family of Western nations. These leaders expressed Russia's eagerness to be recognized by the West as one of its own, and they saw the West as driven by essentially liberal motivations to spread justice and freedom in the world.

Others, like Primakov and Putin, during his first terms in the office, while avoiding direct confrontation with the West, sought to reassert Russia's power. Unlike their liberal predecessors, they were suspicious of the West's power motivations—both geopolitical and geoeconomic—and wanted to restore Russian national pride and independence.

Russia has faced multiple foreign challenges and opportunities in recent decades: the danger of arms races; promises of post–Cold War economic and security cooperation; NATO expansion; threats of global terrorism; regional instability; climate change; and others. Confronted with those challenges and opportunities, some leaders, in Albert Sorel's memorable formulation, arranged "their policy to suit the realities of the world," while others imagined "the world to suit their policy."[3] There will certainly be many other external challenges ahead for Russia, and they are likely to lead to other creative visions of national interest and foreign policy strategy. It is, as the same thinker put it more than a century ago, "the eternal dispute."

LESSONS FOR RUSSIA

What lessons can Russia learn from the past thirty years of its foreign policy? Are there particular steps it should take, or abstain from taking, that would preserve and enhance its status in the world?

Staying Engaged

First and foremost, it is important that in adjusting to new external challenges and solving its more specific domestic problems, Russia stay engaged with the world in general, and the West in particular. Lack of acceptance by the West should not prompt Russian leaders to take an isolationist path; rather, it should encourage them to double their efforts to explain their international policies as being consistent with their vision of a global world. Isolationism cannot be practical in a world that has grown increasingly global in terms of both new opportunities and new threats. Russia should not deprive itself of new opportunities to participate in global flows of information, capital, and labor. Nor can it fully shield itself against new diseases or types of violence, or other crises of a transnational nature.

Isolationism, particularly an anti-Western one, remains strong in Russia. Hard-line Civilizationists, as well as some Statists, continue to argue that Russia is destined to oppose the West's civilizational and political influences across the globe. These forces insist on viewing the world in black-and-white terms and refuse to acknowledge that many of Russia's interests are best accomplished through participation in international organizations and joint activities. They continue to practice the old maxim "The enemy of my enemy is my friend" by recommending that Russia support anti-Western forces and work against those who are supportive of the West. In the post-Western world, these forces may remain powerful, especially if this world proves to be more unstable and dangerous than one where US unipolarity is a factor.

The former Soviet region has emerged as an especially contested area in this respect, and the Russia–Georgia conflict, Russia's annexation of Crimea, and subsequent military intervention in Ukraine have confirmed the failure of international law to preserve peace in the Caucasus and Eastern Europe. Despite all of the flawed policies of New Thinking and Integration with the West, the general effort of these philosophies to move away from anti-Western isolationism must be recognized. One should remember that before their fail-ures, each of these courses had a broad social appeal and expressed some deep Russian aspirations. These aspirations must not be neglected in the future, and they can be assessed based on the criteria of security, welfare, and identity. Russians supported the vision of New Thinking because it promised to prevent a threat of nuclear war and to reform the heavily militarized econ-omy. Society was eager to replace the rigid economic and political system with one that would be more open to the world. In addition, a considerable part of Soviet society identified itself with the West culturally. Many in the post-Stalin generation saw the need to move beyond the discourse of "irrec-oncilable contradictions" between socialism and capitalism and were open to ideas and cultural products from Europe and the United States. Just as many Russians had initially supported New Thinking, they did not initially oppose the strategy of Integration with the West. That strategy, too, was appealing for its openness to the world. It was no accident that in being hard on Gorbachev for his lack of domestic economic reforms, Yeltsin and Kozyrev took New Thinking as their point of departure in building relationships with the West.

The post-Kozyrev Great Power Balancing did not mean to return to Soviet-like isolationism. Indeed, its principal architect, Yevgeni Primakov, had been a New Thinking supporter and a member of Gorbachev's close circle of trusted advisers. Yet, the strategy of balancing the United States and building a multipolar world proved to contain elements of isolationism, some of which were unnecessary and did not serve Russia well. Brought up in the tradition of Soviet class-based geopolitics, the father of Great Power Balancing continued to be a geopolitical thinker and thought more about defending his country's political independence and security perimeter than about Russia's economic opportunities. Condemning NATO's enlargement decision was one thing, but attempting to integrate the former Soviet region at the expense of Russia's scarce resources in response to the enlargement was an entirely different matter. The post-Soviet integration was almost explicitly geopolitically driven and was viewed by many as an isolationist-minded project rather than an engagement-minded one.

Along the same lines, developing closer economic and political cooperation with non-Western nations in Asia and the Muslim world was fully justified and appropriate, but inviting them into an essentially anti-American balancing coalition was misleading and counterproductive. Putin's attempts to contain Western influences in the world can have only a limited effect if they are pursued from weak domestic foundations and without coordination with major non-Western powers. The relative weakness of Russia's economy and the lack of China and India's political support for confronting the United States and NATO over European security and Ukraine demonstrated to Moscow the power of global interdependence. Within the globalized world, staying engaged is not just an option, but a foreign policy imperative.

The vision of Russia as Eurasia, if pursued at the expense of Russia's ties with Europe, is also a flawed one. Insistence on Eurasia as anti-American and anti-European did a disservice to Primakov. Even if his own approach was more refined and pragmatic than that of the hard-liners, embracing Eurasia as a traditionally geopolitical notion added to Western perceptions of Russia's new foreign policy as essentially isolationist, and could not resonate with the majority of the Russian public. "Western" and "Eurasian" coexist and overlap within the Russian psyche. Russia continues to be a multicultural, multiethnic, and multireligious community that has coexisted and interacted with Asian and Middle Eastern regions. That alone qualifies it to be a "Eurasian power." Putin's new initiative of building the Eurasian Economic Union, therefore, has a certain public appeal and a chance to be sustained as long as it is not pursued at the expense of Russia's European-rich experience. It is crucial that Russia and the West overcome mutual hostility and engage in cooperation to resolve pressing global issues. The Russia–Western crisis over Ukraine and European security has fundamentally weakened movement in this direction.

Following a National Path

It is no less important that in staying engaged with the world, Russian leaders do not lose sight of what has historically made Russia a special cultural
community. Historically, Russia has played a vital role in European developments, while preserving special relations with Asia and the Muslim world.
This unique geopolitical and geocultural location has not harmed Russia's
own identity development, as the Russians have learned from their neighbors
while remaining a community with a distinct culture and history.

Globalization, too, is unlikely to erase Russia's distinctiveness, although it
does present the great challenge of finding an appropriate national niche in
the new world. Russia must take advantage of the increased global flow of
knowledge, goods, and capital. At the same time, it must avoid some highly
divisive social, economic, and political consequences of globalization, and
that requires considerable national creativity and imagination. Such divisive
consequences manifest themselves in migration crises in the Middle East and
Europe, the tightening of labor markets, and the rising appeal of nationalist
ideas across the world. Russia's foreign policy needs to reflect the realities of
the increasingly global and yet persistently diverse world. It needs to conform
with the old wisdom that foreign policy is as much a science of revealing
patterns of behavior as it is an art of following them by creatively synthe-
sizing national and global imperatives. Both vision and power are critical
here—vision, for a reality-grounded strategy formulation, and power, for its
implementation. Or, in E. H. Carr's terms, utopia and reality, free will and
determinism, are essential in successful foreign policymaking.

Russia's post-Soviet experience suggests errors, as well as accomplishments, in constructing a national path toward a globalizing world. New
Thinking and, especially, Integration with the West did not withstand the test
of time partly because their proponents overestimated the liberal nature of
globalization and underestimated the forces of divisiveness and conflict in
the world. As a result, their international engagement was not sufficiently
supported at home, and it came at a very high price of domestic political,
social, and economic disintegration. Both New Thinkers and Integrationists
sought to solve their domestic problems by obtaining external material and
institutional recognition. Both lost control over the economy—Gorbachev,
as a result of destroying the old centralized system of state orders without
having a new one in place, and Yeltsin, as a result of introducing price liberalization under the monopolistic structural environment. Both leaders had
been stripped of some of their political power—Gorbachev ceded power to
radical Westernizers, and Yeltsin made serious concessions to Statists and
incorporated them into the ruling establishment. Most importantly, both had
little faith in the ability of the state to lead the process of global adjustment.

This, too, was a consequence of placing a much higher premium on transnational and global developments than on searching for a national formula of adaptation to these developments.

Great Power Balancing and Pragmatic Cooperation showed greater sensitivity to the national tradition in searching for a path toward globalization. Primakov's major accomplishment had to do with restoring some important attributes of foreign policy sovereignty. Working under the conditions of Russia's continuous economic decline and under a president committed to the previously articulated Westernist vision, the father of Great Power Balancing was able to take and sustain a considerably more independent line in Russia's relations with Yugoslavia, Iraq, and the former Soviet region. He also showed that Russia was in a position to improve its security environment in the former Soviet Union, once it had been willing to invest important diplomatic resources in it. Continuing to be engaged in the tough defense of what Primakov saw as Russia's national interest, while maintaining dialogue with the West, became an important example for Putin to follow. While softening Primakov's preoccupation with geopolitics and strengthening the emphasis on globalization and economic modernization, Putin followed the line of defending Russia's national interest as different from those of Western nations. Sensitive to the national tradition, the initiator of Pragmatic Cooperation differentiated himself and his strategy of globalization sharply from those associated with New Thinking and Integration with the West.

After being reelected to a third—and then a fourth—term as president, Putin has sought to revive Russia's national interest and values in an effort to strengthen the country's position from which to maintain relations with Western nations in economic and security areas. However, he has also engaged in a tough defense of Russia's perceived priorities, including by methods of assertiveness in information, cyber, and military areas. This dilemma manifested itself in Ukraine when Moscow sacrificed its relations with the West in order to assert its interests in Ukraine, at the expense of international law. Russia also intervened in Syria, developed new weapons systems, and meddled in Western elections. In 2022, the Kremlin went so far as to challenge the West by demanding security guarantees from NATO, and by invading Ukraine. This course resulted in political confrontation and mutual economic sanctions, further increasing Russia's isolation from the West.

LESSONS FOR THE WEST

Russia is sufficiently big and powerful to limit the West's ability to influence its developments. Vast territory, enormous natural resources, military capabilities, and a significant political and diplomatic weight in the world have allowed, and will continue to allow, Russia considerable room for foreign policy maneuvering. It is hard to believe that the West will ever possess enough power to fully determine the shape and direction of Russia's developments. Yet, as this book has argued, the West remains Russia's significant Other, and therefore should act with this in mind by avoiding serious disagreements, and sending Russia a unified, rather than a conflicted, message. Engagement, reciprocity, and patience should be the main principles guiding Western actions toward this nation. Carefully applied, these principles in time can bring more security and stability to the world.

Staying Engaged

The first principle that should guide Western actions toward Russia is engagement. A genuine Russia–West engagement is critical for making progress in arms control, counterterrorism, the establishment of regional security, and cooperation in economic and energy matters.

Yet, the West's engagement with Russia has been modest, and following Russia's invasion of Ukraine in 2022, the engagement stopped. A majority of the political class in Western nations have continued to mistrust Russia well after the Soviet disintegration, mainly focusing on reducing nuclear threats coming from the region. Despite Gorbachev's and Yeltsin's expectations, the West never introduced anything remotely similar to the post–World War II Marshall Plan. Western leaders went only so far as to extend Russia some symbolic forms of recognition, such as membership in the G-7, while abstaining from more serious commitments to transforming postcommunist economic and political institutions.

The efforts by President Barack Obama to "reset" relations with Russia promised a new way of engaging, but proved to be limited and misguided. The fact that Obama's approach evolved from the "reset" to sanctions is of course partly the Kremlin's responsibility. However, the US side also bears responsibility for not trying to create a mutually beneficial engagement. A number of important issues that Russia views as of key significance remained unresolved. The Kremlin was critical of the US proposal to develop the Missile Defense System jointly with the Europeans but separately from Russia. Western nations were rhetorically supportive of the former Soviet states' bid for NATO membership, whereas Russia maintained its right to protect its interests in the former Soviet region. The Kremlin also criticized the West's handling of the Middle Eastern crisis by going after regime change in Libya and Syria. By the time Western nations and Russia confronted the Ukrainian revolution, the Kremlin had little trust left in the other side's intentions.

Opponents of engagement with Russia in the West were strong, and have gotten even stronger since the Ukraine crisis. Many of these opponents see problems with Russia's human rights record under Putin. Others charge that Russia presents a threat to the West's strategic interests and that it collaborates with dangerous regimes. Still others point to Russia's policy in the former Soviet region and assertiveness in cyber and information areas as evidence of the Kremlin's neo-Soviet imperialism. In the new climate of anti-Russian sanctions, many within the Western political class insist that isolating and punishing Russia for its actions is the only appropriate response. Instead of engaging in a dialogue with the Kremlin, the West has gone through several rounds of sanctions against the Russian economy, offered military training for the Ukrainian army, and strengthened NATO forces on Russia's western border.

Punishing or isolating Russia has not disciplined it, however. Russia continues to be in a position to withstand pressures from the West. Against expectations, such pressures have served to push Russia further away from Western nations. Anti-Western forces within and outside Russian leadership have presented an image of the West as a threat and are grateful to Western politicians for assisting them in constructing such an image. The examples of NATO's expansion, military interventions in Kosovo and the Middle East, as well as sanctions against the Russian economy, teach us that ignoring Russia or viewing it exclusively as a threat leads to a more defiant, not a more cooperative, Russia.

Engaging on Mutually Acceptable Terms

Engagement will be especially effective when conducted on a reciprocal or mutually acceptable basis. Anything short of reciprocity might result in cheating by the sides involved. Hegemonic engagement on Western terms will come at the cost of Russia's own interests and perceptions. As Thomas Graham wrote, "It is not Russia's strength that generates and feeds the fear of it; it is the weakness of the West and its lack of confidence."[4] Rather than trying to dictate policies, the United States should acknowledge that Russia can be a responsible protector of its own interests in the world. On the other hand, attempts to appease Russia by jeopardizing the West's own interests are equally dangerous. Former Cold War enemies will develop the required trust only when they openly engage in direct negotiations of mutually acceptable relations. Unfortunately, the support in the West for hegemonic engagement with Russia is stronger than for a reciprocal engagement. Russia's insistence on its own interests and specifics often gets dismissed as reflecting the remnants of Soviet and anti-Western thinking. Despite the West's political polarization and decline relative to the rise of non-Western economies, many in the

Western part of the world continue to believe that Western civilization is in a position to teach the rest of the world about appropriate institutions, values, and moral standards. This attitude remains a serious obstacle to the mutual understanding required for reciprocal engagement.

As Western nations have continued to display this hegemonic attitude, Russia's negative perceptions of the West have grown stronger. In particular, Russians have resented the expansion of US and EU economic, political, and security institutions in Eurasia and elsewhere, while dismissing Russia's opposition as pure paranoia. The conflict with Georgia and Ukraine, too, became possible in part because the balance of power in the region had long ago been violated by NATO's and the EU's decisions to expand its infrastructure at the expense of Russia's interests. International law was silent in the Caucasus and Ukraine, just as it had been previously silent when Yugoslavia and Iraq were attacked by Western powers without the approval of the United Nations, of which Russia is a member. Even Russia's meddling in Western elections cannot be fully understood without noting that the West has frequently interfered with Russia's political affairs and has criticized Russia's human rights record without considering how unpopular such criticisms are inside Russia. As the world struggles to meet the challenges of the COVID-19 pandemic, economic development, and climate change, it is important that the West engage with others without patronizing them.

A genuinely successful engagement is therefore difficult to design and maintain. Given the history of hostilities between Russia and the West, as well as divergent current interests, there will always be differences in the two nations' approaches to solving existing problems. Nevertheless, in light of the alternative—an isolated and resentful Russia—engagement on mutually acceptable terms is worth a serious effort. When such engagement is in place, the two sides will be able to deliver important results, such as strategic treaties and agreements on counterterrorism and nonproliferation of the most dangerous weapons.

Tempering Expectations

In addition to engagement and reciprocity in relations with Russia, the West ought to be patient and not expect miracles. Unreasonable expectations about Russia have not been uncommon in the past, and should not be a guide in the future. Although many hoped for Russia to quickly leave its past behind and emerge as a market democracy with special relationships with Western nations, the reality proved to be different. Russia has built not a free-market model of capitalism, but rather oligarchical capitalism, with the economy largely controlled by individuals with special ties to the Kremlin. In the area of political and legal institutions, Russia has developed a super-presidential system with few formal checks and balances. As far as the relationship with the West is concerned, several polls indicate that many Russians see the West as a potential threat, rather than as a friend or strategic partner.

The West bears a share of the responsibility for these unattractive outcomes. After all, Western officials pushed aggressively for shock therapy as a model for economic reform in Russia, and deepened their relationship with Yeltsin beyond a reasonable level. The choice to expand NATO by excluding Russia from it, despite available alternative ways to provide security in Europe, also did not—and could not—improve Western credibility in the Russians' eyes. Finally, the United States' strategy of global regime change and gaining political and military influence in the post-Soviet region served to exacerbate the Kremlin's perception of security vulnerability and regional instability.

To change the skeptical attitudes of Russians and the Kremlin, it is important to formulate some long-term objectives and to organize relationships with Russia with these objectives in mind. First, nations should select the bilateral relationships' most vital and pressing issues that would reflect broad social needs and the interests of whole societies. For example, the issue of domestic transformation should be put on the agenda only if it reflects the desires of both Russian and Western societies. Today, most experts in Russia do not see internal developments as a basis for a long-term relationship; instead, they emphasize the significance of global issues, such as counterterrorism, nuclear arms reduction, cybersecurity, public health, and environmental sustainability. The second and related point is that Western policymakers must avoid developing exclusive relationships with or demonizing either the ruling elite or the opposition.

Determining and developing an issue-based agenda in relations with Russia is likely to take time, but may prove more productive and help to weaken the current image of the West as overly pushy and opportunistic. As the world moves further into the twenty-first century, it will be increasingly important to recognize the economic, political, and geostrategic significance of Russia as a potential partner.

NOTES

1. Edward Hallett Carr, *The Twenty Years' Crisis, 1919–1939* (New York: Harper & Row, 1964), 11.

2. As quoted in Andrew Kuchins's notes from a meeting with Medvedev at the Valdai Discussion Club in September 2008 (Georgie Anne Geyer, "Russia First to Test New President," *Chicago Tribune*, November 14, 2008, www.chicagotribune.com/news/nationworld/chi-oped1114geyernov14,0,7013815.story).

3. Carr, *The Twenty Years' Crisis*, 11.

4. Thomas Graham, "Dialektika sily i slabosti," *Vedomosti*, June 29, 2007.

Further Reading

OFFICIAL VIEWS

Antonov, A. "We Have to Fight Lies and Fake News Virtually on a Daily Basis." *The National Interest*, August 1, 2021.

Kozyrev, A. V. "Russia: A Chance for Survival." *Foreign Affairs* 71, no. 2 (1992).

Lavrov, S. "Russia's Foreign Policy in a Historical Perspective." *Russia in Global Affairs* 1 (January–March, 2018).

———. "The World at a Crossroads and a System of International Relations for the Future." *Russia in Global Affairs* 4 (October–December, 2019).

Medvedev, D. Speech at meeting with Russian ambassadors and permanent representatives in international organizations. July 12, 2010, Kremlin.ru.

Primakov, Ye. *Russian Crossroads: Toward the New Millennium*. New Haven: Yale University Press, 2004.

Putin, V. "Rossiya na rubezhe tysyacheletiy." *Nezavisimaya gazeta*, December 30, 1999.

———. Speech at the Munich Conference on Security Policy. Munich, February 10, 2007. Kremlin.ru.

———. "Russia and the Changing World." *Moskovskiye novosti*, February 26, 2012.

———. Address to the United Nations, New York, September 29, 2015.

———. Meeting of the Valdai International Discussion Club, October 22, 2020. http://president.kremlin.ru.

———. Presidential Address to the Federal Assembly, April 21, 2021. http://president.kremlin.ru.

BOOKS

Allison, R. *Russia, the West, and Military Intervention*. Oxford: Oxford University Press, 2013.

Askerov, A., and S. Brooks, eds. *Post-Soviet Conflicts: The Thirty Years' Crisis.* Lanham, MD: Lexington Books, 2020.

Bechev, D. *Rival Power: Russia in Southeast Europe.* New Haven: Yale University Press, 2017

Bordachev, T. V. *Europe, Russia and The Liberal World Order.* London: Routledge, 2021.

Borshchevskaya, A. *Putin's War in Syria.* London: I. B. Tauris, 2021.

Cadier, D., and M. Light, eds. *Russia's Foreign Policy: Ideas, Domestic Politics and External Relations.* London: Palgrave, 2015.

Charap, S., and T. Colton. *Everyone Loses: The Ukraine Crisis and the Ruinous Contest for Post-Soviet Eurasia.* London: Routledge, 2017.

D'Anieri, P. *Ukraine and Russia: From Civilized Divorce to Uncivil War.* Cambridge: Cambridge University Press, 2019.

Donaldson, R. H., and V. Nadkarni. *The Foreign Policy of Russia*, 6th ed., Armonk, NY: M. E. Sharpe, 2019.

Fridman, O. *Russian Hybrid Warfare: Resurgence and Politicisation.* New York: Oxford University Press, 2018.

Hill, W. H. *No Place for Russia: European Security Institutions Since 1989.* New York: Columbia University Press, 2018.

Hopf, T. *Social Construction of International Politics: Identities and Foreign Policies, Moscow, 1955 and 1999.* Ithaca, NY: Cornell University Press, 2002.

Kanet, R., ed. *The Russian Challenge to the European Security Environment.* New York: Palgrave, 2017,

Legvold, R., ed. *Russian Foreign Policy in the 21st Century and the Shadow of the Past.* New York: Columbia University Press, 2007.

———. *New Cold War.* London: Polity, 2016.

Libman, A., and E. Vinokurov. *Eurasian Integration: Challenges of Transcontinental Regionalism.* London: Palgrave, 2012.

Lukin, A. *Russia and China: The New Rapprochement.* London: Polity, 2018.

Lukin, A., and G. Diesen, eds. *Russia in a Changing World.* New York: Palgrave, 2020.

Lukyanov, F., ed. *Rossiya v global'noi politike: Novye pravila ili igra bez pravil.* Moscow: Eksmo, 2015.

———. Russia and the Middle East: *Viewpoints, Policies, Strategies.* Minneapolis, MN: East View Press, 2019.

Marsh, C., and N. Gvosdev. *Russian Foreign Policy: Interests, Vectors, and Sectors.* London: CQ Press, 2013.

Mérand, F., and M. Dembińska, eds. *Cooperation and Conflict Between Europe and Russia.* London: Routledge, 2022.

Molchanov, M. A. *Eurasian Regionalism and Russian Foreign Policy.* London: Ashgate, 2015.

Monaghan, A. Power in Modern Russia: Strategy and Mobilization. Manchester, England: Manchester University Press, 2017.

Mouritzen, H., and A. Wivel. *Explaining Foreign Policy: International Diplomacy and the Russo-Georgian War.* Boulder, CO: Lynne Rienner, 2012.

Renz, B. *Russia's Military Revival*. London: Polity, 2018.

Sakwa, R. *Russia Against the Rest: The Post–Cold War Crisis of World Order*. Cambridge: Cambridge University Press, 2017.

Shakleyina, T. A., ed. *Vneshnyaya politika i bezopasnost' sovremennoi Rossiyi, 1991–2002*. 4 vol. Moskva: ROSSPEN, 2002.

Sotiriou, S. *Russian Energy Strategy in the European Union, the Former Soviet Union Region, and China*. Lanham, MD: Lexington Books, 2014.

Stent, A. *The Limits of Partnership: U.S.–Russian Relations in the Twenty-First Century*. Princeton, NJ: Princeton University Press, 2015.

Stoner, K. E. *Russia Resurrected: Its Power and Purpose in a New Global Order*. New York: Oxford University Press, 2021.

Toal, G. *Near Abroad:* Putin, *the West and the Contest over* Ukraine *and the Caucasus.* New York: Oxford University Press, 2017.

Trenin, D. *What Russia Is Up to in the Middle East.* London: Polity, 2017.

Tsygankov, A. P. *Russia and the West from Alexander to Putin: Honor in International Relations*. Cambridge: Cambridge University Press, 2012.

———, ed. *The Routledge Handbook of Russian Foreign Policy*. London: Routledge, 2018.

———. *Russia and America: the Asymmetric Rivalry*. Cambridge: Polity Press, 2019.

Valeriano, V., and R. Maness. Russia's *Coercive Diplomacy: Energy,* Cyber, *and Maritime Policy as New Sources of Power.* New York: Palgrave, 2015.

ARTICLES AND REPORTS

Abdelal, R., and I. Makarov. *The Fragmentation of the Global Economy and U.S.–Russia Relations.* Cambridge: Working Group on the Future of U.S.–Russia Relations, Working Group Paper 8 (2017).

Adamsky, D. "From Moscow with Coercion: Russian Deterrence Theory and Strategic Culture." *Journal of Strategic Studies* 41 (2018).

Bogdanov, A. "Contested 'Logic of Anarchy' in the Post-Soviet Space: The 'Near Abroad' Faces Russia's Power." *Problems of Post-Communism* 68, 6 (2021).

Boklan, D., V. Kashin, et al. *Arkticheskaya politika Rossiyi*. Moscow: Vysshaya shkola ekonomiki, May 9, 2021.

Casula, P. "Russia's and Europe's Borderlands." *Problems of Post-Communism* 61, no. 6 (2014).

Charap, S., D. Massicot, et al. *Russian Grand Strategy*. Washington, DC: RAND, 2021.

Cooley, A. "A Post-American Central Asia." *Foreign Affairs*, August 23, 2021.

Dannreuther, R. "Understanding Russia's Return to the Middle East." International Politics (2018).

Denisov, I., and A. Lukin. "Russia's China Policy: Growing Asymmetries and Hedging Options." *Russian Politics* 6, 4 (2021).

Diesen, G., and C. Keane. "The Offensive Posture of NATO's Missile Defence System." *Communist and Post-Communist Studies* (2018).

Flonk, D. "Emerging Illiberal Norms: Russia and China as Promoters of Internet Content Control." International Affairs 97, no. 6 (November 2021).

Forsberg, T., R. Heller, and R. Wolf, eds. "Status and Emotions in Russian Foreign Policy." A special issue of *Communist and Post-Communist Studies* 47, nos. 3–4 (2014).

Gunitsky, S., and A. P. Tsygankov. "The Wilsonian Bias in the Study of Russian Foreign Policy." *The Problems of Post-Communism* 65 (2018).

Istomin, I. "The Logic of Counterpoint: Aspirations of Liberal Hegemony and Counter-Ideological Alignment." *Russia in Global Affairs* 2 (March–April 2019).

Kaczmarski, M. "China's New Silk Road and Russia's Eurasian Economic Union." *International Affairs* 93, 6 (2017).

Kertysova, K. "The Prospects for US–Russia Climate Engagement Under Moscow's Chairing of the Arctic Council." *Russia Matters*, May 19, 2021.

Kolsto, P., and H. Blakkisrud. "Russia's Neighborhood Policy and Its Eurasian Client States: No Autocracy Export." *Russia in Global Affairs* 2 (April–June 2021).

Kuhrt, N., and V. Feklyunina, eds. *Assessing Russia's Power: A Report.* King's College, London and Newcastle University, 2017.

Laruelle, M., and K. Limonier. "Beyond 'Hybrid Warfare': A Digital Exploration of Russia's Entrepreneurs of Influence." *Post-Soviet Affairs* (2021).

Lewis, D. G. "Geopolitical Imaginaries in Russian Foreign Policy: The Evolution of 'Greater Eurasia.' " *Europe-Asia Studies* 70, 10 (2018).

Monaghan, A. *How Moscow Understands War and Military Strategy.* Washington, DC: CNA, 2020.

Østensen, Å. G., and T. Bukkvoll. "Private Military Companies: Russian Great Power Politics on the Cheap?" *Small Wars and Insurgencies* 33, nos. 1–2 (September 2021).

Petro, N. N. *Russia's Orthodox Soft Power.* New York: Carnegie Council, 2015. http://www.carnegiecouncil.org/publications/articles_papers_reports/727.

Pieper, M. "*Russkiy Mir*: The Geopolitics of Russian Compatriots Abroad." *Geopolitics* (2018).

Remington, T., C. Spirito, E. Chernenko, O. Demidov, and V. Kabernik. *Toward U.S.–Russia Bilateral Cooperation in the Sphere of Cybersecurity.* Boston: Harvard University, Working Group on the Future of U.S.–Russia Relations, Paper 7, May 2016.

Silaev, N. "Russia and Its Allies in Three Strategic Environments." Europe-Asia *Studies* (2021).

Slater, M. R., M. Purcell, and A. M. Del Gaudio, eds. *Considering Russia: Emergence of a Near Peer Competitor.* Quantico, VA: Marine Corps University, 2017.

Stent, A. "Trump's Russia Legacy and Biden's Response." *Survival*, July 27, 2021.

Toward the Great Ocean—6. The Valdai Club's Report, 2018.

Trenin, D. V. "U.S. Elections and Russia–U.S. Relations." *Russia in Global Affairs* 1 (January–March 2020).

Tsygankov, A. P. "The Sources of Russia's Fear of NATO." *Communist and Post-Communist Studies* (2018).

————. "The Revisionist Moment: Russia, Trump, and Global Transition." *Problems of Post-Communism* (2020).

Ven Bruusgaard, K. "Russian Strategic Deterrence." *Survival* 58, 4 (2016).

Way, L. A., and A. Casey. "Russian Foreign Election Interventions Since 1991." *PONARS Eurasia Policy* Memo No. 520, March 2018.

Wilson, J. L. "Cultural Statecraft and Civilizational and Cultural Themes as a Component of Russian and Chinese Domestic and Foreign Policy." *Politics* (2015).

Zevelev, I. "Russia in the Post-Soviet Space: Dual Citizenship as a Foreign Policy Instrument." *Russia in Global Affairs* 2 (April–June 2021).

Ziegler, C. E. "Russian–American Relations: From Tsarism to Putin." *International Politics* 51, no. 6 (2014).

INTERNET SITES

Eurasia Daily Monitor, Jamestown Foundation. http://jamestown.org/edm.

Foreign Ministry of Russian Federation. http://www.mid.ru.

Johnson's Russia List, Center for Defense Information. http://www.cdi.org/russia/johnson/default.cfm.

PONARS Eurasia Policy Program. http://www.ponarseurasia.org.

Russia in Global Affairs. http://eng.globalaffairs.ru.

Russian and Eurasian Program, Carnegie Endowment for International Peace or Moscow Center. http://www.carnegieendowment.org/programs/russia.

Russia's President. www.kremlin.ru.

Valdai Discussion Club. https://valdaiclub.com.

Essay Questions

Chapter 1: Understanding Change and Continuity in Russia's Foreign Policy

1. Which schools of Russian foreign policy thinking are discussed in the chapter? Which goals and interests of Russia do these schools capture? Which conditions of Russia's change does each of them stress?

2. What are some of the Western theories of Russian foreign policy? What are their analytical strengths and weaknesses? Why is a single theory not sufficient?

3. By which normative standards should one assess the effectiveness of Russian foreign policy? Which policy can be viewed as more/less effective? Why?

Please provide examples in support of your answers.

Chapter 2: The Cold War Crisis and Soviet New Thinking, 1985–1991

1. What schools and disagreements within the political establishment can be identified during perestroika? Which political and rhetorical strategies were followed by conservatives to challenge Gorbachev's proposed changes?

2. What conclusions do you draw from the data on the decline of economic performance and oil output, the referendum on the future of the Union, and your knowledge of the Soviet system, and Gorbachev's actions? Was the Soviet breakup inevitable? Was it caused by the system, Gorbachev's actions, or some combination of these factors? What was the role played by Western nations?

3. What role did Gorbachev's foreign policy play in ending the Cold War and the Soviet system? Was Gorbachev's military withdrawal from Europe and acceptance of Germany's reunification advantageous to his legitimacy at home and abroad?

Please provide examples in support of your answers.

Chapter 3: The Post-Soviet Decline and Attempts at Cooperation, 1991–2004

1. Please describe Yeltsin's worldview in terms of available schools of Russian foreign policy. How did changes that he advocated in domestic and foreign policy differ from those proposed by Gorbachev?
2. Why was Yeltsin not successful in implementing his ideas?
3. What role, if any, did the West play in Russia's transformation during the 1990s?
4. Why did Yeltsin replace Andrei Kozyrev with Yevgeny Primakov as foreign minister in the mid-1990s? Which policies came to replace those of Yeltsin and Kozyrev?
5. Did Primakov's priorities reflect Russia's interests? Were these priorities supported at home and successfully implemented?
6. Please assess Putin's ideology of the early 2000s using evidence from his background, actions, or speeches. Is he a liberal, Russian nationalist, Communist, strong state supporter, or a combination thereof? What does Putin's ideology and foreign policy tell you about the nature of Russia's political system? How does Putin's approach to foreign policy differ from that of Kozyrev, on the one hand, and Primakov, on the other?

Please provide examples in support of your answers.

Chapter 4: Recovery and Assertiveness, 2005–2019

1. How did Putin's foreign policy vision change since the mid-2000s? Did he become more or less cooperative in relations with the West?
2. What are key points of Putin's criticism of the West in the Munich speech? Is Putin calling for a change of world order or a change in US foreign policy?
3. What explains the change in Putin's foreign policy? Which academic theory is better at explaining the change?

4. Was Dmitri Medvedev's course of modernization and deepening ties with the West radically different from Putin's policy? What were Medvedev's proposed changes and continuities relative to Putin's policy?
5. Why was Medvedev not successful in developing a new security framework with Europe and the United States following Russia's conflict with Georgia?
6. What were some of Medvedev's disagreements with Putin? How did these disagreements contribute to Putin's return to the presidency? Do old and new assertive policies by Putin differ?
7. Why has Russia become more assertive in relations with the West? In what ways do realist, liberal, and constructivist explanations differ in explaining the shift in Russian foreign policy?
8. Please identify up to five chronological points that made the Russia–West conflict in Ukraine more likely?
9. How can one explain Russia's interference in US elections in 2016?
10. What explains the Russia–China entente and the reasons for turning toward Asia?
11. Which crises and examples of tensions in US–Russia relations can be identified since 2016?
12. Using your imagination, consider what might happen if Russia deploys nuclear missiles in proximity to the United States—say, in Cuba, as the Soviet Union did in 1961. Would such deployment be likely, and would it reflect Russia's interests? How might the United States react?

Please provide examples in support of your answers.

Chapter 5: From Assertiveness to Isolation? 2019–2022

1. Has Russian foreign policy changed since 2019? Has Russia continued its assertiveness, or has it become more cooperative or defensive in relations with the West? What evidence can be cited in support of your answer?
2. Have Russia's relations with non-Western nations in general—and China, in particular—changed? How can these relations be described in terms of their continuity and change relative to the period of 2005–2018?
3. To the extent that Russia's overall direction has changed, what do you think led to this change? Which theory may assist us in making sense of the new policy direction?
4. Based on an analysis of Russia's relative power and contemporary beliefs, what can be expected from the country's foreign policy in the future? Are there any particular actions or policy directions that can

be excluded? Is Russia more or less likely to cooperate with Western nations in addressing issues of global security?

Please provide examples in support of your answers.

Chapter 6: Conclusions and Lessons

1. What lessons can be drawn from Russia's foreign policy and relations with Western nations? Are these the lessons that the Russian leadership has drawn?
2. In what areas are Russia and the United States likely to cooperate in the near future? What areas are likely to generate continuous disagreements and even result in crises? Why? What strategies do you recommend to manage these crises and disagreements?

Please provide examples in support of your answers.

Topics for Discussion or Simulation

Depending on their objectives, instructors can organize discussions around general or more specific topics related to Russia's foreign policy. For instance, one could assess a strategic international direction of Russia in terms of available courses of action as advocated by the Kremlin's critics at home.

Alternatively, a discussion can begin at the micro level of a specific foreign policy decision and its explanation by a variety of external, domestic, and psychological factors. Here, key questions should be (1) what forces/factors influenced the decision; and (2) what alternative course was available, if any.

Both options should assist in deepening student understanding of Russia-specific forces at play, as well as concepts commonly used in analysis of foreign policy and theory of international relations.

What follows is a tentative list of possible themes and decisions broken down by relevant chapters. In each case, themes and questions may be specified further, particularly if the instructor assigns students specific actors and roles to play (simulation). Additional readings may be assigned as well.

CHAPTER 1: UNDERSTANDING CHANGE AND CONTINUITY IN RUSSIA'S FOREIGN POLICY

Please discuss Russia's strategic choices from perspectives alternative to that of the Kremlin. Select one such perspective—pro-Western liberal, Civilizationist, or another—and then propose some historical intersections at which the Russian state could have acted differently. Examples might include state behavior before World War I and World War II, or others. Consider what a different course of action could have meant for the country's overall direction and relations with specific foreign countries. Which policy course would have been best? Why or why not?

CHAPTER 2: THE COLD WAR CRISIS AND SOVIET NEW THINKING, 1985–1991

Strategic Alternatives: The Soviet conservative reforms at home and a limited dialogue with the West.

Individual Decision: Gorbachev's military withdrawal from Europe and acceptance of Germany's reunification, 1989.

CHAPTER 3.1: RUSSIA'S LIBERAL WESTERNISM, 1991–1993

Strategic Alternatives: Limited market reforms at home, defense of great power and multipolar balance of power abroad.

Individual Decision: Intervention in Moldova to prevent spread of violence and civil war, spring–summer 1992.

CHAPTER 3.2: GREAT POWER BALANCING, 1994–1999

Strategic Alternatives: Instead of trying to contain NATO expansion, focus on counterterrorist cooperation with the West.

Individual Decision: Pressure on Serbia to accept Western conditions for peace after the NATO bombing campaign, June 1999.

CHAPTER 3.3: PUTIN'S PRAGMATIC COOPERATION, 2000–2005

Strategic Alternatives: Continuation of Primakov's policy of multipolarity and reintegration of the former Soviet region.

Individual Decision: Support for the United States following the 9/11 terrorist attacks, September 2001.

CHAPTER 4.1: GREAT POWER ASSERTIVENESS, 2005–2008

Strategic Alternatives: Continuation of Putin's earlier course of Pragmatic Cooperation with the West.

Individual Decision: Official acceptance of the Orange Revolution in Ukraine, November 2004.

CHAPTER 4.2: MEDVEDEV'S MODERNIZATION AND PRAGMATISM, 2008–2011

Strategic Alternatives: Return to Primakov's policy of building strategic ties with China and India.

Individual Decision: No veto on the UNSC resolution of the use of force against Libya, March 2011.

CHAPTER 4.3: "CIVILIZATIONAL" TURN AND NEW ASSERTIVENESS, 2012–2018

Strategic Alternatives: Continuation of Medvedev's course of modernization and deepening ties with the West.

Individual Decision 1: Military support and annexation of Crimea, February–March 2014.

Individual Decision 2: Intervention in the US presidential elections, November 2016.

CHAPTER 5: FROM ASSERTIVENESS TO ISOLATION? 2019–2022

Strategic Alternative 1: Concessions to the West in order to lift sanctions and improve relations.

Strategic Alternative 2: Continuation of assertiveness by increasing pressures on Ukraine and intervening elsewhere in Europe or Eurasia.

Individual Decision 1: Renewal of START, January–February 2021.

Individual Decision 2: Participation in US-organized climate conference, March 2021.

CHAPTER 6: CONCLUSIONS AND LESSONS

Strategic Alternatives for the West: Patient, interest-based engagement with lowered pressures for democratization and protection of human rights.

Individual Decision: The US president's decision to preserve dialogue with Russia on issues of vital importance, such as nuclear security, cybersecurity, and preventing further climate change.

Index